MEDIA
LAW
&
HUMAN
RIGHTS

SECOND EDITION

Andrew Nicol QC

Gavin Millar QC

Andrew Sharland

OXFORD

UNIVERSITY PRESS

OXFORD
UNIVERSITY PRESS

Great Clarendon Street, Oxford OX2 6DP

Oxford University Press is a department of the University of Oxford.
It furthers the University's objective of excellence in research, scholarship,
and education by publishing worldwide in

Oxford New York

Auckland   Cape Town   Dar es Salaam   Hong Kong
Karachi   Kuala Lumpur   Madrid   Melbourne   Mexico City   Nairobi
New Delhi   Shanghai   Taipei   Toronto

With offices in

Argentina   Austria   Brazil   Chile   Czech   Republic   France   Greece
Guatemala   Hungary   Italy   Japan   Poland   Portugal   Singapore
South Korea   Switzerland   Thailand   Turkey   Ukraine   Vietnam

Oxford is a registered trademark of Oxford University Press
in the UK and in certain other countries.

Published in the United States
by Oxford University Press Inc., New York

First published 2009

British Library Cataloguing-in-Publication Data
Data Available

Library of Congress Cataloguing-in-Publication Data
Data Available

Typeset by Cepha Imaging Private Ltd, Bangalore, India
Printed by the MPG Books Group in the UK

ISBN 978–0–19–921750–2

1 3 5 7 9 10 8 6 4 2

CONTENTS

Table of Cases   xiii
Table of Legislation   xxvii

1. **Freedom of Expression and Privacy: An Introduction**

    1.01 Introduction   1

    1.05 Freedom of Expression Theory   2
          1.05 Mill's argument from truth   2
          1.06 Democratic self-governance   3
          1.07 Self-fulfilment   4
          1.08 The relevance of the rationales for protecting freedom
                of expression   4

    1.10 Privacy Theory   5
          1.10 The right to be left alone: Warren and Brandeis   5
          1.12 Prosser: the four privacy torts   6

    1.14 English Law's Approach to Freedom of Expression Prior to
          the Incorporation of the ECHR   6

          1.14 Historical perspective   6
          1.18 Developments immediately prior to the incorporation
                of the ECHR: 1980s and 1990s   8

    1.21 English Law's Approach to the Right to Privacy Prior to the
          Incorporation of the ECHR   9

2. **Freedom of Expression and the Right to Respect for Private Life
    and Media Law: General Principles**

    2.01 Introduction   11

    2.02 Principles of Interpretation of the ECHR   11

          2.03 The teleological approach   12
          2.06 The principle of effectiveness   13
          2.07 Recourse to other human rights instruments   13

2.08 The Law of the ECHR: Article 10 Freedom of Expression   13
    2.08 Introduction   13
    2.11 Article 10(1)   15
    2.35 Article 10(2)   25

2.51 Other Convention Rights of Particular Importance to
    Media Law   35
    2.52 Article 6(1): Reporting of judicial proceedings   35
    2.55 Article 8: The right to respect for private life   36
    2.59 Article 14: The right not to be discriminated against   38
    2.63 Article 15: Restrictions in time of war or other public
        emergency threatening the life of the nation   39
    2.65 Article 17: Restrictions on activities subversive of
        Convention rights—the problem of hate speech   40

3. The Human Rights Act 1998

3.01 Introduction   41

3.03 'Convention Rights'   42
    3.03 Omitted rights   42
    3.11 Strasbourg case law   44

3.16 Interpreting Legislation Consistently with Convention
    Rights   45
    3.16 Introduction   45
    3.20 Primary and secondary legislation   47
    3.22 Declarations of incompatibility   48
    3.27 Matters covered by European Community Law   49

3.29 Public Authorities' Duty to Comply with Convention Rights   50
    3.29 Introduction   50
    3.30 Incompatible primary legislation   50
    3.31 Meaning of 'public authority'   50
    3.41 Omissions to act   54

3.42 Enforcement of Convention Rights: Standing   54

3.54 Enforcement of Convention Rights: Which Court?   58
    3.54 Introduction   58
    3.56 Independent proceedings to enforce Convention Rights   59
    3.57 Limitation period   59
    3.58 Human rights claims in other proceedings   59

3.61 Enforcement of Convention Rights: Remedies   60
    3.61 Introduction   60

3.63	Damages	61
3.66	Damages for judicial acts	62

3.67 **Special Provisions Concerning Freedom of Expression** 62
  3.67 Criminal proceedings 62
  3.68 Restrictions on relief without notice 63
  3.69 Restrictions on pre-trial injunctions 63
  3.73 Prior publicity, public interest, and privacy 64

4. **When Rights have not been Brought Home: Taking a Case to Strasbourg**

  4.01 Introduction 67

  4.03 The Strasbourg Court 68
    4.03 The permanent Court 68
    4.05 The judicial structures of the Court 69
    4.06 The Registry 69

  4.07 Legal Aid 70

  4.08 Making a Complaint 70
    4.09 The time limit for submitting complaints 70
    4.10 The application form 71

  4.12 Admissibility 72
    4.12 Initial inadmissibility 72
    4.17 The applicant must be a 'victim' 73
    4.21 Exhaustion of all effective domestic remedies 75
    4.26 Procedure for determining admissibility 77

  4.27 Consideration of the Complaint 78

  4.30 Just Satisfaction 80

5. **Defamation**

  5.01 Introduction 81

  5.04 Who may Complain of an Article 10 Violation? 82

  5.06 'Without Interference by Public Authority' 82
    5.07 Prior restraint 83
    5.08 Damages awards 83
    5.09 Orders to publish 83
    5.10 Criminal libel 83
    5.11 Final injunctions 84

5.12 Legitimate Aim   84
   5.13 Protecting reputation   84
   5.15 Prevention of disorder   84

5.16 Restrictions 'Necessary in a Democratic Society'   85
   5.22 Assessing the facts   87
   5.28 The form of the expression: fact and value judgment 88
   5.32 The unique position of the press as 'watchdog'   89
   5.35 Public interest considerations   90
   5.50 Reportage   94
   5.54 Responsible and irresponsible journalism   95
   5.56 Excessive sanctions   95

5.59 The Defendant's Right to a Fair Hearing   96

5.61 The Impact of the HRA 1998 on Domestic Law   97
   5.61 Criminal libel   97
   5.63 The civil law of defamation   98

6. Privacy and Confidentiality

6.01 Introduction   103

6.06 State Interference: Searches, Warrants, and Production
    Orders   104

6.10 State Interference: Media Sources   106
   6.10 Compelling disclosure   106
   6.19 Penalizing sources—whistleblowers   110

6.21 Intrusions on Privacy by the Media: Strasbourg   111
   6.21 Protection of privacy and confidentiality as justification for
      restricting freedom of expression   111
   6.26 Article 8: positive obligation   113

6.30 Intrusions by the Media: The UK   115
6.45 Remedies   121
6.48 Threats to Life   122

7. Racial and Religious Hatred

7.01 Introduction   125

7.02 Domestic Law   125

7.09 Discrimination Under the ECHR   127

7.13	Limiting Racist Expression	129
	7.15 Race hate propaganda	129
	7.20 Holocaust denial	132
	7.22 *Lehideux and Isorni* v *France*	133
7.25	Exposing Racism in the Public Interest	134
7.33	The Wider Picture	136

8. Obscenity and Blasphemy

8.01	Introduction	139
	8.06 Domestic law: obscenity	141
	8.10 Domestic law: blasphemy	141
8.13	Obscenity: ECHR	142
	8.13 'Interference by a public authority'	142
	8.14 'Prescribed by law'	143
	8.15 'Legitimate aim'	143
	8.16 'Necessary in a democratic society'	143
	8.20 Selective enforcement	145
8.21	Blasphemy: ECHR	146
	8.21 'Interference by a public authority'	146
	8.22 'Prescribed by law'	146
	8.24 'Legitimate aim'	147
	8.27 'Necessary in a democratic society'	148
	8.33 'Discrimination'	151
8.35	The Impact of the HRA on Domestic Law	152
	8.35 Obscenity	152
	8.40 Blasphemy	155

9. Court Reporting and Contempt of Court

9.01	Introduction	157
9.03	Whose Right? Standing to Complain	158
	9.03 Article 10	158
	9.04 Article 6	158
9.10	'Interference'	160
9.12	'Legitimate Aim'	161
9.14	'Prescribed by Law'	162

9.16	'Necessary in a Democratic Society'	163
9.16	*Sunday Times* v *UK*: the thalidomide articles injunctions	163
9.19	Prejudicial publicity: other cases	165
9.22	Pre-trial injunctions	166
9.23	Criticism of the judiciary	166
9.29	Criticism by lawyers	169
9.33	Access to courts and tribunals	170
9.38	Article 6 and the extent of the obligation to hold 'public hearings'	173
9.45	Publicity of court proceedings and privacy interests	175
9.48	Adverse impact of publicity on third parties	177
9.52	Court reporting and threats to life	178
9.54	Broadcasting coverage of court proceedings	179
9.56	Infringement of court secrecy requirements	180

10. Reporting on Elections and Parliament

10.01	Introduction	183
10.05	Elections	184
10.08	Campaigning	184
10.12	Party election broadcasts	186
10.16	*Bowman* v *UK*	189
10.21	Election law: other possible challenges	190
10.24	Parliament	191
10.24	Parliamentary privilege	191
10.30	Contempt of Parliament	194

11. Licensing and Regulation of the Media

11.01	Introduction	195
11.02	Broadcast Licensing and Regulation	195
11.02	The proviso for licensing in Article 10(1)	195
11.10	Public service broadcasting	198
11.11	Broadcasting bans	198
11.13	Access to broadcasting	199
11.16	Advertising restrictions	200
11.18	Newspaper Licensing	201
11.20	Media Regulators	202
11.21	Article 6: applicability	202
11.31	Article 6(1): rights granted	205
11.42	Article 6: issues for media regulation	209

12. Commercial Speech and Advertising

12.01 Introduction   211
     12.03 What is commercial speech?   212
     12.04 Why protect commercial speech?   212
     12.05 Competing interests   212
     12.06 Categorization   213

12.07 ECHR Case Law   214
     12.07 Commercial speech: general principles   214
     12.10 Commercial speech and advertising by
          professionals   215
     12.15 Commercial speech and advertising critical of
          competitors or products   218
     12.18 Political and religious advertising   219
     12.21 Speech by commercial organizations on matters
          of public concern   221

12.23 The Impact of the HRA on Domestic Law   222
     12.23 Misleading, false, and deceptive advertising   222
     12.24 Truthful and comparative advertising   223
     12.26 Tobacco advertising   223
     12.33 Advertising directed at vulnerable groups such as
          children   227
     12.34 Political advertising   227
     12.35 Public expression of professionals   228
     12.36 Advertising by professionals   229

**13. Official Secrets, National Security, Terrorism, and
Public Disorder**

13.01 Introduction   231

13.06 ECHR Case Law   233
     13.06 National security: general principles   233
     13.08 Publication or disclosure of secret information   233
     13.21 Suppression of speech that threatens public order   239
     13.26 Suppression of speech that threatens national
          security or the territorial integrity of the State   240

13.31 The Impact of the HRA on Domestic Law   243
     13.31 The criminal law: Official Secrets   243
     13.36 The criminal law: encouraging and glorifying
          terrorism   245
     13.37 The civil law   246

Appendices

Appendix 1: Human Rights Act 1998   251

Appendix 2: Convention for the Protection of Human Rights and
       Fundamental Freedoms as Amended by Protocol No.11
       with Protocol Nos. 1, 4, 6, 7, 12 and 13   273

Index   299

TABLE OF CASES

United Kingdom	xiii	Canada	xviii
European Community	xviii	European Court of Human Rights	xviii
European Court of Justice	xviii	Ireland	xxv
Other Jurisdictions	xviii	New Zealand	xxv
American Court of Human Rights	xviii	South Africa	xxv
Australia	xviii	United States of America	xxv

UNITED KINGDOM

A and others, *re* [2006] EWCA Crim 4, [2006] 1 WLR 1361 .... 9.08
A Local Authority v PD and GD (by her guardian Cathy Butcher) [2005] EWHC
    1832 (Fam), [2005] EMLR 35.. 9.49
A Local Authority v W [2005] EWHC 1564 (Fam), [2006] 1 FLR 1 .... 9.49
Ahnee v DPP [1999] 2 AC 294 .... 9.28
Al-Fagih v HH Saudi Research and Marketing (UK) Ltd [2001] EWCA Civ 1634,
    [2003] EMLR 13 .... 5.72
Al Meghrahi v Times Newspapers Ltd 2000 JC 22 .... 9.21
American Cyanamid Co v Ethican Ltd [1975] AC 396 .... 3.70
Anufrijeva v Southwark LBC [2003] EWCA Civ 1406, [2004] 3 All ER 833, CA 3.65
Ashdown v Telegraph Ltd [2001] EWCA Civ 1142, [2002] Ch 149, CA 3.75
Ashworth Hospital Authority v MGN Ltd [2002] UKHL 29, [2002] 1 WLR 2033, HL... 6.16
Asst Deputy Coroner for Inner West London v Channel 4 Television Corp [2007]
    EWHC 2513 (QB), [2008] 1 WLR 945 .... 6.17
Aston Cantlow PCC v Wallbank [2003] UKHL 37, [2004] 1 AC 546 .... 3.09, 3.33, 3.37
Attorney-General v Associated Newspapers Ltd [1994] 2 AC 238..................... 9.58
Attorney-General v Guardian Newspapers Ltd (No 2) 1990 1 AC 109 .... 1.18, 3.01, 13.11
Attorney-General v Newspaper Publishing plc (1988) Ch 33 .... 9.14
Attorney-General v Scotcher [2005] UKHL 36, [2005] 3 All ER 1, HL................ 9.58
Attorney-General v Times Newspapers Ltd [1973] 1 All ER 815;
    [1974] AC 273 .... 1.17, 10.27
Attorney-General v Times Newspapers Ltd [2001] EWCA Civ 97 .... 13.40

BBC v Rochdale Metropolitan BC [2005] EWHC 2862 (Fam), [2006] EMLR 6 .... 9.04
BBB Petitioners (No 1) 2000 JC 419 .... 9.54
Belfast City Council v Miss Behavin' Ltd [2007] UKHL 19, [2007]
    1 WLR 1420.................................... 3.29, 8.04, 8.13, 8.35, 8.37
Benjamin v Minister of Information and Broadcasting [2001] WLR 1040 .... 11.15
Berezovsky v Forbes Inc (No 2) [2001] EMLR 45 .... 5.73
Boehringer Ingelheim Ltd v Vetplus Ltd [2007] EWCA Civ 583 .... 12.24
Bonnard v Perryman [1891] 2 Ch 269................................. 2.49, 3.72, 5.63
Bonnick v Morris [2002] UKPC 31, [2003] 1 AC 300, PC 5.69
Bowman v Secular Society [1917] AC 406...................................... 8.11

Brandon Webster (A Child), *re*: Norfolk County Council v Webster [2006] EWHC
　　2733 (Fam), [2007] EMLR 7 . . . . 9.41
Brind v Secretary of State for the Home Department [1991] AC 696 . . . . 11.11
Buchanan v Jennings [2004] UKPC 36, [2005] 1 AC 115 . . . . 10.26

Cable and Wireless (Dominica) Ltd v Marpin Telecommunications and Broadcasting
　　Co Ltd (2001) 9 BHRC 486 . . . . 2.14
Calder v Powell [1965] 1 QB 509 . . . . 8.09
Camelot Group plc v Centaur Communications Ltd [1998] 1 All ER 251, CA 6.16
Campbell v MGN Ltd [2004] UKHL 22, [2004] 2 AC 457 . . . . 2.58, 3.77, 6.31–6.32,
　　　　　　　　　　　　　　　　　　　　　　　　　　　　　　6.34, 6.38, 6.43, 6.45
Campbell v MGN Ltd (No 2) [2005] UKHL 61, [2005] 1 WLR 3394, HL 6.46
Central Broadcasting Services Ltd v A-G of Trinidad and Tobago [2006] UKPC 35,
　　[2006] 21 BHRC 577, PC 11.05
Charman v Orion Publishing Group Ltd [2007] EWCA Civ 972, [2008] 1 All ER 750 . . . 5.69
Church of Scientology of California v Johnson-Smith [1972] 1 QB 522 . . . . 10.25
Connolly v DPP [2007] EWHC 237 (Admin.) 8.36
Council of Civil Service Unions v Minister for the Civil Service [1985] AC 374 . . . . 13.01
Cream Holdings Ltd v Banerjee [2004] UKHL 44, [2005] 1 AC 253 . . . . 3.71, 6.47, 13.41
Culnane v Morris [2005] EWHC 2438 (QB), [2006] 1 WLR 2880 . . . . 10.11

D v Secretary of State for the Home Department [2006] EWCA Civ 143, [2006] 3 All
　　ER 946, CA 9.37
Derbyshire County Council v Times Newspaper Ltd [1993] AC 534 (HL) 1.02, 3.01, 5.63
Director of Public Prosecutions v A & BC Chewing Gum Ltd [1968] 1 QB 159 . . . . 8.09
Douglas v Hello! Magazine Ltd [2001] QB 967; [2001] 2 All ER 289, CA 3.60, 3.73, 6.34
Douglas v Hello! Magazine Ltd (No 3) [2006] QB 125, CA 6.34, 6.45, 6.46, 6.47
Dunn v Parole Board [2008] EWCA Civ 374, (2008) HRLR 32 . . . . 3.57

E (by her Litigation Friend the Official Solicitor) v BBC [2005] EMLR 30 . . . . 6.44

Fothergill v Monarch Airlines Ltd [1981] AC 251 . . . . 2.02
Fraser v Evans [1969] 1 QB 349 . . . . 3.72

Galloway v Telegraph Group Ltd [2006] EWCA Civ 17, [2006] EMLR 11 . . . . 5.69
Ghaidan v Godin-Mendoza [2004] UKHL 30, [2004] 2 AC 557, HL 3.18
Gleaves v Deakin [1980] AC 477, HL 5.62
Green Corns Ltd v Claverley Group Ltd [2005] EWHC 958 (QB), [2005] EMLR 31 . . . . 6.38
Greene v Associated Newspapers Ltd [2004] EWCA Civ 1462, [2005]
　　QB 972, CA 3.72, 5.63

Hamilton v Al Fayed [2000] 2 All ER 224, HL 10.25, 10.29
Hamilton and Greer v Hencke and others (1995) 10.29
Hellewell v Chief Constable of Derbyshire [1995] 1 WLR 804 . . . . 1.22
Hodgson v Imperial Tobacco [1998] 2 All ER 673 . . . . 9.38

Interbrew SA Ltd v Financial Times Ltd [2002] EWCA Civ 274, [2002] EMLR 24, CA . . 6.17
Interfact Ltd v Liverpool City Council [2005] EWHC 995 (Admin), [2005]
　　1 WLR 3118 . . . . 8.36

Jameel v Dow Jones & Co Inc [2005] EWCA Civ 75, [2005] QB 946 . . . . 5.74
Jameel v Wall Street Journal Europe Sprl [2006] UKHL 44, [2007]
　　1 AC 359, HL 5.68–5.70, 5.74

Kaye v Robertson [1991] FSR 62 .... 1.21

Lady Archer v Williams [2003] EWHC 1670 (QB), [2003] EMLR 38 .... 6.45
Lambeth BC v Kay [2006] UKHL 10, [2006] 2 AC 465 .... 3.19
LM (Reporting Restrictions: Coroner's Inquest), re [2007] EWHC 1902 (Fam),
    (2008) 99 BMLR 11, Fam 9.50
London Regional Transport v Mayor of London [2001] EWCA Civ 1491 .... 2.15
Long Beach Ltd and Denis Sassou Nguesso v Global Witness Ltd [2007] EWHC
    1980 (QB), [2007] EWHC 1980 (QB) 6.40
Lord Advocate v Scotsman Publications [1989] 2 All ER 852 .... 13.33
Lord Browne of Madingley v Associated Newspapers Ltd [2008] EWHC 1777 (QB) 6.42
Loutchansky v Times Newspapers Ltd (No 2) [2001] EWCA Civ 1805, [2002]
    QB 783, CA 5.70
Loutchansky v Times Newspapers Ltd (No 4) [2001] EWCA Civ 536, [2001]
    EMLR 38 .... 5.69
Loutchansky v Times Newspapers Ltd (No 6) [2002] EWHC 2490 .... 5.70

Maxine Carr v News Group Newspapers Ltd [2005] EWHC 971 (QB) 6.48
Mazher Mahmood v Galloway [2006] EMLR 26 .... 6.49
McCartan Turkington Breen (A Firm) v Times Newspapers Ltd [2001]
    2 AC 277 .... 2.19, 5.67, 5.68
McKennitt v Ash [2006] EWCA Civ 1714, [2008] QB 73, CA 2.58, 6.35, 6.45
McKerr, re [2004] UKHL 23, [2004] 1 WLR 807 HL 3.08
Medicaments and Related Classes of Goods, re (No 2) [2001]
    1 WLR 700, CA 11.36, 11.44
Mersey Care NHS Trust v Ackroyd (No 2) [2007] EWCA Civ 101, [2008]
    EMLR 1, CA 6.16
Mosley v News Group Newspapers Ltd [2008] EWHC 687 (QB); [2008]
    EWHC 1777 (QB)... 6.37, 6.39, 6.45
Murray v Big Pictures (UK) Ltd [2008] EWCA Civ 446; [2008] EMLR 12.... 2.58, 6.36, 6.38

OBG Ltd v Allan [2007] UKHL 21, [2008] 1 AC 1 .... 6.46
Observer and Guardian v UK (1991) 14 EHRR 153............................. 6.23
Observer Publications Ltd v Campbell (2001) 10 BHRC 252, PC 11.05
Officer L, re [2007] UKHL 36, [2007] 1 WLR 2135 .... 9.53
O'Riordan v DPP [2005] EWHC 1240 (Admin) 9.15

P v BW (Children Cases: Hearings in Public) [2004] Fam 155, CA 9.41
Parmeter v Copeland (1840) 6 M & W 105 .... 5.01
Persey v Secretary of State for the Environment, Food and Rural Affairs [2002]
    EWHC 371 (Admin), [2003] QB 794 .... 9.37
Porter v Magill [2001] UKHL 67, [2002] 2 AC 357 .... 11.36
Prebble v Television NZ [1995] 1 AC 321 .... 10.29
Prince Albert v Strange (1849) 2 De G & Sm 652, 64 ER 293; (1849) 1 Mac & G 25,
    41 ER 1171 .... 1.11, 1.21

Quartz Hill Consolidated Mining Co v Beal [1882] 20 ChD 501 .... 3.72

R v A [2001] UKHL 25, [2002] 1 AC 45 .... 3.18
R v Advertising Standards Authority ex p City Trading Ltd [1997] COD 202 .... 3.36
R v Advertising Standards Authority ex p Direct Line Financial Services Ltd [1998]
    COD 20 .... 3.36
R v Advertising Standards Authority ex p Insurance Service plc (1990) 2 Admin LR 77 ... 3.36

R v Advertising Standards Authority ex p Matthias Rath BV [2001] EMLR 582;
  (2001) The Times, 10 January 2.37, 12.23
R v Advertising Standards Authority ex p Vernon Pools Organisation Ltd [1992]
  1 WLR 1289. . . . . 2.49, 3.36
R v BBC ex p Referendum Party [1997] 9 Admin LR 553 . . . . 10.13, 10.22
R v Broadcasting Standards Commission ex p BBC [2000] 3 All ER 989, CA 3.48
R v Central Criminal Court ex p Bright [2001] 1 WLR 662 QBD 6.08
R v Central Criminal Court ex p The Guardian, The Observer and Martin Bright
  [2000] UKHRR 796 . . . . 13.03
R v Central Independent Television plc [1994] Fam 192. . . . . 8.30
R v Chief Constable of North Wales ex p Thorpe [1999] QB 396, CA. 6.39
R v Croydon Crown Court ex p Trinity Mirror plc [2008] EWCA Crim 50, [2008]
  QB 770. . . . . 9.49
R v DPP ex p Kebilene [2000] 2 AC 326. . . . . 3.14, 3.17
R v Gough [1993] AC 646 . . . . 11.44
R v Graham-Kerr (1989) 88 Cr App R 302 (CA) 8.39
R v Hicklin (1868) LR QB 360 . . . . 8.07
R v Holding [2005] EWCA Crim 3185, [2006] WLR 1040, CA 10.08
R v Horsham Justices ex p Farquharson [1982] QB 762 . . . . 3.51
R v Keogh [2007] EWCA Crim 528 . . . . 13.35
R v Khan [1997] AC 558 . . . . 1.23
R v Lemon and Gay News Ltd [1979] AC 617 . . . . 8.22
R v McLeod (2000) The Times, 20 December, CA 9.07
R v Perrin [2002] EWCA Crim 747. . . . . 8.38
R v Press Complaints Commission ex p Stewart-Brady [1997] EMLR 185 . . . . 3.37
R v Secretary of State for Health ex p Associated Newspapers Ltd [2001] 1 WLR 292. . . . . 9.37
R v Secretary of State for Health ex p C [2000] UKHRR 639, CA 11.27
R v Secretary of State for Health ex p Imperial Tobacco Ltd [2004] EWHC 2493 . . . . 12.32
R v Secretary of State for Health ex p Wagstaff [2000] UKHRR 875, QBD 9.37
R v Secretary of State for Social Services ex p Child Poverty Action Group [1990]
  2 QB 540 . . . . 3.50
R v Secretary of State for the Home Department, ex p Brind [1991] 1 AC 696 . . . . 3.29, 13.27
R v Secretary of State for the Home Department, ex p Chahal [1994] Imm AR 107 . . . . . 13.01
R v Secretary of State for the Home Department, ex p Chlebak [1991] 1 WLR 890 . . . . . 13.01
R v Secretary of State for the Home Department, ex p Simms [2000]
  2 AC 115 . . . . 1.02, 1.08, 1.18
R v Securities and Futures Appeal Tribunal ex p Fleurose [2001] EWCA Civ 2015,
  [2002] IRLR 297, CA 11.30
R v Shayler [2002] UKHL 11, [2003] 1 AC 247. . . . . 2.19, 13.04, 13.34
R v Skirving [1985] QB 819. . . . . 8.09
R v Smethurst [2001] EWCA Crim 772, [2002] 1 Cr App R 6 . . . . 8.39
R v Tuchin (1704) Holt 424 . . . . 1.14
R (A) v Lord Saville of Newdigate (No 2) [2001] EWCA Civ 2048, [2002]
  1 WLR 1249, CA. 9.53
R (Al-Skeini) v Secretary of State for Defence [2007] UKHL 26, [2008]
  1 AC 153 HL 3.07, 3.12
R (Alconbury Developments Ltd) v Secretary of State for Environment, Transport and
  the Regions [2001] UKHL 23, [2003] 2 AC 295 . . . . 11.34
R (Amin) v Secretary of State for the Home Department [2003] UKHL 51, [2004]
  1 AC 653 . . . . 9.37
R (Animal Defenders International) v Secretary of State for Culture, Media and Sport
  [2008] UKHL 15, [2008] 2 WLR 781 HL 3.14, 3.26, 10.12,
                                                                                    11.16, 12.02, 12.34

R (BBFC) v Video Appeals Committee [2008] EWHC 203 (Admin), [2008]
    1 WLR 1658 . . . . 3.36
R (British American Tobacco and others) v The Secretary of State for Health [2004]
    EWHC 2493 . . . . 12.02
R (Ellis) v Chief Constable of Essex [2003] EWHC 1321 (Admin), [2003]
    2 FLR 566, DC 6.39
R (Farrakhan) v Secretary of State for the Home Department [2002] EWCA Civ 606,
    [2002] QB 1391 . . . . 2.22
R (Green) v The City of Westminster Magistrates' Court and others [2007]
    EWHC 2785 . . . . 8.09
R (Greenfield) v Secretary of State for the Home Department [2005] UKHL 14,
    [2005] 2 All ER 240, HL 3.65
R (Heather Moore and Edgecomb Ltd) v Financial Ombudsman Service [2008]
    EWCA Civ 642 . . . . 11.37
R (Malik) v Manchester Crown Court [2008] EWHC 1362 (Admin) 6.08, 6.18
R (Morgan Grenfell) v Special Commissioner of Income Tax [2002] UKHL 21 . . . . 6.16
R (North Cyprus Tourism Centre Ltd) v Transport for London [2005]
    EWHC 1698 . . . . 12.25
R (Pelling) v Bow County Court [2000] UKHRR 165, QBD 9.35, 9.41
R (ProLife Alliance) v BBC [2003] UKHL 23, [2004] 1 AC 185 . . . . 2.46, 3.14, 3.40,
    10.14, 10.15, 11.08, 11.15
R (Rusbridger) v A-G [2003] UKHL 38, [2004] 1 AC 357 . . . . 3.46
R (Ullah) v Secretary of State for the Home Department [2004] UKHL 26, [2004]
    2 AC 323 . . . . 3.12, 8.40
R (Wildman) v Office of Communications [2005] EWHC 1573 (Admin), [2005]
    EMLR 3 . . . . 11.06
Raja v Van Hoogstraten [2004] EWCA Civ 968, [2004] 4 All ER 793, CA 11.29
Roddy (A Child) (Identification: Restrictions on Publication), re [2003] EWHC 2927
    (Fam), [2004] 2 FLR 949 . . . . 6.44
Red Dot Technologies Ltd v Apollo Fire Detectors Ltd [2007] EWHC 166 . . . . 12.24
Redmond-Bate v DPP (1999) 7 BHRC 375 . . . . 1.19
Reynolds v Times Newspapers [1999] 3 WLR 1010; [2001] 2 AC 127 . . . . 1.18, 3.01,
    5.65, 5.68, 5.69–5.72, 5.73
Reynolds v Times Newspapers Ltd [2001] 2 AC 127 . . . . 3.01
Roberts v Gable [2008] 2 WLR 129; [2006] EWHC 1025 (QB), [2007]
    EMLR 457 . . . . 5.69, 5.72

S (a child) (identification: restriction on publication), re [2004] UKHL 47, [2005]
    AC 593 . . . . 6.32, 9.48
S (Minor) (Care Order: Implementation of Care Plan), re [2002] UKHL 10, [2002]
    2 AC 291 . . . . 3.09, 3.16
Schering Chemicals Ltd v Falkman [1982] QB 1 . . . . 1.18
Secretary of State for the Home Department v MB [2007] UKHL 46, [2008]
    1 AC 440 . . . . 3.18
Sim v Stretch (1936) 52 TLR 669 . . . . 5.01
Smith Kline Beecham plc v Advertising Standards Authority, 17 January 2001 . . . . 12.23
St Peter and St Paul's Chingford, re [2007] Fam 67 . . . . 8.36
Starrs and Chalmers v Procurator Fiscal, Linlithgow 2000 JC 208 . . . . 11.35, 11.44

T (by her Litigation Friend the Official Solicitor) v BBC [2007] EWHC 1683 (QB),
    (2008) 1 FLR 281 . . . . 6.44
Thompson and Venables v News Group Newspapers Ltd [2001] Fam 430 . . . . 6.48, 6.49
Tillery Valley Foods v Channel Four Television [2004] EWHC 1075 (QB) 6.43

Venables and Thompson v News Group Newspapers Ltd, [2001] Fam 430 . . . . 3.38, 3.60

Wason v Walter [1868] LR 4 QB 73 . . . . 10.27
Whitehouse v Gay News Ltd and Lemon [1979] AC 617 . . . . 8.10

X (a Woman Formerly Known as Mary Bell) and Y v News Group Newspapers Ltd
    [2003] EWHC 1101 (QB), [2003] EMLR 37 . . . . 6.48
X Ltd v Morgan-Grampian (Publishing) Ltd [1991] 1 AC 1 . . . . 1.18, 6.11

YL (by her litigation friend the Official Solicitor) v Birmingham City Council [2007]
    UKHL 27, [2008] 1 AC 95 . . . . 3.34
Youssoupoff v MGM (1934) TLR 581 . . . . 5.01

EUROPEAN COMMUNITY

European Court of Justice

Elleniki Radiophonia Teleoraissi AE v Pliroforissis (Case C-260/89) [1991]
    ECR 1-2925 . . . . 12.28
Germany v European Parliament (Case C-376/98) 12.27, 12.32
Herbert Karner Industrie-Auktionen GmbH v Trootswijk GmbH [2004]
    ECR 1-3025 . . . . 12.23
Marleasing SA v La Commercial Internacional de Alimentacion SA Case C-106/89
    [1992] CMLR 305 . . . . 3.17
R v Secretary of State for Health ex p Imperial Tobacco Ltd (Case C-74/99) [2000]
    All ER (EC) 769, ECJ 12.27
RTL Television Gmbh v Niederachsische Landesmedienanstalt Fur Privarten
    Rundfunk Case C-245/01 . . . . 11.17
Vereinigte Familiapress Zeitungsverlags-und vertriebs GmbH v Henrich Bauer Verlag
    (Case C-368/95) [1997] ECR 1-3689 . . . . 12.28

OTHER JURISDICTIONS

American Court of Human Rights

Claude Reyes v Chile Case 12.108, Judgment of 19 September 2006 . . . . 2.30–2.31

Australia

Lange v ABC (1997) CLR 520 . . . . 5.71

Canada

Irwin Toy v Quebec [1989] 1 SCR 927 . . . . 1.08, 12.33
R v Keegstra [1990] 3 SCR 697 . . . . 7.34
RJR MacDonald v A-G of Canada (1995) 127 DLR (4th) 1 . . . . 12.02, 12.26, 12.31
Rocket v Royal College of Dental Surgeons [1990] 1 SCR 232 . . . . 12.36

EUROPEAN COURT OF HUMAN RIGHTS

A v UK (2002) 13 BHRC 623 . . . . 10.28
Abdulaziz, Cabales and Balkandali v UK (1985) 7 EHRR 471 . . . . 7.10–7.11
Ahmed v UK (1995) 20 EHRR CD 72 . . . . 3.51
Ahmed and others v UK (1998) 29 EHRR 1 . . . . 2.11, 2.13, 2.41, 2.47
Airey v Ireland (1979) 2 EHRR 305 . . . . 2.06

Akdivar v Turkey (1996) 23 EHRR 143 . . . . 4.03
Albert and Le Compte v Belgium (1983) 5 EHRR 533 . . . . 11.34
Ali Erol v Turkey (App No 35076/97), 20 June 2002 . . . . 4.28
Amihalachioaie v Moldova (App No 60115/00), 20 April 2004 . . . . 9.29
Amnesty International (UK) v UK (App No 38383/97), 18 January 2000 . . . . 12.06, 12.19
Appleby and others v UK (2003) 37 EHRR 38 . . . . 2.25
Arrowsmith v UK (1978) 3 EHRR 218 . . . . 13.21, 13.23, 13.24
Arslan v Turkey (App No 23462/94), 8 July 1999 . . . . 13.28
Artico v Italy (1980) 3 EHRR 1 . . . . 2.06
Associated Newspapers Ltd v UK (App No 24770/94), 30 November 1994 . . . . 9.58
Association Ekin v France (2002) 35 EHRR 1207 . . . . 2.50
Atkinson, Crook and The Independent v UK App No 13366/87 (1990)
    67 DR 244 . . . . 2.54, 9.09, 9.35
Autronic AG v Switzerland (1990) 12 EHRR 485 . . . . 2.07, 2.14, 2.44,
    3.48, 9.54, 11.03, 11.09
Axen v Germany (1983) 6 EHRR 182 . . . . 9.43
Aydin Tatlav v Turkey (App No 50692/99), 2 May 2006 . . . . 8.32
Ayuntamiento v Spain App No 15090/89 (1991) 68 DR 209 . . . . 3.49

B and P v UK (2002) EHRR 529 . . . . 2.53, 9.41, 9.44
Bader v Austria App No 26633/95 22 EHRR CD 213 . . . . 10.22
Bankovic v Belgium (2001) 11 BHRC 435 . . . . 4.14
Barfod v Denmark (1989) 13 EHRR 493 . . . . 5.41, 9.24
Barthold v Germany (1985) 7 EHRR 383 . . . . 2.16, 2.43, 2.46, 12.10
Baskaya and Okcuoglu v Turkey (App Nos 23536/94 and 24408/94), 8 July 1999 . . . . . . 13.28
BBC v UK (App No 25798/94) (1996) 84-A DR 129 missing bracket on proof 6.09, 9.09
Beh El Mahi and others v Denmark (App No 5653/06) 8.40
Belgian Linguistic Case (No 2) (1968) 1 EHRR 252 . . . . 2.61, 7.12
Benham v UK (1996) 22 EHRR 293 . . . . 11.30
Benthem v Netherlands (1985) 8 EHRR 1 . . . . 11.24, 11.26
Berdzenishvili v Russia (App No 31697/03), 29 January 2004 . . . . 4.09
Bergens Tidende v Norway (2001) EHRR 16 . . . . 2.18, 2.46, 3.64, 4.30, 5.26, 5.47
Bladet Tromsø and Stensaas v Norway (1999) 29 EHRR 125 . . . . 2.22, 2.46, 2.47,
    5.08, 5.25, 5.47, 5.54
Blake v UK (App No 68890/01), 26 September 2006 . . . . 13.18
Bowman v UK (1998) 26 EHRR 1 . . . . 2.46, 3.45, 10.06, 10.16–10.20
Brind v UK App No 18714/91 (1994) 77 DR 42 . . . . 11.11, 13.27
Bryan v UK (1995) 21 EHRR 342 . . . . 11.34, 11.43
Burden v UK (App No 13378/05), Judgment, 12 December 2006 . . . . 4.25
Busuioc v Moldova (2006) 42 EHRR 14 . . . . 2.46

C v UK (App No 14132/88), 13 April 1989 . . . . 9.21
Campas Dâmazo v Portugal (App No 17107), 24 April 2008 . . . . 9.60
Campbell and Fell v UK (1984) 7 EHRR 165 . . . . 2.53, 9.41, 11.34, 11.35
Cardot v France (1991) 13 EHRR 853 . . . . 4.21
Casado Coca v Spain (1994) 18 EHRR 1 . . . . 2.11, 2.23, 2.46, 9.31, 12.12, 12.36
Castells v Spain (1992) 14 EHRR 445 . . . . 2.46, 5.15, 5.59, 10.15
Cettin v Turkey App Nos 40153/98 and 40160/98, 13 February 2003 . . . . 13.25
Ceylan v Turkey (1999) 30 EHRR 73 . . . . 7.19, 13.28
Chahal v UK (1996) 23 EHRR 413 . . . . 4.23, 13.01
Chappell v UK (1989) 12 EHRR 1 . . . . 4.22
Chauvy v France (2005) 41 EHRR 29 . . . . 5.19, 5.21
Chorherr v Austria (1993) 17 EHRR 358 . . . . 2.16, 13.22, 13.24

Choudhury v UK (App No 17439/90), 5 March 1991 . . . . 8.33
Colman v UK (1993) 18 EHRR 119 . . . . 12.13
Colombani v France (App No 51279/99), 25 September 2002 . . . . 5.25, 5.49
Confédération des Syndicats Médicaux Français v France (1986) 47 DR 225 . . . . 3.51
Costello-Roberts v UK (1993) 19 EHRR 112 . . . . 3.33
Council of Civil Service Unions v UK (1987) 50 DR 228 . . . . 3.52
Craxi v Italy (No 2) (2004) 38 EHRR 995 . . . . 9.51
Cumpana v Romania (2005) 41 EHRR 14 . . . . 5.06, 5.19–5.20,
5.21, 5.27, 5.49, 5.58

Dalban v Romania (App No 28114/95), 28 September 1999; (2000)
8 BHRC 91 . . . . 3.53, 4.20, 5.40, 5.49
De Haes & Gijsels v Belgium (1997) 25 EHRR 1 . . . . 5.09, 5.28, 5.32, 9.25
Delcourt v Belgium (1969) 1 EHRR 355 . . . . 11.33
Demicoli v Malta (1991) 14 EHRR 47 . . . . 3.31
Demuth v Switzerland (App No 38743/97), 5 November 2002 (2004)
38 EHRR 20 . . . . 2.34, 11.03, 12.03
Dichand v Austria (App No 29271/95), 26 February 2002 . . . . 5.30
Diennet v France (1995) EHRR 554 . . . . 2.52, 9.39, 11.24
Du Roy and Malaurie v France (App No 34000/96), 3 October 2000 . . . . 9.59
Dupuis and others v France (App No 1914/02), 7 June 2007 . . . . 9.60
Dyuldin and Kislov v Russia (App No 25968/02), 31 July 2007 . . . . 5.23, 5.43

Earl Spencer v UK App Nos 28851/95 and 28852/95 (1998) 25 EHRR CD 105 . . . . 4.22
East African Asians v UK (1981) 3 EHRR 76 . . . . 7.12
Ediciones Tiempo SA v Spain App No 13010/87 (1989) 62 DR 247 . . . . 5.09
Editions Plon v France (2006) 42 EHRR 36 . . . . 6.25
Ekbatani v Sweden (1988) 13 EHRR 504 . . . . 9.43
Engel and others v Netherlands (1976) 1 EHRR 647 . . . . 2.04, 2.11, 2.47, 11.29, 13.06
Erdogdu and Ince v Turkey (App Nos 25067/94 and 25068/94), 8 July 1999 . . . . 13.28
Ettl v Austria (1987) 10 EHRR 255 . . . . 11.34

Fairfield v UK (App No 24790/04), 8 March 2005 . . . . 3.53
Falakaoglu and Saygili v Turkey (App Nos 22147/02 and 24972/03) 13.29
Faurisson v France (1997) 2 BHRC 1 . . . . 7.21
Fayed v UK (1994) 18 EHRR 393 . . . . 11.27
Feldek v Slovakia (App No 29032/95) 12 July 2001 . . . . 2.22, 5.22, 5.31
Flux v Moldova (No 6) (App No 22824/04), 29 July 2008 . . . . 5.55
Fredin v Sweden (1991) 13 EHRR 784 . . . . 11.24
Fressoz and Roire v France (2001) 31 EHRR 28 . . . . 6.22
Fuentes Bobo v Spain (App No 39293/98), 29 February 2000; (2000)
31 EHRR 1115 . . . . 2.24, 2.25, 4.13
Funke v France (1993) 16 EHRR 297 . . . . 6.07

Garaudy v France (App No 65831/01), 24 June 2003 . . . . 7.21
Gaskin v UK (1989) 12 EHRR 36 . . . . 2.28, 10.22
Gaweda v Poland App No 26229/95 (2004) 39 EHRR 4 . . . . 2.40, 11.19
Gay News Ltd and Lemon v UK (1982) 28 DR 77; (1982) 5 EHRR 30 . . . . 8.21, 8.22,
8.24, 8.25, 8.27
Gerger v Turkey (App No 24919/94), 8 July 1999 . . . . 13.28
Giniewski v France (2007) 45 EHRR 23 . . . . 5.49
Glas Nadezhda Eood and Elenlov v Bulgaria (App No 14134/02), 11 October 2007 . . . . . 11.05
Glasenap v Germany (1986) 9 EHRR 25 . . . . 2.13

Glimmerveen and Hagenbeek v Netherlands App Nos 8348/78 and
　　8406/78 (1979) 18 DR 187 . . . . 2.46, 2.65, 7.15, 7.21
Golder v UK (1975) 1 EHRR 524 . . . . 2.03, 2.04, 2.06
Goodwin v UK (1996) 22 EHRR 123 . . . . 2.07, 2.20, 2.22
Goodwin v UK (1997) 25 EHRR 1 . . . . 6.11–6.13, 6.14, 6.15, 6.16
Goodwin v UK (2002) 35 EHRR 447 . . . . 2.05
Grigoriades v Greece (1997) 27 EHRR 464 . . . . 2.17
Grinberg v Russia (2006) 43 EHRR 45 . . . . 5.36
Groppera Radio AG and others v Switzerland (1990) EHRR 321 . . . . 2.16, 11.03, 11.09, 12.30
Grupo Interpres SA v Spain App No 32849/96 (1997) 89 DR 150 . . . . 9.35
Guchez v Belgium App No 10027/82 (1984) 40 DR 100 . . . . 2.53
Guerra and others v Italy (1998) 26 EHRR 357 . . . . 2.29, 9.34
Guja v Moldova (App No 14277/04), 12 February 2008 . . . . 6.19

Hachette Filipacci Associes v France (App No 71111/01), 14 June 2007 . . . . 6.25
Hadjianastassiou v Greece (1992) 16 EHRR 219 . . . . 13.06, 13.16, 13.31
Haider v Austria App No 25060/94 (1995) 83 DR 66 . . . . 10.21, 10.22, 11.14
Hakansson v Sweden (1990) 13 EHRR 1 . . . . 9.04
Handyside v UK (1976) 1 EHRR 737 . . . . 1.09, 1.19, 2.04, 2.10, 2.16, 2.22,
　　　　　　　　　　　　　　　　2.42, 2.46, 4.14, 5.16, 7.23, 8.02, 8.16, 8.28, 8.31
Harman v UK App No 10038/82 (1984) 38 DR 53 . . . . 4.28, 9.54, 9.56, 11.29
Hashman and Harrup v UK (2000) 8 BHRC 104 . . . . 2.40
Herczegfalvy v Austria (1992) 15 EHRR 437 . . . . 2.40
Hertel v Switzerland (1998) 28 EHRR 534 . . . . 2.46, 5.46, 12.06, 12.16
Hewitt and Harman v UK (1989) 67 DR 88 . . . . 6.06
Hilton v UK (1988) 57 DR 108 . . . . 3.47
HN v Italy App No 18902/91 (1998) 94 DR 21 . . . . 11.19
Hoare v UK App No 31211/96 [1997] EHRLR 678 . . . . 8.13, 8.17
Hocagullari v Turkey (App No 77109/01) 13.29
Hodgson and Channel 4 v UK App Nos 11553/85 and 11658/85 (1988) 56 DR 156 . . . . 4.28
Hodgson, D Woolf Productions Ltd and National Union of Journalists v UK
　　App Nos 11553/85 and 11685/85 (1987) 51 DR 136 . . . . 9.03, 9.09
Holding and Barnes v UK (App No 2352/02), 11 March 2002 . . . . 11.34
Honsik v Austria App No 25062/94 (1995) 83 DR 77 . . . . 7.21
Hrico v Slovakia (App No 41498/99), 20 July 2004 . . . . 9.27
Huggett v UK App No 24744/94 (1995) 82 DR 98; 20 EHRR CD 104 . . . . 10.21, 11.14
Hummatov v Azerbaijan (App No 9852/03), 29 November 2007 . . . . 9.40

IA v Turkey (2007) 45 EHRR 30 . . . . 8.21, 8.31–8.32
Independent News and Media and Independent Newspapers Ireland Ltd v Ireland
　　(2006) 42 EHRR 46 . . . . 5.57
Informationsverein Lentia and others v Austria (1993) 17 EHRR 93 . . . . 2.24, 11.03, 11.06
Ireland v UK (1978) 2 EHRR 25 . . . . 2.63
Isabel Hilton v UK App No 12015/86 (1988) 57 DR 108 . . . . 4.09

Jacubowski v Germany (1994) 19 EHRR 64 . . . . 12.15
Janowski v Poland (1999) 29 EHRR 705 . . . . 2.46
Jersild v Denmark (1994) 19 EHRR 1 . . . . 2.07, 2.19, 2.21, 2.46,
　　　　　　　　　　　　　　　　　　5.22, 5.28, 5.51, 7.26, 7.32, 9.10
Jerusalem v Austria (App No 26958/95), 27 February 2001 . . . . 5.59
Jerusalem v Austria (No 2) (2003) 37 EHRR 567 . . . . 5.29, 5.44
Jorbedo Foundation of Christian Scools v Sweden App No 11533/85 (1987)
　　61 DR 92 . . . . 11.26

K v Austria (1993 Series A No 255-B 2.13
K v Federal Republic of Germany (App No 17006/90), 2 July 1991 .... 12.23
Karatas v Turkey (App No 23168/94), 8 July 1999 .... 13.28, 13.36
Karhuvaara v Finland (App No 53678/00), 16 November 2004 .... 6.25
Karkin v Turkey (App No 43928/98), 23 September 2003 .... 7.19
Kingsley v UK (2002) 35 EHRR 10 .... 11.24, 11.35, 11.36, 11.44
Kjeldsen, Busk Madsen and Pedersen v Denmark (1976) 1 EHRR 711 .... 2.04
Klass v Germany (1978) 2 EHRR 214 .... 3.50, 4.17
Kobenter and Standard Verlags Gmbh v Austria (App No 60899/00),
    2 November 2006 .... 9.26
Kolompar v Belgium (1993) 16 EHRR 197 .... 4.24
Kommerstant Moldova v Moldova (App No 41827/02) 13.30
König v Germany (1978) 2 EHRR 170 .... 11.23
Krone Verlag GmbbH & Co v Austria (No 3) (2004) EHRR 42 ....2.46, 12.06, 12.17
Kuhnen v Federal Republic of Germany App No 12194/86 (1988) 56 DR 205 .... 7.17
Kyprianou v Cyprus (2007) 44 EHRR 27 .... 9.05

Langborger v Sweden (1989) 12 EHRR 11.36
Latif and others v UK (App No 72819/01), 29 January 2004 .... 4.09
Lawless v Ireland (No 3) (1961) 1 EHRR 15 .... 7.14
Le Compte, Van Leuven and De Meyere v Belgium (1981) 4 EHRR 1 .... 11.24
Leander v Sweden (1987) 9 EHRR 433 .... 2.13, 2.27, 2.28, 9.34, 9.37, 9.54, 10.22
Lebideux and Isorni v France (1998) 5 BHRC 540 .... 7.22, 7.24
Lehideux and Isorni v France (2000) 30 EHRR 665 .... 2.66, 12.19
Leigh v UK App No 10039/82 (1984) 38 DR 74 .... 9.56
Leigh, Guardian Newspapers Ltd and Observer Ltd v UK App No 10039/82 (1984)
    38 DR 74; (1985) 7 EHRR 442 .... 3.45, 4.19
Leiningen-Westerburg v Austria App No 26601/95 (1997) DR 85 .... 9.32
Liberty v UK (App No 58243/00), 1 July 2008 .... 6.06
Lindner v Germany (App No 32813/96), 9 March 1999 .... 12.12
Lingens v Austria (1986) 8 EHRR 407 ....2.46, 3.64, 3.73, 5.10, 5.29, 5.31, 5.36–5.37
Loersch v Switzerland App No 23868/94 (1995) 80 DR 162 .... 9.11
Loizidou v Turkey (1996) 23 EHRR 513 .... 4.14
Lombardo v Malta (App No 7333/06), 24 April 2007 .... 5.43

Malone v UK (1984) 7 EHRR 14 .... 6.06
Markt Intern Verlag and Klaus Beerman v Germany (2003)
    37 EHRR 161 .... 2.46, 12.07, 12.30
Mathieu-Mohin and Clerfayt v Belgium (1987) 10 EHRR 1 .... 2.06, 10.06
McVicar v UK (2002) 35 EHRR 22 .... 2.22, 5.59, 5.73
Meltex Ltd and Mesrop Movseyan v Armenia (App No 32283/04), 17 June 2008 .... 11.05
Müller v Switzerland (1988) 13 EHRR 212 ....2.16, 2.46, 8.03, 8.13,
                                                           8.14, 8.17, 8.18, 8.19
Murphy v Ireland (2003) 38 EHRR 212 ....10.12, 11.16, 12.06, 12.19, 12.20, 12.34
Muslum Gunduz v Turkey (No 1) (2005) 7.19

News Verlags GmbH & Co KG v Austria (App No 31457/96) 11 January 2000
    (2001) 31 EHRR 8 .... 9.10, 9.20
Niemietz v Germany (1992) 16 EHRR 97 .... 3.48, 6.06
Nilsen and Johnsen v Norway (1999) 30 EHRR 878 .... 5.46
Nordisk v Denmark (App No 40485/02), 8 December 2005 .... 6.14
Norwood v UK (App No 23131/03), 16 November 2003 (2004)
    40 EHRR SE 111 .... 2.66, 7.18

Oberschlick v Austria (No 1) (1991) 19 EHRR 389 . . . . 5.37, 7.28
Oberschlick v Austria (No 2) (1997) 25 EHRR 357 . . . . 5.38
Observer and Guardian v UK (1991) 14 EHRR 153 . . . . 1.18, 2.19, 2.22, 2.41, 2.49,
               3.48, 5.07, 5.17, 5.32, 7.28, 9.22, 13.02,
          13.06, 13.07, 13.08, 13.11, 13.17, 13.18, 13.21
Okcuoglu v Turkey (App No 24246/94), 8 July 1999 . . . . 13.28
Open Door Counselling and Dublin Well Woman v Ireland (1992)
  15 EHRR 244 . . . . 2.15, 2.22, 3.45, 3.64, 12.21–12.22, 12.31
Osman v UK (1988) 29 EHRR 245; 1 FLR 198 . . . . 6.48, 9.52, 9.53, 11.25
Osterreichischer Rundfunk v Austria (App No 35841/02), 7 December 2006 . . . . 3.39
Otto-Preminger-Institut v Austria (1994) 19 EHRR 34 . . . . . 2.46, 8.21, 8.25, 8.28–8.30, 8.32
Özgür Gündem v Turkey (2001) 31 EHRR 1082 . . . . 2.25

P4 Radio Hele Norge ASA v Norway (App 76682/01) Decision of 6 May 2003 . . . . 9.55
Peck v UK (2003) 36 EHRR 41 . . . . 4.23, 6.29
Pedersen and Baadsgaard v Denmark (2006) 42 EHRR 24 . . . . 5.39, 5.40, 5.49
Perna v Italy (2004) 39 EHRR 563 . . . . 5.23, 5.27, 5.55, 5.58
Piermont v France (1995) 20 EHRR 301 . . . . 2.11, 2.17, 2.22, 5.15, 13.26
Pierre-Bloch v France (1998) 26 EHRR 202 . . . . 11.23
Piersack v Belgium (1982) 5 EHRR 169 . . . . 11.36
Plattform 'Artze für das leben' v Austria (1988) 13 EHRR 204 . . . . 2.24
Polat v Turkey (App No 23500/94), 8 July 1999 . . . . 13.28
PP and T v UK (1996) 22 EHRR CD 148 . . . . 4.19
Prager and Oberschlick v Austria (1995) 21 EHRR 1 . . . . 2.20, 2.22, 5.23, 5.31,
                    5.41, 9.23, 9.25
Pretto v Italy (1983) 6 EHRR 182 . . . . 2.52, 9.44
Pretty v UK (2002) 35 EHRR 1 . . . . 8.19
Pudas v Sweden (1987) 10 EHRR 380 . . . . 11.24
Purcell v Ireland App No 15404/89 (1991) 70 DR 262 . . . . 2.17, 11.11, 13.27

Radio ABC v Austria (1997) 25 EHRR 185 . . . . 11.10
Radio France v France App No 53984/00 (2005) 40 EHRR 29 . . . . 3.39, 5.09
Radio Twist v Slovakia (App No 62202/02), 19 December 2006 . . . . 6.25
Rees v UK (1986) 9 EHRR 56 . . . . 2.05
Riepan v Austria (App No 35115/97), 14 November 2000 . . . . 9.40
Ringeisen v Austria (1971) 1 EHRR 455 . . . . 11.23
Rizos & Daskas v Greece (App No 65545/01), 27 May 2004 . . . . 5.49
Robins v UK (1997) 26 EHRR 527 . . . . 9.38
Roemen and Schmit v Luxembourg (App No 51772/99), 25 February 2003 . . . . 2.20, 6.13

S & G v UK (App No 17634/91), 2 September 1991 . . . . 8.37
Scarth v UK (1998) 26 EHRR CD 154 . . . . 9.38
Scherer v Switzerland (App No 17116/90) 14 January 1993 . . . . 2.50, 8.17
Schöpfer v Switzerland (App No 25405/94) 2.11, 9.29
Schuler-Zgraggen v Switzerland (1993) 16 EHRR 405 . . . . 2.54
Sciacca v Italy (2006) 43 EHRR 20 . . . . 2.58, 6.28
Scozzari and Giunta v Italy (2002) 35 EHRR 12 . . . . 4.30
Selisto v Finland (2006) 42 EHRR 8 . . . . 5.48
Shabanov v Russia (App No 5433/02), 14 December 2006 . . . . 9.47
Silver v UK (1983) 5 EHRR 347 . . . . 2.37
Skalka v Poland (App No 43425/98), 27 May 2003 . . . . 9.27
Smith and Grady v UK (2000) 29 EHRR 493 . . . . 4.23
Soering v UK (1989) 11 EHRR 439 . . . . 2.04, 4.14, 4.23

SRG v Switzerland (App No 43524/98) 12.16
Stambuk v Germany (2003) 37 EHRR 42 . . . . 2.46, 12.14
Steel and Morris v UK (2005) 41 EHRR 22 . . . . 2.22, 5.33, 5.43, 5.49,
                                                    5.57, 5.60, 5.68, 5.73, 5.74
Steel and others v UK (1998) 28 EHRR 603 . . . . 2.13, 2.16, 2.39
Steur v Netherlands (2004) 39 EHRR 33 . . . . 2.22
Stewart-Brady v UK (App No 36908/97), 21 October 1998 . . . . 3.37
Stoll v Switzerland (2008) 47 EHRR 59 . . . . 2.20, 13.19–13.20
Stubbings and Others v UK (1996) 23 EHRR 213 . . . . 5.19, 5.20
Sunday Times v UK (App No 6538/74) (1979) 2 EHRR 245 . . . . 1.17, 2.09, 2.35, 2.46,
                                 2.56, 5.18, 5.32, 6.33, 9.12, 9.14, 9.16, 9.19, 9.22
Sunday Times v UK (No 2) (1991) 14 EHRR 229 . . . . 13.08
Surek and Ozdemir v Turkey (App Nos 23927/94 and 24277/94), 8 July 1999 . . . . 13.28
Surek v Turkey (Nos 1, 2, 3 and 4) (App Nos 26682/95, 24122/94 and 24762/94),
    8 July 1999 . . . . 7.32, 13.28
Sutter v Switzerland (1984) 6 EHRR 272 . . . . 9.44
Szucs v Austria (1997) 26 EHRR 310 . . . . 9.44

T v Belgium App No 97777/82 (1983) 34 DR 158 . . . . 7.20–7.21
T v UK (2000) 30 EHRR 121 . . . . 9.42
Tammer v Estonia (2003) 37 EHRR 43 . . . . 5.45
Tete v France App No 11123/84 (1987) 54 DR 52 . . . . 11.14
Thoma v Luxembourg (2003) 36 EHRR 21 . . . . 5.53
Thorgiersen v Iceland (1992) 14 EHRR 843 . . . . 2.46, 5.12
Tillack v Belgium (App No 20477/05), 27 November 2007 . . . . 6.13
Times v UK (App No 18897/91), 12 October 1992 . . . . 9.14
Times Newspapers Ltd v UK (App No 14631/89), (1990) 65 DR 307 . . . . 3.45, 4.18, 5.05
Tolstoy Miloslavsky v UK (1995) 20 EHRR 442 . . . . 2.22, 4.18, 5.11, 5.55
Tourancheau and July v France (App No 53886/00), 24 November 2005 . . . . 9.60
Tre Traktörer Aktiebolag v Sweden (1989) 13 EHRR 309 . . . . 11.24
Tyrer v UK (1978) 1 EHRR 1 . . . . 2.04

Ukrainian Media Group v Ukraine (2006) 43 EHRR 25 . . . . 5.36
Unabhangige Initiative Informations Vielfalt v Austria (2003) 37 EHRR 33 . . . . 2.11, 5.30
United Christian Broadcasting Ltd v UK (App No 44802/98), 7 November 2000 . . . . 11.04

Veraart v Netherlands (App No 10807/04), 30 November 2006 . . . . 9.30
Verein gegen Tierfabriken v Switzerland (2002) EHRR 159 . . . . 10.14
Vereiniging Weekblad Bluf! v Netherlands (1995) 29 EHRR 189 . . . . 6.23, 9.57, 13.17
Vereinigung Blidender Künstler v Austria App No 68354/01 (2008)
    47 EHRR 5 . . . . 2.46, 8.18, 8.35
Vereinigung Demokratischer Soldaten Österreichs and Gubi v Austria (1994)
    20 EHRR 56 . . . . 2.32, 2.47, 2.61, 13.06
Verlangsgruppe News Gmbh v Austria (No 2) (App No 10520/02), 14 December 2006 . . . 6.28
VgT Verein Gegen Tierfabriken v Switzerland (2001) 34 EHRR 159 . . . . 2.24, 3.26, 11.16,
                                       12.18, 12.19, 12.20, 12.34
Vides Aizsardzibas Klubs v Latvia (App no 57829/00), 25 May 2004 . . . . 5.49
Vogt v Germany (1995) 21 EHRR 205 . . . . 2.11, 2.46, 2.47, 13.06
Von Hannover v Germany (2005) 40 EHRR 1 . . . . 2.58, 5.19, 5.20, 6.27–6.28, 6.31, 6.34
Voskuil v Netherlands (App No 64752/01), 22 November 2007 . . . . 6.13, 6.14

W and K v Switzerland (App No 16564/90), 8 April 1991 . . . . 8.20
Weber v Switzerland (1990) 12 EHRR 508 . . . . 9.57, 13.17

Werner v Austria (1997) 26 EHRR 310 . . . . 9.44
Wille v Liechtenstein (2000) 30 EHRR 558 . . . . 2.11, 2.47
Wingrove v UK (1996) 24 EHRR 1 . . . . 2.23, 2.48, 2.50, 4.21,
8.21, 8.23, 8.26, 8.30, 8.32, 8.34, 8.40
Witzsch v Germany (App No 7485/03), 13 December 2005 . . . . 7.21
Worm v Austria (1997) 25 EHRR 454. . . . . 4.09, 9.19

X and the Association of Z v UK (App No 4515/70), 11 July 1971 . . . . 10.12, 10.22
X and Y v Netherlands (1985) 8 EHRR 235 . . . . 2.57
X v Belgium (1980) 23 DR 237 . . . . 2.53
X v Federal Republic of Germany (1982) 29 DR 194 . . . . 7.20, 7.21
X v Federal Republic of Germany App No 8383/79 (1979) 17 DR 227 . . . . 2.26
X v Germany App No 9235/81 (1982) 29 DR 192 . . . . 2.16
X v UK (1970) 30 CD 70. . . . . 9.38

Yankov v Bulgaria (2005) 41 EHRR 854 . . . . 2.46
Young and O'Faolain v Ireland App Nos 25646/94 and 29099/95 [1996]
EHLRR 326 . . . . 10.28

Z v Finland (1997) 25 EHRR 371 . . . . 9.45–9.46
Z v UK (2002) 34 EHRR 3 . . . . 11.25
Zana v Turkey (1997) 27 EHRR 667 . . . . 5.15
Zand v Austria App No 7360/76 (1978) 15 DR 70 . . . . 11.35
Zihlman v Switzerland App No 21861/93 (1995) DR 12 . . . . 9.31

IRELAND

Corway v Independent Newspapers (Ireland) Ltd [2001] 1 IRLM 426. . . . . 8.23

NEW ZEALAND

Lange v Atkinson [2000] 3 NZLR 385 . . . . 1.18

SOUTH AFRICA

National Media v Bogoshi 1998 (4) SA 1196 (SCA) 5.71

UNITED STATES OF AMERICA

44 Liquormart v Rhode Island 116 S Ct 1495 (1996) 12.26

Abrams v US 250 US 616 (1919). 1.05, 1.08, 13.21, 13.28

Bates v Bar of Arizona 433 US 350 (1977). 12.12
Brandenburg v Ohio 395 US 444 (1969). 13.23, 13.24, 13.28, 13.36

Central Hudson Gas v Public Services Commission 447 US 557 (1980) 12.02, 12.23
Collin v Smith 439 US 916 (1978) 7.34

Florida Star v BJF 491 US 524 (1989) 1.13

Gertz v Robert Welch Inc 418 US 323 (1974). 5.71
Grayned v City of Rockford 408 US 104 . . . . 2.38

Jacobellis v Ohio 378 US 184 (1964) 8.14

Lorillard Tobacco Co v Riley (2001) 533 US 525 . . . . 12.34

NAACP v Button 371 US 415 (1963) 2.38
Near v Minnesota 283 US 697 (1931) 1.17, 13.37
New York Times v Sullivan 376 US 254 (1964) 2.46, 5.71
New York Times v US; Washington Post v US 403 US 713 (1971) 1.17, 2.50, 13.15, 13.38

Pittsburgh Press Co v The Pittsburgh Commission on Human Relations 413
    US 3376 (1973) 12.23
Posadas de Puerto Rico Associates v Tourism Company of Puerto Rico 478
    US 328 (1986) 12.26
Procunier v Martinez 416 US 396 (1974) 1.07

RAV v City of St Paul 505 US 377 (1992) 7.34
Roth v US 354 US 476 (1957) 8.13
Rubin v Coors Brewing Co 115 S Ct 1585 (1995) 12.26

Snepp v US 444 US 507 (1980) 13.12, 13.18
St Amant v Thompson 390 US 727 (1968) 5.71

Texas v Johnson 491 US 397 (1989) 2.17
Time Inc v Hill 385 US 374 (1967) 1.13

Virginia State Board of Pharmacy v Virginia Citizens Consumer Council 425
    US 748 (1976) 12.04, 12.12, 12.32
Virginia v Black 538 US 343 (2003) 7.34

TABLE OF LEGISLATION

Statutes and Statutory		European Community	xxx
Instruments	xxvii	Germany	xxx
Official Publications	xxix	International	xxx
Australia	xxix	Ireland	xxx
Canada	xxix	Switzerland	xxxi
Council of Europe	xxix	United States of America	xxxi

STATUTES AND STATUTORY INSTRUMENTS

Bill of Rights 1688
Art 9 . . . . 10.24–10.29
Civil Procedure Rules 1998 (SI
1998/3132)
Pt 7, r 7.11 . . . . 3.56
Pt 25, r 25.3(1) 3.68
Pt 39, r 39.2 . . . . 9.38
Practice Direction 39, para 1.4A 9.41
r 31.22 . . . . 9.56
Communications Act
2003 . . . . 3.26, 11.06, 12.01
s 319 . . . . 10.12, 11.07, 12.34
s 319(2)(f) 10.14
s 321 . . . . 10.12, 12.34
s 333 . . . . 10.13
s 336 . . . . 11.11
Companies Acts 11.18
Contempt of Court Act 1981
s 2 . . . . 9.17–9.18, 9.21
s 4(1) 9.18
s 5 . . . . 9.18
s 8 . . . . 9.58
s 9 . . . . 9.54
s 10 . . . . 6.10, 6.16
Crime and Disorder Act 1998
s 31 . . . . 7.07
Criminal Justice Act 1925
s 41 . . . . 9.54
Criminal Justice and Immigration
Act 2008
s 79 . . . . 8.12, 8.40
Data Protection Act 1998 . . . . 3.37
s 32(3) 3.76

Defamation Act 1952
s 10 . . . . 10.11
Defamation Act 1996 . . . . 5.63
s 13(1) 10.29
s 13(5) 10.26
Sch 1, para 2 . . . . 4.29
Sch 1, para 16(3)(b) 4.29
Electoral Administration Act 2006 . . . 10.02
European Communities Act 1972 . . . . 3.28
Human Rights Act 1998 . . . . 1.11, 1.20,
3.01–3.02, 3.37, 4.02, 4.23, 5.03,
5.64, 5.65, 7.09, 9.09, 10.04, 11.12,
11.35, 11.42, 12.23–12.24,
13.33, 13.37
s 2 . . . . 3.11–3.12
s 21(1) 3.21, 3.31
s 2(2)–(3) 3.15
s 22(4) 3.58
s 3 . . . . 3.18–3.19, 3.67, 9.18
s 3(1) 3.16
s 3(2)(a) 3.19
s 3(2)(b) 3.20
s 3(2)(c) 3.21
s 4 . . . . 3.22
s 4(6) 3.22
s 4(6)(a)–(b) 3.25
s 6 . . . . 3.32, 3.38, 3.67, 4.23, 5.63
s 6(1) 3.29, 3.32, 3.40, 3.72
s 6(2)(a)–(b) 3.30
s 6(3)–(4) 3.31
s 6(3) 10.31
s 6(3)(a) 3.31
s 6(3)(b) 3.32
s 6(5) 3.32
s 6(6) 3.41

Human Rights Act 1998 (*cont.*)
ss 7–9 .... 3.42
s 7 .... 3.10, 3.58
s 7(1) 3.43, 3.54
s 7(1)(a) 3.56
s 7(1)(b) 3.58
s 7(2) 3.56
s 7(3) 3.50
s 7(5) 3.57
s 7(6)(a) 3.58
s 8(1),(6) 3.61
s 8(2)–(4) 3.63
s 9(1)–(2) 3.59
s 9(3)–(5) 3.66
s 10 .... 3.22
s 11 .... 3.13, 3.55, 3.67, 6.30
s 12 .... 3.60, 3.67, 3.67–3.68,
            6.05, 6.40, 13.40
s 12(1) 3.67
s 12(2) 3.68, 6.47
s 12(3) 3.69–3.72, 6.47, 10.23, 13.41
s 12(4) 3.73, 3.74, 6.04, 6.33
s 12(4)(a) 3.67
s 12(4)(a)(i) 6.37
s 12(4)(b) 6.43
s 12(5) 3.67
s 19(1) 3.26
s 19(1)(a) 12.34
Sch 1 .... 3.03–3.09
Sch 2 .... 3.22
Incitement to Disaffection Act 1934
ss 1–2 .... 13.21
Law of Libel Amendment Act 1888 ... 8.22
s 8 .... 5.61
Libel Act 1843
s 6 .... 5.61
Malicious Communications Act 1988
s 1(1) 8.36
Newspaper Libel and Registration
act 1881 .... 11.18
Northern Ireland Act 1973
s 38(1)(a) 3.20
Northern Ireland Act 1998 .... 3.20
Obscene Publications Act 1959 ...... 8.16
s 1 .... 8.08
s 1(1) 8.38
s 2(1) 8.38
s 4 .... 8.27
Obscene Publications Act
1964 .... 8.16, 8.38
Official Secrets Act 1911
s 1 .... 13.31
s 2 .... 13.31–13.32

Official Secrets Act 1989 .... 13.31
ss 1–6 .... 13.32
s 1 .... 13.34
s 1(1) 13.32
s 2 .... 13.35
s 3 .... 13.35
s 4 .... 13.34
s 5 .... 13.33
Police and Criminal Evidence Act
1984 .... 6.08
Political Parties, Elections and
Referendums Act 2000
ss 28, 28A, 28B, 29 .... 10.01
s 37 .... 10.13
s 87(2)(a) 10.10
s 131 .... 10.08
Protection of Children Act 1978
s 1(a) 8.39
Public Interest Disclosure Act 1998 ... 6.20
Public Order Act 1936 .... 7.03
Public Order Act 1986 .... 7.07
Part 3 .... 7.04, 7.05, 7.06
Part 3A 7.05, 7.06
s 19(1) 7.04
ss 21–23 .... 7.04
ss 29A-29N 7.05
Race Relations Act 1965
s 6 .... 7.03
Race Relations Act 1976
s 3A 7.02
Racial and Religious Hatred Act
2006 .... 7.05, 8.12
Regulation of Investigatory Powers
Act 2000 .... 6.06
Representation of the People Act
1983 .... 10.02
s 66A 10.10
s 75 .... 10.16–10.20
s 75(1) 10.08, 10.09
s 93 .... 10.10
s 106(1) 10.11
s 106(3) 10.11, 10.23
s 160(4) 10.09
s 168(a)(ii) 10.09
s 173(a) 10.09
Serious Organised Crime Act 2005
ss 82–94 .... 6.50
Supreme Court Act 1981
s 29(3) 3.59
s 31(3) 3.50
Terrorism Act 2000
Sch 5 .... 6.18
Terrorism Act 2001 .... 13.36

Terrorism Act 2006
  s 1 .... 13.36
Theatres Act 1968
  s 2(4) 8.10
Tobacco Advertising and
  Promotion Act 2002 .... 12.32
Tobacco Advertising and Promotion
  (Brandsharing) Regulations
  2004 (SI 2004/1824) 12.32
Trades Descriptions Act 1968 .... 12.01
Treason Felony Act 1848 .... 3.46
Video Recordings Act 1984 .... 3.36,
                               8.36
  s 4(1) 8.23

OFFICIAL PUBLICATIONS

Bar Code of Conduct 12.35
BBC Editorial Guidelines for
  Elections 10.10
BBC License and Agreement 11.11
BBC Royal Charter 2007 .... 10.13
Fifth Report of the Committee on
  Standards in Public Life
  (Cm 4507-1, 1998) 10.01
Ofcom Broadcasting Code
  rules 6.8 to 6.13 .... 10.10
Reform of section 2 of the Official
  Secrets Act 1911 (Cm 408,
  1988) 13.34

AUSTRALIA

New South Wales Defamation Act
  2005 .... 5.71

CANADA

Canadian Charter of Rights
  ss 1, 2(b) 1.03
Canadian Criminal Code
  s 319 .... 7.34

COUNCIL OF EUROPE

Committee of Ministers
  Recommendation R (89) 9.46
Committee of Ministers
  Recommendation R(2000) 23
  Art 10 .... 11.05
Committee of Ministers
  Recommendation R(2003)
  (13) 9.60, 10.01

Convention for the Protection
  of Human Rights and
  Fundamental Freedoms
  1950
  (European Convention on Human
  Rights) 1.18, 2.01–2.07
  Section II 4.03
  Art 1 .... 3.04, 3.07, 4.01
  Art 2 .... 2.63, 3.53, 4.23, 6.39,
                          9.37, 9.52–9.53
  Art 3 ...... 2.63, 4.23, 7.10, 7.16, 10.18
  Art 4 .... 2.63
  Art 5 .... 3.66, 7.14, 10.31
  Art 6 ...... 5.60, 5.74, 6.18, 7.14, 7.15,
       9.01, 9.04–9.09, 9.33, 9.37–9.44,
       10.11, 10.31, 11.01, 11.20–11.30,
             11.42–11.44, 13.35
  Art 6(1) 2.52–2.54, 9.01, 9.19,
            9.35, 9.41, 10.28–10.29,
            11.23–11.24, 11.28,
            11.31–11.42, 13.18
  Art 6(2) 11.38
  Art 6(3) 11.39
  Art 7 .... 2.63, 11.40
  Art 8 ...... 1.23, 2.05, 2.55–2.58, 3.07,
       3.47–3.48, 3.65, 4.22, 5.14, 5.19,
       5.20, 6.01, 6.03, 6.06, 6.09,
       6.26–6.30, 6.32–6.34, 6.36, 6.39,
       6.44–6.45, 9.45–9.46, 9.48, 10.28
  Art 8(2) 6.02, 6.07
  Art 9 .... 8.25, 8.33, 8.40
  Art 10 ..... 1.03, 1.09, 1.18, 2.08–2.10,
       2.54–2.57, 2.61, 2.66, 3.01, 3.26,
       3.44, 3.46–3.49, 3.60, 3.64, 4.13,
       4.18, 4.28, 5.03, 5.04, 5.06, 5.07,
       5.12, 5.13, 5.15, 5.18, 5.19, 5.28,
       5.30, 5.32–5.34, 5.40, 5.53, 5.54,
       5.56, 5.60, 5.62, 5.63, 5.73, 5.74,
       6.09, 6.11, 6.18, 6.19, 6.22–6.26,
       6.32, 6.33, 6.36, 6.44, 7.15,
       7.17–7.19, 7.21, 7.23, 7.28, 8.04,
       8.13, 8.16, 8.21, 8.24, 8.25, 8.31,
       8.32, 8.35–8.37, 8.39, 8.40, 9.04,
       9.10, 9.11, 9.14, 9.18, 9.19, 9.21,
       9.22–9.37, 9.47, 9.48, 9.56–9.60,
       10.01, 10.06, 10.14, 10.21, 10.31,
       11.13–11.17, 12.02, 12.04,
       12.06–12.12, 12.14–12.15, 12.17,
       12.19, 12.22–12.25, 12.27, 12.32,
       12.34, 13.09, 13.12–13.14,
       13.16–13.19, 13.21, 13.24,
       13.28–13.30, 13.34, 13.36,
              13.39–13.40

Art 10(1) 2.09, 2.11–2.34, 5.16,
       7.01, 7.11, 7.26, 9.01, 9.03,
      10.12, 10.17, 10.22, 11.02–11.09
Art 10(2) 2.09, 2.11, 2.13,
    2.34–2.50, 3.73, 5.08, 5.16, 5.17,
    5.21, 5.31, 5.36, 5.54, 6.07, 6.21,
    7.13, 7.17, 7.20, 7.21, 7.24, 7.26,
    8.02, 8.19, 9.01, 9.12, 9.13, 9.15,
      9.16, 9.35, 9.41, 10.11,
      10.12, 11.03, 11.14, 11.19,
        13.07, 13.28
Art 13 . . . . 3.05, 3.09–3.10,
      3.62, 4.01, 4.23
Art 14 . . . . . 2.59–2.62, 7.09, 7.10–7.12,
    7.15, 7.16, 8.20, 8.33, 8.40,
      10.11, 10.22, 11.04
Art 15 . . . . 2.63–2.64
Art 17 . . . . . 2.65–2.66, 7.13, 7.14, 7.15,
    7.16, 7.18, 7.21, 7.23, 7.24
Art 19 . . . . 4.03
Art 27 . . . . 4.05
Art 28 . . . . 4.26
Art 29(3) 4.26
Art 30 . . . . 4.05
Art 33 . . . . 4.02
Art 34 . . . . 3.35, 3.43,
    3.49–3.50, 4.03, 4.17, 9.03
Art 35 . . . . 4.16
Art 35(1) 4.09, 4.21
Art 35(2)–(3) 4.12
Art 36 . . . . 4.29
Art 38 . . . . 4.27
Art 40(1) 4.29
Art 40(2) 4.12
Art 41 . . . . 4.03, 4.10, 4.17, 4.30
Art 43 . . . . 4.05
Art 46 . . . . 4.03
Protocol No 1, Art 3 . . . . 10.01, 10.05
Protocol No 11 . . . . 4.03, 4.04, 4.14
Protocol No 12, Art 1 . . . . 7.09
Protocol No 14 . . . . 4.04,
      4.05, 4.16, 4.27
Protocol No 14, r 15–16 . . . . 4.06
Protocol No 14, r 26(1)(a) 4.05
Protocol No 14, r 39 . . . . 4.26
Protocol No 14, r 44(2) 4.29
Protocol No 14, r 49 . . . . 4.05
Protocol No 14, r 53(3) 4.26
Protocol No 14, r 4.26
Protocol No 14, r 54 . . . . 4.26
Protocol No 14, r 56 . . . . 4.26
Protocol No 14, r 59 . . . . 4.27
Protocol No 14, r 62 . . . . 4.27

Protocol No 14, r 72 . . . . 4.05
Protocol No 14, r 73 . . . . 4.05
Protocol No 14, r 91–92 . . . . 4.07
Convention on Transfrontier
   Television 1989 . . . . 2.07
Parliamentary Assembly
   Recommendation 1516
   (2001) 10.01
Rules of Procedure of the European
   Court of Human Rights 1998
   r 61 . . . . 3.50

EUROPEAN COMMUNITY

Directive 2003/33/EC 12.32
Directive 98/43/EC 12.27

GERMANY

Unfair Competition Act 1909
   s 13 . . . . 12.10

INTERNATIONAL

American Convention on Human
   Rights 1969
   Art 13 . . . . 2.30–2.31
Beijing Statement of Principles of
   the Independence of the
   Judiciary in the LAWASIA
   Region 1991 . . . . 9.42
Convention for the Protection of
   Individuals with Regard to
   Automatic Processing of
   Personal Data 1981 . . . . 9.46
International Convention on the
   Elimination of All Forms of
   Racial Discrimination 1965 . . . . . 2.07
   Art 4 . . . . 7.33
International Covenant on Civil
   and Political Rights 1966
   Art 19 . . . . 7.21
   Art 20(2) 7.33
   Art 26 . . . . 7.09
UN Convention on the Rights of
   the Child 1989 . . . . 9.42
Vienna Convention on the Law of
   Treaties 1969 . . . . 2.02
   Art 31(1) 2.03

IRELAND

Constitution

Art 40(3) (Eighth Amendment) . . . 12.22

SWITZERLAND

Federal Unfair Competition Act
  1986 . . . . 12.16

UNITED STATES OF AMERICA

Bill of Rights
  First Amendment 7.34
Constitution
  First Amendment 1.03

1

FREEDOM OF EXPRESSION AND PRIVACY: AN INTRODUCTION

Introduction	1.01	to the Incorporation of the	
Freedom of Expression Theory	1.05	ECHR	1.14
Privacy Theory	1.10	English Law's Approach to the	
English Law's Approach to		Right to Privacy Prior to the	
Freedom of Expression Prior		Incorporation of the ECHR	1.21

Introduction

This book is aimed at practitioners in the media law field, but it is hoped that **1.01** it will be of interest to students of media law and human rights law. It is not intended to be a definitive text on media law; for this see Geoffrey Robertson QC and Andrew Nicol QC, *Media Law*.[1] Neither is it intended to be a comparative academic work; if this is what is required, see Professor Eric Barendt's work entitled *Freedom of Speech*.[2]

The dual focus of this book is the jurisprudence of the European Court of **1.02** Human Rights ('the European Court') and the case law of the domestic courts since the HRA came into force.[3] Decisions of the European Commission of Human Rights ('the Commission') are referred to where necessary.[4] We hope to give a comprehensive analysis of all relevant case law in the media law field.

---

[1] Sweet & Maxwell (5th edn, 2007).
[2] Oxford: OUP (2nd edn, 2005), which examines the protection of freedom of speech in England, Germany, the USA and under the European Convention.
[3] The majority of the case law comes from the English Courts, although there is discussion of Scottish and Northern Irish case law when relevant.
[4] The European Commission ceased to exist on 1 November 1998 when a full-time European Court came into being as a result of the Eleventh Protocol to the European Convention on Human Rights coming into force.

However, we also intend to draw on jurisprudence from other jurisdictions, particularly the USA and Canada. The US jurisprudence necessarily does not provide all the answers to questions concerning media law, freedom of expression, and privacy, but it is by far the most developed in this field, and consistently grapples with human rights issues. Additionally, prior to the incorporation of the European Convention on Human Rights (ECHR), English courts were willing to draw on US case law in the field of freedom of expression,[5] although not the right to respect for privacy.

1.03 Canadian jurisprudence is useful because, unlike the US First Amendment,[6] the right to freedom of expression contained in Section 2(b) of the Canadian Charter of Rights, guaranteeing everyone the 'fundamental freedom' of 'freedom of thought, belief, opinion and expression, including freedom of the press and other media of communication', is subject to express limitations contained in Section 1 of the Charter which provides that limitations on freedom of expression are permissible if they are 'such reasonable limits prescribed by law as can be demonstrably justified in a free and democratic society.' This approach mirrors that of Article 10 ECHR.

1.04 This chapter briefly examines the philosophical justifications underpinning the right to freedom of expression and the right to privacy. While this might seem out of place in a work aimed at practitioners, it is both useful and necessary to understand how the jurisprudence in the media law field has developed in the past and how it is likely to develop in the future. This discussion is followed by a brief outline of English law's treatment of the right to freedom of expression and the right to privacy prior to incorporation of the ECHR. The substantive chapters address the post incorporation case law in detail and therefore it is not analysed here.

Freedom of Expression Theory[7]

Mill's argument from truth

1.05 The argument from truth is the predominant and most durable of the underlying rationales for the protection of speech. Today it is most commonly associated

---

[5] See, eg *Derbyshire County Council* v *Times Newspapers Ltd* [1993] AC 534 (HL) and *R* v *Secretary of State for the Home Department, ex p Simms* [2000] 2 AC 115.

[6] The First Amendment to the US Constitution provides: 'Congress shall make no law . . . abridging the freedom of speech, or of the press'.

[7] For a more learned (and lengthy) discussion of the philosophical underpinnings of the right to freedom of expression, see Schauer, F, *Free Speech: A Philosophical Enquiry* (Cambridge: CUP, 1982).

with John Stuart Mill, who in his book *On Liberty* argued that suppression of opinion was wrong, because it is only by the 'collision of adverse opinions' that truth is discovered or confirmed. This argument had been advanced two centuries earlier by Milton.[8] The rationale was taken up by Justice Holmes in *Abrams* v *US*[9] who asserted that all truths were relative and that they can only be judged 'in the competition of the market'. Holmes concluded that 'The best test of truth is the power of the thought to get itself accepted in the competition of the market' (at 630). This argument for the protection of freedom of expression posits that freedom of expression is not an end in itself but a means of identifying and accepting truth. The argument involves a scepticism both of the state and of accepted beliefs and 'acknowledged truths'. This truth or 'marketplace of ideas' rationale for freedom of expression extends not only to political speech, but also to the ideas of philosophy, history, the social sciences, the natural sciences, other branches of human knowledge, and commercial speech. However, it is of little or no application to obscene speech or personal abuse which often contains no factual assertions.

Democratic self-governance[10]

This argument is associated, particularly in the USA, with Alexander Meiklejohn.   **1.06**
His view was that the main purpose of protecting freedom of expression was to protect the rights of citizens to understand matters of political concern so as to enable them to participate meaningfully in the democratic process. Meiklejohn stated that: 'The principle of the freedom of speech springs from the necessities of the program of self-government. It is not a Law of Nature or Reason in the abstract. It is a deduction from the basic American agreement that public issues shall be decided by universal suffrage.'[11]

This rationale explains the importance placed on political speech by, amongst others, the European Court. However, the disadvantage with the rationale, and the reason why, by itself, it is insufficient to justify the extensive protection of freedom of expression, is that it potentially excludes large areas of expression that are traditionally considered important, such as artistic and literary expression.

---

[8] See Milton, J, 'Areopagitica: A Speech for the Liberty of Unlicensed Printing (1644)' in *Prose Writings* (London: Everyman's edn, 1958).

[9] 250 US 616, 630–1 (1919).

[10] See Laws, Sir J, 'Meiklejohn, the First Amendment and Free Speech in English Law' in Professor I Loveland (ed), *Importing the First Amendment, Freedom of Speech and Expression in Britain, Europe and the USA* (Oxford: Hart Publishing, 1998) for a critique of Meiklejohn's theory.

[11] Meiklejohn, A, *Political Freedom: The Constitutional Powers of the People* (Oxford: OUP, 1965) at 27.

Self-fulfilment

1.07 While Mill's argument from truth and Meiklejohn's argument from self-governance justify the protection of freedom of expression as a means to an end, freedom of expression can also be an end in itself. Under this theory, freedom of expression is protected not just to create a better government and not merely to discover the truth, but to 'enlarge the prospects for individual self-fulfilment' or to allow 'personal growth and self-realisation'. In the words of Justice Thurgood Marshall of the US Supreme Court in *Procunier* v *Martinez*[12] '[Freedom of expression] serves not only the needs of the polity but also those of the human spirit—a spirit that demands self-expression.' This rationale for protecting expression is of broadest application, embracing the protection of expression such as obscenity which would not receive protection under either of the two other rationales.

The relevance of the rationales for protecting freedom of expression

1.08 All three rationales for protecting freedom of expression have been recognized in US and Canadian law[13] and by the House of Lords in *R* v *Secretary of State for the Home Department, ex p Simms*,[14] where Lord Steyn stated:

> Freedom of expression is, of course, intrinsically important: it is valued for its own sake. But it is well recognised that it is also instrumentally important. It serves a number of broad objectives. First, it promotes the self-fulfilment of individuals in society. Secondly, in the famous words of Holmes J (echoing John Stuart Mill), 'the best test of truth is the power of the thought to get itself accepted in the competition of the market'.[15] Thirdly, freedom of speech is the lifeblood of democracy. The free flow of information and ideas informs political debate. It is a safety valve: people are more ready to accept decisions that go against them if they can in principle seek to influence them. It acts as a brake on the abuse of power by public officials. It facilitates the exposure of errors in the governance and administration of justice of the country.[16]

1.09 The European Court has also made reference to the underlying rationales for protecting the right to freedom of expression. In one of the first major judgments on Article 10, the Court stated:

> Freedom of expression constitutes one of the essential foundations of a society, one of the basic conditions for its progress and for the development of every man.

---

[12] 416 US 396, 427 (1974).
[13] See, eg *Irwin Toy* v *Quebec* [1989] 1 SCR 927, at 968–71.
[14] [2000] 2 AC 115, at 126.
[15] *Abrams* v *US* 250 US 616 (1919), at p 630 per Holmes J (dissent).
[16] See Stone, Seidman, Sunstein and Tushnet, *Constitutional Law* (3rd edn, 1999) pp 1078–86.

Subject to paragraph 2 of Article 10, it is applicable not only to 'information and ideas' that are favourably received or regarded as inoffensive but also to those that offend, shock or disturb the state or any sector of the population. Such are the demands of pluralism, tolerance and broad mindedness without which there is no 'democratic society'.[17]

This quotation encapsulates two of the three main theoretical rationales for the protection of expression: (i) freedom of expression enables citizens to participate effectively in a democracy; and (ii) freedom of expression is an integral aspect of each citizen's right to self-development and fulfilment.[18] The third rationale—namely Mill's argument from truth, which is closely linked to the utilitarian tradition in moral philosophy—has been less influential in the jurisprudence of the European Court than in the US and Canadian Supreme Courts.

Privacy Theory

The right to be left alone: Warren and Brandeis[19]

In arguably one of the most influential academic legal articles ever written, **1.10** Warren and Brandeis famously discovered the 'right to privacy' implicit in the (predominantly English) common law. The authors drew on case law in the field of defamation, breach of confidence, copyright, and trespass to conclude that these cases were merely instances and applications of a general 'right of privacy'. They stated: 'The intensity and complexity of life, attendant upon advancing civilization, having rendered necessary some retreat from the world, and man, under the refining influence of culture, has become more sensitive to publicity, so that solitude and privacy have become more essential to the individual; but modern enterprise and invention have, through invasions upon his privacy, subjected him to mental pain and distress, far greater than could be inflicted by merely bodily injury.'[20]

This article had a profound influence on the development of US law[21] with **1.11** nearly every American state recognizing a 'right to privacy'. However, even

---

[17] *Handyside* v *UK* (1976) 1 EHRR 737, para 49.
[18] See, eg Scanlon, T, 'Freedom of Expression and Categories of Expression' (1979) 40 U Pittsburgh L Rev 519.
[19] Warren, SD and Brandeis, LD, 'The Right to Privacy' (1890) 4 Harv L Rev 193, reprinted in Wacks, R, *Privacy and the Law,* vol II (International Library of Essays in Law and Legal Theory) (London: Dartmouth, 1993; New York: New York University Press, 1993).
[20] Ibid, at 196.
[21] See discussion in Wacks, R, *Privacy and Press Freedom* (London: Blackstone Press, 1995), ch 1, at 11–12.

though the authors relied almost exclusively on English cases, most notably the defamation decision in *Prince Albert* v *Strange*,[22] no such development occurred in the more judicially conservative English courts prior to the incorporation of the HRA 1998.

Prosser: the four privacy torts[23]

1.12 William Prosser classified the tort (or more accurately torts) of breach of privacy in US law as follows:

(a) intrusion on seclusion, solitude, or private affairs;
(b) publication of embarrassing private (but true) facts;
(c) publicity which portrays a person in a false light;
(d) appropriation of a person's name or likeness (now often known as the right of publicity).[24]

1.13 Prosser's article, like Warren and Brandeis's, had a profound impact on American law. These four privacy torts have been recognized in most states, although the extent of protection varies from state to state with New York and California leading the way in protecting privacy rights. The second and third privacy torts have given rise to difficulties under the First Amendment—see *Time Inc* v *Hill*[25] (false light privacy) and *Florida Star* v *BJF*[26] (disclosure of identity of rape victim)—because they limit the right of the press to publish truthful information. The fourth tort is more concerned with protecting the valuable commercial interests of an individual's name and image rather than the 'right of privacy' as it is commonly understood.

English Law's Approach to Freedom of Expression Prior to the Incorporation of the ECHR

Historical perspective

1.14 The absence of any constitutional or statutory provision protecting freedom of expression means that the right to freedom of expression has been largely residual. *Blackstone's Commentaries* do not mention the right to freedom of speech, although there is some discussion of freedom of the press. Dicey wrote

---

[22] (1849) 2 De G & Sm 652, 64 ER 293; (1849) 1 Mac & G 25, 41 ER 1171.
[23] Prosser, W, 'Privacy' (1960) 48 Calif L Rev 383, reprinted in Wacks, (n 19 above) at 47.
[24] Ibid, at 389.
[25] 385 US 374 (1967).
[26] 491 US 524 (1989).

that: 'Freedom of discussion is . . . in England little else than the right to write or say anything which a jury, consisting of twelve shopkeepers, think it expedient should be said or written.'[27] Thus unpopular or unorthodox expression went unprotected. The suppression of expression critical of the government was viewed as necessary to maintain the reputation of government. Lord Holt, in *R v Tuchin*,[28] reasoned: 'If men should not be called to account for possessing the people with an ill opinion of the government, no government can subsist; for it is very necessary for every government, that the people should have a good opinion of it. And nothing can be worse to any government, than to endeavour to produce animosities as to the management of it. This has always been looked upon as a crime, and no government can be safe unless it be punished.'

One of the main tools utilized to suppress expression critical of the King or his agents was seditious libel. Truth was not a defence on the grounds that 'the greater the truth, the greater the libel' against the government. Neither was it necessary to prove intent to incite insurrection, because merely intending to publish criticism was unlawful as it found 'fault with his masters and betters'.[29] **1.15**

The second method used to control expression was the elaborate system of licensing, which English writers had to contend with until it was abolished in 1695. All writing had to be licensed prior to publication, otherwise the publication was unlawful. The abolition of the licensing system led to the development of a concept of freedom of the press that prohibited the existence of prior restraints. In 1765, Blackstone wrote that: 'The liberty of the press is indeed essential to the nature of a free state; but this consists in laying no *previous* restraints on publications, and not in freedom from censure for criminal matter when published. Every free man has an undoubted right to lay what sentiments he pleases before the public; to forbid this is to destroy the freedom of the press; but if he publishes what is improper, mischievous or illegal, he must take the consequences of his own temerity.'[30] **1.16**

English courts, while wary of prior restraints, have not adopted the near absolute bar on prior restraints that the US Supreme Court jurisprudence has developed.[31] **1.17**

---

[27] Dicey, AV, *Introduction to the Study of the Law of the Constitution* (London: Macmillan, 1959), ch VI. Such a view is diametrically opposed to the jurisprudence of the European Court, which has repeatedly emphasized the importance of protection of unpopular minority speech.

[28] (1704) Holt 424.

[29] See Chafee, Z, *Free Speech in the United States* (Cambridge, Mass: Harvard University Press, 1941), at 19.

[30] Blackstone, W, *Commentaries on the Laws of England*, Book IV, at 151–2 (1765).

[31] Contrast *Near v Minnesota* 283 US 697 (1931) and *New York Times v US* 403 US 713 (1971) (the *Pentagon Papers* case) with *Attorney-General v Times Newspapers Ltd* [1974] AC 273 (concerning an injunction preventing the publication of an article on the dangers of thalidomide,

**Developments immediately prior to the incorporation
of the ECHR: 1980s and 1990s**

1.18   The English judiciary, subject to certain notable exceptions,[32] consistently failed
to give sufficient regard to the right to freedom of expression in the period prior
to the incorporation of the ECHR into domestic law. Lord Goff, in *Attorney-
General* v *Guardian Newspapers Ltd (No 2)*,[33] expressed the opinion that there
was no difference in principle between English law on freedom of expression
and Article 10 of the Convention (a view reiterated by Lord Keith in *Derbyshire
County Council* v *Times Newspapers Ltd*).[34] The number of cases in which English
law has been held to contravene Article 10 suggests that the protection of freedom
of expression afforded by English law is generally less full than that afforded by
Article 10. Due in large part to the absence of a binding code of rights, English
law lacked the developed principles of US and Canadian law. The development
of such principles commenced prior to the incorporation of the ECHR,[35] and
has continued post incorporation.[36]

1.19   Sedley LJ, in *Redmond-Bate* v *DPP*,[37] echoing the sentiments of the European
Court in *Handyside* v *UK*,[38] emphasized the importance of protecting unpopular
or offensive speech. Ms Redmond-Bate and her colleagues were Christian
fundamentalist preachers who were arrested for breach of the peace after refusing
to comply with a police officer's instruction to stop preaching on the steps
of Wakefield Cathedral. They were subsequently convicted of obstructing a
police officer in the execution of his duty. Sedley LJ, allowing the appeal against
conviction, stated:

---

which was later held, by the European Court of Human Rights, to be a violation of Art 10 ECHR
in *Sunday Times* v *UK* (1979) 2 EHRR 245).

[32] One notable exception is Lord Denning's dissenting judgment in *Schering Chemicals Ltd* v
Falkman [1982] QB 1. Examples of cases where English courts have failed to give sufficient regard
to the right to freedom of expression include *X Ltd* v *Morgan-Grampian (Publishing) Ltd* [1991]
1 AC 1. *Reynolds* v *Times Newspapers* [1999] 3 WLR 1010 has been seen as similarly deficient by
the New Zealand Court of Appeal: *Lange* v *Atkinson* [2000] 3 NZLR 385, at 399.

[33] [1990] 1 AC 109, at 283–4. This case concerned publication of extracts from *Spycatcher* by
Peter Wright. *Observer and Guardian* v *UK* (1991) 14 EHRR 153, held that the UK was in breach
of Art 10 because the injunction restraining the publication of such extracts was not necessary in
a democratic society after *Spycatcher* had been published in the USA and was therefore no longer
secret.

[34] [1993] AC 534.

[35] See, eg Lord Steyn's speech in *R* v *Secretary of State for the Home Department, ex p Simms*
[2000] 2 AC 115.

[36] See generally, chs 2 and 5–13.

[37] (1999) 7 BHRC 375.

[38] (1976) 1 EHRR 737.

Free speech includes not only the inoffensive but the irritating, the contentious, the eccentric, the heretical, the unwelcome and the provocative provided it does not tend to provoke violence. Freedom only to speak inoffensively is not worth having. What Speakers' Corner (where the law applies as fully as anywhere else) demonstrates is the tolerance which is both extended by the law to opinion of every kind and expected by the law in the conduct of those who disagree, even strongly, with what they hear. From the condemnation of Socrates to the persecution of modern writers and journalists, our world has seen too many examples of state control of unofficial ideas. A central purpose of the European Convention on Human Rights has been to set close limits to any such assumed power.

In the first edition of this work, we predicted that these judicial pronouncements **1.20** appeared to indicate that some members of the English judiciary would take a robust approach towards the protection of freedom of expression after the 1998 Act came into force. The extent to which this prediction came true is discussed in detail in chapters 5–13.

English Law's Approach to the Right to Privacy Prior to the Incorporation of the ECHR

Historically, English law has not recognized a positive 'right to privacy', although **1.21** the courts have developed the common law, in a number of areas, to protect what today would be described as privacy rights.[39] More recently, the existence of a right to privacy has been the subject of judicial comment. In the notorious case of *Kaye* v *Robertson*,[40] the star of a television series suffered serious head injuries in a car crash. While he was lying in his hospital bed, semiconscious, a reporter and photographer from the *Sunday Sport* newspaper entered his hospital room uninvited and took photographs of him. The Court of Appeal concluded that the newspaper could publish the pictures, provided they did not say that the actor had agreed to be photographed or interviewed. Glidewell LJ stated (at 66): 'It is well-known that in English law there is no right to privacy, and accordingly there is no right of action for breach of a person's privacy. The facts of the present case are a graphic illustration of the desirability of Parliament considering whether and in what circumstances statutory provision can be made to protect the privacy of individuals.'

Legatt LJ said (at 71) that the right to privacy 'has so long been disregarded **1.22** here that it can be recognized only by the legislature.' However, this conservative

---

[39] See Warren and Brandeis (n 19 above) and *Prince Albert* v *Strange* at para 1.11.
[40] [1991] FSR 62.

attitude is by no means accepted by all the judiciary. Laws J (as he then was) stated in *Hellewell* v *Chief Constable of Derbyshire:*[41] 'If someone with a telephoto lens were to take from a distance and with no authority a picture of another engaged in some private act, his subsequent disclosure of the photograph would, in my judgement, as surely amount to a breach of confidence as if he had found or stolen a diary in which the act was recounted and proceeded to publish it. In such a case, the law would protect what might reasonably be called a *right of privacy,* although the name accorded to the cause of action would be breach of confidence.' (emphasis added)

1.23   Laws J's approach reflects the ideas of Warren and Brandeis and Prosser. Lord Nicholls of Birkenhead, in *R* v *Khan,*[42] (a case concerning the use of covertly gathered evidence) stated: 'I prefer to leave open for another occasion the important question whether the present, piecemeal protection of privacy has now developed to the extent that a more comprehensive principle can be seen to exist.' Chapter 6 discusses, in detail, the considerable impact that incorporation of Article 8 EHCR has had on domestic law.

---

[41] [1995] 1 WLR 804, at 807H.
[42] [1997] AC 558, at 582H–583A.

2

FREEDOM OF EXPRESSION AND THE RIGHT TO RESPECT FOR PRIVATE LIFE AND MEDIA LAW: GENERAL PRINCIPLES

Introduction	2.01	Other Convention Rights of	
Principles of Interpretation of the		Particular Importance to	
ECHR	2.02	Media Law	2.51
The Law of the ECHR: Article 10			
Freedom of Expression	2.08		

Introduction

This chapter examines the general principles of the ECHR as they are relevant to **2.01** media law. The main focus of this chapter is Article 10, which concerns the right to freedom of expression, but it also briefly discusses Articles 6(1) concerning reporting of judicial proceedings, Article 8 and the right to respect for privacy, Article 14's prohibition on discrimination in relation to other Convention rights, Article 15's restrictions in the time of war, and Article 17 concerning restrictions on activities subversive of Convention rights. Where relevant, we have included case law from domestic courts as well as the European Court. First, we outline some general principles applicable to the interpretation of the Convention.

Principles of Interpretation of the ECHR[1]

The ECHR is an international treaty, and therefore it is interpreted in accordance **2.02** with public international law principles of which the main source is the Vienna

---

[1] See generally, Lester, A and Pannick, D (eds), *Human Rights Law and Practice* (2nd edn, 2004) ch 3.

Convention on the Law of Treaties 1969. Although the Vienna Convention is not retrospective and therefore does not expressly apply to the 1950 European Convention on Human Rights and Freedoms, it is generally understood to encapsulate the prior principles of public international law on the interpretation of treaties.[2] The principles of interpretation developed by the European Court represent a significant departure from common law canons of construction.

The teleological approach

2.03 The basic principle of interpretation applied by the European Court is one grounded in a 'teleological approach' which reflects the Vienna Convention. Article 31(1) of the Vienna Convention provides that: 'A treaty shall be interpreted in good faith in accordance with the ordinary meaning to be given to the terms of the treaty in their context and in light of its objects and purpose.'[3]

2.04 The objects and purpose of the ECHR have been described as 'the protection of human rights',[4] and the maintenance and promotion of 'the ideals and values of a democratic society'.[5] The European Court has held that important features of a democratic society include 'pluralism, tolerance and broadmindedness',[6] the rule of law and access to the courts.[7] The teleological principle permits the meaning of the Convention rights to adapt and change according to the evolving social norms of the Member States. The European Court has noted that the Convention is: 'A living instrument which . . . must be interpreted in the light of present day conditions.'[8]

2.05 This dynamic approach to interpretation means that the older a decision of the Court or Commission, the greater the care that is needed to consider whether changing conditions have undermined its basis.[9] Although there is no formal doctrine of precedent under the Convention, consistency of approach is recognized as desirable in the interests of legal certainty.

---

[2] See *Fothergill* v *Monarch Airlines Ltd* [1981] AC 251, at 282C–D, *per* Lord Diplock.
[3] The European Court indicated that it will apply the Vienna Convention: see *Golder* v *UK* (1975) 1 EHRR 524, at 532.
[4] See *Soering* v *UK* (1989) 11 EHRR 439.
[5] See *Kjeldsen, Busk Madsen and Pedersen* v *Denmark* (1976) 1 EHRR 711, at para 53.
[6] *Handyside* v *UK* (1976) 1 EHRR 737, at 754.
[7] *Golder* v *UK* (1975) 1 EHRR 524, at 535. See also *Engel* v *Netherlands* (1976) 1 EHRR 647.
[8] See *Tyrer* v *UK* (1978) 2 EHRR 1, para 16.
[9] See, eg the European Court's jurisprudence on the Art 8 ECHR rights of transsexuals. Compare *Rees* v *UK* (1986) 9 EHRR 56 (Art 8 ECHR did not require that a transsexual could alter her birth certificate to reflect her new gender) and *Goodwin* v *UK* (2002) 35 EHRR 447 (the lack of legal recognition of an individual's new gender did breach Art 8 ECHR).

The principle of effectiveness

The Court in *Artico* v *Italy*,[10] asserted that 'the Convention is intended to **2.06** guarantee not rights that are theoretical or illusory but rights that are practical and effective'. So any conditions imposed on the exercise of rights must not 'impair their very essence and deprive them of effectiveness'.[11] Thus the Court must focus on the realities of the situation. This principle of effectiveness has led the European Court to impose positive obligations on states in certain circumstances (see 2.24–2.25). It has also led the Court to imply rights such as the right of access to the courts.[12]

Recourse to other human rights instruments

The European Court is increasingly examining other human rights instruments, **2.07** emanating from both the Council of Europe and other international organizations, to assist in the interpretation of the ECHR. In the media law context, the European Court took into account the Council of Europe's Convention on Transfrontier Television when assessing whether Switzerland's refusal to grant a company a licence to receive and retransmit programmes from a satellite was 'necessary in a democratic society'.[13] In *Goodwin* v *UK*,[14] the Court drew on a resolution of the European Parliament. In *Jersild* v *Denmark*,[15] it examined the International Covenant on the Elimination of All Forms of Racial Discrimination when deciding the extent to which racist speech was afforded protection by Article 10 ECHR (see 7.25–7.32).

The Law of the ECHR: Article 10 Freedom of Expression

Introduction

Article 10 of the ECHR provides: **2.08**

1. Everyone has the right to freedom of expression. This right shall include freedom to hold opinions and to receive and impart information and ideas without interference by public authority and regardless of frontiers.

---

[10] (1980) 3 EHRR 1, at para 33.
[11] *Mathieu-Mohin* v *Belgium* (1987) 10 EHRR 1, at para 52.
[12] See *Golder* v *UK* (1979) 1 EHRR 524. See also *Airey* v *Ireland* (1979) 2 EHRR 305 para 26 where the Court implied the right to civil legal aid in certain cases.
[13] See *Autronic AG* v *Switzerland* (1990) 12 EHRR 485.
[14] (1996) 22 EHRR 123.
[15] (1994) 19 EHRR 1.

This Article shall not prevent States from requiring the licensing of broadcasting, television or cinema enterprises.

2. The exercise of these freedoms, since it carries with it duties and responsibilities, may be subject to such formalities, conditions, restrictions or penalties as are prescribed by law and are necessary in a democratic society, in the interests of national security, territorial integrity or public safety, for the prevention of disorder or crime, for the protection of health or morals, for the protection of the reputation or rights of others, for preventing the disclosure of information received in confidence, or for maintaining the authority and impartiality of the judiciary.

2.09 Article 10(1) sets out the positive freedom, while Article 10(2) sets out the limitations on that freedom. The Court has stated that, when adjudicating on Article 10 cases, the Court is faced: 'not with a choice between two conflicting principles, but with a principle of freedom of expression that is subject to a number of exceptions which must be narrowly interpreted . . . It is not sufficient that the interference belongs to that class of the exceptions listed in Article 10(2) which has been invoked; neither is it sufficient that the interference was imposed because its subject matter fell within a particular category or was caught by a legal rule formulated in general or absolute terms: the Court has to be satisfied that the interference was necessary having regard to the facts and circumstances prevailing in the specific case before it.'[16]

2.10 The importance of freedom of expression has constantly been emphasized. In one of the first major judgments on Article 10, the Court stated: 'Freedom of expression constitutes one of the essential foundations of a society, one of the basic conditions for its progress and for the development of every man. Subject to para 2 of Article 10, it is applicable not only to "information and ideas" that are favourably received or regarded as inoffensive but also to those that offend, shock or disturb the state or any sector of the population. Such are the demands of pluralism, tolerance and broad mindedness without which there is no "democratic society".'[17] However, notwithstanding these noble sentiments, the European Court has often afforded limited protection to offensive expression particularly when such expression relates to religious matters.[18]

---

[16] *Sunday Times* v *UK* (1979) 2 EHRR 245, at p 281, para 65.
[17] *Handyside* v *UK* (1976) 1 EHRR 737, at para 49.
[18] See generally, ch 8 and the cases discussed therein.

Article 10(1)

Who benefits from the right?

The first sentence of Article 10(1) provides that *'Everyone* has the right to freedom of expression' (emphasis added). Those able to claim the protection of the right include legal as well as natural persons.[19] As far as natural persons are concerned, there is no class of person to which the prima facie right has been held not to apply.[20] Article 10(1) extends not just to journalists but also publishers and editors.[21] Members of the armed forces,[22] civil servants,[23] judges,[24] and lawyers[25] benefit from the protection of Article 10(1), although their status is likely to be relevant in determining whether any interference is proportionate under Article 10(2).

2.11

Which activities are covered by the right?

The right guaranteed by Article 10 protects more than simply expression in the sense of public communications of opinion. It expressly includes, but is not limited to, the right to hold opinions and to receive information and ideas, as well as the right to impart them.

2.12

The European Court has avoided defining exactly which activities are covered by Article 10(1), though the arguments of contracting States that a particular type of activity is not expressive are usually unsuccessful. Governments have unsuccessfully contended that Article 10 was not applicable in *Glasenapp* v *Germany*[26] and *Leander* v *Sweden*.[27] Both of these cases concerned the State's refusal to recruit the applicants to civil service posts because of their extremist political opinions (both right wing and left wing). However, although Article 10 was held to be engaged by the State's refusal to recruit individuals because

2.13

---

[19] See, eg *Autronic AG* v *Switzerland* (1990) 12 EHRR 485, at para 47.

[20] The only possible exception to this broad statement is 'aliens'. Art 16 provides that 'Nothing in Articles 10, 11 and 14 shall be regarded as preventing the High Contracting Parties from imposing restrictions on the activities of aliens.' See generally, Harris, DJ, O'Boyle, M and Warbrick, C, *Law of the European Convention on Human Rights* (London: Butterworths, 1995) at 508–10. There is no Court jurisprudence on this issue other than *Piermont* v *France* (1995) 20 EHRR 301. Art 16 is looking increasingly out of place and out of date; see Lester, A and Pannick, D (eds), *Human Rights Law and Practice* (2nd edn, 2004), at para 4.16.1.

[21] See, eg *Unabhangige Initiative Informations Vielfalt* v *Austria* (2003) 37 EHRR 33.

[22] eg *Engel and Others* v *Netherlands* (1976) 1 EHRR 647.

[23] eg *Vogt* v *Germany* (1995) 21 EHRR 205 and *Ahmed* v *UK* (1998) 29 EHRR 1.

[24] *Wille* v *Liechtenstein* (2000) 30 EHRR 558.

[25] eg *Casado Coca* v *Spain* (1994) 18 EHRR 1 and *Schöpfer* v *Switzerland* (App No 25405/94), 20 May 1998.

[26] (1986) 9 EHRR 25.

[27] (1987) 9 EHRR 433.

of their political views, the infringement was held to be justified pursuant to Article 10(2). In *Ahmed* v *UK*,[28] where the applicants challenged regulations restricting the political activities of local government officers in 'politically restricted posts', it was common ground that Article 10(1) was engaged; again, however, the Court found that the infringement was justified. The UK government unsuccessfully contended that Article 10 did not apply to non-peaceful protests where two of the applicants physically impeded the activities of others.[29] The right to freedom of expression has been held, in certain circumstances, to include the negative right not to speak or to remain silent.[30]

2.14 Furthermore, in *Autronic AG* v *Switzerland*,[31] the Court said: 'Article 10 applies not only to the content of information but also to the means of transmission or reception since any restriction imposed on the means necessarily interferes with the right to receive or impart information.' In *Cable and Wireless (Dominica) Ltd* v *Marpin Telecommunications and Broadcasting Co Ltd*,[32] the Privy Council drew on this authority to find that a State monopoly on the provision of telecommunications interfered with the rights of would-be competitors. As Lord Cooke said: 'Some significant hindrance to a would-be competitor's freedom is normally inherent in any requirement that he provide to his customers certain services only if permitted and on terms laid down by a monopolist.'

The right to receive information

2.15 Article 10 includes the right to receive as well as to impart information. This means that 'victims' who have standing to bring proceedings before the European Court, or in domestic proceedings under the HRA 1998, can potentially include newspaper readers or television viewers (see 3.42–3.53). A good example of the European Court recognizing the right of individuals to receive information is *Open Door Counselling and Dublin Well Woman* v *Ireland*,[33] where the Court ruled that an injunction, imposed by Irish courts, which effectively restrained staff at the applicants' clinics from imparting information to pregnant women concerning abortion facilities outside Ireland, by way of non-directive counselling, was contrary to Article 10. The Court permitted the applicants contesting the injunction to include two women of child-bearing age (who were not pregnant) as they belonged to a class of women of child-bearing age which

---

[28] (1998) 29 EHRR 1.
[29] See *Steel and others* v *UK* (1998) 28 EHRR 603.
[30] See, eg *K* v *Austria* (1993) Series A No 255–B, p 38.
[31] (1990) 12 EHRR 485, at para 47.
[32] (2001) 9 BHRC 486.
[33] (1992) 15 EHRR 244.

might be adversely affected by the injunction because it prevented them from receiving information about abortion services in the UK. The Court of Appeal has recognized the importance of the right to receive information, describing it as 'the lifeblood of a democracy'.[34]

To which types of expression does Article 10 apply?

The right to freedom of expression in Article 10(1) is not limited on the basis of the content of the particular expression at issue. The Court has confirmed that it extends to opinions and ideas that are viewed as offensive by the State, or by a proportion of the State's population.[35] It applies to commercial[36] and artistic[37] speech as well as to speech the primary purpose of which is political (see 2.46). Expression includes words both spoken and written, the display or dissemination of pictures and images, and also certain forms of conduct (for example, a peaceful march or demonstration, the purpose of which is to communicate a political message[38]). The Court has held that Article 10(1) applies even where the expression consists of light music and commercials transmitted by cable.[39] The protection of Article 10(1) also applies to expression regardless of the medium by which it is conveyed, whether by newspapers, cinema, television, radio, or the Internet. It also extends to the distribution of leaflets,[40] the display of banners,[41] and the exhibition of paintings.[42] **2.16**

Article 10(1) is likely to extend to symbolic speech or expressive conduct such as flag burning.[43] The High Court has concluded that it extends to defacing the US flag.[44] Its protection has extended to an expulsion order which was specifically intended to restrict the freedom of expression of an individual.[45] The only potential limit on the type of expression covered by Article 10(1) is **2.17**

---

[34] See *London Regional Transport* v *Mayor of London* [2001] EWCA Civ 1491, *per* Sedley LJ, at para 55.

[35] See *Handyside* v *UK*, quoted at para 2.10.

[36] *Barthold* v *Germany* (1985) 7 EHRR 383, at para 42.

[37] *Müller* v *Switzerland* (1988) 13 EHRR 212, at para 27.

[38] See, eg *Steel and others* v *UK*, discussed above at para 2.13.

[39] *Groppera Radio AG and others* v *Switzerland* (1990) 12 EHRR 321.

[40] See, eg *Chorherr* v *Austria* (1993) 17 EHRR 358.

[41] *X* v *Germany* App No 9235/81, (1982) 29 DR 194.

[42] *Müller* v *Switzerland* (1988) 13 EHRR 212.

[43] See the concurring opinion of Judge Jambrek in *Grigoriades* v *Greece* (1997) 27 EHRR 464, where he drew on the US flag-burning cases including *Texas* v *Johnson* 491 US 397 (1989).

[44] See *Percy* v *DPP* [2002] Crim LR 835.

[45] See *Piermont* v *France* (1995) 20 EHRR 301.

expression that is anti-democratic in its sentiment[46] or hate speech (an issue which is discussed in depth in chapter 7).

The special position of the media

2.18   The European Court has recognized that the press and other media have a special place in a democratic society as 'purveyor of information and public watchdog', and thus restrictions directed against such organizations tend to be scrutinized very closely. In *Bergens Tidende* v *Norway*[47] the Court emphasized: 'Where . . . measures taken by the national authorities are capable of discouraging the press from disseminating information on matters of legitimate public concern, careful scrutiny of the proportionality of the measures on the part of the Court is called for.'

2.19   The freedom of expression guaranteed by Article 10 includes freedom of the press.[48] The media receives particularly strong protection under Article 10 because it has a duty to impart, in a manner consistent with its obligations and responsibilities, information and ideas on all matters of public interest.[49] The House of Lords, in *McCartan Turkington Breen* v *Times Newspapers Ltd*,[50] has similarly recognized the importance of the media in a modern democracy. Lord Bingham stated:

> In a modern, developed society it is only a small minority of citizens who can participate directly in the discussions and decisions which shape the public life of that society. The majority can participate only indirectly, by exercising their rights as citizens to vote, express their opinions, make representations to the authorities, form pressure groups and so on. But the majority cannot participate in the public life of their society in these ways if they are not alerted to and informed about matters which call or may call for consideration and action. It is very largely through the media, including of course the press, that they will be so alerted and informed. The proper functioning of modern participatory democracy requires that the media be free, active, professional and inquiring. For this reason the courts, here and elsewhere, have recognized the cardinal importance of press freedom.[51]

---

[46]   See, eg *Purcell* v *Ireland* App No 15404/89, (1991) 70 DR 262 concerning expression in support of terrorists.

[47]   (2001) 31 EHRR 16.

[48]   See, eg *Observer and Guardian* v *UK* (1991) 14 EHRR 1537.

[49]   See, eg *Jersild* v *Denmark* (1994) 19 EHRR 1, at para 31.

[50]   [2001] 2 AC 277.

[51]   Ibid, at pp 290G–291A. See also, *R* v *Shayler* [2003] 1 AC 247, *per* Lord Bingham, at para 21, where he commented on the potent and honourable 'role of the press in exposing abuses and miscarriages of justice'.

This journalistic freedom allows a degree of exaggeration, or even provocation.[52] **2.20**
Although the European Court has, at times, taken into account the perceived
quality of the journalism in deciding how much protection the expression
should receive.[53] Article 10 has also been held to include the protection of
informants who provide confidential sources to the press, since without such
information the press could not perform its vital role as a 'public watchdog'.[54]
This protection is part of the Article 10 rights of both the press and the source.
Both parties would be victims of an interference with their right to impart and
receive information if disclosure was ordered.

Article 10 requires deference to the media as to the methods of objective and **2.21**
balanced reporting; the Court in *Jersild* v *Denmark* stated that it is not for the
courts, whether domestic or European: 'to substitute their own views for those
of the press as to what technique of reporting should be adopted by journalists.
In this context the Court recalls that Article 10 protects not only the substance
of the ideas and information expressed, but also the form in which they are
conveyed.'

'Interference by a public authority'

In most cases this is not an issue. Interferences with the right to freedom of **2.22**
expression include, in civil proceedings, a damages award,[55] the imposition of
an injunction,[56] an order to disclose a source,[57] the refusal of legal aid to defend
defamation proceedings,[58] the admonishment of a lawyer,[59] an order to publish a
judicial judgement in a newspaper,[60] and the seizure or destruction of material.[61]

---

[52] See *Prager and Oberschlick* v *Austria* (1995) 21 EHRR 1, at para 38.

[53] See, eg *Stoll* v *Switzerland* (2008) 47 EHRR 59 (concerning a report relating to confidential
negotiations relating to compensation for Holocaust victims) discussed in ch 13.

[54] See *Goodwin v UK* (1996) 22 EHRR 123 and *Roemen and Schmit* v *Luxembourg* (App
No 51772/99), discussed in ch 6.

[55] *Tolstoy Miloslavsky* v *UK* (1995) 20 EHRR 442 and *Bladet Tromso and Stensaas* v *Norway*
(1999) 29 EHRR 125 para 50.

[56] *Open Door Counselling and Dublin Well Woman* v *Ireland* (1992) 15 EHRR 244; *Observer
and Guardian* v *UK* (1991) 14 EHRR 153.

[57] *Goodwin* v *UK* (1996) 22 EHRR 123.

[58] See *Steel and Morris* v *UK* (2005) 41 EHRR 22. The European Court placed considerable
weight on the massive imbalance of resources between the Claimant, McDonald's the multinational
corporation and two unemployed individuals with no legal experience. Cf *McVicar* v *UK* (2002)
35 EHRR 22 where the refusal of legal aid was found not to violate Art 10 ECHR.

[59] See *Steur* v *Netherlands* (2004) 39 EHRR 33.

[60] *Feldek* v *Slovakia* (App No 29032/95), 12 July 2001.

[61] *Handyside* v *UK* (1976) 1 EHRR 737.

In the criminal field, interferences include convictions,[62] fines, and the length of a custodial sentence. An expulsion from a country together with a ban on re-entry constitutes an interference.[63]

2.23   An 'interference by a public authority' includes restrictions upon freedom of expression which are imposed by a private body which is exercising public law functions. For example, in *Wingrove* v *UK*,[64] the British Board of Film Classification refused to grant a certificate for a video, which effectively led to a ban on the distribution of that video. While the Board is a private body, it is designated under s 4 of the Video Recordings Act 1984 as the authority responsible for the issue of certificates for videos. It was treated by the Court as a public authority.[65] In some circumstances, a State's failure to prevent or control interferences with freedom of expression by *private parties* can give rise to an interference with an applicant's right to freedom of expression by the State because its 'positive obligation' to protect freedom of expression is engaged. It is to this matter which we now turn.

Positive obligations

2.24   Article 10(1) ECHR does not simply prevent States from imposing restrictions on freedom of expression; it imposes a positive obligation on the State to facilitate the exercise of that right.[66] The extent of a State's positive obligations under Article 10 ECHR is hard to discern, not least, because the European Court has refused to articulate any general theory as to their scope.[67] In determining whether or not a positive obligation exists, regard must be had to the fair balance that has to be struck between the general interest of the community and the interests of the individual. The European Court has imposed positive obligations on States in a variety of contexts. In *Fuentes Bobo* v *Spain*,[68] the applicant was a producer at a State television company (TVE). He was dismissed as a result of voicing offensive and insulting criticism of senior management of TVE in

---

[62] *Prager and Oberschlick* v *Austria* (1995) 21 EHRR 1.

[63] *Piermont* v *France* (1995) 20 EHRR 301. See also, *R (Farrakhan)* v *Secretary of State for the Home Department* [2002] QB 1391 (exclusion of Mr Farrakhan, a US preacher, found to interfere with his Art 10 ECHR rights and thus required justification).

[64] (1996) 24 EHRR 1. See also, *Casado Coca* v *Spain* (1994) 18 EHRR 1 (disciplinary penalty imposed by Barcelona Bar Council treated as attributable to the State).

[65] This treatment accords with the approach taken by the HRA 1998 to 'public authorities'; see paras 3.31–3.40.

[66] See, eg *Plattform 'Ärtze für das Leben'* v *Austria* (1988) 13 EHRR 204 (concerning freedom of peaceful assembly, although the reasoning is equally applicable to freedom of expression) and *Informationsverein Lentia and others* v *Austria* (1993) 17 EHRR 93 (concerning a state monopoly broadcaster): see further, ch 11.

[67] See *VgT Verein Gegen Tierfabriken* v *Switzerland* (2001) 34 EHRR 159, at para 46.

[68] (2000) 31 EHRR 1115.

two radio programmes. The applicant complained to the domestic employment tribunals that his dismissal was unfair. On appeal, the Spanish courts held that the applicable employment legislation afforded no remedy. The Spanish government argued that it could not be held responsible for the applicant's dismissal, as the relationship between the applicant and the employer was governed by private rather than public law. The Court rejected this argument because the State has a positive obligation, in certain circumstances, to protect individuals from interferences with their right to freedom of expression even by private persons. The Court concluded that domestic legislative provisions which had failed to afford a remedy should themselves be regarded as an interference with the applicant's right to freedom of expression, for which the State was responsible.

In *Özgür Gündem v Turkey*[69] the Court concluded that Turkey had failed, in **2.25** breach of its positive obligations, to protect a Kurdish newspaper and staff from attacks by private persons and as such had violated Article 10 ECHR. *Fuentes Bobo* and *Özgür Gündem* can be contrasted with *Appleby and others* v *UK*[70] where the majority of the European Court refused to impose a positive obligation on the State to ensure that the applicants were able to peacefully campaign in a privately owned shopping centre which dominated the town. The Court stated:

> not withstanding the acknowledged importance of freedom of expression, [it] does not bestow any freedom of forum for the exercise of that right. While it is true that democratic, social, economic and technological developments are changing the ways in which people move around and come into contact with each other, the Court is not persuaded that this requires the automatic creation of rights of entry to private property, or even, necessarily, to all publicly owned property. . . .Where however the bar on access to property has the effect of preventing any effective exercise of freedom of expression or it can be said that the essence of the right has been destroyed, the Court would not exclude that a positive obligation could arise for the State to protect the enjoyment of Convention rights by regulating property rights. The corporate town, where the entire municipality was controlled by a private body, might be an example.[71]

---

[69] (2001) 31 EHRR 1082.
[70] (2003) 37 EHRR 38.
[71] Ibid, at para 47.

Access to information[72]

2.26 Article 10 ECHR includes the right to *receive* as well as to impart information. In the late 1970s a draft additional protocol to the ECHR was discussed which expressly extended the right to freedom of expression to include the freedom to seek information. Unfortunately, this draft protocol failed to secure widespread support and was abandoned.[73] Initially it appeared that Article 10 would be interpreted broadly to include some form of right of access to information held by States without the need for an additional protocol. In *X* v *Federal Republic of Germany*,[74] the European Commission on Human Rights stated: 'It follows from the context in which the right to receive is mentioned . . . that it envisages first of all access to general sources of information . . . the right to receive information may under certain circumstances include a right of access by the interested person to documents which although not generally accessible are of particular importance.'[75]

2.27 However, subsequent case law from the European Court has not interpreted this as requiring a State to provide access to information. In *Leander* v *Sweden*,[76] the Court held, in relation to the State's refusal to reveal secret information: 'The right to freedom to receive information basically prohibits a Government from restricting a person from receiving information that others wish or may be willing to impart to him. Article 10 does not, in circumstances such as those of the present case, confer on the individual a right of access to a register containing information on his personal position, nor does it embody an obligation on the Government to impart such information to the individual.'

2.28 The same approach was adopted in *Gaskin* v *UK*,[77] where the applicant complained that he had been refused access to a case record relating to him created when he was a minor and held by a local authority. The Court found that there had been no violation of Article 10.[78] However, in both *Leander* and

---

[72] Other organs of the Council of Europe have encouraged states to protect the right of access to information. See Parliamentary Assembly Resolution 1087 (1996), where, in relation to access to environmental information, it was stated that 'public access to clear and full information . . . must be viewed as a basic human right'.

[73] See generally, Malinverni, G, 'Freedom of Information in the European Convention on Human Rights and the International Covenant on Civil and Political Rights' (1983) 4 Human Rights LJ.

[74] App No 8383/78, (1979) 17 DR 227.

[75] Ibid, at 228–9.

[76] (1987) 9 EHRR 433, at para 74.

[77] (1989) 12 EHRR 36.

[78] However, the European Court concluded that the applicant was entitled to the information he sought pursuant to Art 8 because it was essential to his private life.

Gaskin, the information sought related to a specific individual and its disclosure could not be said to be in the public interest.

In the late 1990s, the European Commission held that Article 10 places States not only under an obligation to make environmental information accessible to the public, but also under a positive obligation to collect, process, and disseminate information which, by its very nature, is not directly accessible and which cannot be known to the public unless the authorities act accordingly. However, the European Court refused to adopt the same approach and concluded that Article 10 was not applicable in the circumstances of the case.[79] However, the Court concluded that the failure to supply such information was a violation of the right to respect of family life protected by Article 8. **2.29**

The Strasbourg jurisprudence can be contrasted with that of the Inter-American Court of Human Rights which has concluded that Article 13 of the American Convention on Human Rights, the freedom of expression provision of the Convention which has a similar, albeit not identical, structure to Article 10 ECHR, includes a right of access to information. In *Claude Reyes* v *Chile,*[80] the Inter-American Court of Human Rights stated: **2.30**

> With respect to the facts of the present case, the Court concludes that Article 13 of the Convention, which specifically establishes the rights to 'seek' and 'receive' information protects the right of all persons to request access to information held by the State, with the exceptions permitted by the restrictions regime of the Convention. As a result, this Article supports the right of persons to receive such information and the positive obligation on the State to supply it, so that the person may have access to the information or receive a reasoned response when, on grounds permitted by the Convention, the State may limit access to it in the specific case. The said information should be provided without a need to demonstrate a direct interest in obtaining it, or a personal interest, except in cases where a legitimate restriction applies. Disclosure to one person in turn permits it [the information] to circulate in society in such a way that it can be known, obtained and evaluated. In this way, the right to freedom of thought and of expression contemplates protection of the right of access to information under State control.[81]

The Inter-American Court ordered Chile to provide the information requested, which related to a major logging project, or adopt a reasoned decision as to why it was not providing it. The Court further required the State to train public officials on the right of access to information. It remains to be seen whether *Claude Reyes* v *Chile* has any influence on the European Court's thinking on the issue. **2.31**

---

[79] *Guerra and others* v *Italy* (1998) 26 EHRR 357.
[80] Case 12.108, Judgment of 19 September 2006.
[81] Ibid, at para 77.

The Strasbourg Court may seek to distinguish such case law on the basis that Article 13 of the Inter-American Convention, unlike Article 10 ECHR, includes the right to 'seek information' rather than merely receive and impart information.

2.32 Notwithstanding the lack of a general right to obtain information under Article 10, if the State supports the dissemination of certain materials, it is not permitted to discriminate between types of publication on the basis of the publication's content. This issue was addressed in *Vereinigung Demokratischer Soldaten Österreichs and Gubi v Austria*,[82] where the Court concluded that the failure of the State to distribute *Der Igel* to Austrian soldiers while distributing other magazines for soldiers was a violation of Article 10.

Licensing of broadcasting, television, and cinema

2.33 The third sentence of Article 10(1) provides that broadcasting, television, and cinema may be subject to a licensing system. The European Court has stated that the purpose of the third sentence is:

> To make it clear that states are permitted to regulate by a licensing system the way in which broadcasting is organised in their territories, particularly in its technical aspects . . . Technical aspects are undeniably important, but the grant or refusal of a licence may also be made conditional on other considerations, including such matters as the nature and objectives of a proposed station, its potential audience at a national, regional or local level, the rights and needs of a specific audience and the obligations deriving from international legal instruments. This may lead to interferences whose aims will be legitimate under the third sentence of paragraph 1, even though they do not correspond to any of the aims set out in paragraph 2. The compatibility of such interferences must nevertheless be assessed in the light of the other requirements of paragraph 2.[83]

2.34 Therefore, while the State has a considerable degree of autonomy in its licensing system, any restriction must comply with the requirements of Article 10(2) (see 2.35). One recent example of the Court considering licensing restrictions against the requirements of Article 10(2) is *Demuth v Switzerland*.[84] In *Demuth*, the Court rejected a complaint by the applicant who had been refused a licence to broadcast a television programme about cars because the programme was not able to offer the 'required valuable contribution to comply with the general instructions for radio and television.' The applicant alleged that the refusal of a licence was discriminatory and arbitrary. The Court rejected the applicant's argument; the programme was essentially commercial, focusing on increasing

---

[82] (1994) 20 EHRR 56.
[83] *Informationsverein Lentia and others v Austria* (1993) 17 EHRR 93, at para 32.
[84] (2004) 38 EHRR 20.

car sales, and did not conform with the Swiss licensing requirements because it did not contribute to the provision of objective information, education, or entertainment. The Court concluded that there had been no breach of Article 10(2); the Swiss government was entitled to impose qualitative requirements on broadcasting provided they were not arbitrary or disproportionate.

Article 10(2)

Introduction

In *Sunday Times* v *UK*,[85] the Court set out the issues which arise when considering whether an infringement of the right to freedom of expression meets the Article 10(2) conditions: **2.35**

(a) Is the restriction on freedom of expression 'prescribed by law'?
(b) Does the restriction have a legitimate aim?
(c) Is the restriction 'necessary in a democratic society'?
(d) Is the restriction within the State's 'margin of appreciation'?

If any of these questions are answered in the negative, the restriction on freedom   **2.36**
of expression is a violation of Article 10. Each substantive chapter in this book will deal with these conditions in detail. However, the general principles are analysed below.

'Prescribed by law'

The requirement that a restriction must be 'prescribed by law' ensures that any   **2.37**
restriction on the right to freedom of expression must satisfy the requirements of the rule of law. In the British context, a permissible restriction must, as a minimum, be authorized by or pursuant to statute, statutory instrument, by a common law rule, or by EU legislation. Restrictions authorized by government circulars, with no statutory underpinning, will lack a sufficient legal basis to be 'prescribed by law'.[86] In *R* v *Advertising Standards Authority, ex p Matthias Rath BV*[87] the Administrative Court held at the permission stage that the British Codes of Advertising and Sales Promotion had sufficient statutory underpinning and were sufficiently clear, precise, and accessible for their requirements to be 'prescribed by law'. However, a legal basis for a restriction is not in itself sufficient.

---

[85] (1979) 2 EHRR 245. The European Court concluded that the House of Lords' decision that the Sunday Times had been in contempt of court violated Article 10 because it was not necessary in a democratic society'. This led to the enactment of the Contempt of Court Act 1981 discussed fully at paras 9.15–9.17.

[86] See *Silver* v *UK* (1983) 5 EHRR 347.

[87] [2001] EMLR 582, at para 26.

Restrictions must also be reasonably precise and accessible. The European Court has held that: 'the law must be adequately accessible: the citizen must be able to have an indication that is adequate in the circumstances of the legal rules applicable to a given case. [Further], a norm cannot be regarded as a "law" unless it is formulated with sufficient precision to enable the citizen to regulate his conduct: he must be able—if need be with the appropriate advice—to foresee, to a degree that is reasonable in the circumstances, the consequences which a given action may entail.'[88]

2.38   The need for foreseeability is of particular importance in relation to Article 10 because vague or imprecise laws have the tendency to 'chill' legitimate expression. In the USA, vague statutes impinging on the right to freedom of speech are invariably struck down as unconstitutional because of their chilling effect on protected speech.[89] The US Supreme Court in *Grayned* v *City of Rockford*[90] explained the void for vagueness doctrine in the following terms:

> Vague laws offend several important values. First, because we assume that man is free to steer between lawful and unlawful conduct, we insist that laws give the person of ordinary intelligence a reasonable opportunity to know what is prohibited, so that he may act accordingly. Vague laws may trap the innocent by not providing fair warning. Second, if arbitrary and discriminatory enforcement is to be prevented, laws must provide explicit standards for those who apply them. A vague law impermissibly delegates basic policy matters to policemen, judges, and juries for resolution on an ad hoc and subjective basis, with the attendant dangers of arbitrary application. Third, but related, where a vague statue 'abut[s] upon sensitive areas of basic First Amendment Freedoms' [protecting freedom of speech] it 'operates to inhibit the exercise of [those] freedoms.' Uncertain meanings inevitably lead citizens to 'steer far wider of the unlawful zone' . . . than if the boundaries of the forbidden areas were clearly marked.[91]

2.39   The European Court has unfortunately not adopted such a robust approach and has been very reluctant to find that an interference with an applicant's right to freedom of expression is not 'prescribed by law'. It might be thought that common law systems, in which the precise scope of a rule of law may have to be drawn from the ratios of several judicial decisions, are more likely than

---

[88]   *Silver* v *UK*, at para 49.
[89]   See, eg *NAACP* v *Button* 371 US 415 (1963), which concerned a Virginia Statute prohibiting attorneys from soliciting prospective clients and had been used against the National Association for the Advancement of Colored People (NAACP) for informing individuals of their rights and referring them to lawyers. See generally, Nowak, J and Rotunda, R, *Constitutional Law* (5th edn) (St Paul, Minn: West Publishing, 1995), at 1001–2 for a discussion of the void for vagueness doctrine.
[90]   408 US 104.
[91]   Ibid, at 108–9.

civil law systems to fail to satisfy the requirement of precision. However, in *Steel and others v UK*,[92] the Court concluded that even the notoriously obscure conditions under which a police constable's power of arrest for breach of the peace arises, were defined with sufficient precision at common law to meet the requirements of Article 10(2) even though there was a conflict of judicial authority.

One rare example where the Court found the domestic law lacking is *Herczegfalvy* **2.40** *v Austria*,[93] which concerned interference with the correspondence of mental patients. The person interfering with the correspondence had an unfettered discretion as to whether, and if so when, to do so. The Court concluded from this that the interference was not 'prescribed by law'. Further, in *Hashman and Harrup v UK*,[94] the Court found that binding over orders requiring persons to be 'of good behaviour' were insufficiently precise to be regarded as 'prescribed by law'.[95]

Legitimate aim

The requirement that the restriction must have a legitimate aim simply means **2.41** that the purpose of the interference with the freedom of expression must be one of the aims listed in Article 10(2). This long list is intended to be exhaustive. However, a number of the permitted aims, such as 'the prevention of disorder' and the 'protection of the rights of others', are inherently broad.[96] The Court has, in general, not sought to go behind the purpose for which a particular restriction is said to be imposed. In *Observer and Guardian v UK*,[97] for example, the Court accepted that the government had applied for an interlocutory injunction to restrain publication of extracts from *Spycatcher* in order to protect national security. The fact that the book was widely available throughout the world (including the USA and Australia) did not affect the Court's willingness to believe that the restriction had been imposed for a legitimate purpose. The real question was whether the restriction was 'necessary in a democratic society' (see 2.42–2.43). The Court concluded that the injunction against the newspapers

---

[92] (1998) 28 EHRR 603, at para 94.
[93] (1992) 15 EHRR 437.
[94] (2000) 8 BHRC 104.
[95] See also, *Gaweda v Poland* App No 26229/95 (refusal to register a periodical entitled *Germany, A thousand year enemy of Poland* on the basis that it was 'inconsistent with the real state of things' was not prescribed by law).
[96] See, eg *Ahmed and others v UK* (1998) 29 EHRR 1, where the Court concluded that ensuring the effectiveness of a system of local political democracy was included in the concept of 'rights of others'.
[97] (1991) 14 EHRR 153.

failed the test of necessity in so far as it prevented publication when the book was widely available elsewhere.

Necessary in a democratic society

2.42   The third, and by far the most important, requirement is that every restriction must be 'necessary in a democratic society'. This means that it must correspond to 'a pressing social need' and be proportionate to meet that need. The European Court has explained that 'necessary' is not synonymous with 'indispensable', but it does not have the flexibility of such expressions as 'useful', 'reasonable', or 'desirable'.[98]

2.43   The necessity of a restriction must be 'convincingly established'.[99] In the vast majority of cases, the question whether a violation is established depends on whether the restriction imposed is necessary and proportionate. The Court has adopted a number of approaches to the issue of proportionality:[100] if the need could be achieved by less restrictive means, the restriction will fail the test for proportionality; if the measure is unsuitable for achieving the legitimate objective, the measure will fail the test for proportionality. An example of the doctrine of proportionality in operation is the case of *Barthold* v *Germany* (above) which concerned a ban on veterinary surgeons advertising their services. The applicant was prohibited from repeating various remarks he had made in a newspaper interview about the lack of emergency veterinary services as a result of the profession's unwillingness to work unsociable hours. The Court concluded that the ban was disproportionate because it risked 'discouraging members of the liberal professions from contributing to public debate on topics affecting the life of the community if even there is the slightest likelihood of their utterances being treated as entailing, to some degree, an advertising effect' (at para 58). The Court recognized that the State had a legitimate aim in protecting the rights of other veterinary surgeons from unfair competition but the restrictions, as drafted, were overbroad as they extended to discussion of matters of public concern. The Court acknowledged the 'chilling effect' of such broad restrictions on veterinary surgeons' speech.

Margin of appreciation

2.44   The final element of the Court's analysis of restrictions on freedom of expression is the 'margin of appreciation', which refers to the latitude allowed to Member

---

[98]   *Handyside* v *UK* (1976) 1 EHRR 737, at para 48.
[99]   *Barthold* v *Germany* (1985) 7 EHRR 383, at 403.
[100]   See Lester, A and Pannick, D (eds), *Human Rights Law and Practice* (2nd edn, 2004) ch 3 for a discussion of the doctrine of proportionality.

States in their observance of the Convention. The Court has held that the 'margin of appreciation': 'goes hand in hand with European supervision, whose extent will vary according to the case. Where . . . there has been an interference with the exercise of the rights and freedom guaranteed in paragraph(1) of Article 10, the supervision must be strict, because of the importance of the rights in question; the importance of these rights has been stressed by the Court many times. The necessity for restricting them must be convincingly established.'[101]

The extent of the 'margin of appreciation' varies depending on the subject matter. The margin has tended to be broad in cases concerning obscenity, blasphemy, national security, the protection of morals, and commercial speech; whereas in cases of political expression the European Court has applied stricter scrutiny. The Court's use of the margin of appreciation has been described as 'illustrat[ing] a disappointing lack of clarity'[102] although certain factors such as the type of expression in issue, the severity of the sanction, and the degree of consensus between Member States on a particular issue tend to be relevant. The applicability of the doctrine of 'margin of appreciation' in domestic law is discussed at 3.13–3.14.   **2.45**

Factors relevant to the test of necessity in Article 10(2)

Categories of expression The case law in Strasbourg has tended to deal specifically with three main classes of expression—political, artistic, and commercial— with political expression receiving the most protection. However, care should be taken not to apply this threefold classification too rigidly, because the expression at issue may fall within more than one category. One such example of expression that fell into more than one category was *Hertel v Switzerland*,[103] which concerned newspaper articles detailing the alleged dangers of microwave ovens. The manufacturers of microwaves sued under the Unfair Competition Act. The government sought to argue that the expression in question was commercial in nature, and therefore the State should be afforded a wide margin of appreciation. The Court rejected this contention as the expression was not purely commercial but was part of a debate affecting the public interest over public health (at para 47).   **2.46**

   (a) *Expression on matters of general public concern* The European Court attaches the highest importance to the protection of political expression, which it has defined expansively to include speech on matters of general public concern.

---

[101] *Autronic AG v Switzerland* (1990) 12 EHRR 485, at para 61.
[102] Judge MacDonald, 'The Margin of Appreciation' in *The European System for the Protection of Human Rights*, MacDonald, Matscher and Petzold (eds) at 85.
[103] (1998) 28 EHRR 534

The Court has viewed expression concerning litigation,[104] alleged police malpractice,[105] the alleged cruelty to seals inflicted by hunters,[106] the practice of cosmetic surgeons,[107] and even comments on the quality of local veterinary services[108] to be expression on matters of public concern worthy of strong protection. In *Lingens* v *Austria*[109] (discussed fully in chapter 5), the applicant was a journalist who had alleged that the then Chancellor of Austria had protected and assisted former Nazis. Mr Lingens was convicted and fined for criminal libel. The Court emphasized the importance of freedom of political debate in a free and democratic society: 'it is incumbent on the press to impart information and ideas on political issues just as those in other areas of public interest. Not only does the press have the task of imparting such ideas: the public also has a right to receive them . . . The limits of acceptable criticism are . . . wider as regards a politician as such than as regards a private individual: unlike the latter, the former inevitably and knowingly lays himself open to close scrutiny of his every word and deed by both journalists and the public at large, and must consequently display a greater degree of tolerance' (at paras 41–42).

The Court makes clear in the above passage that the limits of permissible criticism depend, to some extent, on the identity of the person being criticized. Restrictions on public criticism will be more closely supervised when those criticized are politicians. Police officers and civil servants apparently fall into an intermediate category. Though there is a public interest in accurate information about their professional conduct, they do not—unlike politicians—knowingly lay themselves open to close scrutiny of their words and deeds.[110] Recently, however, the European Court has sought to limit the scope of this intermediate category to law enforcement officers and prosecutors.[111]

But, although the European Court has said that politicians should not expect to escape criticism, it has also emphasized the importance of not restricting their own freedom of speech. In *Castells* v *Spain*,[112] the Court drew attention to the importance of the rights of politicians, especially members of opposition parties: 'In [a] democratic system the actions or omissions of the government must be subject to close scrutiny not only of the legislative and judicial

---

[104] *Sunday Times* v *UK* (1979) 2 EHRR 245.

[105] *Thorgeirson* v *Iceland* (1992) 14 EHRR 843.

[106] *Bladet Tromsø and Stensaas* v *Norway* (1999) 29 EHRR 125.

[107] *Bergens Tidende* v *Norway* (2001) 31 EHRR 16.

[108] *Barthold* v *Germany* (1985) 7 EHRR 383.

[109] (1986) 8 EHRR 407.

[110] See *Janowski* v *Poland* (1999) 29 EHRR 705. Contrast *New York Times* v *Sullivan* 376 US 254 (1964), in which the US Supreme Court held that a public official could not sue for libel except in respect of allegations which he could establish had been made with 'actual malice'. The plaintiff in *Sullivan* was a police officer.

[111] See *Busuioc* v *Moldova* (2006) 42 EHRR 14. See also, *Yankov* v *Bulgaria* (2005) 41 EHRR 854, where the Court concluded that speech by a prisoner that was critical of prison officers should receive heightened protection because it related to matters of general public concern.

[112] (1992) 14 EHRR 445, at para 45.

authorities but also of the press and public opinion. Furthermore, the dominant position which the government occupies makes it necessary to display restraint in resorting to criminal proceedings, particularly where other means are available for replying to the unjustified attacks and criticisms of its adversaries or the media.'

The House of Lords has adopted a similar approach to political expression. In *R (ProLife Alliance) v BBC*[113] Lord Nicholls stated: 'Freedom of political speech is a freedom of the very highest importance in any country which lays claim to being a democracy. Restrictions on this freedom need to be examined rigorously by all concerned, not least the courts.'[114]

It is particularly important to have a free flow of opinions and information during the run-up to elections.[115] Where, however, the expression is directed at the undermining of democracy and human rights themselves, the State is not required by Article 10 to confer the same protection as it would be obliged to provide in the case of orthodox political expression. This has been applied in particular to expression by extreme left-wing and neo-Nazi groups.[116] Even in this context, however, the more recent case law from Strasbourg suggests that the collapse of communism in Eastern Europe has meant that it is no longer so necessary to impose restrictions on the speech of communist sympathisers.[117]

(b) *Commercial expression*[118] Though it is now clear that Article 10(1) extends to cover commercial expression, the European Court has frequently invoked the margin of appreciation to justify restrictions on such expression. It has held that consumer protection is a legitimate justification for a ban on false and misleading advertising.[119] In *Casado Coca v Spain*,[120] the Court went further and held that a near complete ban on advertising by lawyers, even when truthful and accurate, was permissible in order to maintain confidence in the proper administration of justice and the dignity of the legal profession. In view of the wide divergences of approach to this question between contracting States, national authorities and courts were best placed to determine how to strike the balance between these legitimate purposes and the public right to receive information about the provision of legal services.[121] However, in *Krone Verlag*

---

[113] [2004] 1 AC 185.

[114] Ibid, at 224.

[115] See *Bowman* v *UK* (1998) 26 EHRR 1

[116] See, eg *Glimmerveen and Hagenbeek* v *Netherlands* App Nos 8348/78 and 8406/78, (1979) 18 DR 187, see paras 7.15–7.16; see also the Court's decision in *Jersild* v *Denmark* (1994) 19 EHRR 1, discussed in ch 7.

[117] See, eg *Vogt* v *Germany* (1995) 21 EHRR 205, which concerned dismissal of a teacher on the grounds that she was a member of the communist party. This was held to be a violation of the Convention by the Court of Human Rights.

[118] See chapter 12 for a detailed discussion of Commercial Speech and Advertising.

[119] *Markt Intern Verlag and Klaus Beermann* v *Germany* (1989) 12 EHRR 161, at para 26.

[120] (1994) 18 EHRR 1.

[121] Ibid, at para 55. Cf *Stambuk* v *Germany* (2003) 37 EHRR 42 (violation in relation to fine of ophthalmologist for breach of rules of professional conduct relating to his appearance in a newspaper article detailing his laser operation techniques).

GmbbH & Co v *Austria (No 3)*,[122] the European Court, for the first time, concluded that a restriction on pure commercial speech violated Article 10. The Austrian Courts prohibited the applicant from placing advertisements contrasting the cost of his newspaper with that of a local rival, unless the advertisement explained the differences in reporting styles of coverage of political and economic matters between the newspapers in question. This restriction on the applicant's ability to advertise was found to be overly broad, very difficult to comply with, and impairing the very essence of comparative advertising. As such it was disproportionate to the legitimate aim of protecting the rights of others and not 'necessary in a democratic society'. It remains to be seen whether *Krone Verlag* heralds a more protective approach to commercial speech. However, at least at present the Court's jurisprudence in this area is less developed than that of the US Supreme Court, which provides near absolute protection for truthful and accurate commercial speech except in relation to 'sinful' but lawful products or services such as alcohol, tobacco, and gambling where some limited restrictions are permitted.[123]

(c) *Artistic expression*[124] Artistic expression has been less well-protected in Strasbourg than either political or commercial expression. Although the Court has consistently held that Article 10 extends to artistic expression, including the public exchange of cultural and social information of all kinds (see *Müller* v *Switzerland,* at 2.16), the protection afforded to this type of expression has been minimal. The Court has permitted States a wide 'margin of appreciation' in this field, particularly in relation to expression which has the potential to offend religious or moral sensibilities.[125] In *Otto-Preminger-Institut* v *Austria*,[126] the applicants complained about the seizure and confiscation of a film which, in the view of the Austrian authorities, was likely to offend religious feelings. The Court upheld the State's action, even though the film was shown only in private to members of a film club who had been fully informed of its theme and content. Other cases in which interference with expression has been upheld by the Court include *Müller* v *Switzerland*,[127] which concerned a conviction for obscenity and confiscation of paintings which were shown in an exhibition of contemporary art; and *Handyside* v *UK*,[128] which concerned a ban on *The Little Red Schoolbook* in England and Wales even though this book was widely

---

[122] (2004) 39 EHRR 42.

[123] The distinction between the jurisprudence can, at least partially, be explained by the difference in the underlying rationales for the protection of freedom of expression by the two legal systems. The jurisprudence of the US Supreme Court, but not of the European Court, has accepted that one of the justifications for the protection of expression is the pursuit of truth (including truth as to the quality of various products or services).

[124] See ch 8, Obscenity and Blasphemy, which considers the Court's jurisprudence on artistic expression in more detail.

[125] The case law in the area falls short of judicial pronouncements that Art 10 applies to offensive and shocking expression; see *Handyside* v *UK,* discussed at para 2.10.

[126] (1994) 19 EHRR 34.

[127] (1988) 13 EHRR 212.

[128] (1976) 1 EHRR 737.

available throughout Continental Europe (and, indeed, in Scotland where a prosecution under Scots obscenity law had failed).

In 2008, nearly 20 years after *Müller*, the European Court again considered the protection that should be afforded to offensive art. *Vereinigung Blidender Künstler v Austria*[129] concerned the exhibition of a controversial painting called 'Apocalypse' which was a collage of 34 public figures, including Mother Teresa, all naked and involved in various sexual activities. The Court found that the imposition of an injunction preventing the display of the art was not 'necessary in a democratic society'. The injunction was not limited in time or space and, as such, was disproportionate, taking into account the satirical nature of the expression in question. It is too early to say whether *Vereinigung Blidender Künstler v Austria* heralds more robust protection of artistic expression.

Duties and responsibilities of the applicant Article 10(2) provides that the exercise **2.47** of the right to freedom of expression carries with it 'duties and responsibilities'. This phrase is occasionally invoked by governments when seeking to limit the right to freedom of expression of a particular class of individuals, such as members of the armed forces,[130] judges,[131] and civil servants.[132] It is difficult to define what this phrase adds, as the identity of the applicant is taken into account by the Court when deciding whether a particular restriction is 'necessary in a democratic society' and within the State's 'margin of appreciation'. The 'duties and responsibilities' of certain classes of applicants are enhanced—for example, journalists because of their role as 'public watchdog' provided, of course, they are acting in a professional capacity (see 2.18). Recently the Court has played down this phrase and has emphasized that regardless of an applicant's particular status, they are still 'individuals' who benefit from the full protection of the Convention.[133] In *Bladet Tromsø and Stensaas v Norway*,[134] the Court interpreted the phrase 'duties and responsibilities' as meaning that the freedom of expression of journalists was subject to the proviso that they were acting in good faith in order to provide accurate and reliable information in accordance with the ethics of journalism.

The medium of the expression The European Court has considered the medium **2.48** of the expression when deciding whether a given restriction is legitimate. For example, in relation to television and radio, which have a very wide potential

---

[129] App No 68354/01, (2008) 47 EHRR 5.
[130] eg *Engel and others v Netherlands* (1976) 1 EHRR 647.
[131] See *Wille v Liechtenstein* (2000) 30 EHRR 558, at para 64.
[132] eg *Vogt v Germany* (1995) 21 EHRR 205 and *Ahmed and others v UK* (1998) 29 EHRR 1.
[133] See, eg *Vereinigung Demokratischer Soldaten Österreichs and Gubi v Austria* (1994) 20 EHRR 56, at para 36.
[134] (1999) 29 EHRR 125, at para 65.

audience and are, by their nature, more intrusive, the State is likely to find it easier to justify a restriction than with a medium with a small potential audience, such as a film show in a licensed sex shop.[135] The Court has taken into account the difficulty of controlling the circulation of videos once they have been put into circulation when deciding on draconian restrictions on the blasphemous video, *Visions of Ecstasy*.[136]

2.49 *Prior restraint or ex post facto sanction?* The Court has made clear that Article 10 is engaged whether the restriction imposed is a prior restraint or a sanction imposed after publication. However, it will be considerably more difficult to justify prior restraints (eg injunctions)[137] than subsequent punishment (eg committal for contempt of court), or civil liability (eg damages for defamation).[138] In *Observer and Guardian* v *UK,* the Court held: 'The dangers inherent in prior restraints are such that they call for the most careful scrutiny on the part of the Court. This is especially so as far as the press is concerned, for news is a perishable commodity and to delay its publication for even a short period may well deprive it of all its value and interests.'[139]

2.50 *In* Association Ekin *v* France[140] the Court concluded that a Minister's wide-ranging power to impose prior restraints on certain publications would only be compatible with Article 10 if it was subject to strict scrutiny by the Courts to prevent any abuse of the power.[141] In his dissenting judgment in *Wingrove* v *UK,*[142] Judge de Meyer went further, taking the view that all prior restraints are unacceptable interferences in the field of freedom of expression. This view has never commanded majority support from the Court.[143]

---

[135] See *Scherer* v *Switzerland* (App No 17116/90), 14 January 1993.

[136] *Wingrove* v *UK* (1996) 24 EHRR 1.

[137] See generally, Barendt, E, *Freedom of Speech* (Oxford: OUP, 2007), 2nd edn, ch 4.

[138] This distinction is already to some extent recognized in English law, eg, in the rule that an interlocutory injunction will not generally issue in proceedings for defamation where the defence of justification has been raised (*Bonnard* v *Perryman* [1891] 2 Ch 269); see also, the rule that interim relief will not normally be granted to prevent publication of an adjudication by a public regulatory authority (*R* v *Advertising Standards Authority, ex p Vernon Pools Organisation Ltd* [1992] 1 WLR 1289).

[139] (1991) 14 EHRR 153, at para 60.

[140] (2002) 35 EHRR 1207.

[141] Section 12 HRA, discussed in detail at paras 3.67–3.77, provides such a legal framework in the UK.

[142] (1996) 24 EHRR 1, at 36.

[143] A near absolute ban on prior restraints exists in the USA: see, eg *New York Times* v *US*; *Washington Post* v *US* 403 US 713 (1971).

Other Convention Rights of Particular Importance to Media Law

There are a number of other Convention Articles that may be relevant in deciding **2.51** whether restrictions on freedom of expression are permissible.

Article 6(1): Reporting of judicial proceedings

(See generally, chapter 9 for a more detailed analysis of this area.) Article 6(1) **2.52** is concerned with the right to a fair trial. The starting position is that a fair trial requires a public trial because a public trial 'protects litigants from the administration of justice in secret'[144] and it maintains public confidence in the judicial system.[145] However, the right to a public hearing is not unqualified; Article 6(1) expressly permits some restrictions on the reporting of judicial proceedings: 'In the determination of his civil rights and obligations or of any criminal charge against him, everyone is entitled to a fair and public hearing within a reasonable time by an independent and impartial tribunal established by law. *Judgment shall be pronounced publicly but the press and public may be excluded from all or part of the trial in the interests of morals, public order or national security in a democratic society, where the interests of juveniles or the protection of the private life of the parties so require, or to the extent strictly necessary in the opinion of the court in special circumstances where publicity would prejudice the interests of justice.*' (emphasis added)

The scope of Article 6(1) has given rise to a great deal of case law.[146] **2.53** It applies to all criminal proceedings, and to all ordinary civil litigation between private parties including tort, contract, restitution, family law, and employment law. Article 6(1) also applies to most licensing decisions[147] and professional disciplinary tribunals.[148] The Court has held that prison disciplinary proceedings, although within the ambit of Article 6(1), can be conducted inside a prison without public or media access for 'reasons of public order and security'.[149] However, such an exclusion is not permissible in ordinary

---

[144] *Pretto* v *Italy* (1983) 6 EHRR 182.

[145] *Diennet* v *France* (1995) 21 EHRR 554, at para 33.

[146] See generally, Lester, A and Pannick, D (eds), *Human Rights Law and Practice* 2004 (2nd edn) ch 4 pp 203–55.

[147] See *X* v *Belgium* (1980) 23 DR 237 (licence to run a public house terminated as a result of the applicant's conviction for keeping a brothel).

[148] See *Guchez* v *Belgium* App No 10027/82, (1984) 40 DR 100 (concerning suspension of the applicant by the disciplinary board of the Architects' Association for canvassing custom).

[149] *Campbell and Fell* v *UK* (1984) 7 EHRR 165.

criminal proceedings (at para 87). While Article 6(1), unlike Article 10, does not require that any restriction or interference be 'necessary in a democratic society', the Court in *Campbell and Fell* considered the restrictions under a similar proportionality analysis. In *B and P* v *UK*[150] the Court rejected the applicants' complaint that their Children Act 1989 proceedings for residence orders had been held in private and had therefore breached Article 6 (1) ECHR. The Court thought that these were 'prime examples of cases where the exclusion of the public may be justified to protect the privacy of the child and parties and to avoid prejudice and in the interests of justice.'

2.54   A litigant may waive his or her right to a public hearing, provided this waiver does not run counter to any important public interest.[151] The media have unsuccessfully asserted their right to attend a criminal hearing. In *Atkinson, Crook and The Independent* v *UK*,[152] the Commission rejected an application under Article 10 brought by two journalists complaining about the decision of a trial judge to hold sentencing proceedings in camera. The Commission rejected the applicant's argument that the State could not restrict a person from receiving information that others wish to impart to him, because the rights of the defendant and the interests of justice also had to be taken into account.

Article 8: The right to respect for private life[153]

2.55   Article 8 concerns various privacy rights, of which the right to respect for private life is relevant to media law. An individual's right to respect for private life can potentially conflict with the media's right to freedom of expression under Article 10.

Article 8 provides:

1. Everyone has the right to respect for his private and family life, his home and his correspondence.
2. There shall be no interference by a public authority with the exercise of this right except such as is in accordance with the law and is necessary in a democratic society in the interests of national security, public safety or the economic well-being of the country, for the prevention of disorder or crime, for the protection of health or morals, or for the protection of the rights and freedoms of others.

---

[150] (2002) 34 EHRR 529.
[151] *Schuler-Zgraggen* v *Switzerland* (1993) 16 EHRR 405.
[152] App No 13366/87, (1990) 67 DR 244.
[153] See ch 6 for a detailed discussion of the issues relating to privacy and the media.

As with Article 10, the first paragraph of Article 8 asserts the positive right, **2.56** namely the right to respect for private life, while the second paragraph sets out how and when restrictions on that positive right can be justified. The methodology of Article 8 is the same as Article 10, and therefore the first stage is to identify an interference with the right. If such an interference exists, first, it must be 'in accordance with the law', which is identical in meaning to the Article 10 requirement that the interference is 'prescribed by law' (see *Sunday Times* v *UK*, at 2.37–2.40); secondly, the interference must achieve a legitimate aim; and, thirdly, the interference must be 'necessary in a democratic society' and within the State's 'margin of appreciation.'

In the media law context, invasions of privacy are likely to be perpetrated **2.57** by private bodies such as newspapers and television stations rather than by the State.[154] However, as discussed at 2.24–2.25 above in relation to Article 10, States have a positive obligation to ensure the effective protection of the right to respect for private life. The concept of a positive obligation in relation to protection of this right is more developed than the Article 10 jurisprudence. The Court has stated that the positive obligation will extend to requiring action to protect an individual from the acts of other private parties: 'The Court recalls that although the object of Article 8 is essentially that of protecting the individual against arbitrary interference by the public authorities, it does not merely compel the State to abstain from such interference: in addition to this primarily negative obligation, there may be positive obligations inherent in an effective respect for private or family life. These obligations may involve the adoption of measures designed to secure respect for private life even in the sphere of the relations of individuals between themselves.'[155]

In the seven years since the first edition of this book was published, the European **2.58** Court had developed the doctrine of positive obligations in relation to the protection of privacy from intrusion by media organizations. This development is arguably the most significant change to media law in the last decade. In *Von Hannover* v *Germany*[156] the Strasbourg Court concluded that the lack of protection from intrusive media afforded to public figures by German law breached Article 8 ECHR. The Court concluded that public figures, like other individuals, were entitled to a zone of privacy. The photographs in issue showing Princess Caroline of Monaco shopping, skiing, and on holiday contributed

---

[154] But some television stations such as the BBC are likely to be public authorities under the Human Rights Act and therefore an individual will be able to rely directly on Article 8; see chapter 3, at paras 3.31–3.40.

[155] *X and Y* v *Netherlands* (1985) 8 EHRR 235, at para 23.

[156] (2005) 40 EHRR 1.

nothing to the public debate about matters of general importance; as such the failure of the State to regulate such intrusions breached her right to respect for her private life.[157] Domestic courts have similarly developed the action for breach of confidence to provide significant protection for individuals from intrusion from the media subject to a public interest defence.[158]

Article 14: The right not to be discriminated against[159]

2.59   The ECHR's discrimination provision is not freestanding but is limited to those rights embodied in the Convention and the Protocols. To invoke Article 14, it is necessary to show that the facts in question fall 'within the ambit' of one or more of the Convention rights. Article 14 ECHR provides: 'The enjoyment of the rights and freedoms set forth in this Convention shall be secured without discrimination on any ground such as sex, race, colour, language, religion, political or other opinion, national or social origin, association with a national minority, property, birth, or other status.'

2.60   Article 14 sets out a number of categories of prohibited discrimination, but it is clear from the use of words 'such as' and 'other status' that these categories are not closed.

2.61   Article 14 does not prohibit all kinds of differential treatment, merely differential treatment which has 'no reasonable justification'. The existence of such justification depends on the aim and effect of the measure in question, and whether the measure is proportionate to the aim that is sought to be realised.[160] One example of discrimination in the media law field where one would have expected the European Court to have recourse to Article 14, is *Vereinigung Demokratischer Soldaten Österreichs and Gubi* v *Austria*,[161] which concerned the failure of the State to distribute *Der Igel* to Austrian soldiers while distributing other magazines for soldiers. The Court concluded that there was a violation of Article 10, because the State was not permitted to discriminate between types of publication on the basis of the publication's content. However, the Court reached this conclusion without recourse to Article 14.

---

[157]   See also, *Sciacca* v *Italy* (2006) 43 EHRR 20.
[158]   See, eg *Campbell* v *MGN Ltd* [2004] 2 AC 457, *McKennitt* v *Ash* [2008] QB 73 and *Murray* v *Big Pictures (UK) Ltd* [2008] EWCA Civ 446 discussed in ch 6.
[159]   See ch 7 for a further discussion of the issues relating to discrimination.
[160]   *Belgian Linguistic Case (No 2)* (1968) 1 EHRR 252.
[161]   (1994) 20 EHRR 56.

Other areas of media law where Article 14 may be relevant include the criminal **2.62** law of blasphemy, which explicitly discriminates against non-Christian religions. See generally, chapter 8.

Article 15: Restrictions in time of war or other public emergency threatening the life of the nation

Article 15 permits the suspension of various Convention rights in times of **2.63** war and other public emergencies threatening the life of the nation. Article 15 provides:

1. In time of war or other public emergency threatening the life of the nation any High Contracting Party may take measures derogating from its obligations under this Convention to the extent strictly required by the exigencies of the situation, provided that such measures are not inconsistent with its other obligations under international law.
2. No derogation from Article 2, except in respect of deaths resulting from lawful acts of war, or from Articles 3, 4 (paragraph 1) and 7 shall be made under this provision.
3. Any High Contracting Party availing itself of this right of derogation shall keep the Secretary-General of the Council of Europe fully informed of the measures which it has taken and the reasons therefor. It shall also inform the Secretary-General of the Council of Europe when such measures have ceased to operate and the provisions of the Convention are again being fully executed.

This Article may be relevant to reporting on wars. Despite the language of **2.64** Article 15(1) restricting it to measures that are 'strictly required', the Court has recognized a margin of appreciation for the contracting State in assessing whether such an emergency exists and, if so, what steps are necessary to overcome it.[162] Van Dijk and van Hoof[163] contend, correctly in our view, that the exceptions provided for in Article 15 can never be applicable to the 'freedom to hold opinions' contained in Article 10, since an exception to that right can in no circumstances be 'strictly required' in the sense of Article 15(1).

---

[162] See *Ireland* v *UK* (1978) 2 EHRR 25, at paras 91–2.
[163] *Theory and Practice of the European Convention on Human Rights* (4th edn, Kluwer Law International, 2006), at p 816.

Article 17: Restrictions on activities subversive of Convention rights—the problem of hate speech

2.65 (See chapter 7) Article 17 permits restrictions on those who seek to destroy the Convention rights of others and has been invoked in relation to prosecutions for hate speech.[164] Article 17 ECHR provides: 'Nothing in this Convention may be interpreted as implying for any state, group or person any right to engage in any activity or perform any act aimed at the destruction of any of the rights and freedoms set forth herein or at their limitation to a greater extent than is provided for in the Convention.'

2.66 In *Lehideux and Isorni* v *France*[165] the Court stated that speech negating 'clearly established historical facts', such as the Holocaust, 'would be removed from the protection of Article 10 by Article 17', although, on the facts of the case, the Court concluded that the expression in issue was not revisionist and as such did fall within the ambit of Article 10. A similar approach was adopted in *Norwood* v *UK*[166] to speech attacking Islam. The applicant was convicted of a racially aggravated offence under the Public Order Act 1986 for putting up a poster linking Islam with the attacks on the World Trade Centre in 2001 and calling for 'Islam out of Britain—Protect the British People'. The Court rejected his complaint pursuant to Article 10 as inadmissible because Article 17 removed protection for the gratuitous attack on a religion.

---

[164] See, eg *Glimmerveen and Hagenbeek* v *Netherlands* App Nos 8348/78 and 8406/78, (1979) 18 DR 187.
[165] (2000) 30 EHRR 665.
[166] (2004) 40 EHRR SE 111.

3

THE HUMAN RIGHTS ACT 1998

Introduction	3.01	Enforcement of Convention	
'Convention Rights'	3.03	Rights: Standing	3.42
Interpreting Legislation		Enforcement of Convention	
Consistently with Convention		Rights: Which Court?	3.54
Rights	3.16	Enforcement of Convention	
Public Authorities' Duty to		Rights: Remedies	3.61
Comply with Convention		Special Provisions Concerning	
Rights	3.29	Freedom of Expression	3.67

Introduction

The long title to the Human Rights Act (HRA) 1998 declares its purpose to 'give **3.01** further effect to rights and freedoms guaranteed under the European Convention on Human Rights'. As chapter 1 showed, even before the HRA, the ECHR was referred to with increasing regularity in cases concerning freedom of expression. The House of Lords declared on several occasions that it could see no difference between Article 10 and the common law's approach to the right of freedom of speech.[1] The number of occasions on which the European Court found the UK media law decisions to be in violation of Article 10 suggests that this rosy outlook was not always justified in practice. However, it did mean that Article 10 and its jurisprudence were familiar to the courts in the media law context.

Nevertheless, even this area of law has been affected by the HRA. In particular: **3.02**

(a) It puts an obligation on courts to interpret legislation 'so far as it is possible to do so' compatibly with the Convention. This gives wider

---

[1] *Derbyshire C C v Times Newspapers Ltd* [1993] AC 534; *A-G v Guardian Newspapers Ltd (No 2)* [1990] 1 AC 109; *Reynolds v Times Newspapers Ltd* [2001] 2 AC 127.

scope to read UK legislation in conformity with the Convention than the traditional common law approach to statutory interpretation would allow.

(b) It puts an obligation on all public authorities (including the courts) to act in conformity with the Convention. This was new and gave new scope for invoking respect for freedom of expression.

(c) It provides new remedies where a public authority has violated a Convention right.

(d) It contains special provisions concerning freedom of expression (s 12).

(e) It supports those trends that could be detected in the common law in favour of freedom of expression.

'Convention Rights'

Omitted rights

3.03 It is convenient shorthand to refer to the HRA as 'incorporating the Convention into UK' law, but it is not completely accurate. In the first place, it is not the whole of the Convention and its Protocols which are referred to when the Act speaks of 'Convention rights'. Unsurprisingly, they do not include those Protocols to which the UK is not a party, or situations where the UK has entered a reservation to the Convention or a Protocol (see HRA, Schedule 3). Schedule 1 to the Act sets out those parts of the Convention and Protocols which *are* included in the term 'Convention rights'.

3.04 There are two provisions of the Convention which are not included in Schedule 1 even though the UK has agreed to be bound by them—Article 1 and Article 13. Article 1 provides:

Article 1 Obligation to respect human rights

The High Contracting Parties shall secure to everyone within their jurisdiction the rights and freedoms set out in Section I of this Convention.

3.05 Article 13 provides:

Article 13 Right to an effective remedy

Everyone whose rights and freedoms as set forth in this Convention are violated shall have an effective remedy before a national authority notwithstanding that the violation has been committed by persons acting in an official capacity.

3.06 The government explained these omissions by saying that the 1998 Act itself was the means by which the Convention rights were to be secured, and the HRA itself ensured that there would be an effective remedy. To the extent that the HRA did not provide a complete remedy (in particular, where primary legislation was indisputably in conflict with the Convention), this reflected deliberate government policy that the Act should leave untouched Parliament's ultimate power to legislate, even in a manner which conflicted with human rights.

The omission of Article 1 has and is likely to have little practical effect. **3.07** The Article does not itself confer rights but it does elaborate on the territorial scope of other provisions which do create rights. As such, the UK courts will take it into account (and Strasbourg interpretation of it) when construing those other rights.[2] Similarly, the European Court of Human Rights has referred to Article 1 when developing its idea of 'positive obligations' inherent in other parts of the Convention (eg Article 8). Where those other rights are listed in the Schedule to the HRA, the UK courts have had no trouble in treating these ancillary positive obligations as also included.

However, the UK courts have stressed that the legislative technique of listing **3.08** specified rights in the Schedule rather than simply incorporating the Convention into British law can have other real consequences. Thus, for instance, for the most part the domestic rights created by the HRA arise only in relation to events that take place after the commencement of the Act (2nd October 2000).[3] The UK's international responsibility dates from 1953 for the Convention itself and the various dates on which it has ratified various protocols.

The omission of Article 13 may be more significant. Again, there can be **3.09** situations where this provision will help inform the meaning of other parts of the Convention which are incorporated,[4] but, because it is not included in the Schedule, it is not possible for the UK courts to rely on it directly in order to establish a breach of UK law.[5]

Section 7 of the Act (which provides for remedies) is the domestic equivalent **3.10** of Article 13. It will be unreal to expect the UK courts to disregard entirely the case law which Strasbourg has built up as to what is required of an 'effective remedy'.

---

[2] See, eg *R (Al-Skeini)* v *Secretary of State for Defence* [2008] 1 AC 153 HL.
[3] See *Re McKerr* [2004] 1 WLR 807 HL.
[4] See, eg *Aston Cantlow PCC* v *Wallbank* [2004] 1 AC 546 at [44].
[5] See, eg *Re S (Minors) (Care Order: Implementation of Care Plan)* [2002] 2 AC 291.

Strasbourg case law

3.11 At a European level, 'Convention rights' mean more than the plain text of the Convention and its Protocols. As chapter 2 showed in the context of the provisions that most affect the media, a considerable body of case law has grown up which explains and to some extent amplifies the meaning which is to be given to the treaties themselves. Section 2 of the Act requires this case law to be taken into account whenever any question has to be determined in connection with a Convention right.

3.12 The obligation, though, is only to 'take into account' the European case law. This choice of phrase was deliberate. Clearly, where the European Court has established principles in relation to the Convention rights, the UK courts will have to follow them. As Lord Bingham said in *R (Ullah)* v *Secretary of State for the Home Department*,[6] 'The duty of national courts is to keep pace with the Strasbourg jurisprudence as it evolves over time: no more, but certainly no less.' In *Al-Skeini* (see 3.07) Lord Brown suggested that this sentence could as well have ended 'no less, but certainly no more'. He observed that if a national court construed the Convention rights too strictly, the aggrieved individual could find a remedy in Strasbourg, but if the national court was too generous, an aggrieved government had no right of petition to the European Court of Human Rights.

3.13 The application of principles to the facts of the particular cases will usefully illustrate how the European Court regards those principles as having to be applied in practice. Yet there are some respects in which the role of the European Court is different from that of the domestic courts. This can be seen most strikingly in the Court's concept of the 'margin of appreciation'. This is a jurisprudential tool which the Court has adopted because of its position as an international court. It reflects the Court's sensitivity to the fact that it is composed of international judges and does not have the same contact with, or experience of, the legal system and culture of a particular contracting State as do the domestic courts of that State. In any case, the function of the European Court is not to act as a further tier of appeal within the domestic judicial scheme. Many of the decisions of the Court reflect on the one hand the pull towards restraint which the concept of the margin of appreciation implies, and on the other hand the opposite pull of the need to maintain European supervision. These concepts and the struggle between them are not material for domestic courts, tribunals, or other decision-makers. So, when 'taking account' of the case law, courts will have to assess how much they need to make allowance for a concern which they need not share.

---

[6] [2004] 2 AC 323 at [20].

Similarly, the Convention rights are intended to establish a floor of rights, not a ceiling: s 11 of the HRA makes clear that the Act is intended to add to, not detract from, existing rights.

However, while the 'margin of appreciation' is an immaterial concept for a **3.14** domestic court, some discretionary area of judgment may still be left to the legislature and the government.[7] The extent of this area varies according to the rights in issue and the nature of the act of the public authority in question. In the media field, for example, the courts have allowed considerable latitude to Parliament to determine that there should be no advertising by organizations with political aims—*R (Animal Defenders International)* v *Secretary of State for Culture, Media and Sport*,[8] and that all programmes, including party election broadcasts should be subject to the taste and decency standard—*R (ProLife Alliance)* v *BBC*.[9]

Courts take judicial notice of the case law of UK courts. In practice, they have also **3.15** taken judicial notice of the case law of the Strasbourg organs. However, strictly speaking, this is a matter of evidence, and the Act gives the Lord Chancellor the power to prescribe by Rules the manner of proving it (HRA, s 2(2) and (3)). Instead of Rules, a Practice Direction has been adopted which requires the citation of 'an authoritative and complete report' and for copies to be provided to the court and other parties not less than three days before the hearing. Printouts from the European Court's database (HUDOC) can be used.[10] Applicants before the European Court can choose whether to use English or French. The judgment (at least initially) is given in the applicant's language of choice. Linguistically challenged practitioners can find a useful summary of the French judgments in the Court's press releases which are issued at the same time and which can also be accessed from the Court's database.

Interpreting Legislation Consistently with Convention Rights

Introduction

(1) So far as it is possible to do so, primary legislation and subordinate legislation **3.16** must be read and given effect in a way which is compatible with Convention rights.[11]

---

[7] *R* v *DPP, ex p Kebilene* [2000] 2 AC 326.
[8] [2008] 2 WLR 781 HL.
[9] [2004] 1 AC 185.
[10] See Practice Direction to CPR Part 39, para 8.1.
[11] HRA, s 3(1).

This provision is one of the cornerstones of the 1998 Act. Thus recourse to the Convention is not confined to situations where the legislation is ambiguous. Nor are the courts merely to take account of the requirements of the Convention. On the contrary, they must, so far as possible, achieve an interpretation of domestic legislation which is compatible with Convention rights.[12]

3.17 This statutory obligation carries the qualification 'so far as it is possible to do so'. The phrase deliberately echoes the way in which the courts of Member States of the EU are required to interpret their domestic legislation compatibly with EU legislation so far as it is possible to do so.[13] This means that where more than one interpretation of the legislation is possible, the court must choose that which is consistent with the Convention right. Lord Cooke has described it as 'a strong adjuration', and accurately predicted that a provision in a criminal statute which appeared to put the legal burden of proof on a defendant might in some circumstances be interpreted as no more than an evidential burden.[14] In the same case, Lord Hope drew an analogy between issues under the HRA and the approach of the Privy Council to constitutional protections for individual rights. Both called for a generous and purposive construction.

3.18 In consequence the courts have been willing to read down a statute or read words into it, if this has been necessary to achieve a Convention-compliant result.[15] What s 3 does not permit, however, is for the courts to 'interpret' legislation in a way that is contrary to one of its fundamental features. They should also be wary of making use of s 3 where a Convention-compliant result could be achieved in one of several different ways. Both these courses would overstep their constitutional role and turn the courts into legislators. Even the HRA does not allow this.[16]

3.19 The interpretative obligation under s 3 is a different approach to statutory construction than that which the courts normally employ. It means, for instance, that the intention of the legislator is not a reliable guide to meaning. It cannot be, because the new interpretative obligation applies whenever the legislation was enacted, even if this was before the 1998 Act was passed.[17] It also follows that pre-HRA judicial decisions as to the meaning of legislation will have to be re-examined if their conclusions conflict with Convention rights. However, save

---

[12] *Re S (Minors) (Care Order: Implementation of Care Plan)* [2002] 2 AC 291.
[13] Case C–106/89 *Marleasing SA* v *La Commercial Internacional de Alimentacion SA* [1992] CMLR 305.
[14] *R v DPP, ex p Kebilene* [2000] 2 AC 326.
[15] eg *R v A* [2002] 1 AC 45; *Secretary of State for the Home Department* v *MB* [2008] 1 AC 440.
[16] *Ghaidan* v *Godin-Mendoza* [2004] 2 AC 557, HL.
[17] HRA, s 3(2)(a).

in very exceptional circumstances, the usual rules of precedent apply. Thus the ratio decidendi of a higher court in the judicial hierarchy will remain binding even if a lower court thinks that it conflicts with a decision of the Strasbourg court. The lower court would, of course, be free to call attention to the conflict in its judgment and, if the issue was critical to its decision in the case, grant permission to appeal.[18]

Primary and secondary legislation

The obligation applies to primary and secondary legislation. However, primary **3.20** legislation remains valid if, even when adopting this method of interpretation, it is incompatible with the Convention and the legislation's continuing operation or enforcement is not affected.[19] 'Primary legislation' is defined as meaning: a public general act; a local and personal act; a private act; a Church Assembly Measure; a Measure of the General Synod of the Church of England; an Order in Council made under the Royal Prerogative; an Order in Council made under s 38(1)(a) of the Northern Ireland Act 1973 or the corresponding provision of the Northern Ireland Act 1998; or an Order in Council amending a public, private, or local Act. 'Primary legislation' also includes an order or other instrument under primary legislation bringing the legislation into force or amending primary legislation. However, this later category does not include an order or instrument by the National Assembly of Wales, a member of the Scottish Executive, a Northern Ireland Minister, or a member of a Northern Ireland department.[20]

With subordinate legislation,[21] there are two elements to the inquiry: (i) the **3.21** meaning of the subordinate legislation; and (ii) the power under the primary legislation to make subordinate legislation. The courts must interpret the subordinate legislation so far as it is possible to do so compatibly with the Convention, and they will likewise try to interpret the enabling primary legislation as conferring power to act in accordance with the Convention. However, this may not be possible. If (disregarding any possibility of revocation) primary legislation prevents removal of the incompatibility, the validity of both the primary legislation and its subordinate offshoot are valid, and the continuing operation and enforcement of the incompatible subordinate legislation are unaffected.[22]

---

[18] *Kay* v *Lambeth BC* [2006] 2 AC 465.
[19] HRA, s 3(2)(b).
[20] HRA, s 21(1).
[21] As defined by HRA, s 21(1).
[22] HRA, s 3(2)(c).

Declarations of incompatibility

3.22   While primary legislation and this restricted class of subordinate legislation remain valid and effective even if it is impossible to read them compatibly with Convention rights, the courts are not completely powerless. Any court or tribunal can, of course, express its view as part of its decision. The cogency of its arguments may have the force of persuasion that amending legislation is necessary. However, the High Court (and the higher appellate courts) can go further and formally make a 'declaration of incompatibility'.[23] Once again, the declaration does not affect the validity, continuing operation, or enforcement of the provision,[24] but it does give the government the power to amend the legislation by an expedited procedure.[25]

3.23   The courts which can make declarations of incompatibility do not include magistrates' courts or the Crown Court, even though the judges of the latter include High Court judges. Where a criminal case raises such an issue, the matter must therefore reach (in England or Wales) the Court of Appeal or, if the case proceeds by way of judicial review or an appeal by case stated, the High Court, before a declaration can be made. County courts cannot make declarations of incompatibility. A case can be transferred from the county court to the High Court if there is a real prospect that a declaration of incompatibility will be made.[26] Within the High Court declarations of incompatibility can only be made by High Court judges, and a deputy High Court judge, master, or district judge cannot try a case where a claim is made for such a declaration or in respect of a judicial act under the HRA.[27]

3.24   If a court is considering whether to make a declaration of incompatibility, the Crown is entitled to 21 days' notice and to be joined as a party to the proceedings.[28]

3.25   A declaration of incompatibility does not affect the validity, continuing operation, or enforcement of the provision as a matter of law.[29] However, in practice, the government would be under considerable political pressure to bring UK law into conformity with what our courts have said the Convention requires. If the government thought that the UK courts had misunderstood

---

[23] HRA, s 4.
[24] HRA, s 4(6).
[25] HRA, s 10 and Sch 2.
[26] See CPR, r 30.3(2)(g).
[27] CPR, PD 2B, para 7A.
[28] CPR, Pt 19, r 19.4A; the court can specify an alternative period of notice.
[29] HRA, s 4(6)(a).

the Convention's obligations, it could conceivably refuse to pass the necessary legislation and contest the inevitable complaint to the European Court. The Act makes clear that the decision of the UK courts is not binding on the parties to the proceedings[30] so that, as a matter of UK law, there would be no formal obstacle to the government taking such an obdurate stance.

The HRA intended that future legislation (at least public bills) would be **3.26** compatible with Convention Rights. Section 19(1) requires the sponsoring minister to make a statement that he or she believes this to be so, or alternatively to state expressly that it is not so, but the minister nonetheless wants Parliament to consider the bill. The second option has only been taken once since the section came into effect. The Secretary of State sponsoring the Communications Bill (which subsequently became the Communications Act 2003) said that he thought the bans on political advertising were compatible with the Convention rights but, because of the judgment of the Strasbourg Court in *VgT* v *Switzerland*,[31] could not be sure. Unsurprisingly this led an NGO (which happened also to be campaigning against cruelty to animals) to seek a declaration of incompatibility when broadcasters refused to show its advertisements on the grounds that the organization had political aims. However, the House of Lords held that the provisions in the Communications Act were compatible with Article 10—*R (Animal Defenders International)* v *Secretary of State for Culture, Media and Sport* (see 3.14).

Matters covered by European Community Law

Although generally speaking the courts can only make a declaration of **3.27** incompatibility if primary legislation is unavoidably in conflict with Convention rights, their powers are greater if the legislation in question concerns a matter covered by European Community law. The European Court of Justice has declared on numerous occasions that it will be guided by general principles of law common to the Member States, including their shared commitment to the protection of fundamental human rights. The ECHR is a valuable source for determining the content of those rights.

Consequently, Community measures will be assessed in the light of the **3.28** obligations in the ECHR. Correspondingly, domestic implementation of those measures must also accord with the principles of the Convention. If domestic law—even primary legislation—cannot be reconciled with the Convention's

---

[30] HRA, s 4(6)(b).
[31] (2001) 34 EHRR 159.

requirements, it must give way. This is not a result of the HRA but of the European Communities Act 1972.

Public Authorities' Duty to Comply with Convention Rights

Introduction

3.29   (1) It is unlawful for a public authority to act in a way which is incompatible with a Convention right.[32]

This is the second major innovation of the 1998 Act. In the past, the courts were reluctant to impose even the attenuated duty to have regard to the ECHR in the exercise of statutory powers.[33] This provision goes further. It is not sufficient for authorities to take account of the Convention or to have regard to it; they must not act in a way which is incompatible with a Convention right. But equally the courts are here concerned with substance not form. So the decision of a public authority will not be unlawful for failing to take account of a Convention right unless its decision did actually infringe the right.[34]

Incompatible primary legislation

3.30   Once again, the duty is qualified in the case of primary legislation which requires incompatible behaviour so that the 'authority could not have acted differently',[35] or where the authority was acting so as to give effect to or to enforce primary legislation provisions which 'cannot be read or given effect in a way which is compatible with the Convention rights'.[36] The strength of this language is a reminder of how keenly Parliament wishes the courts to strive in carrying out their interpretative duty to find a reading of even primary legislation which is compatible with Convention rights.

Meaning of 'public authority'

3.31   The Act does not try to list 'public authorities'. It expressly *includes* courts and tribunals;[37] 'tribunal' means any tribunal in which legal proceedings may be brought:[38] It expressly *excludes* either House of Parliament (except the House

---

[32]   HRA, s 6(1).
[33]   *R v Secretary of State for the Home Department, ex p Brind* [1991] 1 AC 696.
[34]   See, eg *Belfast City Council v Miss Behavin' Ltd* [2007] 1 WLR 1420, HL.
[35]   HRA, s 6(2)(a).
[36]   HRA, s 6(2)(b).
[37]   HRA, s 6(3)(a).
[38]   s 21(1).

of Lords in its judicial capacity) or a person exercising functions in connection with proceedings in Parliament.[39] This exclusion is intended to continue the immunity which proceedings in Parliament have from judicial scrutiny as a result of the Bill of Rights. The immunity, though, does not extend to Strasbourg, where the UK will remain liable for any breaches of Convention rights as a result of Parliamentary proceedings or the acts of Parliamentary officials.[40]

Departments of central government, local authorities, and the police are all obvious examples of what is meant by 'public authorities'. All of their activities are subject to the obligation in s 6(1) to act compatibly with Convention rights. However, the term 'public authority' is meant to extend beyond these easy examples. This is clear from the further partial definition that includes 'any person certain of whose functions are functions of a public nature'.[41] In the case of a hybrid body some only of whose functions are of a public nature, the duty under s 6 does not apply if the nature of the particular act in question was private.[42] **3.32**

There are other areas of law which rely on a similar distinction between 'public' bodies (or functions) and those which are private. A decision needs, for instance, to have a public character in order to be amenable to judicial review. Another example is the effect of directives of the Commission of the EU. Even without implementing domestic legislation they are directly applicable to public bodies, or 'emanations of the State'. Precedents from these other areas of law may be helpful in deciding whether a particular body or function is 'public' for the purposes of the HRA, but it is dangerous to read them across without further thought. The HRA was intended to allow remedies in the domestic courts for breaches of the Convention which would otherwise have to be addressed in Strasbourg. Thus the governing consideration in deciding whether a body is a 'public authority' for the purpose of this Act is whether the UK would be responsible for its actions or decisions before the European Court of Human Rights.[43] The Court has certainly treated a State as responsible for the decisions of its courts even though (as the Convention requires) courts are independent of the government. Likewise, it is responsible if it has delegated obligations to private individuals or bodies.[44] **3.33**

---

[39] HRA, s 6(3) and (4).
[40] See, eg *Demicoli* v *Malta* (1991) 14 EHRR 47.
[41] HRA, s 6(3)(b).
[42] HRA, s 6(5).
[43] *Aston Cantlow PCC* v *Wallbank* [2004] 1 AC 546.
[44] See, eg *Costello-Roberts* v *UK* (1993) 19 EHRR 112.

3.34   On this basis the House of Lords has, for instance, decided that the owners of a private care home were not a 'public authority' although many of their residents were financially supported by their local authorities.[45]

3.35   Another consideration is that only *non-governmental* organizations can claim to be 'victims' of a violation of Convention rights—see Article 34 ECHR. Therefore the courts will ask whether, in respect of a particular function of a hybrid body, Parliament intended that the body should be outside the Convention's guarantees.

3.36   In the media context, the statutory regulator, Ofcom, is clearly a public authority. The Advertising Standards Authority (ASA) is a company limited by guarantee. It operates on a voluntary basis, but it does so within a framework of Community law[46] and the power of the Director-General to obtain an injunction to control misleading advertisements.[47] The ASA is subject to judicial review[48] and will be a public authority for the purpose of the HRA. The British Board of Film Classification (BBFC) is another example of a private body which has been brought within a statutory system of regulation. It has been designated by the Home Secretary for the purpose of operating the system of classifying videos which the Video Recordings Act 1984 requires. It would therefore be a 'public authority' when discharging these duties. So, too, would the Video Appeals Committee which hears appeals from decisions of the BBFC.[49]

3.37   The Press Complaints Commission (PCC), on the other hand, is a private body and an example of voluntary self-regulation. Legislation does not give it any powers or the ability to enforce its rulings. It has had no statutory underpinning, although both the HRA and the Data Protection Act 1998 have the potential to make use of its Code of Conduct. It may also be said that the Commission is an example of a self-regulatory body set up by the press in the shadow of implicit (and sometimes express) threats to impose governmental regulation if self-regulation cannot be made to work. In the context of public law, this has sometimes been sufficient to make the industry's own regulator amenable to judicial review. Indeed, the PCC itself has faced judicial review proceedings, although it has never been necessary for a court to rule definitively

---

[45]   *YL (by her litigation friend the Official Solicitor)* v *Birmingham City Council* [2008] 1 AC 95.
[46]   Dir 84/450.
[47]   Consumer Protection from Unfair Trading Regulations 2008, SI 2008/1277.
[48]   See *R* v *Advertising Standards Authority Ltd, ex p Insurance Service plc* (1990) 2 Admin LR 77; *R* v *Advertising Standards Authority Ltd, ex p Vernon Organisation Ltd* [1992] 1 WLR 1298; *R* v *Advertising Standards Authority, ex p City Trading Ltd* [1997] COD 202; *R* v *Advertising Standards Authority Ltd, ex p Direct Line Financial Services Ltd* [1998] COD 20.
[49]   See *R (BBFC)* v *Video Appeals Committee* [2008] 1 WLR 1658.

on the matter.[50] The government said in the course of the HRA debates that it considered that the PCC undertook public functions but the press did not.[51]

Newspapers, themselves, are clearly private bodies which will not owe the duty **3.38** under s 6 even though they operate in the public domain and fulfil a public service.[52]

The broadcast media will generally be regarded as non-governmental organiza- **3.39** tions and therefore able to rely on Convention rights. This is so even though, in the case of the BBC and Channel 4, they are publicly owned. In *Radio France* v *France*[53] admissibility decision 23 September 2003, the Court said that 'In order to determine whether any given legal person other than a territorial authority falls within [the category of governmental organization] account must be taken of its legal status and, where appropriate, the rights that status gives it, the nature of the activity it carries out and the context in which it is carried out, and the degree of its independence from the political authorities.' *Osterreichischer Rundfunk* v *Austria* [54] is to the same effect. The BBC and Channel 4 act independently in putting out their own material or their commissioned programmes. This would mean that in doing so they both qualify as non-governmental organizations and have the protection (in regard to these matters) of Convention rights. Correspondingly, in these matters the broadcasters are not 'public authorities'.

However, for certain purposes the broadcasters do exercise regulatory functions. **3.40** Thus, for instance, election broadcasts are put together by political parties, but the broadcasters are responsible for seeing that they observe the Ofcom Codes. In this respect the broadcasters are carrying out public functions. They are amenable to judicial review and must comply with the duty in s 6(1) of the HRA.[55]

---

[50] *R* v *Press Complaints Commission, ex p Stewart-Brady* [1997] EMLR 185. Stewart-Brady's subsequent complaint to the Commission under Art 8 was dismissed as inadmissible (App No 36908/97, 21 October 1998).

[51] Hansard HC Debs, 6th ser, col 414. However, in *Aston Cantlow PCC* v *Wallbank* (para 3.33 above), the House of Lords deprecated the use of Hansard to illustrate which organizations were to be 'public authorities' for the purpose of the HRA.

[52] *Venables and Thompson* v *News Group Newspapers Ltd* [2001] Fam 430 para D1.

[53] App No 53984/00.

[54] (App No 35841/02), 7 December 2006.

[55] See, eg *R (ProLife Alliance)* v *BBC* [2004] 1 AC 185.

Omissions to act

3.41   The prohibition in s 6 against 'acting' in a way which is incompatible with a Convention right also applies to failing to act. There is a qualification for failure to introduce legislation or to make any primary legislation or remedial order.[56]

Enforcement of Convention Rights: Standing

3.42   The third key element in the HRA is its provision for the enforcement of Convention rights. They can be relied upon in the course of proceedings which have some independent purpose, or in proceedings brought specifically to enforce the Convention right. They can be raised in an appeal or on judicial review.[57]

3.43   However, a Convention right can only be enforced by a person who has been or would be a 'victim' of the violation (or potential violation) of the right.[58] The concept of 'victim' comes from the Convention itself, which allows any 'person, non-governmental organisation or group of individuals claiming to be the victim of a violation by one of the High Contracting Parties of the rights set forth in Convention or the Protocols' to make an application to the European Court of Human Rights.[59] This right of individual petition to the Court was a major step forward in the growth of international human rights law. Initially, it was not an integral part of the Convention but an optional extra. Thus, although the UK was one of the original signatories to the Convention, it did not allow the right of individual petition until 1966. It then did so for renewable periods of five years. However, the right of individual access has now come to be seen as an indispensable part of the Convention's structure and is no longer optional. Those who believe that their Convention rights have been violated despite the HRA can still complain to Strasbourg (see chapter 4). Decisions of the UK courts which directly address Convention issues are likely to be treated with greater respect by the Court, but there are plenty of instances where the Court has found violations from countries which have incorporated the Convention's requirements into their domestic laws.

3.44   A 'victim' must be directly affected by the violation or prospective violation of the Convention. In most cases concerning freedom of expression, this has not given

---

[56]   HRA, s 6(6).
[57]   HRA, ss 7–9.
[58]   HRA, s 7(1).
[59]   Art 34 ECHR.

rise to any problems—it has been relatively easy to identify whether the applicant has been directly affected. Applications have been accepted from publishers, printers, and individual journalists. The reach of Article 10 is even wider because it protects the right to *receive* as well as the right to *impart* information and ideas. Thus women of child-bearing age could be considered to be victims of an Irish Supreme Court injunction prohibiting the publication of information about abortion facilities provided outside Ireland.[60] Nonetheless, it is important to observe some of the comments which the Court and Commission have made in developing the autonomous meaning of the concept of 'victim'.

The Irish case illustrates another proposition—that complaints can be made   **3.45**
in advance by those who would be directly affected. The Court accepted that women of child-bearing age were potentially affected by the injunction and so were able to come within the category of 'victims' even if they were not actually pregnant. It is not easy to predict precisely when the Court will regard the potential future application of a general measure as sufficient to make a person a victim. In *Times Newspapers Ltd* v *UK*,[61] it found that a newspaper publisher could in principle claim to be a victim of defamation laws that were too vague, but that on the facts of the case Times Newspapers failed because it could not point to any particular jury award which had inhibited any particular article. The Commission also rejected the complaint of a journalist to whom discovered documents had been shown by a solicitor after the documents had been read out in court. The solicitor had been treated as in contempt of court and she was therefore a victim, but no action had been taken against the journalist and the alleged chilling effect of the court's ruling against the solicitor was not sufficient to constitute him a victim.[62] In *Bowman* v *UK*,[63] an anti-abortionist was able to complain of restrictions on election campaign spending even though criminal proceedings against her had been unsuccessful. She had succeeded on a technicality (the charge, which was a summary one, had not been laid within the requisite time limit). The Court accepted that the risk of further prosecutions in future campaigns was sufficiently real to mean that she could still claim to be a victim.

But the risk of interference must be real. The editor of *The Guardian* sought a   **3.46**
declaration that the Treason Felony Act 1848 was incompatible with Article 10. This statute, passed in the wake of Fenian outrages and a febrile revolutionary

---

[60] *Open Door Counselling and Dublin Well Woman* v *Ireland* (1992) 15 EHRR 244.
[61] App No 14631/89, (1990) 65 DR 307.
[62] *Leigh, Guardian Newspapers Ltd and Observer Ltd* v *UK* App No 10039/82, (1984) 38 DR 74.
[63] (1998) 26 EHRR 1.

climate in many countries, penalizes the advocacy of the abolition of the monarchy. The Attorney-General refused to give an assurance that the newspaper and its journalists would not be prosecuted if they ran a campaign for a republican style of government in the UK. The House of Lords said that it was not the function of the courts via declarations of incompatibility to clean up the statute book of redundant but unused legislation.[64] As Lord Scott put it, 'Mr Sales is a very good lawyer. So, too, is Mr Robertson QC. But you do not have to be a very good lawyer to know that to advocate the abolition of the monarchy and its replacement by a republic by peaceful and constitutional means will lead neither to prosecution nor to conviction. All you need to be is a lawyer with common sense.'

3.47 In many cases involving Article 10 and the media it will be all too obvious that a restriction on freedom of expression has been imposed. That will not always be the case with breaches of other Convention rights. The rights to private life and security of correspondence in Article 8, for instance, may be violated by secret surveillance. The test which the Commission used is that there must be a reasonable likelihood that some such measure had been taken against the complainant.[65]

3.48 In principle a company can claim to be a victim of a violation of Convention rights. Article 10 has frequently been invoked by companies in Strasbourg applications.[66] However, not all the Convention rights are capable of applying or are intended to apply to artificial persons. In particular, the right to a private life under Article 8 may well be essentially a right which can only be claimed by individuals. The issue was raised but not decided in a challenge by the BBC to a decision of the Broadcasting Standards Commission (BSC) upholding a complaint by the company which owned Dixons stores. The Court of Appeal held that on the proper interpretation of the Broadcasting Act 1990, the BSC could receive a complaint that a company had suffered an unwarranted infringement of its privacy. It did so expressly on the basis that the statutory jurisdiction of the BSC was not necessarily the same as the meaning of 'private life' in Article 8.[67] A further right under Article 8 is a right to respect for 'correspondence'. This may include business as well as personal

---

[64] *R (Rusbridger)* v *A-G* [2004] 1 AC 357.

[65] *Hilton* v *UK* (1988) 57 DR 108.

[66] eg, *Observer and Guardian* v *UK* (1991) 14 EHRR 153; *Autronic AG* v *Switzerland* (1990) 12 EHRR 485.

[67] *R* v *Broadcasting Standards Commission, ex p BBC* [2000] 3 All ER 989, CA.

communications[68] and it may well be that the restrictions on State surveillance or intrusion protect corporate as well as individual communications.

It seems clear from Article 34 that an organ of the State cannot be a victim **3.49** since only *non-governmental* organizations can bring applications. Thus the Commission rejected as incompetent a complaint by a Spanish local authority.[69] The Court has decided that State-owned broadcasters can still qualify as non-governmental organizations if they have sufficient independence of the State—see 3.39. Consequently, the BBC, Channel 4, and SC4 are able, for instance, to rely on Article 10 and the other Convention rights.

Strasbourg has set its face against allowing individuals or groups to bring **3.50** complaints on behalf of those affected.[70] The *actio popularis* is not recognized by Article 34 ECHR. This means that the concept of 'victim' has a narrower meaning than the qualification for bringing an application for judicial review. The test in that context is whether the applicant has a 'sufficient interest',[71] and this has been liberally interpreted to allow public interest groups (especially those with an established reputation) to test the legality of the decisions of public authorities.[72] The government remained firm in its view that challenges under the Act would have to satisfy the 'victim' criterion. This is reflected in s 7(3), which says that: 'If the proceedings are brought on an application for judicial review, the applicant is to be taken to have a sufficient interest in relation to the unlawful act only if he is, or would be, a victim of that act.' Strasbourg has on occasions allowed interest groups to present argument as 'intervenors'.[73] Groups apply to the President of the Chamber who, if permission is granted, will normally restrict it to written observations. As human rights litigation has developed in the UK, there has been an increasing willingness to allow similar interventions in domestic proceedings.

The position is different where the organization represents the interests of **3.51** those who are or will be directly affected. Strasbourg has accepted that professional bodies, trade unions, and non-governmental organizations can represent members in this way, but they must be prepared to identify the affected members and establish that they do in fact have authority to act on

---

[68] See, for instance, *Niemietz* v *Germany* (1992) 16 EHRR 97.
[69] *Ayuntamiento* v *Spain* App No 15090/89, (1991) 68 DR 209.
[70] eg, *Klass* v *Germany* (1978) 2 EHRR 214.
[71] See Supreme Court Act 1981, s 31(3).
[72] eg *R* v *Secretary of State for Social Services, ex p Child Poverty Action Group* [1990] 2 QB 540.
[73] Rules of Procedure of the European Court of Human Rights, r 61.

their behalf.[74] In these circumstances, the individuals become the applicants (a matter which, domestically, may have profound consequences in terms of costs of unsuccessful proceedings). In judicial review, trade unions have sufficient standing to represent the interests of affected members.[75]

3.52 Of course, an organization may on occasions allege that it is itself a victim of a violation of a Convention right.[76] So, for instance, the refusal to allow a pressure group to advertise on the television or radio may lead to a claim by the group that its own right to freedom of expression has been violated.

3.53 The requirement for a complainant to be directly affected by the alleged violation has also precluded applications being instituted on behalf of a victim who has died.[77] It is otherwise if the application had begun before the victim's death,[78] or where the complaint itself concerns the victim's death or the failure to investigate it as required by Article 2, or where the complaint directly concerns the interests of the deceased's family or representatives (as may be the case where publicity has unreasonably intruded on the family's grief in the immediate aftermath of death—see chapter 6).

Enforcement of Convention Rights: Which Court?

Introduction

3.54 Assuming that the complainant satisfies the test of 'victim', there are essentially two ways in which Convention rights can be enforced:

(a) in proceedings brought specifically to enforce the Convention right;
(b) in the course of other legal proceedings.[79]

3.55 The Act makes clear that these procedures are intended to be additional to any other rights which the person might have under domestic law and are not intended to restrict his or her right to make any other claim or bring any other proceedings apart from these new remedies under the 1998 Act.[80]

---

[74] *Confédération des Syndicats Médicaux Français* v *France* (1986) 47 DR 225 and *Ahmed* v *UK* (1995) 20 EHRR CD 72.

[75] See *R* v *Horsham Justices, ex p Farquharson* [1982] QB 762, holding that the National Union of Journalists had sufficient standing to challenge an order of magistrates postponing reporting of committal proceedings.

[76] eg *Council of Civil Service Unions* v *UK* (1987) 50 DR 228.

[77] eg *Fairfield* v *UK* (App No 24790/04), 8 March 2005.

[78] eg *Dalban* v *Romania* (App No 28114/95), 28 September 1999.

[79] HRA, s 7(1).

[80] HRA, s 11.

Independent proceedings to enforce Convention rights

A right to bring proceedings specifically to enforce Convention rights is created **3.56**
by s 7(1)(a) of the Act.[81] The proceedings must be brought in the 'appropriate
court or tribunal'.[82] These are defined by rules, which materially only stipulate
that a claim under s 7(1)(a) in respect of a judicial act must be brought in the
High Court. Other claims under s 7(1)(a) may be brought in any court.[83]

Limitation period

There is a one-year time limit for bringing independent proceedings. The court **3.57**
has a power to extend this limit if it considers that it would be equitable to do so
having regard to all the circumstances.[84] This gives the court a wide discretion.[85]
However, if the procedure which is adopted sets a stricter time limit, that will
prevail.[86] Thus, where the challenge is made by judicial review, claimants will
still have to observe the requirement to apply promptly, and in any event within
three months of the act complained of (but with the court having power to
extend time).[87]

Human rights claims in other proceedings

The second alternative is for the Convention claim to be made in proceedings **3.58**
which have an independent life.[88] This includes legal proceedings which are
brought by or at the instigation of a public authority.[89] This provision had
particular importance in the early days of the implementation of the Act.
Ordinarily it is not possible to enforce Convention rights by any of the methods
established by s 7 if the act complained of took place before that section came into
force (2 October 2000). However, an exception is made where the Convention
right is sought to be enforced in legal proceedings brought by or at the instigation
of a public authority. In that case, a Convention right can be enforced whenever
the act in question took place.[90]

---

[81] These will be civil proceedings. The Act does not create any new criminal offences: s 7(8).
[82] HRA, s 7(2).
[83] CPR, Pt 7, r 7.11.
[84] HRA, s 7(5).
[85] *Dunn* v *Parole Board* (2008) HRLR 32.
[86] HRA, s 7(5).
[87] Supreme Court Act 1981, s 31(4).
[88] HRA, s 7(1)(b).
[89] HRA, s 7(6)(a).
[90] HRA, s 22(4).

3.59   We have seen that courts and tribunals are included in the category of 'public authority' (see 3.31). It follows that they have their own duty to act compatibly with Convention rights. A complaint that a lower court or tribunal has failed in this duty cannot be the subject of independent proceedings; it can be raised only by exercising a right of appeal or making an application for judicial review.[91] This does not derogate from any rule of law which prevents a court from being the subject of judicial review.[92] Thus the prohibition in the Supreme Court Act 1981, s 29(3), which prevents judicial review of matters relating to trial on indictment, remains.

3.60   Because courts are public authorities, any orders which they make which would have the effect of restricting freedom of expression will have to satisfy the Convention right under Article 10. Thus the possibility of raising Convention issues in proceedings which have an independent existence is not confined to proceedings which are brought by or at the instigation of a public authority. Ordinary libel litigation, actions for breach of confidence, actions for copyright infringement, or indeed any of the media torts could potentially raise issues under Article 10 ECHR. This conclusion is reinforced by the special measures required by s 12 of the HRA.[93]

Enforcement of Convention Rights: Remedies

Introduction

3.61   If a court finds that an act of a public authority is or would be unlawful because of a conflict with a Convention right, it can grant such relief or remedy or make such order within its powers as it considers just and appropriate.[94]

3.62   These are broad words, and the government intended that through the scheme of remedies established by the Act it would have complied with its obligation under Article 13 ECHR to provide effective remedies for alleged breaches of Convention rights.[95]

---

[91]   HRA, s 9(1).

[92]   HRA, s 9(2).

[93]   See below and *Douglas v Hello!* [2001] QB 967, *per* Sedley LJ, at para 134 and *Venables and Thompson* v *News Group Ltd* [2001] Fam 430 para D2–3.

[94]   HRA, s 8(1) and (6).

[95]   HL Debs, col 475, 18 November 1997.

Damages

The remedy can include damages, but there are three important restrictions: **3.63**

(a) the court or tribunal must have the power to award damages or order the payment of compensation in civil proceedings;[96]

(b) the court must be satisfied that damages are necessary to afford 'just satisfaction' having regard to any other remedy that is granted and the consequences of any decision in respect of the challenged act;[97]

(c) the court must be guided, in deciding whether to award damages and the amount of any damages which it does give, by the principles of the European Court in awarding compensation.[98]

The Strasbourg approach to damages is generally parsimonious. There are three **3.64** headings under which it will consider loss: pecuniary; non-pecuniary; costs and expenses. Understandably, there must be a causal link between the violation and the pecuniary loss which is alleged, and the loss must actually have occurred. Journalists fined in situations where the Court has found a violation of Article 10 have been awarded the amount of the fine.[99] That will not be necessary in the domestic context if (as would be likely) the court considering the allegation of Article 10 infringement would be able to quash the fine. Otherwise the establishment of pecuniary loss to the satisfaction of the European Court has been rare.[100] So far as non-pecuniary loss is concerned, the court has tended to hold that the finding of a violation amounts to just satisfaction.

The UK courts have also allowed only modest sums for non-pecuniary loss.[101] **3.65** The courts ought not to use analogous domestic remedies (such as measures of damages in tort) as a guide[102] and this has generally been reflected in the size of damage awards where the courts have found media intrusions contrary to Article 8—see chapter 6.

---

[96] HRA, s 8(2).

[97] HRA, s 8(3). The phrase 'just satisfaction' is taken from Art 41 ECHR, which requires the Court if necessary after finding a violation to 'afford just satisfaction to the injured party'.

[98] HRA, s 8(4). This refers expressly to Art 41 of the Convention. Prior to the adoption of the Eleventh Protocol, remedies were granted by the European Court of Human Rights under Art 50. The UK courts are likely to look at decisions under both provisions, which are not materially different.

[99] eg *Lingens* v *Austria* (1986) 8 EHRR 407.

[100] Unusual examples were the *Open Door* case (see 3.44) where the pregnancy counselling service was awarded £25,000 Ir for pecuniary loss and *Bergens Tidende* v *Norway* (2001) 31 EHRR 16 where the Norwegian government had to pay over £400,000 to compensate the applicants for their pecuniary loss.

[101] See *Anufrijeva* v *Southwark LBC* [2004] 3 All ER 833, CA.

[102] *R (Greenfield)* v *Secretary of State for the Home Department* [2005] 2 All ER 240, HL.

Damages for judicial acts

3.66 Special restrictions apply where a 'judicial act' is found to be unlawful because it violates a Convention right. 'Judicial act' means a judicial act of a court, and includes an act done on the instructions of or on behalf of a 'judge'. For these purposes, 'judge' includes a member of a tribunal, a magistrate, and a clerk or other officer entitled to exercise the jurisdiction of a court.[103] Damages cannot be awarded in respect of a judicial act unless it is to compensate for unlawful detention[104] or the act was not done in good faith.[105] In these special cases, the award of damages is against the Crown, but the Minister responsible for the court concerned, or a person or government department nominated by him, must first be joined to the proceedings.[106]

Special Provisions Concerning Freedom of Expression

Criminal proceedings

3.67 Section 12 of the HRA makes several specific provisions relating to freedom of expression. They apply whenever a court (or tribunal) is considering whether to grant relief which, if granted, might affect the exercise of the Convention right to freedom of expression.[107] 'Relief' is defined to include any remedy or order 'other than in criminal proceedings'.[108] The qualification means that the specific provisions in s 12 cannot be invoked when a criminal court is, for instance, considering an application for reporting restrictions. However, s 12 does not derogate from the interpretative obligation in s 3 or the duty on all courts (including criminal courts) as public authorities to act compatibly with Convention rights in s 6. These obligations would anyway require the courts to have regard to the extent to which the material is or is about to become available to the public, or to the public interest in the material being published.[109] Neither does s 12 affect s 11, which makes clear that the new obligations are cumulative and do not restrict any pre-existing rights. The exclusion of criminal courts from s 12 should not therefore affect the case law which has already accumulated as to the principles to be applied in dealing with applications for reporting restrictions of criminal proceedings.

---

[103] HRA, s 9(5).
[104] See Art 5(5) ECHR.
[105] HRA, s 9(3).
[106] HRA, s 9(4).
[107] HRA, s 12(1).
[108] HRA, s 12(5).
[109] See s 12(4)(a).

Restrictions on relief without notice

Where s 12 does apply it restricts the grant of relief which is given without **3.68** notice to the respondent and which would affect Convention rights concerning freedom of expression. The court must be satisfied that the applicant has taken all practicable steps to notify the respondent, or that there are compelling reasons why the respondent should not be notified.[110] These requirements are not significantly different from the practice which prevails in any event,[111] but the requirement is now peremptory and statutory.

Restrictions on pre-trial injunctions

Section 12(3) makes provision for pre-trial injunctions (whether or not notice **3.69** of the application was given to the respondent):

(3) No such relief is to be granted so as to restrain publication before trial unless the court is satisfied that the applicant is likely to establish that publication should not be allowed.

This makes clear that courts cannot in freedom of expression cases simply apply **3.70** the test in *American Cyanamid Co* v *Ethicon Ltd*,[112] of deciding whether the claimant has shown an arguable case and then determining whether or not to grant an injunction on the balance of convenience. In cases concerning breach of confidence, in particular, *American Cyanamid* has led the courts to be ready to grant pre-trial injunctions in order to preserve the status quo. That will no longer be a proper approach. Difficult as it may be in the rushed circumstances in which applications are often heard, and with the evidence then only in an incomplete state, the court will have to determine the likelihood of the claimant succeeding at trial. The onus is on the claimant, who will, presumably, have to address and dispose of any likely defences which the defendant might advance at trial.

The House of Lords considered the effect of s 12(3) in *Cream Holdings Ltd* v **3.71** *Banerjee*.[113] The court had to decide whether the claimant's prospects of success at trial were sufficiently favourable to justify an interim order. Normally this would mean that the claimant had to show that it was more likely than not that the claim would succeed. Departure from this balance of probabilities test would be justified if, for instance, the adverse consequences of publicity would be particularly grave or where a short-term injunction was necessary to prevent

---

[110] HRA, s 12(2).
[111] See CPR, Pt 25, r 25.3(1).
[112] [1975] AC 396.
[113] [2005] 1 AC 253.

immediate harm and there was not time for the court to give proper consideration to the merits of the claim.

3.72   The test of likely success at trial is lower than the test which is applied in libel cases. A claimant will not succeed in obtaining a pre-trial injunction to restrain a defamatory publication if the defendant states that he is prepared to justify the truth of the publication at trial (or defend it as fair comment or a publication on a privileged occasion).[114] Here it is not enough for the claimant to show that he will be likely to succeed at trial. In exceptional cases, if the claimant could show that the libel was plainly untrue or (in the case of fair comment or qualified privilege) plainly malicious, he might succeed despite the defendant's intention to defend, but it is an extremely difficult hurdle for the claimant to overcome. Section 12(3) was not intended to affect these principles; nor does s 6(1) of the HRA. The investigation of whether the claimant has a reputation which ought to be vindicated is carried out at the trial, and it cannot be said that there is any violation of this right by the court until that exercise has taken place. Accordingly, the *Bonnard* v *Perryman* principles have survived the HRA.[115]

Prior publicity, public interest, and privacy

3.73   In dealing with matters which might affect freedom of expression, the court is required to have 'particular regard to the importance of the Convention right to freedom of expression'.[116] This is harmonious with the approach of the European Court, which on several occasions has spoken of the special importance of freedom of expression in a democracy.[117] Although in applying this principle, the courts will need to consider the qualifications on that right in Article 10(2).[118]

3.74   Section 12(4) gives more specific direction where the proceedings relate to material which the respondent claims, or which appears to the court, to be

---

[114] See *Bonnard* v *Perryman* [1891] 2 Ch 269 (justification); *Quartz Hill Consolidated Mining Co* v *Beal* [1882] 20 ChD 501 (privilege); *Fraser* v *Evans* [1969] 1 QB 349 (fair comment).

[115] *Greene* v *Associated Newspapers Ltd* [2005] QB 972, CA.

[116] HRA, s 12(4).

[117] eg *Lingens* v *Austria* (1986) 8 EHRR 407, at 418–19.

[118] *Douglas* v *Hello!* (n 93 above), at para 137.

journalistic, literary, or artistic material (or to conduct connected with such material). In these cases, the court must have particular regard to:

(a) the extent to which—

    (i)   the material has, or is about to, become available to the public; or

    (ii) it is, or would be, in the public interest for the material to be published;

(b) any relevant privacy code.

Paragraph (a) represents considerations which the court would presently take **3.75** into account in any event, at least in connection with breach of confidence claims. In copyright claims, the Court of Appeal has accepted that there may be cases where the public interest would justify the use of material in which someone else owned copyright (though this may depend on whether the claimant was seeking by injunction to impose a prior restraint on publication, or compensation for a publication which had already taken place. The right of freedom of expression was likely to be stronger in the former case).[119]

The reference to a relevant privacy code is not further defined. This contrasts **3.76** with the Data Protection Act 1998, which allows the government to specify a relevant code by subordinate legislation.[120] The obvious candidates include the codes of Ofcom and the PCC. However, because the court can have regard to *any* relevant privacy code, there is the possibility that other codes (such as codes adopted within a particular media organization) may also be examined by the court.

The courts have from time to time referred to the PCC's Code. Thus in *Campbell* **3.77** v *MGN Ltd*[121] it was thought that the Code deprecated the use of long-lens photography of people even in public places if there was a reasonable expectation of privacy.

---

[119] *Ashdown* v *Telegraph Ltd* [2002] Ch 149, CA.
[120] See s 32(3) of that Act.
[121] [2004] 2 AC 457.

4

WHEN RIGHTS HAVE NOT BEEN BROUGHT HOME: TAKING A CASE TO STRASBOURG

Introduction	4.01	Admissibility	4.12
The Strasbourg Court	4.03	Consideration of the Complaint	4.27
Legal Aid	4.07	Just Satisfaction	4.30
Making a Complaint	4.08		

Introduction

By Article 1 ECHR, contracting States assume two fundamental obligations. **4.01** First, they must ensure that 'their domestic body of law is compatible with the Convention, and if need be to make any necessary adjustments to this end';[1] secondly, they must remedy any breaches when they occur. Although the Convention leaves each contracting state to decide how best to ensure enforcement through its domestic law, Article 13 requires an effective remedy before a national authority where a violation has occurred. The substance of a complaint to the European Court of Human Rights is that a State which is a party to the Convention has failed to honour its obligations, and thereby to 'secure' one or more of the Convention rights and freedoms 'to everyone within their jurisdiction' within the meaning of Article 1.

The HRA 1998 seeks to ensure that the UK honours these obligations by **4.02** introducing the Convention into our own legal system. It gives the domestic courts the means to prevent violations, so removing the need for complainants to go to Strasbourg. However, there will still be cases where they will have to go to

---

[1] 214/56 Yearbook 234.

Strasbourg for their remedy. The most obvious examples are where the domestic courts cannot remedy a breach because of primary legislation which cannot be interpreted compatibly with Convention rights and which the government will not amend; or because of the lack of specific legislative 'tools' where the common law or interpretation of more general legislation cannot be used to provide the remedy. Cases will also still be brought where the domestic courts fail to recognize a breach of the ECHR. Although Article 33 permits one contracting State to bring another before the Court, this happens very rarely. This chapter is therefore concerned only with complaints by victims whose rights have been infringed, whether about the law, acts of government bodies, or decisions of domestic courts.

The Strasbourg Court

The permanent Court

4.03   Section II of the ECHR deals with the Court. Before 1 November 1998, two organs were involved: the European Commission and the European Court of Human Rights. On that date Protocol No 11 ('P11') came into force. This brought about a radical change in the procedures for enforcement. Both existing institutions were abolished. For the first time individuals were given direct access to a newly constituted European Court of Human Rights. Whereas previously the Court sat only part-time, now the Court functions on a permanent basis to 'ensure the observance' of the obligations of contracting States.[2] States must not 'hinder in any way the effective enforcement of this right' by obstructing the applicant's communications with the Court or exerting pressure to withdraw or modify the complaint.[3] P11 also revised the role of the Committee of Ministers of the Council of Europe in the Convention process. Its only important remaining function is to receive the final, binding judgments of the Court and ensure that the relevant Member State complies.[4] The Court consists of 47 judges each elected by the Parliamentary Assembly of the Council of Europe from a list of nominees put forward by the contracting States. The full plenary Court is convened only for administrative decisions. A President and Vice-President, responsible for the administration of the Court, are elected by the plenary Court. In outline, the Court receives complaints, considers whether they are

---

[2]   See Art 19.
[3]   See Art 34 for the right of individual petition and *Akdivar* v *Turkey* (1996) 23 EHRR 143, at para 105.
[4]   See Art 46.

'admissible', and, if they are, decides whether the Convention has been violated. Under Article 41, it may order the State to pay compensation and costs to the successful applicant. The current Rules of Procedure of the European Court of Human Rights came into effect on 1 November 2003.

The workload of the Court increased dramatically in the years after P11. In 2004 **4.04** the Committee of Ministers adopted Protocol No 14 ('P14') which aims to simplify and speed up the Court system. At the time of writing it has not come into force because Russia is refusing to ratify it. Whether it will ever do so remains unclear. The main changes intended by P14 are, however, identified below.

The judicial structures of the Court

All complaints are initially referred to a single judge known as a 'Judge **4.05** Rapporteur', who reports on the question of admissibility to either a Chamber of seven judges or, in weaker cases, to a Committee of three judges.[5] P14 would amend Article 27 ECHR to allow the Court to sit in single-judge formation in deciding admissibility as well as merits. When deciding cases Chambers include at least one judge from the State against whom the complaint is made.[6] The highest judicial body within the Court structure is the Grand Chamber, consisting of 17 judges. This may determine complex and serious cases 'relinquished' to it by a Chamber with the agreement of the parties[7] and may hear appeals from Chambers' judgments on the merits.[8] Permission for such an appeal is required from a screening panel of five judges, but will be given if 'the case raises a serious question affecting the interpretation of the Convention . . . or a serious issue of general importance'. There is no appeal against Committee or admissibility decisions.

The Registry

This consists of lawyers and support staff, and carries out most of the day-to- **4.06** day administration of the Court. It is headed by a Registrar and two Deputies appointed by the plenary Court.[9] The Registry lawyer assigned to the case will be the applicant's point of contact with the Court. For this reason, he or she will usually be a national of the State concerned.

---

[5] r 49. P14 would allow a Committee, as well as a Chamber, to admit a case and give an immediate judgment in favour of the applicant where appropriate.

[6] r 26(1)(a).

[7] Art 30 ECHR and r 72.

[8] Art 43 ECHR and r 73.

[9] rr 15 and 16.

Legal Aid

4.07   At present our domestic legal aid scheme does not cover the bringing of a complaint to the Court. However, lawyers may enter into conditional fee agreements to pursue cases to Strasbourg. Legal aid may be granted by the Court towards the end of the examination of a complaint's admissibility.[10] It will be granted, if necessary for the proper conduct of the case, where the applicant has insufficient means to meet all or part of the costs.[11] The contracting party may be asked to submit its comments on the question of 'sufficient means'. The UK responds to such requests through the Legal Services Commission which indicates whether the applicant would be eligible for civil legal aid in this country. If so, the Court will invariably grant legal aid and it may do even if the applicant does not meet the domestic entitlement criteria. The Court's legal aid involves the payment of set amounts for specified pieces of work, such as drafting the application or the reply to the government's response, and representing the applicant at hearings. The amounts are modest and would not match the professional fees in our legal system. The Court will usually pay for only one lawyer. Travelling and hotel costs are paid for attendance at hearings. A successful complainant may be awarded costs, though again these are not generous.

Making a Complaint

4.08   The procedure for making a complaint is relatively straightforward but moves slowly. The majority of cases are rejected as inadmissible without a hearing. It is therefore vital that complaints explain why the admissibility criteria are met (see below) and set out in full the facts, domestic law, and the arguments of Convention law as to why the grievance amounts to a violation.

The time limit for submitting complaints

4.09   Under Article 35(1) ECHR, a complaint may be considered only if it is made 'within a period of six months from the date on which the final decision was taken' in any domestic proceedings. The 'final decision' is the final decision in an effective domestic remedy pursued. Time cannot be artificially extended

---

[10] r 91. If granted it is retrospective so payments will be made towards the earlier costs—eg of preparing the initial application.
[11] r 92.

by pursuing ineffective, or hopeless, domestic remedies. The six-month rule is applied strictly, save that time is taken to run from the date upon which the applicant receives the reasons for the decision.[12] Where there are no domestic remedies, and therefore no proceedings, the six months run from the applicant's date of knowledge of the incident, act, or decision complained of.[13] However, a complaint may be about the continuing operation of a law, and the complainant a potential, rather than an actual, victim of the law (see below). Or it may be about a continuing state of affairs, such as a ban on particular publications. Where the complaint is of this type and there is no effective domestic remedy, time does not begin to run until the law is repealed or the situation ends. Where a doubtful domestic remedy is pursued which may, in the end, prove to be ineffective (for example, because leave to appeal is refused), an applicant should protect his or her position by submitting an appeal within six months of the previous decision.[14] A claim is submitted as at the date of the initial written communication, which may be a letter or fax to the Court, provided it sets out basic details of the complaint.[15]

The application form

There is a standard application form. If this has not been used as the initial **4.10** communication, the Court will reply by sending one. Once this has been returned completed, the complaint will be registered. The form requires:

(a) the applicant's name, age, address, nationality, sex, and occupation;

(b) the name, occupation, and address of any representative;

(c) the name of the respondent country;

(d) a succinct statement of the relevant facts, including dates;

(e) identification of the Articles of the Convention said to have been violated and the arguments (with reference to case law) to support these allegations;

(f) a clear statement as to why the admissibility criteria (see 4.12) are met. The six-month rule and the requirement to exhaust domestic remedies must be addressed;

(g) information as to the overall object of the complaint (for example, repeal of legislation) and any 'just satisfaction' including compensation sought under Article 41 ECHR (see 4.30);

(h) copies of relevant documents, including decisions;

---

[12] *Worm* v *Austria* (1997) 25 EHRR 454, at para 33.
[13] *Isabel Hilton* v *UK* App No 12015/86, (1988) 57 DR 108, at 113.
[14] See, eg *Berdzenishvili* v *Russia* (App No 31697/03), 29 January 2004.
[15] *Latif and others* v *UK* (App No 72819/01), 29 January 2004.

(i) an indication of what, if any, other international procedures have been used in the attempt to remedy the grievance.

4.11 If the form is lacking in detail or unclear, the complainant runs the risk that the Judge Rapporteur who considers it will be unable to identify a proper Convention point and will make a recommendation for rejection of the complaint through the Committee procedure.

Admissibility

Initial inadmissibility

4.12 Complaints will fall at the first hurdle if they do not comply with the following requirements of Article 35(2) and (3) ECHR:

(a) The complainant must have been identified. The Court will not consider anonymous applications. Although the applicant may ask to be identified only to the respondent government, such a request will be granted only in exceptional and duly justified cases.[16]

(b) The complaint must not be substantially the same as one already examined by the Court or some other international body, and must not be 'incompatible with the . . . Convention . . ., manifestly ill-founded, or an abuse of the right of application.'

4.13 A complaint is 'incompatible' if it is clearly outside the scope of the Convention altogether, for example because it does not concern a right protected by the ECHR or is about the acts or omissions of private persons rather than the failure of the State to protect such a right. However, the Court appears increasingly willing to use the concept of 'positive obligation' to uphold complaints arising out of disputes between private persons, particularly in the context of Article 10 ECHR. See for example *Fuentes Bobo* v *Spain*,[17] where the applicant had been dismissed by the state television company for speaking out publicly against management in a labour dispute. The Spanish High Court had found the dismissal to be lawful in employment law, and the Constitutional Court had dismissed a subsequent appeal by the applicant based on his right to freedom of expression. A majority of the European Court, however, held that the dismissal amounted to a violation of his Article 10 right, emphasizing that Article 10

---

[16] Since this is a departure from the principle in Art 40(2) ECHR that all documents deposited at the Registry are presumed to be public, where confidentiality is requested the application must contain a statement of reasons: r 47(3).

[17] (App No 39293/98), 29 February 2000.

ECHR applies to relations between an employer and employee governed by private law, and that a State has a positive obligation in some such cases to protect freedom of expression.

The applicant must be a 'victim' (see below) and the violation must occur within the jurisdiction of the State concerned, but not necessarily within its territory. The question is whether the state has de facto control over the events in issue.[18] In *Loizidou* v *Turkey*,[19] for example, it was held that Turkey exercised sufficient control over the administration in Northern Cyprus. Thus although a State has no control over standards of justice in other countries, it may be liable if it deports a person knowing that he or she will face torture or inhuman or degrading treatment or punishment in that country[20] Complaints cannot be brought in respect of protocols which the contracting State has not yet ratified. However, P11 precludes a State ratifying a protocol but refusing to accept that there is a right of individual petition in connection with it.   **4.14**

The cases do not establish any clear or consistent approach to the application of the 'manifestly ill-founded' ground of rejection. The best that can be said is that it represents a threshold merits test. If a complaint discloses prima facie grounds that there has been a breach of the Convention and the Court considers that a full examination of its merits is justified, it will pass the threshold test.   **4.15**

Perhaps the most controversial change intended by P14 is the addition of a further admissibility criterion to Article 35 ECHR. According to this a case can be declared inadmissible if: i) the applicant has not suffered a 'significant disadvantage', and; ii) unless respect for human rights requires an examination of the case on the merits, and; iii) provided that no case may be rejected on this ground which has not been duly considered by a domestic tribunal.   **4.16**

The applicant must be a 'victim'

A complaint may be brought only by a person, non-governmental organization (such as a commercial company, voluntary organization, or political party), or a group of individuals 'claiming to be the victim of a violation'.[21] The Court recognizes three types of victim with standing to pursue an application—actual, potential, or indirect. An 'actual victim' must already have been personally affected by the violation. Such a victim does not have to show that damage or detriment has been suffered, though whether it has been will be relevant to   **4.17**

---

[18] See *Bankovic* v *Belgium* (2001) 11 BHRC 435.
[19] (1996) 23 EHRR 513.
[20] eg *Soering* v *UK* (1989) 11 EHRR 439.
[21] Art 34 ECHR.

the nature of just satisfaction under Article 41 (see 4.30). A 'potential victim' is at risk of being personally affected. In one case the Court accepted that a group of German lawyers could challenge laws permitting secret phone tapping even though there was no evidence of a particular risk that their lines would be tapped. The fact that any tapping would be secretive was regarded as an important factor by the Court in treating them as potential victims.[22] An 'indirect victim' is one who is immediately affected by the direct violation of the rights of another person—for example, the family of a prisoner.

4.18   In *Leigh, Guardian Newspapers and Observer Ltd* v *UK* [23] the applicant journalists complained under Article 10 of restrictions on the use that could be made of documents disclosed to parties in litigation and then read out in court. The Court considered that any detriment to them, as journalists interested in the cases, was too indirect or remote for them to be considered actual 'victims'. Similarly in 1990, Times Newspapers tried to challenge the use of juries, with unrestricted powers to award damages, to try libel actions. The applicant complained of the 'chilling effect' on journalistic freedom of expression of a series of recent large jury awards in the High Court. The Commission declined to characterize Times Newspapers as a victim of this state of affairs. Rather, it was simply trying to challenge 'the general state of the law relating to jury trial in defamation actions'.[24] The Commission observed that the applicant could have been regarded as a victim if it had identified a particular article or allegation which it had decided not to publish because of the risk of a high damages award (at 312).[25]

4.19   However, there is no requirement that the complainant be a citizen of, or in some way physically present in, the State concerned, or indeed any State of the Council of Europe. Thus an American magazine or newspaper could complain if its freedom to circulate in a contracting State was interfered with by the government. Where the victim is incapacitated, an authorized representative may make the complaint on his or her behalf. A child may complain through a parent, guardian, or other authorized representative, including a lawyer.[26]

---

[22]   *Klass* v *Germany* (1978) 2 EHRR 214, at para 34.
[23]   (1985) 7 EHRR 409.
[24]   *Times Newspapers* v *UK* App No 14631/89, (1990) 65 DR 307, at 312.
[25]   The complaint raised by Times Newspapers was eventually considered by the Court in *Tolstoy Miloslavsky* v *UK* (1995) 20 EHRR 442, where the applicant was 'personally affected' as a defendant against whom a massive damages award had actually been made. This case is discussed in detail in ch 5.
[26]   *PP and T* v *UK* (1996) 22 EHRR CD 148.

Victim status can be lost if the government provides sufficient redress to the   **4.20**
applicant in the teeth of the challenge. However, the redress must be effective
and the national authority must acknowledge that there has been a breach of
the Convention. In *Dalban* v *Romania*,[27] the applicant was a journalist who
had been convicted and ordered to pay damages in criminal libel proceedings.
After the Commission had ruled in his favour he died, and his widow continued
the proceedings. Before the case reached the Court the applicant's conviction
was quashed by the Romanian Supreme Court. The government argued that
this removed his status, and therefore that of his widow, as a 'victim'. This
argument was rejected. The Court noted that the Supreme Court had quashed
his conviction on one of the charges only because of his death, a decision which
did not involve any acknowledgement of breach of the Convention. It also
doubted whether the widow could obtain compensation for the financial losses
through civil proceedings easily or, indeed, at all. This case is discussed in more
detail in chapter 5.

Exhaustion of all effective domestic remedies

Article 35(1) ECHR specifies that the jurisdiction of the Court can be invoked   **4.21**
only 'after all domestic remedies have been exhausted'. Only then can it be
said that the contracting State's own institutions have conclusively failed to
protect the substantive Convention rights in issue. As the Court has put it,
applicants must provide the national courts with a full opportunity 'of preventing
or putting right the violations' before going to Strasbourg.[28] This is one of the key
procedural rules under the Convention, but one which is often misunderstood or
misapplied by applicants and their lawyers, with the result that many complaints
are ruled inadmissible.

The application should set out why the applicant believes that all domestic   **4.22**
remedies have been exhausted. The onus is then on the State to show why
this is not the case. In seeking to do this the State can rely on any effective
and available remedy which would have had some prospect of success. Because
of this, if there is more than one effective possible remedy, they should all
be pursued by the applicant before turning to Strasbourg. In *Earl Spencer* v
UK,[29] the applicant and his wife complained under Article 8 ECHR about the
failure of domestic law to protect them against unwanted tabloid intrusions
into their private lives. Although they had complained to the Press Complaints

---

[27] (2000) 8 BHRC 91.
[28] *Cardot* v *France* (1991) 13 EHRR 853, para 36.
[29] App Nos 28851/95 and 28852/95, (1998) 25 EHRR CD 105.

Commission, their applications to Strasbourg were ruled inadmissible because they had failed to sue the papers concerned and had settled breach of confidence proceedings against two friends suspected of being the source of the stories.[30] If in doubt, claimants should always try to pursue the remedy, or obtain the opinion of a senior lawyer specializing in the relevant area of law that it would be futile to do so. Provided this is fully reasoned and its conclusion cannot be conclusively challenged by the government (for example, because it has failed to take into account a determinative piece of case law), it will normally be accepted by the Court. In *Wingrove* v *UK*,[31] a complaint about a decision of the British Board of Film Censors was admitted on the basis of leading counsel's advice that judicial review was futile. In the past the government has sometimes agreed that further appeals would be pointless where the domestic law is sufficiently clear, although this may not happen so often now because of the HRA 1998. Similarly, where legal aid has been sought to pursue the remedy but refused on the merits, the Court is usually prepared to treat the remedy as exhausted. If it has been refused on grounds of financial ineligibility, however, the claimant must either instruct a lawyer privately, or exercise his or her rights to litigate in person.

4.23   If the State identifies a possible avenue which has not been pursued, the applicant must show why it would have been ineffective, or that there were special circumstances absolving the applicant from the obligation to exhaust. A remedy may be ineffective because it is discretionary, particularly if the discretion lies with a public authority rather than a court. An appeal may be ineffective because it is bound to fail because of binding legal precedent or a statutory provision. The Court has considered the effectiveness of judicial review proceedings under Article 13 ECHR, which guarantees an effective remedy for the enforcement of substantive Convention rights, particularly in the context of decisions to expel and deport. It has accepted that the High Court's power to 'anxiously scrutinize' and, if appropriate, quash such decisions where there is a serious risk to life (Article 2) or of inhuman or degrading treatment (Article 3), means that there is an effective remedy.[32] However, this was not the case where the factual basis for the decision to expel could not be reviewed because of national security considerations;[33] or when the decision under challenge was a government policy

---

[30] See also, *Chappell* v *UK* (1989) 12 EHRR 1, where documents had been wrongly seized under an Anton Piller order. Contempt proceedings, a damages claim, and an application for return of the documents all had to be pursued.

[31] (1996) 24 EHRR 1.

[32] *Soering* v *UK* (see n 20 above); *D* v *UK* (1997) 24 EHRR 423.

[33] *Chahal* v *UK* (1996) 23 EHRR 413.

and the operation of the irrationality test in judicial review effectively excluded consideration of Convention principles—in particular the necessity for the interference.[34] The implementation of the HRA 1998 requires the High Court to scrutinize cases involving infringements of Convention rights even more closely. It therefore increases the effectiveness of the judicial review remedy, in particular through the s 6 requirement that public authorities act compatibly with Convention rights and the Court's consideration of whether infringements are 'necessary in a democratic society' (see further, chapter 3).

The remedy must be effective in all respects. For example, a challenge to an **4.24** extradition order which is said to expose the individual to serious mistreatment will not be effective unless the order is stayed pending the outcome. If the State wishes to argue that there is an effective remedy, it must do so at the admissibility stage and cannot take a different position on 'availability' to that which it took in the national courts.[35] The exhaustion must have occurred by the time admissibility is considered, which may take some time. It is therefore possible to get a 'flying start' by submitting an anticipatory application to the Court as the conclusion of the final stage approaches, in the expectation that the remedy will not be obtained.

So far the Court has ruled that a declaration of incompatibility is *not* an effective **4.25** remedy, principally because the government has a power but not a duty to implement the necessary changes to primary legislation. However, the Court has also indicated that if there developed a sufficiently consistent pattern of ministers exercising this power in practice, the position might be different.[36] The safest course is to both (a) make an initial complaint to Strasbourg within six months of the original act or omission, and (b) pursue an application for a declaration in the UK courts.

Procedure for determining admissibility

The Judge Rapporteur writes a report to the Committee or Chamber to which **4.26** the complaint is referred. Where the Judge Rapporteur considers that it is inadmissible on its face (perhaps after clarification has been sought from the applicant), it will simply be referred to a Committee which (if unanimous) may

---

[34] See, eg *Smith and Grady* v *UK* (2000) 29 EHRR 493 and *Peck* v *UK* (2003) 36 EHRR 41. In which the Court concluded that complaints to media regulatory bodies about the broadcast or publication of CCTV footage of the applicant could not have provided him with an effective remedy because they lacked the power to award damages.

[35] See, eg *Kolompar* v *Belgium* (1993) 16 EHRR 197, para 31.

[36] *Burden* v *UK* (App No 13378/05), Judgment, 12 December 2006.

declare it inadmissible without further formality.[37] Where the case is referred
to a Chamber, whether by the Rapporteur or because the Committee cannot
agree unanimously upon inadmissibility,[38] the Chamber decides how to deal
with the case under r 54. It may also declare the case inadmissible without
taking any further steps.[39] If it does not, it may investigate further with the
complainant and will formally 'communicate' the complaint to the State, asking
it to give its observations on the issues concerning the Court by way of a
response.[40] This will address the merits of the complaint and any admissibility
points the government takes. The applicant replies to this. The Chamber may
then, exceptionally, convene a short oral admissibility hearing before giving its
decision, particularly if the complainant asks for one.[41] It may combine this
with the final merits hearing (Article 29(3) and r 54A(1)). The decision may
be reached by a majority and will be given in writing.[42] While it is considering
a case, the Chamber, or its President, may indicate to the parties an 'interim
measure' which it considers should be adopted in the interests of the parties or
the proper conduct of the proceedings.[43]

Consideration of the Complaint

4.27   Once the Court has decided that a case is admissible it considers the merits of the
complaint. It may invite the parties to submit further evidence and submissions
in writing.[44] The Chamber can decide to hold an oral hearing on the merits,
though this is now the exception rather than the rule.[45] If it does not, and there
was no oral hearing on the merits at the admissibility stage, one of the parties
can request a hearing post-admissibility. After admissibility, the Chamber will
try to reach a negotiated agreement, known as a 'friendly settlement', between
the applicant and the State 'on the basis of respect for human rights as defined
in the Convention'.[46] This gives the State an opportunity to avoid the political

---

[37] Art 28 and r 53(3). P14 would allow a Committee to admit a complaint and give an immediate judgment on the merits if it is manifestly well-founded. This would enable speedy resolution of 'clone' or 'repetitive violation' cases.

[38] r 53(4).

[39] r 54(2).

[40] r 54(2)(b).

[41] r 54(3).

[42] r 56.

[43] r 39; for example, to prevent destruction of an artistic work held to be obscene, though usually the State will postpone irreversible action once it is aware of a complaint to the Court.

[44] r 59(1).

[45] r 59(3).

[46] Art 38 and r 62.

embarrassment of a decision involving censure by the Court. P14 would allow the Court to activate the friendly settlement procedure 'at any stage of the proceedings'.

Settlements have become more common as the jurisprudence of the Court has developed, enabling States to predict more accurately when they may lose a case. However, the Court must be satisfied that any settlement takes account of the general interest. It may therefore require changes in the law, or the convening of an inquiry, or commissioning of an independent report, in addition to compensation and other redress for the complainant. In *Harman* v *UK*,[47] the applicant challenged contempt proceedings brought against her for showing a journalist documents disclosed to her in court proceedings as the solicitor to one of the parties, notwithstanding that the documents had actually been read out in open court. The government accepted the admissibility ruling of the Commission and entered into a friendly settlement which required amendment of the discovery rules of the Supreme Court. In *Hodgson and Channel 4* v *UK*,[48] the television company had been prohibited from using actors to read out daily transcripts of the Clive Ponting official secrets trial in nightly broadcasts. There was no right of challenge to the order of the criminal trial court. The government again entered into a friendly settlement of the applicant's complaint as to the lack of a remedy. This time legislation was introduced granting the media a special right of challenge before the Court of Appeal when excluded or gagged by order of a Crown Court.[49] In *Ali Erol* v *Turkey*,[50] involving the prosecution of a newspaper editor, the Turkish government agreed to bring its law into line with Article 10 ECHR by making a wide-ranging series of amendments to provisions affecting free speech. **4.28**

The President of the Chamber dealing with an application may permit any third party, whether a legal person, a government, or an interested organization, such as Liberty, to intervene and make written, or exceptionally oral, submissions if it is 'in the interest of the proper administration of justice'.[51] The final oral hearing is held in public[52] and is short, being usually no more than half a day with time-limited arguments. Judgments are delivered on a few weeks' notice to the parties and the public, and copies are sent to the parties and their representatives to avoid the need to attend. As indicated above, in important cases the Grand **4.29**

---

[47] App No 10038/82, (1984) 38 DR 53.
[48] App Nos 11553/85 and 11658/85, (1988), 56 DR 156.
[49] See s 159, Criminal Justice Act 1988.
[50] (App No 35076/97), 20 June 2002.
[51] Art 36 and r 44(2).
[52] Art 40(1).

Chamber may hear an appeal on the merits against a Chambers judgment. The Defamation Act 1996, Sch 1, paras 2 and 16(3)(b), gives a qualified privilege to fair and accurate reports of Court judgments. There is immunity in respect of statements made by participants in proceedings before the Court.[53]

Just Satisfaction

4.30 Where a complaint is upheld the Court must consider whether the applicant is entitled to compensation and/or an award of costs.[54] As with the grant of legal aid, any award of costs by the Court will not be generous. The complainant is asked for details of any compensation claim within two months of the admissibility decision. Compensation is intended to place the victim in the same position as if the violation had never happened, and may therefore be substantial if there have been large pecuniary losses.[55] It will only be ordered where there are no other measures available to the State to remedy the consequences of the violation.[56] The Court has no power to make any other orders against a State. Though binding, the Court's judgment does not have any legal effect in the UK, save as relevant authority in later domestic cases.[57]

---

[53] See European Court of Human Rights (Immunities and Privileges) Order 2000 (SI 2000/1817) which gives effect to the Sixth Protocol to the General Agreement on Privileges and Immunities of the Council of Europe (Cm 4727) and the 1996 European Agreement Relating to Persons Participating in Proceedings of the European Court of Human Rights (Cm 4728).

[54] Art 41 ECHR.

[55] See *Bergens Tidende* v *Norway* (2001) 31 EHRR 16, discussed in chapter 5, where some £411,000 was awarded to cover the damages and costs paid out by a newspaper in a defamation case.

[56] See *Scozzari and Giunta* v *Italy* (2002) 35 EHRR 12, paras 249–50.

[57] See HRA 1998, s 2.

5

DEFAMATION

Introduction	5.01	Restrictions 'Necessary in a	
Who may Complain of an		Democratic Society'	5.16
Article 10 Violation?	5.04	The Defendant's Right to a Fair	
'Without Interference by Public		Hearing	5.59
Authority'	5.06	The Impact of the HRA 1998 on	
Legitimate Aim	5.12	Domestic Law	5.61

Introduction

In England a claimant raises a defamation claim by showing publication of a **5.01** defamatory statement referring to him or her. In broad terms the statement is defamatory if it damages the claimant's reputation. Specifically, the question is whether it has a meaning 'lowering the Plaintiff in the estimation of right-thinking members of society generally',[1] or 'exposing him to hatred ridicule or contempt'[2] or causing him to be 'shunned or avoided'.[3] It is presumed that such a statement is false. In libel (written defamation) damage to reputation is presumed. So some damages will always be recovered.

To avoid liability the defendant must establish one of the recognized defences. **5.02** The main ones are truth (known as 'justification'), fair comment on a matter of public interest, or 'privilege'. The publication is 'privileged' if it occurred in circumstances in which the law, for public policy reasons, gives immunity. The privilege may be 'qualified' (by the requirement to have published in good faith) or 'absolute'.

---

[1] *Sim* v *Stretch* (1936) 52 TLR 669, at 671.
[2] *Parmeter* v *Copeland* (1840) 6 M & W 105, at 108.
[3] *Youssoupoff* v *MGM* (1934) TLR 581, at 587.

5.03 In the last decade the HRA 1998 has begun to 'constitutionalize' defamation. Courts increasingly consider the free speech right, as well as the competing rights—to protect reputation, dignity, and privacy—when they decide cases. In this chapter we consider, first, the Article 10 ECHR principles that have informed this process and then the changes that have occurred in our domestic law.

Who may Complain of an Article 10 Violation?

5.04 Applications to Strasbourg may be made by individuals, corporations, and non-governmental organizations. Many of the defamation cases before the Court have been brought by journalists. Anyone who is a 'publisher' at common law can complain of a violation of Article 10 rights. This would include journalists, editors, proprietors, media organizations, printers, and distributors.

5.05 The applicant must *be* a 'victim' of a violation in the sense recognized by the Court. This concept is dealt with in chapters 3 and 4. An application cannot be made in the abstract[4] or on behalf of others who are 'victims'. However, the applicant does not have to be a citizen of, or domiciled in, a contracting State of the Council of Europe. So a publication from outside these territories could complain about interference with its circulation in a contracting State.

'Without Interference by Public Authority'

5.06 Interferences take many different forms in defamation cases. In rare cases publication may be prohibited altogether. Post-publication awards of damages and injunctions are common. Other orders may seek to redress the damage to the complainant's reputation. In many European countries complaints about damage to reputation are pursued through the criminal courts, either by state or private prosecutors. Indeed, more than two-thirds of the Member States of the Council of Europe maintain criminal defamation laws. Some are regularly used against journalists. Sometimes the offences are of 'insulting', or 'violating the honour' of, the complainant. The punishments in such criminal proceedings are closely scrutinized in Strasbourg. In some worrying cases prison sentences, or prohibitions on working,[5] are imposed on the journalist. Even if the Court upholds a finding in defamation it may still conclude that the applicant's Article 10 right has been violated if the sanction imposed is disproportionate.

---

[4] See, eg *Times Newspapers* v *UK* (1990) 65 DR 307.
[5] See *Cumpana* v *Romania* (2005) 41 EHRR 14, at paras 37–58 and 117.

Prior restraint

In defamation cases, prior restraint is rare both for practical and legal reasons. **5.07**
An application for an anticipatory order can only be made if the complainant
learns of the publication in advance. Article 10 protects the media against pre-
publication injunctions or threats (of criminal or civil proceedings). Any such
interference is particularly closely scrutinized by the Court because it inhibits
or prevents the dissemination of ideas and information altogether.[6]

Damages awards

An order to pay damages for defamation, even if the amount is not dispropor- **5.08**
tionate, will amount to an 'interference' with the speaker's Article 10 rights so
that the imposition of liability must be justified in accordance with the principles
of Article 10(2).[7]

Orders to publish

In *Ediciones Tiempo SA* v *Spain*[8] the applicant published an article alleging **5.09**
irregularities in the management of a public company. The domestic court
ordered it to publish an article in response by one of its managers. The
Commission accepted that the order was an interference. In *De Haes & Gijsels*
v *Belgium*,[9] the applicants had been successfully sued by a number of Antwerp
judges over articles alleging bias in their handling of a child custody case. They
were ordered to publish the judgment and to pay for it to be published in six
daily newspapers. These orders were identified by the Court as interferences.
See also *Radio France* v *France*,[10] where a radio station was ordered to broadcast
repeated announcements about an adverse judgment.

Criminal libel

In the landmark case of *Lingens* v *Austria*,[11] the Court rejected an argument **5.10**
that criminal libel proceedings did not 'strictly speaking prevent [the convicted
journalist] from expressing himself', observing that the penalty imposed:

> amounted to a kind of censure, which would be likely to discourage him from
> making criticisms of this kind again in future . . . In the context of political debate

---

[6] *Observer and Guardian* v *UK* (1991) 14 EHRR 153, at para 60.
[7] *Bladet Tromsø and Stensaas* v *Norway* (1999) 29 EHRR 125, para 50.
[8] App No 13010/87, (1989) 62 DR 247.
[9] (1997) 25 EHRR 1.
[10] (2005) 40 EHRR 29, at para 28.
[11] (1986) 8 EHRR 407.

such a sentence would be likely to deter journalists from contributing to public discussion of issues affecting the life of the community. By the same token a sanction such as this is liable to hamper the press in performing its task as purveyor of information and public watchdog. (at para 44)

Final injunctions

5.11 An injunction to prevent repetition of a proven libel is an interference. But it may be a 'logical consequence' of the finding of the domestic court and justified if 'framed precisely to prevent the applicant from repeating the libelous allegations' and nothing more.[12]

Legitimate Aim

5.12 In the defamation cases, the legitimate aim identified by the contracting State is invariably the need to protect the reputation of others. In principle it is a legitimate aim to protect the reputation of 'others', even if they have not been identified in the defamatory material. In *Thorgeirson* v *Iceland*,[13] the applicant had written newspaper articles describing unspecified members of the Reykjavik police as 'beasts in uniform' and 'police brutes'. Although his conviction and sentence for criminal defamation was in violation of Article 10, the Court accepted that it was aimed at protecting the reputations of the officers.

Protecting reputation

5.13 While everyone is in principle entitled to have their reputation protected, the actual protection given under Article 10 may depend on various factors including the extent to which the complainant participates in public life (see 5.35).

5.14 In recent years the Court has identified the right to protection of a person's reputation as 'one of the rights guaranteed by Article 8 of the Convention, as one element of the right to respect for private life'.[14] The effect this may have on how the Court reviews decisions in defamation cases is considered below.

Prevention of disorder

5.15 In *Castells* v *Spain*,[15] the applicant was a Senator of an opposition political grouping which supported Basque independence. He had published an article

---

[12] *Tolstoy Miloslavsky* v *UK* (1995) 20 EHRR 442, at para 54.
[13] (1992) 14 EHRR 843, at para 59.
[14] See *Radio France* v *France* (n 10 above), at para 31.
[15] (1992) 14 EHRR 445.

suggesting that the government had been behind the killings of pro-separatists. He was convicted of an offence of insulting the government under the Spanish Criminal Code following the withdrawal of his Parliamentary immunity. The article had been published shortly after the adoption of the post-Franco Constitution, as the government put it, during 'a sensitive, indeed critical, period for Spain . . . when groups of differing political persuasions were resorting to violence'. The Court accepted that 'in the circumstances obtaining in Spain in 1979' the criminal proceedings had been instituted for the 'prevention of disorder' as well as to protect the reputations of others (at paras 39 and 41). It would be difficult to envisage such an argument succeeding other than in extreme circumstances of political instability, for example those created by terrorism.[16] This potential danger was recognized, but not made out on the facts, in *Piermont* v *France*,[17] in which the expulsion of an MEP and anti-nuclear campaigner from New Caledonia was found to have breached Article 10.

Restrictions 'Necessary in a Democratic Society'

In the defamation cases the Court has always emphasized the importance of   **5.16**
freedom of expression by reference to its observations in *Handyside* v *UK*[18]
that:

> freedom of expression, as secured in paragraph 1 of Article 10, constitutes one of the essential foundations of a democratic society and one of the basic conditions for its progress and for each individual's self-fulfillment. Subject to paragraph 2, it is applicable not only to 'information' or 'ideas' that are favourably received or regarded as inoffensive or a matter of indifference, but also those that offend, shock or disturb. Such are the demands of that pluralism, tolerance and broadmindedness without which there is no 'democratic society'.

It has consistently noted that whilst this freedom is 'subject to exceptions'   **5.17**
identified in Article 10(2), the importance of the right requires these to
'be construed strictly, and the need for any restrictions [to] be established
convincingly'.[19]

As in all other Article 10 cases it is not enough that the restriction was lawfully   **5.18**
imposed as a matter of domestic law. The Court 'has to be satisfied that the

---

[16] See, eg *Zana* v *Turkey* (1997) 27 EHRR 667 (paras 51, 55 and 61).
[17] (1995) 20 EHRR 301, at para 77.
[18] (1976) 1 EHRR 737 para 49.
[19] See *Observer and Guardian* v *UK* (n 6 above), at para 59.

interference was necessary having regard to the facts and circumstances prevailing in the specific case before it'.[20]

5.19   However, in *Chauvy* v *France*,[21] and the subsequent Grand Chamber case of *Cumpana* v *Romania*,[22] recognition of the right to protection of reputation as an aspect of private life led the Court to identify an additional consideration in the review by the Court.

> The Court must also ascertain whether the domestic authorities struck a fair balance between, on the one hand, the protection of freedom of expression as enshrined in Article 10, and on the other hand, the protection of the reputation of those against whom allegations have been made, a right which, as an aspect of private life is protected by Article 8 of the Convention . . . That provision may require the adoption of positive measures designed to secure effective respect for private life even in the sphere of the relations of individuals between themselves.[23]

5.20   Sometimes Article 8 imposes positive obligations on the State to act to prevent interferences with privacy.[24] In this passage in *Cumpana* the Court was saying that media damage to a person's reputation may trigger such an obligation, requiring the national court to intervene between the complainant and the publisher to protect the former's reputation. This might be so even though the court's order would interfere with media freedom of expression.

5.21   Confusingly, in both judgments this 'fair balance' principle was explained after the Court had described the traditional Article 10(2) approach, requiring the State convincingly to establish the need for interference in order to protect reputation.[25] This gives free speech presumptive priority over protection of reputation. No question of a positive obligation to protect reputation under Article 8 arises. However, if such an obligation can now arise in media defamation cases, this presumptive priority may have to give way as it has done in other complaints about media invasion of privacy (see chapter 6). The domestic courts may have to give greater protection to reputation, balancing the rights of the parties on the facts to see which is more deserving of protection.

---

[20]   *Sunday Times* v *UK* (1979) 2 EHRR 245, para 65.
[21]   (2005) 41 EHRR 29, at para 70.
[22]   (2005) 41 EHRR 14.
[23]   See *Von Hannover* v *Germany* (2004) 40 EHRR 1, para 57; *Stubbings and others* v *UK* (1996) 23 EHRR 213, paras 61–2 and *Cumpana*, at para 91.
[24]   See the passages referred to in *Von Hannover* and *Stubbings*.
[25]   See, eg in *Chauvy*, at para 63, and in *Cumpana*, at paras 84–8.

Assessing the facts

When considering the necessity for the restriction, the Court asks whether the **5.22** domestic court has reached an acceptable assessment of the facts.[26] In defamation cases it will readily make its own assessment where it considers that this was not the case.

The Court starts by looking at the particular words or allegations complained **5.23** of. It will be quick to identify and protect an honest value judgment where it has been wrongly characterized as a factual statement by the national court (see 5.29).[27] However, it also looks at the article as a whole, to see what its thrust was and what purpose lay behind it.[28] It will check that the words actually identified the complainant as the subject of the allegations.[29]

Critically, it will also look at the context in which the publication occurred. **5.24** For example, if the journalist was discussing matters of public importance or responding to an attack, the Court is more inclined to protect the speech.

Bladet Tromso and Stensaas v *Norway* is a good example of this approach. The **5.25** applicants' articles had accused seal hunters of cruelty and breaching seal hunting regulations. The hunters obtained damages. In finding a violation, the Court looked at 'the wider context of' the paper's coverage of the seal hunting issue. This had extended over a series or articles. It was balanced, setting out the competing points of view. Its 'thrust' was to discuss the issue, 'not primarily to accuse certain individuals . . . of cruelty to animals'.[30] The coverage was based on an official report by an inspector who had been on the vessel. So the paper was acting responsibly in passing the information on to the public, even though it had not verified the facts or asked the sealers to comment.[31] See also *Columbani* v *France*[32] where the journalist had reported the content of an official EU report on drug-trafficking.[33]

In *Bergens Tidende* v *Norway*,[34] the paper had run a series of articles reporting **5.26** women's complaints about a cosmetic surgeon. He had obtained damages

---

[26] See *Jersild* v *Denmark* (1994) 19 EHRR 1, at para 31; *Feldek* v *Slovakia* (App No 29032/95), 12 July 2001, at para 73.
[27] Even though this is a matter which comes within the margin of appreciation *(Prager & Oberschlick* v *Austria* (1995) 21 EHRR 1, at para 36).
[28] *Perna* v *Italy* (2004) 39 EHRR 563 at para 47.
[29] *Dyuldin and Kislov* v *Russia* (App No 25968/02), 31 July 2007, at para 43.
[30] Para 63.
[31] Paras 68 and 70.
[32] (App No 51279/99), 25 September 2002.
[33] Para 65.
[34] (2001) 31 EHRR 16.

because the articles created the 'impression' that he had been reckless. In finding a violation, the Court drew heavily on the wider context. It noted in particular that 'according to the evidence Dr R had been responsible for carrying out over 8,000 operations in a period of some ten years' and that the women had contacted the paper after reading a favourable report it published about him.[35]

5.27 This willingness to reappraise the material can, however, work against the journalist. In *Perna* v *Italy* the applicant had accused a prosecutor in Palermo of participating in a communist plot to take over public prosecutors' offices across Italy. The Grand Chamber rejected his argument that the allegations were simply 'critical judgements which there was no need to prove'.[36] In *Cumpana* v *Romania* the Court agreed with the assessment of the national court that the published allegations of criminality 'had presented a distorted view of reality and had not been based on actual facts'.[37]

The form of the expression: fact and value judgment

5.28 Article 10 protects not only the substance of the ideas and information expressed, but also the form in which the journalist communicates them.[38] The Court has therefore given the media considerable latitude in the methods it uses in publishing and broadcasting. It will not substitute its own views as to what techniques of reporting or presentation should be used to get a story across. This is a matter for the journalist. Nor will it apply its own view as to how an allegation should be counterbalanced, provided balance is present when needed.[39]

5.29 The Court always emphasizes the importance of drawing a 'careful distinction' between expression in the form of statements of fact and the expression of value judgments. This is because 'the existence of facts can be demonstrated, whereas the truth of value judgments is not susceptible of proof'. This makes it impossible for a journalist to defend an expression of opinion if truth is the only available defence.[40]

5.30 An adverse finding for expressing an honest 'value judgment' is very likely to involve a violation of Article 10. See for example *Dichand* v *Austria*,[41] where the newspaper criticized a lawyer MP as unwise in making laws which 'had

---

[35] *Bergens Tidende* v *Norway*, para 51.
[36] At para 47.
[37] At para 103.
[38] See *De Haes & Gijsels* v *Belgium*, at para 48.
[39] *Jersild* v *Denmark*, at para 31.
[40] *Lingens* v *Austria*, at para 46; *Jerusalem* v *Austria (No 2)* (2003) 37 EHRR 567, at paras 42–4.
[41] (App No 29271/95), 26 February 2002.

advantages for his clients'.[42] See also *Unabhangige Initiative Informationsvielfalt v Austria*,[43] where the journalist suggested that Jorg Haider, the leader of the right-wing Austrian Freedom Party, had been engaged in 'racist agitation'.[44]

This does not mean that Article 10(2) can never be successfully invoked in a   **5.31**
comment case. There must still be some established or admitted factual basis
for the expression of the opinion, which must be in good faith.[45] In *Prager &
Oberschlick v Austria*,[46] the Court was satisfied that the journalists had gone too
far by reason of the 'breadth' of their accusations which lacked a 'sufficient factual
basis'.[47] The extent to which a 'link' is needed 'between a value judgment and
its supporting facts' will vary from case to case depending on the circumstances.
Nor does the factual basis have to be spelt out in the published material. It may
lie in the complainant's own published statements about himself or information
'known to the general public'.[48]

The unique position of the press as 'watchdog'

For many years now the Court has acknowledged that the press has a unique   **5.32**
position under Article 10. It has made clear that the press has not only a right
but a duty to impart information and ideas on matters of public interest, which
the public has a corresponding right to receive.[49] It is allowed to interpret the
facts which it presents to the reader.[50] The role of the press as public watchdog
is 'essential . . . in a democratic society'. Indeed, 'journalistic freedom covers
possible recourse to a degree of exaggeration, or even provocation'.[51]

In *Steel and Morris v UK*,[52] the applicants were London Greenpeace campaigners   **5.33**
found to have published leaflets attacking the McDonald's Corporation on
health, environmental, and moral grounds. The government argued that they
'were not journalists' and should not receive enhanced protection under Article
10. The Court appeared to disagree, emphasizing: 'that in a democratic society
even small and informal campaign groups, must be able to carry on their
activities effectively and there exists a strong public interest in enabling such

---

[42] *Dichand v Austria*, at paras 47–50.
[43] (2003) 37 EHRR 33.
[44] At para 46.
[45] *Lingens v Austria*, at para 46, and *De Haes & Gijsels v Belgium*, at para 47.
[46] (1995) 21 EHRR 1.
[47] At para 37.
[48] *Feldek v Slovakia* (App No 29032/95), 12 October 2001, at paras 81–6.
[49] See *Observer and Guardian v UK*, at para 59.
[50] *Sunday Times v UK* (1979) 2 EHRR 245, para 65.
[51] *De Haes & Gijsels v Belgium*, at paras 37 and 46.
[52] (2005) 41 EHRR 22.

groups and individuals outside the mainstream to contribute to public debate by disseminating information and ideas on matters of general public interest such as health and the environment' (para 89).

5.34 Thus the safeguards 'afforded by Article 10 to journalists [and the proviso] that they act in good faith . . . must apply to others who engage in public debate' (para 90).

Public interest considerations

5.35 Since the 1980s the Court has expanded the enhanced protection given to media speech on matters of public interest. It has done this by identifying those who must accept more hard-hitting media coverage. There are numerous decisions in which the Court has distinguished between private and public reputations and ruled that the extent to which the latter may be protected is more limited, particularly where the press is acting as 'watchdog'. It has also done this by identifying issues on which there should be greater freedom to speak out even if this damages reputation.

Politicians and politics

5.36 The leading case is *Lingens* v *Austria*. The applicant had published two articles accusing the Austrian Chancellor, Bruno Kreisky, of protecting and helping former Nazi SS officers for political reasons. Kreisky successfully prosecuted the applicant for an offence of criminal defamation. The Court accepted that the protection of his reputation as a politician was a legitimate aim. However, it emphasized that 'the limits of acceptable criticism' of a politician in his public life are wider than those applying to private individuals. In a classic passage the Court stressed that: 'a politician . . . inevitably and knowingly lays himself open to close scrutiny of his every word and deed by both journalists and the public at large, and he must consequently display a greater degree of tolerance. No doubt Article 10(2) enables the reputation of . . . all individuals to be protected, and this protection extends to politicians too, even when they are not acting in their private capacity; but in such cases the requirements of such protection have to be weighed in relation to the interests of the open discussion of political issue' (at para 42).[53]

5.37 The scope for journalists to attack politicians is greater in a highly charged political climate. In *Lingens* the President of the Austrian Liberal Party, Friedrich Peter, had been identified as a former SS officer by a Jewish pressure

---

[53] See also recently: *Ukrainian Media Group* v *Ukraine* (2006) 43 EHRR 25, at para 67; *Grinberg* v *Russia* (2006) 43 EHRR, at para 32.

group only days after a general election. The next day, hours after ruling out a coalition with the Liberals, Mr Kreisky had compared the pressure group to the 'mafia' in a television interview. In finding that the interference was disproportionate, the Court emphasized that the climate in which the words had been written 'must not be overlooked'. In the 'struggle' represented by the post-election controversy about Mr Peter's past, everyone involved 'used the weapons at his disposal; and these were in no way unusual in the hard-fought tussles of politics' (at para 43). In reaching the same conclusion in *Oberschlick v Austria (No 1)*,[54] the Court relied on the fact that the journalist's opinions were a reaction to the politician's own 'shocking' views, that the State should discriminate against immigrant families in the payment of benefit, expressed in the course of an election campaign.

In *Oberschlick v Austria (No 2)*,[55] the journalist had reported a speech of Jorg   **5.38**
Haider under the headline 'PS: "Idiot" instead of Nazi'. The article stated that this was how he would describe Haider. The speech had praised the Austrian 'soldiers' of the Second World War, including those in the SS or Wehrmacht, for their role as founders of the contemporary, prosperous, Austrian democratic state. The applicant was convicted of 'insult' in a private prosecution brought by Haider. In finding a violation, the Court noted that the applicant's 'polemical' article was 'part of the political discussion provoked by Mr Haider's speech' (para 33). One recent decision of the Court has been heavily criticised for failing to recognize this important principle.[56]

Judges, public servants, and others who enter public life

In general, public servants acting in an official capacity are, like politicians,   **5.39**
subject to 'wider limits of acceptable criticism than private citizens. However, it cannot be said that civil servants knowingly lay themselves open to close scrutiny of their every word and deed the way that politicians do'.[57]

Thus in *Dalban v Romania*[58] the conviction of a journalist for defaming the chief   **5.40**
executive of a state-owned agricultural company (in the form of allegations of serious frauds which were under police investigation) was held to be in violation of Article 10. In *Pedersen and Baadsgaard*, by contrast, the status of the complainant (a chief superintendent of police) was not decisive. The

---

[54] (1991) 19 EHRR 389.
[55] (1997) 25 EHRR 357.
[56] See *Lindon, Otchakovsky-Laurens and July v France* (App Nos 21279/02 and 36448/02), 22 October 2007.
[57] See *Pedersen and Baadsgaard v Denmark* (2006) 42 EHRR 24, at para 80.
[58] (2000) 8 BHRC 91.

applicant television reporters had accused the superintendent of intentionally suppressing vital evidence which would have exonerated the accused in a murder case. They had been convicted of violating his personal honour. The Court found by nine votes to eight that there had been no violation of their Article 10 rights. The majority was swayed by the fact that the applicants did not have a sufficient factual basis for this specific accusation of a 'serious criminal act' (paras 80 and 87).

5.41 Although judges are public servants the Court recognizes particular reasons for protecting their reputations. In *Barfod* v *Denmark*,[59] the applicant journalist had been convicted of defaming two judges by accusing them of bias. The Court refused to find a violation, rejecting an argument that 'the accusations against the judges should be seen as part of a political debate, with its wider limits of legitimate criticism' (para 35). In *Prager and Oberschlick* the journalists had attacked a number of judges in strident terms. While the Court accepted that the press 'is one of the means by which politicians and public opinion can verify that judges are discharging their heavy responsibilities in a manner which is in conformity with the [democratic] aim which is the basis of the task entrusted to them', it also recognized that the judiciary: 'must enjoy public confidence if it is to be successful in carrying out its public duties. It may therefore prove necessary to protect such confidence against destructive attacks that are essentially unfounded, especially in view of the fact that judges who have been criticized are subject to a duty of discretion that precludes them from replying' (para 34).

5.42 Criticism of the judiciary in the context of court reporting is dealt with in chapter 9.

5.43 In *Steel and Morris* v *UK* the Court suggested that large public companies and those who manage them also lay themselves open to close scrutiny and must therefore be subject to wider limits of 'acceptable criticism' than private citizens (para 94). So do local councils.[60]

Who is in the 'public arena'?

5.44 In *Jerusalem* v *Austria (No 2)* the Court made clear that any 'private individuals or associations' could 'lay themselves open to scrutiny when they enter the arena of public debate'. On the facts these included those who cooperated with a political party in making its drug policy.

---

[59] (1989) 13 EHRR 493.
[60] See *Lombardo* v *Malta* (App No 7333/06), 24 April 2007, at para 54 and *Dyuldin and Kislov* v *Russia* (see n 29 above), at para 43.

However, it may be difficult to say who has entered this arena and which aspects of   **5.45**
their lives should be subject to these 'wider limits'. The difficulty is illustrated by
Tammer v *Estonia*.[61] The journalist had been convicted of insulting the second
wife of politician Edgar Savisaar. During Mr Savisaar's first marriage she was
employed by the State as his assistant when he was Minister of the Interior.
She gave birth to his child which she placed in the custody of her parents. He
was forced to resign as Minister when secret recordings of his conversations
with other politicians were published. The complainant admitted she had made
the recordings and resigned as well. She then wrote her memoirs in which she
discussed her affair with Mr Savisaar and the break-up of his first marriage. The
journalist's conviction was for suggesting that the complainant had broken up
Mr Savisaar's first marriage and was an 'unfit mother'. He argued with some
force that the complainant had become 'a public figure in her own right' and
that his comments were on matters of public interest (paras 45–7). The Court
disagreed, concluding that they were not 'justified by considerations of public
concern' (para 68).

Issues of public interest or concern

In *Hertel* v *Switzerland*,[62] the Court emphasized the importance of freedom   **5.46**
of speech 'where what is at stake is . . . participation in debate affecting the
general interest, for example over public health' (para 47). In *Nilsen and Johnsen*
v *Norway*,[63] this approach was adopted in a defamation case arising out of 'a
long and heated debate in Norway about . . . allegations of police violence'
(para 46). The applicants in *Hertel* and *Nilsen* were an academic and police
officers respectively. However, this extended protection for speech on issues of
public interest has principally benefited the media.

In the *Bladet Tromsø* case, the Court stressed that the contents of the articles could   **5.47**
not be looked at 'in isolation of the controversy that seal hunting represented
at the time in Norway' (at para 62). In *Bergens Tidende* v *Norway*, it considered
that the articles raised matters of 'consumer protection of direct concern to the
local and national public'. It declined to find that: 'the undoubted interest of
Dr R in protecting his professional reputation was sufficient to outweigh the
important public interest in the freedom of the press to impart information of
legitimate public concern' (para 60).

See also, in a similar vein, *Selisto* v *Finland*,[64] where allegations that a surgeon   **5.48**

---

[61] (2003) 37 EHRR 43.
[62] (1999) 28 EHRR 534.
[63] (1999) 30 EHRR 878.

had been drinking before an operation in which the patient died painted 'an alarming picture about issues of patient safety' (at para 63).

5.49   Other matters of public interest identified in the cases include: mismanagement of state assets;[65] misconduct by prosecutors, *Rizos & Daskas* v *Greece*;[66] failure to follow conservation laws;[67] the failure of a foreign head of State to combat drug-trafficking;[68] corruption by local government officials;[69] the possible doctrinal origins of the Holocaust;[70] and the activities of 'powerful commercial entities'.[71]

Reportage

5.50   Journalists often publish or broadcast defamatory allegations made by others without agreeing with the speaker. This is sometimes called 'reportage'. It may happen through publication of an interview. Sometimes the journalist ends up being sued. In deciding whether there is a violation of Article 10 in this situation the Court makes allowances for the importance of this form of reporting.

5.51   In *Jersild* v *Denmark*, the Court recognized that news reporting based on interviews 'whether edited or not, constitutes one of the most important means whereby the press is able to play its vital role of "public watchdog".' Consequently: 'The punishment of a journalist for assisting in the dissemination of statements made by another person in interview would seriously hamper the contribution of the press to discussion of matters of public interest and should not be envisaged unless there are particularly strong reasons for doing so' (para 35).

5.52   There is particular protection for journalists who refer to material in official reports. See the cases discussed under 'Assessing the facts' above.

5.53   More difficult questions arise where the journalist appears to be endorsing the defamatory allegations. In *Thoma* v *Luxembourg*,[72] the Court felt that the journalist may have 'adopted' part of a newspaper article which he quoted on the radio (para 60). However, it rejected the argument that there was a 'general requirement' for journalists 'systematically and formally to distance themselves from the content of' defamatory material. It considered that in identifying the

---

[64] (2006) 42 EHRR 8.
[65] *Dalban* v *Romania*, at para 33.
[66] (App No 65545/01), 27 May 2004.
[67] *Vides Aizsardzibas Klubs* v *Latvia* (App No 57829/00), 25 May 2004.
[68] *Colombani* v *France*.
[69] *Cumpana* v *Romania*.
[70] *Giniewski* v *France* (2007) 45 EHRR 23.
[71] *Steel and Morris* v UK.
[72] (2003) 36 EHRR 21.

statement as a quote from a 'strongly worded' and possibly unjustified article he had done enough to retain the protection of Article 10.

Responsible and irresponsible journalism

The recognition in Article 10(2) that the exercise of the right 'carries with it **5.54** duties and responsibilities' is unique in the ECHR. No other right is qualified in this way. Relying on these words the Court has repeatedly said that the media must not 'overstep certain bounds in particular in respect of the reputation and rights of others and the need to prevent disclosure of confidential information'.[73] In *Pedersen and Baadsgaard* v *Denmark*, the Court emphasized that the quid pro quo for the enhanced protection of journalists under Article 10 was that:

> they should act in good faith and on an accurate factual basis and provide 'reliable and precise' information in accordance with the ethics of journalism . . . these 'duties and responsibilities' are liable to assume significance when there is a question of attacking the reputation of a named individual and infringing the 'rights of others'. Thus, special grounds are required before the media can be dispensed from their ordinary obligation to verify factual statements that are defamatory of private individuals. (para 78)

Thus the protection might be lost where sources were not reliable or insufficient **5.55** weight was given to the presumption of innocence when accusing others of crimes. In *Perna* v *Italy*, the journalist's defence was fatally flawed because he had never even tried to prove that the specific criminal conduct alleged 'had actually occurred'.[74]

Excessive sanctions

A disproportionate penalty will result in a violation of Article 10. In *Tolstoy* **5.56** *Miloslavsky* v *UK*,[75] the Court considered the record award of libel damages of £1.5 million made by a High Court jury against the applicant. It observed that a 'high degree of flexibility' could be justified in the law of defamation damages. The well-established matters a jury was required to take into account (such as

---

[73] See, eg the *Bladet Tromsø* case, at paras 58, 59, and 65.
[74] At paras 31 and 47. See also, *Flux* v *Moldova (No 6)* (App No 22824/04), 29 July 2008, where the newspaper failed to verify a defamatory allegation in an anonymous letter it published.
[75] (1995) 20 EHRR 442.

the gravity of the libel, extent of publication, injury to feelings, anxiety caused by having to litigate, absence of an apology, and so on) were sufficient to ensure that the award was 'prescribed by law'. The fact that these did not include the principle of proportionality was not fatal.[76] But the Court ruled unanimously that the sheer amount of the award gave rise to a violation because it did not bear the required 'reasonable relationship of proportionality to the injury to reputation suffered'. Referring back to its earlier finding, it commented that 'An award of the present size must be particularly open to question where the substantive national law applicable at the time fails itself to provide a requirement of proportionality'.[77]

5.57 In *Independent News and Media and Independent Newspapers Ireland Ltd* v *Ireland*,[78] by contrast, the domestic courts had considered whether an award of IR£300,000 was proportionate. Given this, and the margin of appreciation given to States in determining damages, there was no violation. In *Steel and Morris* v *UK*, the Court indicated that a defendant's limited means could be a factor in determining the proportionality of a damages award. The awards of thirty-six and forty thousand pounds against the defendants were considered excessive 'when compared to [their] modest incomes and resources'.[79]

5.58 The Court has made clear that non-financial criminal sanctions are almost certain to be disproportionate. In *Cumpana*, the Court said that without exceptional circumstances, such as an element of 'hate speech or incitement to violence', journalists should not be jailed for defamation. This is so in particular since imprisonment 'by its very nature, will inevitably have a chilling effect'.[80] The Court considered that the secondary sanctions imposed on the applicants, prohibition from exercising civil rights and working as journalists for a year, were also inconsistent with press freedom. Fines and awards of cost will have to be justified as proportionate in the same way as civil damages awards.[81]

The Defendant's Right to a Fair Hearing

5.59 Where the statement is considered to be fact, the journalist must be permitted to call relevant evidence to try to prove truth.[82] Generally the media has to prove

---

[76] At paras 41 and 42.
[77] At para 49.
[78] (2006) 42 EHRR 46.
[79] At para 96.
[80] Paras 115–16.
[81] See *Perna* v *Italy*, at para 48.
[82] *Castells* v *Spain*, at para 48.

truth though exceptionally special grounds may require the claimant to prove falsity.[83] Where the statement is comment the speaker must be given an 'effective opportunity' to support the statements and show they were fair.[84]

In *Steel and Morris*, the Court found that the defendants' rights under Article 6 **5.60** ECHR had been violated because they were denied legal aid to advance a complex defence to McDonald's' claim. The trial lasted 313 days, preceded by 28 interlocutory applications. An appeal took a further 23 days. The Court found an 'unacceptable inequality of arms' and that the defendants could not present their case effectively without specialist legal representation.[85] In consequence their Article 10 rights were also violated given, in particular, the public interest issues at stake and the 'legitimate and important role that campaign groups can play in stimulating public discussion'. The Court noted the difficulty they faced proving truth 'without legal aid'.[86]

The Impact of the HRA 1998 on Domestic Law

Criminal libel

The Law Commission has long since recommended abolition of criminal libel.[87] **5.61** It enables an extremely serious libel to be punished as a crime triable on indictment. Leave of a High Court judge is required before a newspaper or periodical can be prosecuted.[88] However, justification is a defence only if the defendant can persuade the jury that the publication was for the 'public benefit'[89] and it is not even certain that fair comment is a defence.

As indicated above, Article 10 requires an unrestricted defence of truth and **5.62** strong protection for public interest speech by the media, especially in the form of good faith comment. None of these elements is established in criminal libel law. Thirty years ago, in *Gleaves* v *Deakin*,[90] Lord Diplock suggested that the offence would be difficult to reconcile with Article 10. Doubtless this is why there has not been a public prosecution of the media for the common law offence of criminal libel for many years.

---

[83] *McVicar* v *UK* (2002) 35 EHRR 22, para 83.
[84] *Jerusalem* v *Austria* (App No 26958/95), 27 February 2001, at para 46.
[85] Para 72.
[86] Para 95.
[87] Law Commission, *Criminal Law: Report on Criminal Libel* (Law Com No 149, Cm 9618, 1985).
[88] Law of Libel Amendment Act 1888, s 8.
[89] Libel Act 1843, s 6.
[90] [1980] AC 477, HL, at 483.

The civil law of defamation

5.63   The fundamentals of the Article 10 and domestic jurisprudence are similar. There is a comparable common law right to freedom of expression.[91] This is balanced against the right to reputation on a case-by-case basis. Applications for prior restraint orders against the media are closely scrutinized and will fail unless the claimant establishes that no defence can succeed at trial. See *Greene v Associated Newspapers Ltd*[92] in which the Court of Appeal also accepted that the right to protection of reputation was an aspect of private life. There is a fastidious procedural regime, both before and at trial, which should ensure a proper assessment of the facts even where there is a jury trial. The common law defences of justification, fair comment, and privilege can be applied in a way that enables the courts to act compatibly with the principles described above in accordance with HRA 1998, s 6.[93]

5.64   However, the arrival of the HRA has required some adjustment of the common law of defamation. More will occur. The key cultural change for the judges has been the need to apply law which properly reflects the values underpinned by the rights to expression and reputation, as in Strasbourg.

The Reynolds defence for public interest speech

5.65   In *Reynolds* v *Times Newspapers Ltd*,[94] the House of Lords anticipated the implementation of the HRA in considering whether English law should develop a new, subject-matter category of qualified privilege for political speech. The claimant, a former Irish Prime Minister, had sued the *Sunday Times* over an allegation that he had lied to the Irish Parliament. Instead of developing such a privilege their Lordships extended the common law test for qualified privilege (a legal, social, or moral duty to make the statement and a corresponding interest in the recipient in receiving it) to cover media organizations when imparting information to the public on matters of 'serious public concern', provided they do so through balanced responsible journalism. Lord Nicholls identified ten factors that judges might consider in deciding whether a particular publication met this standard. These were:

> 1. The seriousness of the allegation. The more serious the charge, the more the public is misinformed and the individual harmed, if the allegation is not true.
> 2. The nature of the information, and the extent to which the subject matter is

---

[91]   See *Derbyshire CC* v *Times Newspapers Ltd* [1993] AC 534.
[92]   [2005] QB 972 (applying *Bonnard* v *Perryman* [1891] 2 Ch 269).
[93]   Bolstered by the statutory categories of absolute and qualified privilege in the Defamation Act 1996 which protect speech on public interest matters, such as reporting the courts and Parliament.
[94]   [2001] 2 AC 127.

a matter of public concern. 3. The source of the information. Some informants have no direct knowledge of the events. Some have their own axes to grind, or are being paid for their stories. 4. The steps taken to verify the information. 5. The status of the information. The allegation may have already been the subject of an investigation which commands respect. 6. The urgency of the matter. News is often a perishable commodity. 7. Whether comment was sought from the plaintiff. He may have information others do not possess or have not disclosed. An approach to the plaintiff will not always be necessary. 8. Whether the article contained the gist of the plaintiff's side of the story. 9. The tone of the article. A newspaper can raise queries or call for an investigation. It need not adopt allegations as statements of fact. 10. The circumstances of the publication, including the timing. (at 205)

These broadly reflect the matters which, in various cases, have been considered **5.66** by the Strasbourg Court in assessing responsible journalism (see 5.54). Where the privilege applies, the media has immunity from liability in respect of any false allegations of fact.

In a series of wide-ranging speeches their Lordships examined the values **5.67** underlying the interests in play in a defamation case. Reputation was recognized as 'an integral part of [a person's] dignity . . . [I]t should not be supposed that reputation is a matter of importance only to the affected individual . . . Protection of reputation is conducive to the public good' (at 201). People should not be 'unjustly' deprived of their reputation (238). Freedom of expression was identified as a constitutional right (207–8).[95] Echoing the Strasbourg Court, Lord Nicholls acknowledged that 'Without freedom of expression by the media, freedom of expression would be a hollow concept' (at 200), and commented: 'The press discharges vital functions as a bloodhound as well as a watchdog. The Court should be slow to conclude that a publication was not in the public interest and, therefore, that the public had a right to know, especially when the information is in the field of political discussion. Any lingering doubts should be resolved in favour of publication' (at 205).

Lord Bingham commented eloquently to similar effect in *McCartan Turkington* **5.68** *Breen (A Firm)* v *Times Newspapers Ltd*.[96] Indeed, there have been indications, since *Steel and Morris* v *UK*, that the *Reynolds* defence should extend to NGOs and others publishing '*material of public interest in any medium*'.[97] Quite aside from the difficulties in identifying a member of the media in the internet age, this approach is surely correct given the values underlying the free speech right—most importantly democratic self-governance (see chapter 1).

---

[95] See also, *McCartan Turkington Breen,* at para 45.
[96] [2001] 2 AC 277, HL, at 290.
[97] See, eg *Jameel* (n 98 below), at paras 54, 137 and 146.

5.69 In *Jameel* v *Wall Street Journal Europe Sprl*,[98] their Lordships considered how *Reynolds* had been applied. They felt the need to emphasize, in accordance with the principles identified in relation to the form of the expression above, that the Courts should make allowance for editorial judgment when applying the responsible journalism test.[99] It was also necessary to look at the article as a whole, not just the words complained of, to see whether the threshold public interest requirement was met (para 51). In *Jameel* it was. The article alleged official monitoring of a Saudi/UK group of companies for involvement in funding terrorism. Consistently with the Strasbourg cases, the post-*Reynolds* decisions cases have found public interest in reports of: incompetence in the managing of state-owned companies;[100] discreditable activities of public figures;[101] political disputes;[102] and police corruption.[103]

Irresponsible journalism

5.70 The value to the media of the *Reynolds* defence largely depends on how the 'responsible journalism' standard is applied. Up until *Jameel* its value was distinctly limited. The judges tended to ignore the journalist's judgment about what should be published, and in what form, applying a strict 'objective' standard (akin to reasonable care in the law of negligence).[104] They tended to see the Nicholls factors as 'hurdles', all of which the journalist had to jump to access the defence. This resulted in the bar being set too high. Failure to verify information or put the claimant's side of the story[105] tended to be fatal. So did a failure to prove that sources were reliable.[106] In *Jameel* the Lords objected to this restrictive interpretation of the defence, which went against 'the spirit of *Reynolds*'.[107] In *Jameel*, publication of the story was deemed responsible even without the claimant's response. It remains to be seen whether *Jameel* will lead to more *Reynolds*' defences succeeding.

5.71 Other common law jurisdictions apply different standards in this area. In American constitutional law, the media has much greater protection. The claimant must show actual malice, producing evidence that the journalist had

---

[98] [2007] 1 AC 359, HL.
[99] See at paras 33, 51, and 108.
[100] *Bonnick* v *Morris* [2003] 1 AC 300, PC.
[101] *Louchansky* v *Times Newspapers Ltd (No 4)* [2001] EMLR 38 and *Galloway* v *Telegraph Group Ltd* [2006] EMLR 11.
[102] *Roberts* v *Gable* [2008] 2 WLR 129.
[103] *Charman* v *Orion Publishing Group Ltd* [2008] 1 All ER 750.
[104] See *Louchansky (No 2)* [2002] QB 783, CA, at para 40.
[105] See *Reynolds* itself.
[106] *Louchansky (No 6)* [2002] EWHC 2490, paras 31–43.
[107] See Lord Hoffman at para 56.

serious doubt about the truth of the allegation.[108] In the Commonwealth jurisdictions, the tests are closer to the *Reynolds* standard. In Australia, the journalist's conduct has to be reasonable.[109] In South Africa, the test is whether it was reasonable to publish the particular facts in that particular way at that particular time.[110]

Neutral reportage

In dealing with this species of public interest reporting, the courts have respected **5.72** 'the spirit of *Reynolds*'. It is now established that, in reporting on political matters at least, there is no need to verify the content of a repeated allegation. This is so if, considering the 'thrust' of the article as a whole, the allegation is not adopted.[111]

Other possible developments

The presumption of falsity remains one of the most contentious aspects of **5.73** defamation law. Media organizations would like to see the claimant bear the burden of proving falsity, rather than having to prove truth themselves. In *McVicar* and *Steel and Morris*, the Court indicated that, in some cases, this obligation might lead to a violation of Article 10. It remains to be seen whether these cases will arise in England. To date, however, the courts have been steadfast in maintaining the presumption against all Article 10 arguments.[112]

In *Jameel* v *Dow Jones & Co Inc*,[113] the Court of Appeal rejected an argument that **5.74** the presumption of damage was inconsistent with Article 10 principles. However, in the *Jameel* v *Wall Street Journal Europe Sprl* case, the European arm of the same publishing house has applied to Strasbourg for a ruling that the presumption of damages in favour of corporate claimants is inconsistent. In *Jameel* v *Dow Jones & Co Inc*, the court did at least strike out the claim for abuse of process, drawing on the Strasbourg principle that any interference must be proportionate. Only five people read the article, three of whom were associates of the claimant. *Steel and Morris* is unlikely to be the last word on whether the domestic funding arrangements in defamation cases give rise to Article 10 violations. Claimant lawyers acting under conditional fee arrangements can claim an uplift of up to

---

[108] See *New York Times* v *Sullivan* 376 US 254 (1964), *St Amant* v *Thompson* 390 US 727 (1968), and *Gertz* v *Robert Welch Inc* 418 US 323 (1974).
[109] See *Lange* v *ABC* (1997) CLR 520, 576 for political speech; and the statutory defences in individual states—eg the New South Wales Defamation Act 2005.
[110] *National Media* v *Bogoshi* 1998 (4) SA 1196 (SCA).
[111] See *Al-Fagih* v *HH Saudi Research and Marketing (UK) Ltd* [2003] EMLR 13 and *Roberts* v *Gable* [2007] EMLR 16, at para 61(3).
[112] See, eg *Berezovsky* v *Forbes Inc (No 2)* [2001] EMLR 45 para 12 and *Reynolds* at p 192.
[113] [2005] QB 946.

one hundred per cent of their normal fees if they obtain a costs order. This is a massive disincentive to the media to defend defamation cases. The costs liability if they lose after a trial is likely to dwarf the damages awarded. The Article 6 and 10 ECHR issues arising are to be considered in Strasbourg in an application by *The Mirror* arising out of the Naomi Campbell privacy litigation (see chapter 6).

6

PRIVACY AND CONFIDENTIALITY

Introduction	6.01	Intrusions on Privacy by the	
State Interference: Searches,		Media: Strasbourg	6.21
Warrants, and Production		Intrusions by the Media: The UK	6.30
Orders	6.06	Remedies	6.45
State Interference: Media Sources	6.10	Threats to Life	6.48

Introduction

The media were nervous when the Human Rights Bill was being debated in **6.01** Parliament. They feared that it would lead to the introduction of a law of privacy into English law. The source of their worry was Article 8 which provides that:

1. Everyone has the right to respect for his private and family life, his home and his correspondence.
2. There shall be no interference by a public authority with the exercise of this right except such as is in accordance with the law and is necessary in a democratic society in the interests of national security, public safety or the economic well-being of the country, for the prevention of disorder or crime, for the protection of health or morals, or for the protection of the rights and freedoms of others.

The reason for the anxiety is not immediately obvious. The express terms of **6.02** Article 8(2) are directed at intrusions into private lives *by a public authority*. For the most part the media are not public authorities. How, therefore, could this provision affect them?

The answer was the elusive concept of 'positive obligations'. On its face Article 8, **6.03** like many of the other parts of the Convention, contains a negative command. It says to the State and its public authorities what they shall not do. However, the European Court of Human Rights has developed the idea that some of the provisions of the Convention to some (uncertain) extent also contain implied positive obligations. The media were concerned that the European Court would find that there was a positive obligation on the State parties to the Convention to adopt measures that would provide protection for privacy against intrusions by the media. This had not happened by 1998, but there were straws in the wind which pointed in that direction.

6.04   But it should not be thought that privacy was a totally alien concept in English law at the time the HRA was passed. The action for breach of confidence could provide protection against leaked documents and other secrets. The old torts of trespass and nuisance were sometimes brought out against the press, and the regulators of broadcasters had power to investigate allegations that they had intruded unreasonably into private lives. Yet, although these (and particularly breach of confidence) were being expanded by the judges, there was understandable nervousness in the media that the introduction of the Convention rights into English law would see a quantum leap in privacy protection. It was this which led to the following being included as s 12(4) of the Act:

> (4) The court must have particular regard to the importance of the Convention right to freedom of expression and, where the proceedings relate to material which the respondent claims, or which appears to the court, to be journalistic, literary or artistic material (or to be connected with such material), to –
>
> (a)   the extent to which
>
>> (i)   the material has, or is about to, become available to the public; or
>> (ii) it is, or would be, in the public interest for the material to be published;
>
> (b)   any relevant privacy code.

6.05   As we shall see, s 12 has not been the bulwark against the privacy tide which the media may have hoped. However, before looking at that more closely, it is useful to take a step back and consider how the negative command in Article 8 may provide a degree of protection for the media against state intrusion.

State Interference: Searches, Warrants, and Production Orders

6.06   Only individuals in their personal lives can have a 'family life', but businesses, including media organizations, can rely on the protection given to 'correspondence'.[1] So warrants or searches of business premises must also meet the requirements of Article 8. Telephone calls are treated as a form of 'correspondence' and therefore intercepts must be 'prescribed by law', which they were not when the UK was found to be in breach of Article 8 in *Malone* v *UK*.[2] The activities of the security services had to be put on a statutory footing for the same reason.[3] In 2008 the Court found that the UK provisions under the Regulation of Investigatory Powers Act 2000 gave inadequate clarity as to the manner of the exercise of the wide discretion to intercept, examine, share, and destroy intercepted communications between the UK and other countries.[4]

Warrants, intercepts, and searches must not only have a basis in national law. **6.07** They must also in each case be for one of the purposes set out in Article 8(2). It will be rare for them to fail that test. However, the third requirement is that the interference must be 'necessary in a democratic society'. This term, which is the same as is used in Article 10(2), imports the requirement of proportionality. Consequently, over-broad search powers or warrants will infringe Article 8.[5]

In England and Wales, the Police and Criminal Evidence Act 1984 establishes a **6.08** special procedure where the police wish to obtain access to journalistic material. An ordinary search warrant cannot be issued. A production order (or, in very unusual cases, a warrant) must be obtained from a Crown Court judge. Different access conditions have to be satisfied depending on whether or not the material is held in confidence. Even if it is not confidential, the Courts must pay due regard to the principles of freedom of expression.[6]

Nonetheless, whenever there have been violent demonstrations or disorder it **6.09** is now commonplace for the media to face applications for disclosure of their photographs and film, and PACE production orders are almost invariably made. After the Broadwater Farm riots and the death of PC Blakelock, the BBC was compelled by a witness order to provide its untransmitted film at the subsequent trial. It complained to Strasbourg that this was a breach of its rights under Article 10. It argued that its film crews would be exposed to greater risk in the future if it became known that their work could be used by the police. The Commission, however, was unpersuaded: '[It] considers that any risk to film

---

[1] See *Niemietz* v *Germany* (1992) 16 EHRR 97.
[2] (1984) 7 EHRR 14.
[3] See *Hewitt and Harman* v *UK* (1989) 67 DR 88.
[4] *Liberty* v *UK* (App No 58243/00), 1 July 2008.
[5] See, eg *Funke* v *France* (1993) 16 EHRR 297.
[6] See *R* v *Central Criminal Court, ex p Bright* [2001] 1 WLR 662 QBD; *R (Malik)* v *Manchester Crown Court* [2008] EWHC 1362 (Admin).

crews flows from their presence at such incidents as the Broadwater Farm riots and from the fact that they are filming such incidents, rather than from any possibility that untransmitted film may subsequently be made available to the courts.'[7] The obligation to provide the film in response to the summons was part of the BBC's ordinary civic duty and was necessary for maintaining the authority and impartiality of the judiciary. The view, however, persists among cameramen and photographers that they are more at risk if such orders are made. Ultimately, the issue is one of evidence, and the position under Article 10 and Article 8 would no doubt be stronger if there was stronger evidence that such fears were well founded.

State Interference: Media Sources

Compelling disclosure

6.10 Journalists' concerns about privacy and confidentiality become acute when they relate to sources who wish to remain anonymous. Even before the Human Rights Act, Parliament had, to a limited extent, recognized the public interest in preserving the flow of information that comes to the media through confidential sources. The Contempt of Court Act 1981, s 10 provides: 'No court may require a person to disclose, nor is a person guilty of contempt of court for refusing to disclose, the source of information contained in a publication for which he is responsible, unless it is established to the satisfaction of the court that disclosure is necessary in the interests of justice or national security or for the prevention of crime or disorder.'

6.11 This section has been considered by the courts on numerous occasions, including several in the House of Lords. In *X Ltd v Morgan Grampian (Publishers) Ltd*,[8] Lord Bridge said that the 'interests of justice' exception called for a balancing exercise between the particular needs of the claimant and the journalist's presumptive right to preserve source anonymity: 'In this balancing exercise it is only if the judge is satisfied that disclosure in the interests of justice is of such preponderating importance as to override the statutory privilege against disclosure that the threshold of necessity will be reached.' Nonetheless, in that case the House of Lords held that the journalist had been rightly ordered to disclose his source. The journalist, William Goodwin, persisted in his refusal, was fined £5,000, but complained to the European Court of Human Rights.

---

[7] *BBC v UK* App No 25798/94, (1996) 84 DR 129.
[8] [1991] 1 AC 1.

He based his claim squarely on Article 10, arguing that unless a journalist could protect the anonymity of a confidential source, freedom of expression would be jeopardized. The Court agreed and found a violation—*Goodwin v UK*.[9] It said (at para 39):

> Protection of journalistic sources is one of the basic conditions for press freedom, as is reflected in the laws and the professional codes of conduct in a number of contracting states and is affirmed in several international instruments on journalistic freedoms. Without such protection, sources may be deterred from assisting the press in informing the public on matters of public interest. As a result the vital public watchdog role of the press may be undermined and the ability of the press to provide accurate and reliable information may be adversely affected. Having regard to the importance of the protection of journalistic sources for press freedom in a democratic society and the potentially chilling effect an order of source disclosure has on the exercise of that freedom, such a measure cannot be compatible with Article 10 of the Convention unless it is justified by an overriding requirement of public interest.

On the facts of Goodwin's own case, the Court was not convinced that the interests of the claimant, either in neutralizing the threat from this particular leak, or of preventing similar leaks in the future, were sufficient to outweigh the vital public interest in the protection of the journalist's source. **6.12**

The European Court has made clear that the *Goodwin* principle applies equally to searches of journalists' homes or offices, even though nothing is required of the journalist except passivity.[10] Indeed, because of the wide-ranging powers that police will have once they gain access to a journalist's papers, a search is in many ways more intrusive. It is also striking how unsuccessful governments have been in persuading the European Court that other interests ought to prevail over the preservation of source anonymity. So in *Roemen* a violation was found although the investigation was into the proper functioning of public institutions. In *Voskuil v Netherlands*,[11] the journalist had published an article which alleged that the police had fabricated a reason for entering a flat where arms had been found. The convictions of the criminal defendants might have been set aside if the journalist's story had been correct. Yet the measures taken against him to discover his source were found to be a violation of Article 10. In *Tillack v Belgium*,[12] it was alleged that the journalist had bribed an EU official to obtain a story of incompetence or worse in the Community's institutions. Still the Court said that a journalist's **6.13**

---

[9] (1997) 25 EHRR 1.
[10] See *Roemen and Schmidt v Luxembourg* (App No 51772/99), 25 February 2003; *Ernst v Belgium* (App No 33400/96), 15 July 2003.
[11] (App No 64752/01), 22 November 2007.
[12] (App No 20477/05), 27 November 2007.

right not to reveal his or her sources could not be considered a mere privilege to be granted or taken away depending on the lawfulness or unlawfulness of their sources, but was part of the right to information, to be treated with the utmost caution, even more so in the applicant's case, where he had been under suspicion because of vague uncorroborated rumour, as subsequently confirmed by the fact that he had not been charged.

6.14 A rare case where no violation was found was *Nordisk* v *Denmark*.[13] The applicant journalist had gone undercover and secretly filmed a group called the 'Paedophile Association'. After his programme was broadcast he was ordered to hand over the untransmitted footage. He argued that this would disclose the identities of the participants when these had been deliberately disguised in the broadcast. The Court rejected the complaint as manifestly unfounded. The group members had featured in the film unwittingly. Their cooperation had not been dependent on a promise of anonymity. They were not therefore 'sources' within the *Goodwin* principle. Nor were they a 'source' as defined in a recommendation of the Council of Ministers of the Council of Europe on the Protection of Journalistic sources.[14] This is an interesting example of the Court making use of these recommendations as a means of interpreting the Convention and in working out its own jurisprudence. Nor is this an isolated occurrence. In *Voskuil*, the Court also referred to the same recommendation for the principle that generally States ought to try other measures for finding the information in question before pressing a journalist to disclose his source—a principle which the Court referred to as one of subsidiarity.

6.15 The *Goodwin* principle has been adopted by other international courts and expanded. The International Criminal Tribunal for former Yugoslavia had summoned a *Washington Post* reporter, Jonathan Randall, to give evidence at the trial of a Serb politician whom he had once interviewed. The Appeal Chamber set aside the summons. It applied the principle of subsidiarity and ruled that a journalist should not be compelled to testify unless their evidence was vital to the establishment of guilt or innocence and the evidence could not be obtained in any other way.[15] The Special Court for Sierra Leone has extended the *Goodwin* principle to protect researchers for NGOs such as Human Rights Watch and Amnesty International.[16]

---

[13] (App No 40485/02), 8 December 2005.
[14] Recommendation R (2000) 7.
[15] *Prosecutor* v *Brdjanin and Talic: appeal of Jonathan Randall* Case No IT–99–36–T, Judgment of Appeal Chamber, 11 December 2002.
[16] *Prosecutor Brima* Case No SCSL–2004–16–AR73, Judgment of Appeal Chamber, 26 May 2006.

The structure of s 10 of the UK's Contempt of Court Act and the principles   **6.16**
enunciated by the House of Lords in *Morgan Grenfell* are very similar to those
of the Strasbourg Court, but prior to the HRA the outcomes could be radically
different as *Goodwin* itself showed. Shortly after *Goodwin* the Court of Appeal
ordered the owners of the magazine *Marketing Week* to hand over draft financial
accounts for the organizers of the national lottery.[17] This may have been one
of the cases which led the Court of Appeal subsequently to observe that 'the
decisions of the European Court demonstrate that the freedom of the press in
the past carried greater weight in Strasbourg than it has in the courts of this
country'—*Ashworth Hospital Authority* v *MGN Ltd*.[18] In that case, the House of
Lords later upheld an order that the *Daily Mirror* should disclose its source for a
leak of medical records of the Moors murderer, Ian Brady.[19] When it transpired
that the newspaper had only the name of an intermediary who was a freelance
journalist, the Hospital Authority pursued its action against him. However, this
time the Courts said that the ultimate source had probably acted for public
interest reasons. The freelancer had an impressive reputation for performing the
classic 'watchdog' role that Strasbourg envisaged for the media and, in any case,
by this stage many years had passed since the original leak and the Hospital
could hardly show a pressing need to discover the identity of the final source.[20]

Yet the UK courts still appear to be readier than Strasbourg to accept arguments   **6.17**
for disclosure of sources. In *Interbrew SA Ltd* v *Financial Times Ltd*,[21] the Court
thought that a document had been leaked at the time of a brewery takeover
with the intention of affecting the claimant's share price. This may mark out
the case as different (although it may be rather more common for sources to
be disgruntled with the organizations on which they report). In another case,
Lord Justice Scott Baker, who was acting as coroner for the inquest into the
deaths of Princess Diana and Dodi Fayed, succeeded in obtaining disclosure
orders against Channel 4.[22] The channel had broadcast a programme on their
deaths and the role of the paparazzi. The judge who ordered disclosure said that
this was precisely the territory that the inquest was covering. The balance came
down in favour of disclosure—at least to the coroner, who would decide what,
if any, further use should be made of it.

---

[17] *Camelot Group plc* v *Centaur Communications Ltd* [1998] 1 All ER 251, CA.
[18] [2001] 1 WLR 515, CA at para 101.
[19] *Ashworth Hospital Authority* v *MGN Ltd* [2002] 1 WLR 2033, HL.
[20] *Mersey Care NHS Trust* v *Ackroyd (No2)* [2008] EMLR 1, CA.
[21] [2002] EMLR 24, CA.
[22] *Asst Deputy Coroner for Inner West London* v *Channel 4 Television Corp* [2008] 1 WLR 945.

6.18 PACE production orders can only rarely extend to confidential journalistic material. Production orders under the Terrorism Act 2000, Schedule 5 are not so limited, but the court would anyway have to act compatibly with the journalist's Convention rights. In 2008 a production order was made against the author of a biography of Hassan Butt, a self-proclaimed former Islamist activist. The Divisional Court held that the Crown Court was entitled to decide that the police interests in pursuing their terrorist investigation outweighed the journalist's rights under both Article 10 and (because of the potential risk of self-incrimination) Article 6. It did, however, narrow the effect of the order to reduce (for the time being at least) the chance that the material produced would identify sources apart from Mr Butt.[23]

Penalizing sources—whistleblowers

6.19 In *Guja* v *Moldova*,[24] the Grand Chamber had to consider a complaint under Article 10 by a 'whistleblower' who had passed on letters which suggested that political pressure had been applied in the conduct of a prosecution. The Court reiterated that Article 10 applies to the workplace in general and to public servants in particular, but because of their special position they would normally be expected to observe a duty of loyalty, reserve, and discretion. Yet the Court also recognized that corruption and other wrongdoing in the workplace was often impossible to penetrate without the help of an insider. Normally an employee would be expected to raise concerns and complaints with a superior, but there was an important role for wider dissemination if the circumstances required it. The public interest in the disclosure was the first consideration, but the authenticity of the information, the damage which wider disclosure might cause, the motive and good faith of the whistleblower, and the proportionality of any sanction imposed by the employer were also important matters. On the facts of the case the Court unanimously found that Article 10 had been violated.

6.20 In the UK, the Public Interest Disclosure Act 1998 already provides a degree of protection for whistleblowers and, unsurprisingly, adopts a very similar set of considerations in determining whether any detriment imposed by the employer is actionable.

---

[23] *R (Malik)* v *Manchester Crown Court* [2008] EWHC 1362 (Admin).
[24] (App No 14277/04), 12 February 2008.

Intrusions on Privacy by the Media: Strasbourg

Protection of privacy and confidentiality as justification for restricting freedom of expression

The legitimate aims for which Article 10(2) permits restrictions on freedom **6.21** of expression include 'the protection of the rights of others' and 'preventing the disclosure of information received in confidence'. The restrictions must be 'prescribed by law', but where national law does protect privacy or confidential information these restrictions may in principle be compatible with Article 10. They must also, of course, be 'necessary in a democratic society'. It is this requirement that has generated the most controversy.

A good example is *Fressoz and Roire* v *France*.[25] The French satirical magazine, **6.22** *Le Canard Enchaine*, published the tax assessments of the head of Peugeot at the time of an industrial dispute at Peugeot over a pay claim. The assessments showed that the chairman's income had risen by about 45 per cent over two years, while the income of the workers had increased by only 6.7 per cent over the same period. The newspaper was found guilty of handling photocopies of the tax returns and made a complaint to the European Court of Human Rights. The Court noted that although the returns were confidential, under French law local taxpayers could consult records for the taxable income and tax liability of others in their municipality. Thus the essential information in the assessments was accessible to a large number of people. The journalists acted in good faith. The article contributed to a debate on a matter of public interest. The publication of the extracts from the assessments was intended to corroborate the terms of the Article and to show the credibility of its information. The Court concluded that the journalists' rights under Article 10 had been violated.

The prior availability of the material in question may be critical. The UK **6.23** government was found to have breached Article 10 by maintaining the *Spycatcher* injunction even after over a million copies of the book had been sold worldwide.[26] (The Court also held—but only narrowly by 14 votes to 10—that the government had been entitled to seek an injunction on national security grounds prior to publication abroad because of the risk that the book might contain material damaging to the intelligence services.) *Vereinging Weekblad Bluf!* v *Netherlands*[27] elaborated further on the relevance of prior publication.

---

[25] (2001) 31 EHRR 28.
[26] *Observer and Guardian* v *UK* (1991) 14 EHRR 153.
[27] (1995) 20 EHRR 189.

The newspaper applicant had published a leaked Dutch intelligence document and sold some 2,500 copies before the authorities took action to seize the remaining copies. The European Court found that the seizure was a violation of Article 10, even though the numbers sold were very much smaller than in the *Spycatcher* case and, as importantly, even though it was the applicant itself which had put those copies into the public domain. In these two cases the Court accepted that court injunctions or seizures were not necessarily and always a breach of Article 10. However, as forms of 'prior restraint', they called for the most careful scrutiny to see whether they were indeed 'necessary in a democratic society'.

6.24 The death of President Mitterrand was swiftly followed by the publication of his doctor's account of his long battle with cancer. About 40,000 copies were sold before the dead man's family obtained an injunction the following day. The European Court found no breach of Article 10 because of this order. The family's grief was raw and they had moved very fast. The position was different when a permanent injunction was granted nine months later. The family's distress by then must have been less extreme and the public interest in the medical condition of the man who had been the French head of state at the time was entitled to a higher priority.[28] When *Paris-Match* published a photograph of the corpse of the Prefect of Corsica who had been murdered on a public street, his grieving relatives demanded that all the copies of the magazine should be seized because of the infringement of their privacy. The French courts refused this remedy, but they did require the publishers to include a statement saying that the photograph had been included without the consent of the family who considered it an intrusion into the intimacy of their private life. The publishers argued before the Strasbourg Court that the assassination of the Prefect was a public event of huge public interest, but the Court was swayed by the mildness of the measure which had been imposed and the fact that the magazine could not show how this had impacted on their future practice. No violation was found.[29]

6.25 The public interest in the publication or broadcast is a regular theme of the European Court's judgments and it may lead to a finding that a restriction on freedom of expression was inconsistent with Article 10. In *Radio Twist* v *Slovakia*,[30] a broadcaster was fined for playing a tape of a conversation between a government minister and a senior civil servant. They had been discussing a stormy and controversial privatisation of a state-owned insurance company.

---

[28] *Editions Plon* v *France* (2006) 42 EHRR 36.
[29] *Hachette Filipacci Associes* v *France* (App No 71111/01), 14 June 2007.
[30] (App No 62202/02), 19 December 2006.

The intercept had been unlawfully made. The broadcaster had played no part in this illegality but was judged by the Slovakian courts to have infringed the privacy of the participants to the conversation. Emphasizing the good faith of the broadcasters and the public interest in the topic of the discussion, the European Court held that their rights under Article 10 had been violated. In *Karhuvaara v Finland*,[31] the applicant had reported on a case of a drunken lawyer who had been convicted of assaulting a police officer. The newspaper drew attention to the fact that the lawyer's wife was a member of parliament and Chairperson of the Committee of Education and Culture. It had been prosecuted and fined for infringing the wife's privacy. The Court found this to be a violation of Article 10. Although her husband's conviction had had nothing to do with the parliamentarian, some voters might think this relevant to how they wished to vote.

Article 8: positive obligation

The cases considered in the previous section all concerned situations where the national authorities *had* taken action against the media and the Strasbourg Court was required to investigate whether this restriction was compatible with Article 10. Where the State does nothing, the aggrieved applicant will not be the media but the person who complains that his or her privacy or confidentiality was abused. The complaint will be that the lack of any remedy against the media is incompatible with the positive obligation inherent in Article 8.   **6.26**

The leading Strasbourg case on this subject is now *Von Hannover v Germany*.[32]   **6.27**
Princess Caroline von Hannover is a member of the Monaco royal family. She has no official position but she is a fashionable celebrity who features frequently in photo magazines. She tried unsuccessfully to obtain redress from the German courts for the publication of photographs of her which showed her shopping, skiing, horse-riding, or on holiday. Most were taken while she was on public property. The German courts said that she was a public figure who had to tolerate the taking and publication of such photographs. The Strasbourg Court said that this did not do justice to Princess Caroline's right to a private life which even public figures were entitled to enjoy. This included a zone of interaction even in a public context that was protected by Article 8. It was particularly important to maintain this when technological progress meant that intrusion and dissemination were ever easier. The Court was also sympathetic to her

---

[31] (App No 53678/00), 16 November 2004.
[32] (2005) 40 EHRR 1.

complaints of the harassment by the paparazzi and the lack of any public interest justification for the photographs. She was not like a politician who might have to tolerate a narrower zone of privacy. The pictures contributed nothing to the public debate about matters of general importance and the German court's attempt to distinguish between occasions when she was in or out of the public eye was too vague to be workable.

6.28 In *Sciacca* v *Italy*,[33] the Court drew from *Von Hannover* that the concept of 'private life' included a person's right to their image and its publication. Private life also includes a zone of interaction with others even in a public context and the zone is enlarged for an 'ordinary' person. The fact that they were the subject of criminal proceedings did not lead to automatic curtailment. In this case the Italian Revenue Police were investigating the applicant's school which they alleged was bogus. The police released their mugshot of the applicant to the media and it was this action which led to her complaint of a breach of Article 8. The court agreed that releasing the photograph was an 'interference' with her private life and, since there were no regulations for when the police could issue photographs of suspects to the media, the interference was not 'prescribed by law' and consequently constituted a violation of Article 8. If the suspect is a public figure and especially if the circumstances of the offence are matters of public interest, the balance is likely to be different. In those circumstances, the Article 10 interests in freedom of expression are likely to prevail.[34]

6.29 The particular sensitivity of photographic images and absence of any clear-cut division between public and private spaces also characterized the case of *Peck* v *UK*.[35] Peck was a disturbed young man who had tried to commit suicide by slashing his wrists in a back street. He had been seen by the local council's CCTV operator who had sent the police to help him. The council had released stills and short clips of the film as part of its campaign to demonstrate the usefulness of the cameras. However, the European Court found these later actions to be a violation of Peck's Article 8 rights. He was in a public street but not taking part in a public event. He carried a knife but he was not charged with a criminal offence. He risked being seen by a casual passer-by, but not having this distressing event broadcast to the wider public.

---

[33] (2006) 43 EHRR 20.
[34] *Verlangsgruppe News Gmbh* v *Austria (No 2)* (App No 10520/02), 14 December 2006.
[35] (2003) 36 EHRR 41.

Intrusions by the Media: The UK

The positive obligation implied by Article 8 has had a significant impact on **6.30** the development of media law in the UK. The causes of action which existed before the HRA have not been taken away. They could not. Section 11 of the Act makes clear that the rights it introduced were intended to be supplementary to any existing claims. However, under the stimulus of Article 8 the courts have developed the idea that redress may be given where there is a reasonable expectation of privacy. If that expectation exists, it is no longer necessary to show that there was a relationship of confidence between the claimant and the media or between the claimant and the media's source. However, the expectation is not always determinative: any public interest in the publication will always be relevant, and the extent of prior publicity may also tilt the case against intervention.

The House of Lords signalled this change even before the European Court decided **6.31** *Von Hannover.* In *Campbell* v *MGN Ltd*,[36] the supermodel Naomi Campbell was photographed leaving a session of Narcotics Anonymous. The *Daily Mirror* used the picture to illustrate its story which castigated her for telling lies when she denied being a drug user. Campbell could not complain about the exposure of her untruthfulness but the House of Lords held (by a bare majority of 3:2) that the use of the photograph was an intrusion too far. The majority thought that the NA sessions were the equivalent of medical treatment whose privacy the law should be particularly ready to protect. The swing vote was cast by Lord Hope who considered that the photograph was the critical issue. Even though taken on a public street, it was a gross invasion of her privacy because it identified the clinic and showed her as she left.

Campbell was followed by another House of Lords decision in which Articles 8 **6.32** and 10 had been in direct competition. A mother was on trial for the murder of her child. There was evidence that the victim's sibling would suffer psychiatric harm if she and the family were identified in media reporting of the case. An application was made to the High Court to require the coverage to be anonymized. The House of Lords held that the categorization in previous cases, where media restrictions were sought for the benefit of children and vulnerable adults, was now obsolete.[37] Instead the courts should view the matter through

---

[36] [2004] 2 AC 457.
[37] *Re S (Identification: Restrictions on Publication)* [2005] 1 AC 593 at [17].

the lens of these two Convention rights. Lord Steyn identified four principles that needed to be applied:

- Neither article has precedence as such over the other.
- Where the values under the two articles are in conflict, an intense focus on the comparative importance of the specific rights being claimed was necessary.
- The justification for the interference with each right must be taken into account.
- The proportionality test must be applied to each (see further chapter 9).

6.33 The first of these propositions is a striking contrast to that adopted in *Sunday Times* v *UK*[38] which had expressly said that Article 10 did *not* involve a balance between rights, but a general right of freedom of expression which was subject to narrowly drawn qualifications. It may also be thought that it was difficult to square with s 12(4) which required particular regard to be paid to the right of freedom of expression. However, these approaches probably became unsustainable in circumstances where the European Court found that States were under a positive obligation to protect one person's Convention Article 8 rights against another who claimed to be exercising Article 10 Convention rights. Balancing one right against the other in the particular circumstances of the case was then the most likely solution. But it is not easy: the Article 8 right lacks clear definition; the interests to be 'balanced' are not capable of precise measurement; and it is often very difficult to conceptualize a common scale on which all the disparate considerations can be placed.

6.34 *Douglas* v *Hello! Magazine Ltd* also illustrated the effect of the positive obligation in Article 8. Catherine Zeta-Jones and Michael Douglas had a very large and very fashionable wedding in New York. They sold the right to publish exclusive photographs to *OK!* magazine. Guests were not allowed to take pictures of their own. One of the 350 or so people at the occasion took sneak photographs and sold them to *OK!*'s rival, *Hello!* The married couple and *OK!* applied unsuccessfully for an injunction to stop publication of the unauthorized photographs. The Court of Appeal said that because of the deal that they had done, breaches of any remaining rights of confidence or privacy could be compensated in damages.[39] After four years and a trial of the action the case returned to the Court of Appeal. This time the Court said that despite the large number of guests and the sale of rights, the event still remained a private occasion. Guests could describe it in their own words, but photographs were a

---

[38] (1979–80) 2 EHRR 245.
[39] *Douglas* v *Hello! Magazine Ltd* [2001] 2 All ER 289, CA.

different matter. The couple were understandably distressed at the publication of unauthorized pictures. In view of *Campbell* and *Von Hannover* the Court of Appeal thought that they had an unanswerable claim for infringement of their private information and it had been wrong previously to refuse an injunction.[40]

Since then the Canadian folk singer, Loreena McKennitt, has successfully sued **6.35** the author of a book about their lives together which drew on both confidential and private information.[41] The singer had a reasonable expectation of privacy in the material which the book relayed about her personal life, her relationships with others, and her reaction to the death of her fiancé. The author argued that the two of them had lived through these experiences together and her freedom to tell her story was engaged. However, the judge and the Court of Appeal agreed that the balance in this case came down firmly in favour of the singer. She had a reasonable expectation that her former friend and business colleague would preserve her privacy and confidentiality. There was no competing public interest which favoured their publication.

The courts are still trying to give content to the nebulous notion of a reasonable **6.36** expectation of privacy in relation to activities that take place in public. Naomi Campbell had been photographed in a public street but the important additional fact was that she was leaving her NA session. Lady Hale said in that case (at para 154) that Article 8 would not prevent a person being photographed in the street if they had just popped out for a pint of milk. But, according to the Court of Appeal in *Murray* v *Big Pictures (UK) Ltd*,[42] even that may be too simplistic. The author JK Rowling was walking in an Edinburgh street with her husband and 18-month-old child. Without their knowledge, their picture was taken and sold to the media. The child, through his parents, brought an action for infringement of his Article 8 rights. The claim was struck out by the judge but the action was restored by the Court of Appeal which said that whether there had been a reasonable expectation of privacy depended on all the circumstances. It was not determinative that the family had been on a public street, or that they had simply been walking to a local café, or that there had been no element of harassment, or that the child was oblivious to the taking of the photograph or its publication. The Court thought that the judge had given too little attention to the fact that the claim was brought on behalf of the child whose expectation of privacy was greater than that of his world-famous mother. The photograph had not been taken to illustrate an Edinburgh street scene but to capitalize on the public

---

[40] *Douglas* v *Hello! Magazine Ltd (No 3)* [2006] QB 125, CA.
[41] *McKennitt* v *Ash* [2008] QB 73, CA.
[42] [2008] EMLR 12.

appetite for material about his mother. It was not necessary for the claimant to show that the intrusion would be regarded as offensive by reasonable people. If there was a reasonable expectation of privacy, then it would be necessary to consider where the balance came down as between that right of the claimant and the defendant's rights under Article 10.

6.37 Prior publicity must be considered—see HRA, s 12(4)(a)(i) above. It may mean that the claimant has no reasonable expectation of privacy. The provision may also affect the balance between those expectations and the defendant's right of freedom of expression. In *Mosley v News Group Ltd*,[43] video footage had been taken of the claimant with prostitutes. A clip was posted on the defendant's website for twenty-four hours before it was taken down after the claimant's protests. Nonetheless, it had been viewed by about 1.49 million people during that period and the judge concluded that the claimant in those circumstances could no longer have a reasonable expectation of privacy. However, an expedition trial was ordered at which the claimant succeeded in showing that his Article 8 right had been violated.[44]

6.38 There is, however, no hard-edged boundary between material which is in the public domain and that which is not. The *Campbell* and *Murray* cases show that to be so. Another example was *Green Corns Ltd v Claverley Group Ltd*.[45] The owners of children's care homes obtained an injunction to prevent a local newspaper from publishing the addresses of the homes. Previous articles had reported a campaign by local residents against other homes run by the claimant. These had led to a violent demonstration outside one of the homes and it had had to be abandoned. The addresses covered by the injunction might be known in the immediate locality, but not more widely. In these circumstances, there was still a purpose in the injunction which was justified when the rights of the owners of the homes and the children they housed were balanced against those of the newspaper.

6.39 Criminal proceedings (generally) take place in public and so there can usually be no reasonable expectation that convictions will remain private. However, it does not follow that offenders can be named and shamed with impunity. Schemes of this kind that are promoted by public authorities have to be carefully thought through to avoid infringing Article 8 rights,[46] and the disclosure of the identities and addresses of convicted paedophiles can be particularly sensitive because of the

---

[43] [2008] EWHC 687 (QB).
[44] *Mosley v News Group Ltd* [2008] EWHC 1777 (QB) (See 6.41).
[45] [2005] EMLR 31.
[46] *R (Ellis) v Chief Constable of Essex* [2003] 2 FLR 566, DC.

risk of vigilante violence which might entail positive obligations under Article 2 as well as Article 8.[47]

Section 12 of the HRA also requires the court to have regard to the public **6.40** interest in any material which a claimant seeks to restrain. That accords with the approach of the European Court. The public interest argument succeeded in *Long Beach Ltd and Denis Sassou Nguesso v Global Witness Ltd.*[48] The case concerned credit card statements belonging to the son of the President of the Republic of the Congo and the director of the marketing arm of the State's oil company. The statements had been obtained by the NGO, Global Witness, after they had been used in evidence in litigation in Hong Kong. The NGO wrote articles about them and posted them on its website. The judge doubted whether there was any reasonable expectation of privacy in them, but concluded that in any case the claimant was likely to fail on the public interest aspect. The statements provided evidence that part of the revenues from the country's sale of natural resources had been diverted improperly to pay for the claimant's personal living expenses. Once there was good reason to doubt the propriety of a public official there was a public interest in those affairs being open to public scrutiny.

The *News of the World* was unsuccessful at the trial of the Max Mosley privacy **6.41** claim essentially because it was unable to persuade the court that the S&M event which the claimant had arranged with prostitutes also had a Nazi theme or mocked the victims of the Holocaust. The newspaper's other public interest arguments also failed: the S&M activities may have technically been assaults but they did not amount to the serious criminality which would have justified publishing details (and photographs and film) of the intensely private sexual activities, nor could the fact that some people would find the admitted activities intensely unattractive in themselves begin to satisfy the public interest test.[49]

Sometimes different analyses can be used to reach a common conclusion. **6.42** Thus in *Lord Browne of Madingley v Associated Newspapers Ltd,*[50] the former chief executive of BP did not succeed in obtaining a comprehensive injunction against his former gay lover. The story which the man wished to tell included an allegation that Lord Browne had improperly used BP's personnel to help

---

[47] *R v Chief Constable of North Wales ex p Thorpe* [1999] QB 396, CA.
[48] [2007] EWHC 1980 (QB).
[49] See *Mosley v News Group Newspapers Ltd* [2008] EWHC 1777 (QB).
[50] [2008] QB 103, CA.

start up a business which the lover could then run. The Court of Appeal commented that Lord Browne could not obtain an injunction in relation to this information. Either he had no reasonable expectation that such impropriety would remain confidential or private, or, alternatively, the public interest required the defendant's Article 10 right to be given priority.

6.43   HRA, s 12(4)(b) also requires a Court to have regard to any relevant privacy code when deciding issues concerning journalistic, literary, or artistic material. The Press Complaints Commission's Code acknowledged that photography might be unacceptable on private or public property where there was a reasonable expectation of privacy. This encouraged the House of Lords in the *Campbell* case to find that such a reasonable expectation could exist notwithstanding that the model was photographed on a public street. The statutory obligation, though, is only *to have regard to* a relevant code. A contractor who provided chilled meals for several NHS trusts was unable to stop a broadcast of undercover filming which showed poor standards of hygiene. The claimant argued that they had not been given the opportunity to respond and comment on the criticisms of their performance as the broadcasting code would normally require. But the judge ruled that the code was a code of practice for the regulator (whose sanctions did not include prior restraint), it did not embody mandatory requirements which the court had to apply. The claimant was unlikely to show that there had been any breach of confidence and, in any case, there was a strong public interest defence.[51]

6.44   Article 8 does not always work in opposition to Article 10. The right to personal autonomy which lies behind Article 8 may include the right to share personal experiences with others. Munby J has made this point when rejecting applications for injunctions by those seeking to protect a child or vulnerable (but competent) adult.[52] In those cases, Article 8 as well as Article 10 worked in favour of the individual's right to tell his or her story. As long as the individual has the legal competence to take such decisions themselves, it is not for the court to judge whether they are wise or foolish. It is, of course, otherwise, if the individual in question is not competent. Then the Court will have to strike the usual balance between the protection of the privacy rights of the individual against the media's right of freedom of expression.[53]

---

[51] *Tillery Valley Foods* v *Channel Four Television* [2004] EWHC 1075 (QB).
[52] See *Re Roddy (A Child) (Identification: Restrictions on Publication)* [2004] 2 FLR 949 and *E (by her Litigation Friend the Official Solicitor)* v *Channel 4* [2005] EMLR 30.
[53] See, eg *T (by her Litigation Friend the Official Solicitor)* v *BBC* (2008) 1 FLR 281.

Remedies

Although Article 8 has generated new rights in the UK in respect of misuse **6.45** of private information, the level of damages which the courts will award for non-pecuniary loss have been very modest until the Max Mosley case. Naomi Campbell received £2,500 plus a further £1,000 aggravated damages. Michael Douglas and Catherine Zeta-Jones were each awarded £3,500 for the distress arising from the publication of unauthorized photographs of their wedding, plus a further £7,000 between them for the cost and inconvenience of having to hurriedly select authorized photographs to be published by *OK!* magazine. Lady Archer received £2,500 for leaked information about her cosmetic surgery,[54] and Loreena McKennitt obtained judgment for £5,000 for the publication of personal and confidential information in Niema Ash's book. At the Max Mosley trial Eady J ruled that exemplary damages were not available, but he did award £60,000 in compensatory damages.

This is not the whole story. In the *Douglas* v *Hello!* litigation, *OK!* magazine **6.46** successfully pursued an appeal to the House of Lords against the decision of the Court of Appeal that it had no action for breach of confidence against *Hello!*. The Lords restored the judgment of Lindsay J who had found that *OK!* was entitled to approximately £1 million for the financial loss which it had suffered by the publication of *Hello!*'s unauthorized photographs.[55] Even where a claimant cannot prove financial loss, the non-pecuniary damages may only be part of what an unsuccessful defendant has to pay. Naomi Campbell had agreed a conditional fee with her lawyers. When she succeeded in the House of Lords, MGN faced a bill of over £1 million for legal costs. The House of Lords refused to find that this constituted a disproportionate interference with the publisher's freedom of expression.[56]

The modest level of compensation may itself be a reason favouring a pre- **6.47** publication injunction as the Court of Appeal commented in *Douglas* v *Hello!* *(No 3)*—see above. However, the HRA, s 12(3) requires that an interim injunction is only granted if the claimant is likely to succeed at trial. In most cases this means that the claimant must show that it is more likely than not that

---

[54] *Lady Archer* v *Williams* [2003] EMLR 38.
[55] *OBG Ltd* v *Allan* [2008] 1 AC 1.
[56] *Campbell* v *MGN Ltd (No 2)* [2005] 1 WLR 3394, HL.

the claim will ultimately be successful.[57] The HRA, s12(2) also means that it is unusual for such an injunction to be made without hearing representations from the defendant.

Threats to Life

6.48   In rare cases people who have been convicted of particularly notorious crimes have been able to persuade the courts that their lives would be at risk if the new identities which they are given on release were to be revealed. Thompson and Venables, for instance, were found guilty of murdering James Bulger at a time when they were only 11 years old. They were sentenced to indefinite detention but, on the expiry of their 'tariff' terms (the penal as opposed to rehabilitative part of their sentence), they were entitled to apply for parole. The President of the Family Division was persuaded that the risk of a vigilante revenge attack was sufficiently strong that their new identities should be protected by an injunction.[58] Similar orders were made to protect the child killer Mary Bell and Ian Huntley's associate, Maxine Carr, after their release.[59] In Convention terms, these measures were necessary to discharge the State's positive obligation under Article 2 to take reasonable measures to protect them against known real and immediate threats to life.[60]

6.49   Mazher Mahmood, the *News of the World*'s investigative reporter, sought an injunction to prevent the Respect MP, George Galloway, from publishing his photograph on the MP's website for similar reasons. He said that his investigations had aroused so much anger from its subjects that he would be at risk if the publication went ahead. However, the judge refused. He doubted whether the photograph by itself would help an attacker who would need to know more fundamentally how to find the journalist. He thought that the real purpose of the application was to protect Mahmood's earning capacity, but that was not an interest which the Convention protected.[61]

6.50   The Serious Organised Crime Act 2005, ss 82–94 creates a statutory scheme for the protection of vulnerable witnesses, informants, and others involved in the criminal legal process. If new identities are given under this programme, it is

---

[57]   *Cream Holdings Ltd v Banerjee* [2005] 1 AC 253.
[58]   *Thompson and Venables v News Group Newspapers Ltd* [2001] Fam 430.
[59]   *X (a Woman Formerly Known as Mary Bell) and Y v News Group Newspapers Ltd* [2003] EMLR 37; *Maxine Carr v News Group Newspapers Ltd* [2005] EWHC 971 (QB).
[60]   See *Osman v UK* (1998) 29 EHRR 245.
[61]   *Mazher Mahmood v Galloway* [2006] EMLR 26.

an offence to reveal them unless it is unlikely that anyone would be harmed as a result. A lesser measure is to allow a witness to give evidence anonymously—see chapter 9. The scheme under SOCA cannot be used to protect defendants (unless they, too, are informants) and, consequently, when notorious criminals are released in the future and given new names, these will have to be protected, if at all, by a *Thompson and Venables* type of injunction.

7

RACIAL AND RELIGIOUS HATRED

Introduction	7.01	Exposing Racism in the Public	
Domestic Law	7.02	Interest	7.25
Discrimination Under the ECHR	7.09	The Wider Picture	7.33
Limiting Racist Expression	7.13		

Introduction

UK statute law contains a number of provisions limiting freedom to express views **7.01** and ideas which involve race hatred. These are discussed below. In the remainder of this chapter we consider how and why the ECHR allows governments to adopt such measures, notwithstanding the right to freedom of expression in Article 10(1). We also consider how the European Court has approached the difficult issues which arise when the media report the views and activities of racists in the public interest.

Domestic Law

Abuse on grounds of race has long been recognized as a form of discrimination. **7.02** It comes within the statutory tort of 'harassment' in s 3A of the Race Relations Act 1976. The 1976 Act is mainly concerned with discrimination at work but also covers discrimination in other fields, in particular the provision of services to the public. It renders employers and principals liable to pay compensation to victims of such harassment, unless they can show that they took reasonable steps to prevent it from occurring.[1] The bad publicity that results from media

---

[1] s 32.

reporting of racial abuse cases is important in ensuring that employers and service providers take these responsibilities seriously.

7.03 The criminal law has prohibited racist speech more willingly as the years have gone by. Initially the Public Order Act 1936 was used. But this required a probable breach of the peace before police could intervene. Then under s 6 of the Race Relations Act 1965 it was an offence to publish material or make a speech which was threatening, abusive, or insulting, and likely to stir up racial hatred, with intent to cause such hatred. In 1976 this offence was relocated in the 1936 Act and the intent requirement abandoned.

7.04 Part 3 of the Public Order Act 1986 now contains a series of criminal offences involving acts intended or likely, 'having regard to the circumstances', to stir up racial hatred. The best known of these is the use of words or behaviour or display of written material of a threatening, abusive, or insulting nature.[2] However, publishing or distributing such material in writing is also an offence (s 19), as are playing recordings of and broadcasting such material.[3] The latter offence could, in theory, be used against journalists who produce programmes about the racist views of others (see below), though to date this has not happened. It is also an offence under s 23 of the 1986 Act to possess such racially inflammatory material with a view to its use in any of these ways.

7.05 More controversially, the Racial and Religious Hatred Act 2006 has inserted a new Part 3A into the 1986 Act.[4] This finally came into force on 1 October 2007 after some years of legislative debate. The government's long-standing intention was to protect the Muslim community from attacks which were a backlash against Islamic extremism. The general structure of Part 3A corresponds to Part 3, the various equivalent offences being concerned with 'hatred against a group of persons defined by reference to religious belief or lack of religious belief'.[5] However, in this group of offences the act or material concerned must be 'threatening'—it is not enough for it to be 'abusive or insulting'. Also the relevant act must be carried out with the intention to stir up racial hatred. Section 29J, headed 'Protection of Freedom of Expression', has no equivalent at all in Part 3. It makes clear that nothing in Part 3A 'shall be read or given effect in a way

---

[2] s 18. In 2006 the BNP leader, Nick Griffin, was prosecuted but acquitted for this offence after the BBC had screened a speech in which he described Islam as a 'wicked, vicious faith' and said Muslims were turning Britain into a 'multi-racial hell hole'.

[3] ss 21 and 22.

[4] See ss 29A–29N.

[5] s 29A.

which prohibits or restricts discussion, criticism or expressions of antipathy, dislike, ridicule, insult or abuse of particular religions or the beliefs or practices of their adherents, or of any other belief system or the beliefs or practices of its adherents, or proselytising or urging adherents of a different religion or belief system to cease practising their religion or belief system.'

Along with the requirement that the speaker must have intended to stir up racial hatred, this provision will provide a defence to journalists republishing extremist religious speech in their professional work. Prosecutions under Part 3 and 3A can only be brought by or with the consent of the Attorney General. **7.06**

The Crime and Disorder Act 1998 provides for the basic public order offences in the 1986 Act to be treated more severely where they are racially or religiously aggravated.[6] Again, media reporting of criminal proceedings for such crimes is an important deterrent. **7.07**

All of these offences prohibit speech, even though there is no suggestion that it would be likely to cause immediate violence or disorder. The underlying thinking is that allowing speech which abuses racial or religious groups lends respectability to racist views, which in turn may cause a breakdown in public order. Along with the civil law of race discrimination these provisions recognize that there are fundamental rights of others, not to be abused and discriminated against, which must be protected from the evils of racist sentiment. As we will see the ECHR and other international human rights instruments allow, and indeed encourage, such legislation. **7.08**

Discrimination Under the ECHR

The ECHR does not contain a free-standing right not to be discriminated against on grounds of race, or indeed any unlawful grounds. In this sense it lags well behind developments at a global level.[7] However, on 1 April 2005 Protocol 12 came into force having obtained the necessary ten ratifications. It requires that the enjoyment of 'any right set forth by law shall be secured without discrimination'.[8] At present the UK government has no plans to ratify this general non-discrimination provision, or to include **7.09**

---

[6] s 31.
[7] Contrast, for example, Article 26 of the International Covenant on Civil and Political Rights which prohibits discrimination in any field regulated and protected by public authorities.
[8] The list of grounds constituting unlawful discrimination in Article 1 of the Twelfth Protocol are exactly the same as in Article 14 of the Convention.

it as a 'Convention right' for the purposes of the Human Rights Act 1998.

7.10 There is some authority to suggest that discrimination based on race may of itself amount to degrading treatment for the purposes of Article 3 of the ECHR,[9] but the differences of treatment relied upon would have to be so extreme as to denote 'contempt', or be designed to 'humiliate or debase'. However, Article 14 does provide a 'subsidiary', or 'accessory', right to be free from discrimination by stating that: 'The enjoyment of the rights and freedoms set forth in this Convention shall be secured without discrimination on any ground such as sex, race, colour, language, religion, political or other opinion, national or social origin, association with a national minority, property, birth or other status.'

7.11 This enables a complaint of unequal treatment to be made in conjunction with one or more of the substantive rights under the Convention or the Protocols. A violation of Article 14 coupled with the provision creating the substantive right will be established if the complainant can show that the facts in issue in the complaint 'fall within the ambit of the substantive provision'[10] or, put differently, that there has been discrimination in the context of one of the rights or freedoms guaranteed. The connection between the substantive Convention right and the discrimination may be a loose one and it is not necessary to establish a violation of the substantive right in order for a claim under Article 14 to succeed. For example, if a contracting party were to grant a series of new broadcasting licences this would enhance, rather than restrict, freedom of expression. But if it resolved to give them only to its own nationals, although the measure would not involve any interference with the Article 10(1) rights of those excluded, the rights given by Articles 10 and 14 together would be violated.

7.12 Article 14 does not prohibit all differential treatment between those in a comparable situation. The Court has accepted that discrimination may be justified on a 'reasonable and objective' basis.[11] This requires the government to demonstrate a legitimate aim and that the discriminatory measure is proportionate. In any case where the discrimination is because of differing race or nationality, the contracting State will almost certainly fail in any attempt to justify the differential treatment.[12]

---

[9] *Abdulaziz, Cabales and Balkandali* v *UK* (1985) 7 EHRR 471, at para 91.
[10] *Abdulaziz*, at para 71.
[11] *Belgian Linguistics Case (No 2)* (1968) 1 EHRR 252, at para 9.
[12] See, eg *East African Asians* v *UK* (1981) 3 EHRR 76.

Limiting Racist Expression

Although the ECHR does not yet contain a substantive right to be free of discrimination, it does contain provisions which enable contracting parties to control race hate expression. In addition to the limitations on the right of freedom of expression in Article 10(2), which include the protection of the rights of others, Article 17 ECHR provides that: 'Nothing in this Convention may be interpreted as implying for any State, group or person any right to engage in any activity or perform any act aimed at the destruction of any of the rights and freedoms set forth herein or at their limitation to a greater extent than is provided for in the Convention.' **7.13**

In *Lawless* v *Ireland (No 3)*,[13] a complaint was made by a member of the IRA who had been detained without trial. The Court rejected an argument, based on Article 17, that his membership of a terrorist organization was enough to deprive him of the rights of liberty and a fair trial in Articles 5 and 6 ECHR. In doing so the Court stated that: 'the purpose of Article 17, in so far as it refers to groups or to individuals, is to make it impossible for them to derive from the Convention a right to engage in or perform any act aimed at destroying in any activity any of the rights and freedoms set forth in the Convention' (at para 7). **7.14**

Race hate propaganda

The Commission and the Court have consistently drawn upon Articles 10(2), 14, and 17 to resist attempts by propagandists to allege violations of Article 10. In 1979, in the applications of *Glimmerveen and Hagenbeek* v *Netherlands*,[14] the Commission considered Article 17 in the context of a conviction for possessing leaflets inciting racial discrimination, with a view to their distribution. The applicants' political party sought an ethnically homogeneous population without any racial mixing. The previous year it had been declared a prohibited organization under the Dutch Civil Code. The leaflets advocated the 'removal' of all 'Surinamers, Turks and other so-called guest workers from the Netherlands'. Glimmerveen claimed that his conviction violated his rights under Article 10. The Dutch government accepted that it interfered with his right of freedom of expression but argued that Article 17 of the Convention prevented him from exploiting Article 10 to enable him to disseminate racist material. **7.15**

---

[13] (1961) 1 EHRR 15.
[14] App Nos 8348/78 & 8406/78 (1979) 18 DR 187.

The Commission agreed, stating that the 'general purpose of Article 17 is to prevent totalitarian groups from exploiting in their own interests the principles enunciated by the Convention.' It went on: 'To achieve that purpose it is not necessary to take away every one of the rights and freedoms guaranteed from persons found to be engaged in activities aimed at the destruction of any of those rights and freedoms. Article 17 covers those rights which, if invoked, will facilitate the attempt to derive therefrom a right to engage personally in activities aimed at the destruction of any of the rights and freedoms set forth in the Convention' (at p 195).

7.16 The Commission had no difficulty finding that the views expressed in Glimmerveen's leaflets were aimed at the destruction of Convention rights. These were identified as the subsidiary right under Article 14, the possibility that race discrimination might amount to degrading treatment under Article 3 (see above) and the provisions of the Fourth Protocol prohibiting collective or individual expulsion of nationals and collective expulsion of aliens. The Commission concluded that: 'The Netherlands' authorities in allowing the applicants to proclaim freely and without penalty their ideas would certainly encourage the discrimination prohibited by [these] provisions of the Convention . . . [such activities being] contrary to the text and spirit of the Convention' (at p 196).

The application was therefore ruled inadmissible by reason of Article 17.

7.17 In *Kuhnen* v *Federal Republic of Germany*,[15] the applicant was a neo-Nazi journalist who had been convicted of an offence prohibiting the dissemination of anti-democratic propaganda which challenged 'the notion of understanding amongst peoples' by unconstitutional organizations. His leaflets proclaimed that his organization, the 'ANS', was *'against*: capitalism, communism, Zionism, estrangement by means of masses of foreign workers . . .'. The conviction was based on a finding that the ANS was unconstitutional as an organization which sought the revival of the Nazi party (NSDAP) and national socialism in Germany, and with it 'the state of violence and illegality which existed in Germany between 1933 and 1945'. The criminal court also found that the material could revive anti-Semitic and racist sentiments. Kuhnen contended that Article 17 did not apply in his case because the ANS only advocated the reinstatement of NSDAP as a constitutional party by legal means. The Commission declared the application to be manifestly ill-founded. It stated that the interference with Kuhnen's Article 10 rights represented by the conviction had legitimate aims under Article 10(2), namely the interests of national security and public safety

---

[15] App No 12194/86, (1988) 56 DR 205.

and the protection of the rights of others. It also considered that the applicant was indeed trying to use Article 10 in the way prohibited by Article 17 because, as the criminal court had found, by the very act of advocating Nazism his publications were 'aimed at impairing the basic order of freedom and democracy'.[16] Because of this, the interference was 'necessary in a democratic society'.

The Commission's approach in these two cases has been applied consistently by the Court in other race and religious hate cases. In *Norwood* v *UK*,[17] for example, the applicant had placed a BNP poster in his window with a photograph of the Twin Towers on fire and the words 'Islam out of Britain—Protect the British People'. He was convicted of a racially aggravated offence under the Public Order Act 1986. The Court held that Article 17 operated to remove the protection of Article 10 for this act of expression, stating that such a 'general, vehement attack against a religious group, linking the group as a whole with a grave act of terrorism, is incompatible with the values proclaimed and guaranteed by the Convention, notably tolerance, social peace and non-discrimination.'   **7.18**

The Court will, however, look closely at the material to ensure that it really does contain racial or religious hate speech. In *Ceylan* v *Turkey*,[18] the applicant, a prominent Marxist trade unionist, had been convicted for inciting hatred and hostility through a polemical newspaper article. This attacked the government for using 'anti-terrorist' measures to attack Kurdish refugees. But it had not advocated violence in retaliation and had called for the plight of the Kurds to be seen as part of a working class struggle against oppression. The Court acknowledged the racial and other tensions caused by an influx of Kurdish refugees from Iraq but characterized the Article as strong political invective rather than hate speech. On this basis it found a violation of the applicant's Article 10 rights. In *Karkin* v *Turkey*,[19] the Court considered that a speech by another trade union leader which attacked those 'who wanted to destroy the Kurdish people with their dirty war' had not incited hatred on racial grounds. Again a violation was found. In *Muslum Gunduz* v *Turkey (No 1)*,[20] the applicant had been sentenced to two years' imprisonment for the same offence. During an appearance on live television he had attacked contemporary Turkish institutions from an Islamic perspective. The Court considered that his comments were not, in reality, 'hate speech' based on religious intolerance. It found a violation of   **7.19**

---

[16] At pp 209–10.
[17] (App No 23131/03), 16 November 2003.
[18] (1999) 30 EHRR 73.
[19] (App No 43928/98), 23 September 2003.
[20] (App No 35071/97), 4 December 2003.

Article 10 observing that the domestic courts should have given greater weight to his engagement in a lively public debate.

Holocaust denial

7.20 The Commission and Court have also consistently rejected as manifestly ill-founded, complaints asserting the right to engage in holocaust denial. In *X v Federal Republic of Germany*,[21] the applicant had been successfully sued in defamation by a Jewish neighbour after he displayed a pamphlet on his garden fence describing the Holocaust as a 'Zionist swindle'. The Commission agreed with the domestic court that this was an attack on the reputation of his neighbour, whose grandfather had died in Auschwitz, and that the ruling therefore pursued the legitimate aim of protecting the others specified in Article 10(2) ECHR. The restriction was considered proportionate because the pamphlet failed to observe the principles of tolerance and broadmindedness upon which democratic society rests.[22] In *T v Belgium*,[23] the applicant had edited a pamphlet which sought to minimize and justify Nazi atrocities, particularly at Auschwitz. The author, Degelle, had forfeited his right to publish political work through committing wartime national security offences. The applicant had been convicted of availing herself of his forfeited right. She was imprisoned for a year, heavily fined, and all the pamphlets were destroyed. The Commission accepted that these severe measures were aimed at preventing disorder and maintaining the authority of the judiciary within the meaning of Article 10(2) ECHR, and that the interference was necessary in a democratic society 'two hallmarks of which are tolerance and broadmindedness'.[24]

7.21 A series of Court and Commission decisions since *T v Belgium* have made clear that Article 17 removes any denial of the objectively established facts of the Holocaust from the protection of Article 10. See, for example, *Garaudy v France*[25] where the applicant's publication of a book had brought about his conviction for denying crimes against humanity, publishing racially defamatory statements, and inciting religious or racial hatred and violence. In rejecting the application as inadmissible the Court identified Holocaust denial as a form of group libel. It described it as 'one of the most serious forms of racial defamation of Jews

---

[21] (1982) 29 DR 194.
[22] At 197.
[23] App No 9777/82, (1983) 34 DR 158.
[24] At pp 170–1.
[25] (App No 65831/01), 24 June 2003.

and incitement to hatred of them'.[26] Although the Court has never been asked
to rule directly on specific Holocaust denial legislation in one of the countries
where it exists, it seems clear from these cases that in principle such laws can be
regarded as pursuing legitimate aims under Article 10(2) and that it would be
possible to defend their application as 'necessary in a democratic society'. Indeed,
in *Faurisson* v *France*,[27] the UN Human Rights Committee cited *Glimmerveen*
and *X* v *Federal Republic of Germany* (above) in finding that such legislation is
compatible with Article 19 of the International Covenant on Civil and Political
Rights 1966 (which closely corresponds to Article 10 ECHR). The applicant had
been convicted under the French Gayssot Act, passed in 1990, for denying the
Holocaust in a magazine interview. The conviction was found to be a necessary
restriction on his freedom of expression, the Committee noting in particular
evidence that in France 'denial of the Holocaust [is] the principal vehicle for
anti-semitism'.[28]

Lehideux and Isorni v France

In this important case,[29] the Court considered a conviction for 'making a **7.22**
public defence of crimes of collaboration with the enemy'. The applicants
were representatives of two lawful associations which sought to overturn the
conviction of the leader of the wartime Vichy government, Marshal Pétain, for
acts of collaboration with the Nazis. They had placed a pro-Petain advertisement
in a newspaper. While expressly disapproving of the Nazi atrocities, it made no
mention of his involvement in Nazi persecution of French Jews. The applicants
were convicted because they had failed to mention this and had published an
'unqualified . . . eulogy of the policy of collaboration'. In doing so they 'were
justifying the crimes committed in furtherance of that policy'.

The Court re-emphasized that any justification of a pro-Nazi policy or denial of **7.23**
'clearly established historical facts—such as the Holocaust' would be removed
from the protection of Article 10 ECHR by Article 17,[30] and described the
omissions in the text 'about events directly linked with the Holocaust' as 'morally
reprehensible'. However, these omissions had to be considered in the context
of the passage of time since the war, the need for 'every country to debate

---

[26] Other examples are *Honsik* v *Austria* App No 25062/94, (1995) 83 DR 77 at 84, and
Witzsch v *Germany* (App No 7485/03), 13 December 2005.
[27] (1997) 2 BHRC 1.
[28] At para 9.7.
[29] *Lehideux and Isorni* v *France* (1998) 5 BHRC 540.
[30] At paras 47 and 53.

its own history openly and dispassionately'[31] and the fact that the applicants' aims in inserting the advertisement were the same as their organizations' which were lawfully constituted and had never been prosecuted.[32] In light of these considerations, the Court did not consider that conviction for a criminal offence in connection with the advertisement met a 'pressing social need'. In reaching this conclusion the Court invoked the *Handyside* principles of 'pluralism, tolerance and broadmindedness'.

7.24   *Lehideux* v *France* indicates the Court's concern to ensure that Articles 10(2) and 17 are not used to interfere with freedom of political expression in areas other than race hate speech and Holocaust denial, in particular where controversial areas of a State's history are being debated.

Exposing Racism in the Public Interest

7.25   Different issues arise where racist statements are reproduced by the media in reporting on the activities of racists. A balancing exercise is required between two important principles: (i) freedom of dissemination of information; and (ii) the protection of the rights of racial minorities.

7.26   This exercise was undertaken by the full Court in its decision in the case of *Jersild* v *Denmark*.[33] The applicant had compiled a television documentary about a group of openly racist youths in Copenhagen known as the 'Greenjackets'. The broadcast included extracts from a long interview with them. In these the youths made a series of racist comments about 'niggers'. Together with all 'foreign workers', black people were said to be 'animals'. The youths were subsequently convicted of an offence of disseminating racist statements. The applicant was convicted for having 'assisted' their offences. He argued that his conviction violated his Article 10(1) rights. Denmark disputed this, arguing that the interference was 'necessary in a democratic society' to protect the rights of others within the meaning of Article 10(2).

7.27   The case had already split the UN Committee on the Elimination of Racial Discrimination, when it was presented to it by the Danish government, the issue being whether 'due regard' had been paid to the applicant's right of freedom of expression as a journalist.[34] It had also split the Commission, which had found

---

[31] At para 55.
[32] At para 56.
[33] (1994) 19 EHRR 1.
[34] See, at para 21.

a violation by twelve votes to four. It is therefore not surprising that the Court itself was divided on the difficult issue of proportionality. It held, by twelve votes to seven, that the applicant's rights had been violated, the conviction and sentence being disproportionate to the aim of protecting the rights of others.

The majority gave considerable weight to the unique function of the press in **7.28** passing on information to the public as its 'watchdog'.[35] It emphasized once again that 'it is . . . incumbent on [the media] to impart information and ideas of public interest. Not only does the press have the task of imparting such information and ideas: the public also has a right to receive them'. It acknowledged that the potential impact of the particular medium was an important factor in assessing whether the press had complied with its 'duties and responsibilities' and that the audio-visual media often had 'a much more immediate and powerful effect than the print . . . conveying through images meanings which the print media are not able to impart'. But it reiterated that the rights provided for under Article 10 extend to the form as well as to the substance of the expression, so that the courts could not 'substitute their own views for those of the press as to what technique of reporting should be adopted by journalists'[36] and the journalist had a discretion as to the way in which the racist sentiments might be counter-balanced.[37] It also observed, in a passage that has assisted in protecting journalists who republish defamatory statements by interviewees, that: 'News reporting based on interviews, whether edited or not, constitutes one of the most important means whereby the press is able to play its vital role of "public watchdog". The punishment of a journalist for assisting in the dissemination of statements made by another person in an interview would seriously hamper the contribution of the press to discussion of matters of public interest and should not be envisaged unless there are particularly strong reasons for doing so' (at para 35).

The majority found that, on any objective view, the programme could not have **7.29** appeared: 'to have as its purpose the propagation of racist views and ideas. On the contrary, it clearly sought—by means of an interview—to expose, analyse and explain this particular group of youths, limited and frustrated by their social situation, with criminal records and violent attitudes, thus dealing with a matter that already then was of great public concern' (at para 33).

---

[35] See, eg *Observer and Guardian* v *UK* (1991) 14 EHRR 153, at para 59.
[36] At para 31. See also, *Oberschlick* v *Austria* (1991) 19 EHRR 389, at para 67.
[37] At para 37.

7.30   It also noted that the broadcast was a serious Danish news programme intended for a well-informed audience[38] and that it was undisputed that the applicant's aims in compiling the broadcast were journalistic and not racist (at para 36). In the light of these findings of fact, it felt that the conviction of the applicant was disproportionate.

7.31   Even the dissenting opinion in the case was split. Four judges began their opinions by observing poignantly that this was 'the first time that the Court has been concerned with a case of dissemination of racist remarks which deny to a large group of persons the quality of "human beings"', and concluded that the Danish authorities had acted inside the margin of appreciation. They considered it particularly significant that the short section of interview used in the programme represented the 'most crude remarks' made by the youths, 'so it was absolutely necessary to add at least a clear statement of disapproval',[39] which the applicant had failed to do. The other three dissenting judges came down even more strongly against the applicant, observing that the absence of any 'significant reaction on the part of the commentator' to the remarks rendered the statements 'an incitement to contempt not only of foreigners in general but more particularly of black people'. This being so, the defence that the programme would provoke a 'healthy reaction of rejection amongst viewers [displayed] an optimism, which to say the least is belied by experience'.[40]

7.32   The decision in *Jersild* v *Denmark* establishes that the media can report the activities of racists. However, there are certain ground rules. They must take care to maintain their distance and ensure that the presentation does not suggest endorsement of racists' views. Particular care is needed where the media is used as a vehicle for inciteful expression in times of conflict. In *Surek* v *Turkey (No 1)*[41] the applicant newspaper owner had been convicted for publishing readers' letters about military suppression of the Kurds in south-east Turkey. The Court considered the letters were 'an appeal to bloody revenge' and that the tense security situation in the region justified the applicants' conviction.

The Wider Picture

7.33   The European determination to combat hate speech is reflected in Recommendation R (97) 20 of the Committee of Ministers of the Council of Europe which

---

[38]   At para 34.
[39]   At 31, para 3.
[40]   At 32.
[41]   (App No 26682/95), 8 July 1990.

urges States to take 'appropriate steps' to prohibit such speech. Other human rights instruments require strict restraints on the freedom to engage in hate speech. Article 20(2) of the International Covenant on Civil and Political Rights states that 'any advocacy of national, racial or religious hatred that constitutes incitement to discrimination, hostility or violence shall be prohibited by law'. Article 4 of the International Convention on the Elimination of All Forms of Racial Discrimination requires signatories to declare the dissemination of ideas to this effect to be 'an offence punishable by law'. Media incitement to genocide will be severely punished in the international criminal courts and tribunals.[42]

Canada has applied these international norms in its constitutional law.[43]   **7.34**
Australia has a variety of civil and criminal legislation prohibiting race hate speech at both Commonwealth and state levels. In the USA, by contrast, the Supreme Court has used the First Amendment to the Bill of Rights to protect such expression from interference by government because of its content alone. In *Collin* v *Smith*,[44] a local ordinance banning assemblies that would incite hatred of an ethnic, religious, or racial group (intended to prevent the Neo-Nazi party of America marching in Chicago) was struck down. Laws against cross-burning, a Klu Klux Klan method of asserting racial superiority and threatening violence against black people, have proved problematic for the Supreme Court. In the landmark case of *RAV* v *City of St Paul*[45] it considered a local ordinance criminalizing cross-burning which could cause 'anger, alarm or resentment in others on the basis of race, color, creed, religion or gender'. The inclusion in the definition of the offence of the characteristics of the victim/s meant that the expression was being criminalized because of its content and the ordinance was declared unconstitutional. In *Virginia* v *Black*,[46] however, the Court upheld a cross-burning offence which required intent to intimidate without reference to the characteristics of any particular victim/s. Here the offence did not offend the First Amendment because it was prohibiting the cross-burning purely as a 'virulent form of intimidation . . . in light of [its] long and pernicious history as a signal of impending violence'.[47] The expression was therefore being prohibited because it created a risk of imminent violence (not protected by the First Amendment) rather than on the basis of its content.

---

[42] See, most notably, the December 2003 conviction and imprisonment by the Rwanda tribunal of three Hutu radio broadcasters who had called for the 'extermination' of Tutsi 'cockroaches'.

[43] See s 319 of the Canadian Criminal Code prohibiting the wilful promotion of race hate and the Supreme Court case of *R v Keegstra* [1990] 3 SCR 697.

[44] 439 US 916 (1978).

[45] 505 US 377 (1992).

[46] 538 US 343 (2003).

[47] At pp 362–3.

8

OBSCENITY AND BLASPHEMY

Introduction	8.01	The Impact of the HRA on	
Obscenity: ECHR	8.13	Domestic Law	8.35
Blasphemy: ECHR	8.21		

Introduction

Obscene and blasphemous speech (together with racist speech, discussed in **8.01** depth in chapter 7) are regulated, at least in part, because of their ability to offend and shock some or all of the population. Indeed, the protection of individuals from offence as a result of attacks on their religion is really the only justification for prohibiting blasphemous speech.

A number of additional rationales have been advanced for proscribing obscene **8.02** speech, including the harm caused to the individual who is exposed to the obscene material (moral corruption), harm caused by the exploitation of individuals in the making of the obscene material, and more general harms to the population (particularly the female population), by the widespread availability of such material. In relation to restricting expression because it offends, the European Court in *Handyside* v *UK* stated: 'Freedom of expression constitutes one of the essential foundations of a society, one of the basic conditions for its progress and for the development of every man. Subject to paragraph 2 of Article 10, it is applicable not only to "information and ideas" that are favourably received or regarded as inoffensive but also to those that offend, shock or disturb the state or any sector of the population. Such are the demands of pluralism, tolerance and broadmindedness without which there is no "democratic society".'[1]

---

[1] (1976) 1 EHRR 737, at para 49.

8.03 Unfortunately, this worthy sentiment has too often been forgotten by the European Court when deciding cases concerning obscene or blasphemous speech. Obscene and blasphemous speech usually occur in the artistic rather than the political, or commercial, fields. The Court has consistently granted States a substantial margin of appreciation in this regard, first, because the expression in question (unlike political speech) is not considered to be of central importance (see 2.46), and secondly, because the Court is particularly deferential to state regulation of expression where protection of morals is in issue. This is perhaps not surprising given the scope of the European Court's jurisdiction, extending as it does from liberal Northern European States such as The Netherlands to socially conservative Turkey. The Court in *Müller* v *Switzerland*[2] stated: 'It is not possible to find in the legal and social orders of the Contracting states a uniform conception of morals. The view taken of the requirements of morals varies from time to time and from place to place, especially in our era, characterized as it is by a far reaching evolution of opinions on the subject'. (At para 35).

8.04 The domestic courts have adopted a similarly deferential approach to government decision making in this field. Lord Hoffman in *Belfast City Council* v *Miss Behavin' Ltd*[3] stated, in the context of a challenge to a local authority's refusal to licence a sex shop in a central city district:

> If Article 10 . . . [is] engaged at all, [it operates] at a very low level. The right to vend pornography is not the most important right of freedom of expression in a democratic society and the licensing system does not prohibit anyone from exercising it. It only prevents him from using unlicensed premises for that purpose. Even if the council considers that it was not appropriate to have a sex shop anywhere in Belfast, that would only have put its citizens in the same position as most of the rest of the country, in having to satisfy their demand for such products by internet or mail order or going to more liberally governed districts like Soho. This is an area of social control in which the Strasbourg court has always accorded a wide margin of appreciation to the member states, which in terms of the domestic constitution translates into the broad power of judgment entrusted to local authorities by the legislature. If the local authority exercises that power rationally and in accordance with the purposes of the statute, it would require very unusual facts for it to amount to a disproportionate restriction on Convention rights.[4]

8.05 Before discussing the ECHR case law in detail, we briefly outline the domestic law of obscenity and blasphemy.

---

[2] (1988) 13 EHRR 212.
[3] [2007] 1 WLR 1420.
[4] Ibid, *per* Lord Hoffman at para 16. See also, Lady Hale at para 38, where she opined that pornography came below celebrity gossip in the hierarchy of speech which deserves the protection of the law.

Domestic law: obscenity

8.06 The law relating to obscenity and indecency derives from some 20 different statutes and from the common law.[5] It was described by the Williams Committee on Obscenity and Film Censorship as 'a mess'.[6] The simplification that the Williams Committee advocated has, unfortunately, not been adopted by subsequent legislation. Such legislation has, if anything, further complicated the law.

8.07 The common law test for obscenity was laid down in *R* v *Hicklin*[7]: 'whether the tendency of the matter charged as obscenity is to deprave and corrupt those whose minds are open to such immoral influences and into whose hands such a publication might fall.'

8.08 This definition was closely followed by that provided in s 1, Obscene Publications Act 1959: 'an article shall be deemed to be obscene if its effect or (where the article comprises two or more distinct items) the effect of any one of its items is, if taken as a whole, such as to tend to deprave and corrupt persons who are likely, having regard to all relevant circumstances, to read, see or hear the matter contained or embodied in it.'

8.09 Obscene speech is traditionally viewed as relating to sexually explicit material, but the definition is wider than this and extends to, for example, encouraging the use of dangerous drugs[8] or the use of violence.[9]

Domestic law: blasphemy

8.10 The common law offence of blasphemous libel relates to comments about God, holy personages, or articles of the Anglican faith, and is constituted by vilification, ridicule, or indecency. Lord Scarman in *Whitehouse* v *Gay News Ltd and Lemon*,[10] held that the modern law of blasphemy was correctly formulated in Article 214 of *Stephen's Digest of the Criminal Law* (9th edn), which stated: 'Every publication is said to be blasphemous which contains any

---

[5] See Shorts, E and de Than, C, *Civil Liberties, Legal Principles of Individual Freedom* (London: Sweet & Maxwell, 1998), ch 5 for a detailed discussion of the statute and common law in this field.

[6] (1979) Cm 7772.

[7] (1868) LR QB 360.

[8] See, eg *Calder* v *Powell* [1965] 1 QB 509 and *R* v *Skirving* [1985] QB 819.

[9] *Director of Public Prosecutions* v *A&BC Chewing Gum Ltd* [1968] 1 QB 159.

[10] [1979] AC 617. For a more recent consideration of the law of blasphemy, see *R (Green)* v *The City of Westminster Magistrates' Court and others* [2007] EWHC 2785 (High Court rejected claim for judicial review of magistrates' court's refusal to issue a summons for blasphemous libel against the producer of *Jerry Springer: The Opera* and the Director General of the BBC because the prosecution was prevented by Theatres Act 1968, s 2(4) and there was no prima facie case of blasphemous libel).

contemptuous, reviling, scurrilous or ludicrous matter relating to God, Jesus Christ or the Bible, or the formularies of the Church of England as by law established. It is not blasphemous to speak or publish opinions hostile to the Christian religion, or to deny the existence of God, if the publication is couched in decent and temperate language. The test to be applied is as to the manner in which the doctrines are advocated and not to the substance of the doctrines themselves.'

8.11 Thus, the offence relates to 'immoderate or offensive treatment of Christianity or sacred subjects' rather than to moderate and reasoned criticism. The offence is one of strict liability, there being no requirement that the defendant intended to blaspheme.

The rationale for making blasphemers criminally punishable is: 'Their manner, their violence, or ribaldry, or, more fully stated, for their tendency to endanger the peace then and there, to deprave public morality generally, to shake the fabric of society and to be a cause of civil strife.'[11]

8.12 The Law Commission recommended that the offence of blasphemy and blasphemous libel be abolished, but no government has seen fit to follow up this recommendation.[12] Calls to repeal the offence of blasphemy were again heard during discussion of the Bill that eventually became the Racial and Religious Hatred Act 2006.[13] Such calls again fell on deaf ears. However, two years later, Criminal Justice and Immigration Act 2008, s 79, which came into force on 8 July 2008, abolished the common law offences of blasphemy and blasphemous libel in England and Wales.

Obscenity: ECHR

'Interference by a public authority'

8.13 In all the cases concerning obscene speech, the existence of an interference with the applicant's right to freedom of expression has not been seriously disputed. The manner of the interference has included seizure or forfeiture of the offending material,[14] and a criminal conviction followed by a fine[15] or imprisonment.[16] The only argument that could have been invoked by governments to deny an

---

[11] *Bowman* v *Secular Society* [1917] AC 406.
[12] Law Commission, Working Paper No 79, *Offences Against Religion and Public Worship* (1981).
[13] See, eg Liberty's Briefing for Second Reading in the House of Commons on the Racial and Religious Hatred Bill, June 2005, at paras 13–14.
[14] *Müller* v *Switzerland* (1988) 13 EHRR 212.
[15] Ibid.
[16] *Hoare* v *UK* App No 31211/96, [1997] EHRLR 678.

interference with the right to freedom of expression is that obscene publications are not 'expression' within the meaning of Article 10 ECHR. Such an approach has gained some academic[17] and judicial support in the USA, partly as a result of the absolutist nature of the text of the First Amendment (protecting freedom of speech).[18] However, the European Court has, sensibly, rejected this artificial approach, stating in *Müller* v *Switzerland* that Article 10 did not distinguish between the various forms of expression and that artistic expression, including indecent or obscene art, affords the opportunity to take part in the public exchange of cultural, political, and social information and ideas.[19]

'Prescribed by law'

Defining what matters are obscene is notoriously difficult. What to one individual is innocuous, to another is a threat to society. Justice Potter Stuart, in a concurring opinion in *Jacobellis* v *Ohio*,[20] acknowledged that obscenity was difficult (if not impossible) to define, but considered that 'I know it when I see it'. However, this impossibility has not prevented the European Court and Commission from concluding in all cases that the restriction, whatever it may be, is sufficiently certain and predictable to be 'prescribed by law'. **8.14**

'Legitimate aim'

In all the cases concerning obscene speech the legitimate aim is the 'protection of morals'. In *Müller*, the Court intimated that the 'protection of the rights of others' might also be engaged when, as in *Müller*, the obscene material was available by way of exhibition to the general public without adequate warnings. This conclusion was reached in part because individuals had complained about the exhibition of the obscene paintings.[21] **8.15**

'Necessary in a democratic society'

One of the first Article 10 ECHR cases to be heard by the European Court concerned English obscenity legislation. In *Handyside* v *UK*,[22] the European Court enunciated a number of general principles in relation to the right to freedom of expression. *Handyside* concerned a book entitled **8.16**

---

[17] See, eg Schauer, F, *Free Speech: A Philosophical Enquiry* (Cambridge: CUP, 1982) ch 12.
[18] See, eg *Roth* v *US* 354 US 476 (1957).
[19] At para 27. The House of Lords adopted a similar approach in *Belfast City Council* v *Miss Behavin' Ltd* [2007] 1 WLR 1420.
[20] 378 US 184 (1964), at 197.
[21] See para 30.
[22] (1976) 1 EHRR 737.

The Little Red Schoolbook, which was designed to be a reference book for 12- to 18-year-old children. It contained chapters on, *inter alia,* sex (both heterosexual and homosexual), use of drugs, and pornography. The book adopted an anti-authoritarian approach to these topics; for example, when discussing relationships no mention was made of marriage. The police seized both copies of the book and the book matrix. The applicant was convicted under the Obscene Publications Acts 1959 and 1964 and was fined. The magistrates had concluded that the book, bearing in mind its target audience, was likely to 'deprave and corrupt' a substantial proportion of that audience. The magistrates placed reliance, in reaching their conclusion, on the anti-authoritarian nature of the work and the likelihood that it would undermine teaching by parents, the Church, and others in authority. Both the Commission and the Court concluded that the prosecution, conviction, and seizure of the book was 'necessary in a democratic society' and within the State's margin of appreciation. The Court noted that when interferences with freedom of expression are for the 'protection of morals', the State has a significant margin of appreciation. *A fortiori,* where the protection of children is in issue. The applicant contended that the seizure, prosecution, and conviction were not 'necessary in a democratic society' as the book was on sale in a large number of other European States. It had also not been the subject of prosecution in the Isle of Man or Northern Ireland. A prosecution under the Scots law of obscenity had been brought, but it had been unsuccessful. The Court brushed this argument aside by relying on the State's margin of appreciation. The Court noted that a revised edition of the book with the offending passages taken out had been allowed to circulate freely which, notwithstanding the applicant's arguments to the contrary, indicated that the national authorities wished to limit themselves to what was strictly necessary.

8.17 A similar approach was taken by the Court in *Müller* v *Switzerland,*[23] which concerned three paintings in a public exhibition. The national courts considered the paintings obscene as they depicted (amongst other things) sexual relations between men and animals. The national courts convicted the applicants of publication of obscene items, fined them, and ordered the confiscation of the paintings. These paintings were returned eight years later. The Court concluded that both the fine and the confiscation were within Switzerland's margin of appreciation, particularly as the public had free access to the paintings since they were displayed in an exhibition which sought to attract the public at large.[24]

---

[23] (1988) 13 EHRR 212.

[24] See also, *Scherer* v *Switzerland* (App No 17116/90), 14 January 1993 and *Hoare* v *UK* App No 31211/96, [1997] EHRLR 678 for contrasting decisions by the Commission on the exhibiting and sale of pornographic videos.

Nearly twenty years after *Müller* v *Switzerland* was decided, the European Court   **8.18**
again considered the protection that should be afforded to offensive art in
Vereinigung Blidender Künstler v *Austria*.[25] *Künstler* concerned the exhibition
of a controversial painting called 'Apocalypse' which was a collage of thirty-four
public figures, including Mother Teresa, all naked and involved in various sexual
activities. One of the individuals depicted was Mr Meischberger, a former general
secretary of the Austrian Freedom Party. He brought proceedings pursuant to
the Copyright Act, seeking an injunction prohibiting the applicant association
from exhibiting or publishing the painting and requesting compensation. Mr
Meischberger contended that the painting debased him and his political activities. The Austrian Courts granted Mr Meischberger an injunction prohibiting
the applicant association from displaying the painting at exhibitions and ordered
that compensation should also be paid. The majority of the Court concluded
that the injunction, which was not limited in time or space, was disproportionate
and therefore not 'necessary in a democratic society'. The majority noted that the
painting was not meant to suggest reality and that the portrayal of the individuals
amounted to a caricature of the persons concerned using satirical elements. The
Court noted that: 'Satire is a form of artistic expression and social commentary
and, by its inherent features of exaggeration and distortion of reality, naturally
aims to provoke and agitate. Accordingly, any interference with an artist's right
to such expression must be examined with particular care.'

The dissenting judgments disputed the satirical nature of the painting. They   **8.19**
further contended that the majority judgment failed to take into account
Mr Meischberger's right to dignity which, they felt, was covered by the protection
of 'rights of others' in Article 10(2) and had previously been recognized as
being of the very essence of the Convention.[26] The majority's decision affords
artistic expression considerably more protection than *Müller* and as such is to
be welcomed; however, it is too early to say whether it signifies a general shift in
the Court's jurisprudence in this area given that it was a Chamber decision by a
very narrow majority.

Selective enforcement

In *W and K* v *Switzerland*,[27] the applicant challenged a prosecution for selling   **8.20**
and renting obscene material on the basis that the enforcement measures taken
by the State were arbitrary and unfair since a number of other film shops

---

[25] (2008) 47 EHRR 5.
[26] See, eg *Pretty* v *UK* (2002) 35 EHRR 1.
[27] (App No 16564/90), 8 April 1991.

rented similar films but were not prosecuted. The Court concluded that the enforcement was proportionate to the legitimate aim pursued and that as the applicants had failed to demonstrate that their prosecution and conviction stemmed from a particular ground of discrimination stated in Article 14 ECHR, the complaint was inadmissible.

Blasphemy: ECHR

'Interference by a public authority'

8.21   An interference with the right to freedom of expression was not disputed in all four of the decisions relating to blasphemous speech under Article 10 ECHR. The nature of the interference included subsequent prosecution of published blasphemous speech,[28] the seizure and forfeiture of a film prior to its exhibition,[29] the prevention of distribution of a video by the refusal to classify it[30] and a small fine.[31] Both the seizure and the refusal to certify the film in question prevented the expression reaching an audience and thus amounted to a prior restraint. Prior restraints are, theoretically, more difficult to justify, although in both cases the Court concluded that such interferences were justifiable.

'Prescribed by law'

8.22   The first opportunity for the European judicial bodies to consider the English law of blasphemous libel arose in the case of *Gay News Ltd and Lemon* v *UK*.[32] Mrs Mary Whitehouse, in the first prosecution for blasphemy since 1922, brought a private prosecution against the magazine, *Gay News,* which had published a poem about a homosexual's conversion to Christianity which metaphorically attributed homosexual acts to Jesus Christ. Leave was obtained[33] for a private prosecution, the jury deciding that both the editor and the publishing company 'unlawfully and wickedly published or caused to be published a blasphemous libel concerning the Christian religion, namely an obscene poem and illustration vilifying Christ in his life and in his crucifixion'.[34] The European Commission concluded that the application brought by the convicted defendants was

---

[28]   *Gay News Ltd and Lemon* v *UK* (1982) 28 DR 77, (1982) 5 EHRR 123.
[29]   *Otto-Preminger-Institut* v *Austria* (1994) 19 EHRR 34.
[30]   *Wingrove* v *UK* (1996) 24 EHRR 1.
[31]   *IA* v *Turkey* (2007) 45 EHRR 30.
[32]   (1982) 28 DR 77, (1982) 5 EHRR 123.
[33]   Leave from a High Court judge is necessary for prosecutions of newspapers: see Law of Libel Amendment Act 1888.
[34]   *R* v *Lemon and Gay News Ltd* [1979] AC 617.

inadmissible. It considered that the law of blasphemous libel was sufficiently certain to be 'prescribed by law', even though four out of five Law Lords had stated that the issue of whether intention to blaspheme was a necessary requirement of the offence was unclear. Their Lordships decided by 3:2 that intention to blaspheme was not a necessary element of the offence. Two of the judges in the majority (namely, Lords Russell and Scarman) and the two dissenting judges (Lords Diplock and Edmund-Davies) were of the view that the state of the law was unclear. The only judge to regard the law as clear on this issue was Viscount Dilhorne. Furthermore, the Law Commission had criticized the state of the law with regard to its lack of clarity. The European Commission noted that the offence of blasphemy cannot by its very nature lend itself to precise legal definition. The Commission viewed the conclusion of the majority of the House of Lords on the issue of the requisite mens rea as not overstepping the limits of an acceptable clarification of the law. It further concluded that the law was sufficiently accessible to the applicants and that the interpretation was foreseeable with appropriate legal advice. The existence of this certainty is doubtful when one recalls that the definition of the offence requires the publication to be 'contemptuous' or 'ludicrous'—inherently subjective terms, particularly when these matters are questions for the jury.

The European Commission's view as to accessibility and foreseeability was **8.23** reiterated by the European Court in the case of *Wingrove* v *UK*,[35] which arose out of the refusal of the British Board of Film Classification (BBFC) to classify a short film called 'Visions of Ecstasy' on the grounds that it violated the criminal law of blasphemy. The BBFC acted within its statutory powers under s 4(1) of the Video Recordings Act 1984. The Commission found no distinguishing features which would enable it to depart from its earlier conclusion, the common law of blasphemy not having materially changed. The refusal to grant a certificate for distribution of the film on the grounds that it was blasphemous was predictable because the BBFC was enjoined by the Home Secretary to avoid classifying works that 'infringed provisions of the criminal law' and the work in question was, on the advice of counsel, blasphemous.

'Legitimate aim'

The UK government in *Gay News* advanced three potential 'legitimate aims': **8.24** 'prevention of disorder', 'protection of morals', and 'protection of the rights of

---

[35] (1996) 24 EHRR 1. Cf the Irish Supreme Court judgement in *Corway* v *Independent Newspapers (Ireland) Ltd* [2001] 1 IRLM 426, which concluded that a private prosecution for blasphemy brought against a newspaper satirizing the priesthood should not be allowed to go ahead because the law of blasphemy was so uncertain.

others'. The Commission rightly rejected the first two justifications, noting that the public authorities had not viewed it as necessary to prosecute the applicants. This left protection of the rights of others as the only justification. The Commission, ignoring the Court's dicta in *Handyside* v *UK* that Article 10 ECHR extended to offensive and shocking expression, concluded that the protection of the rights of citizens not to be offended in their religious feelings by publications was a legitimate aim.

8.25   The European Court adopted the same approach in *Otto-Preminger-Institut* v *Austria*,[36] which concerned the public exhibition of a satirical film with religious subject matter entitled 'Council of Heaven'. Before its first showing the Public Prosecutor instituted criminal proceedings against the manager of the applicant association and a judicial order for seizure of the film was made. Subsequently an order of forfeiture was made. The European Commission—taking a far more robust approach than in *Gay News* v *UK*—concluded by a majority of 9:5 that the seizure was a violation of Article 10, and by 13:1 that the forfeiture was also a violation of Article 10. The Commission concluded that provisions of the Austrian Penal Code were aimed at protecting the 'rights of others' and 'the prevention of disorder', namely preserving religious peace. The Commission did not, therefore, need to decide whether the forfeiture and seizure were also aimed at the 'protection of morals'. The Court adopted a similar analysis, emphasizing the importance of freedom of religion in a democratic society. The Court stated that certain methods of opposing or denying religious beliefs could 'inhibit those who hold such beliefs from exercising their freedom to hold and express them'. It concluded that the respect for religious feelings of believers as guaranteed in Article 9 ECHR can be violated by provocative portrayals of objects of religious veneration.

8.26   This approach was attacked by the applicant in *Wingrove* v *UK*. The applicant contended that the rights of others only extended to an actual, positive right not to be offended and did not include a hypothetical right held by some Christians to avoid disturbance at the prospect of other people viewing the video work without being shocked. Both the Commission and the Court rejected this narrow definition of 'rights of others', although their analysis is somewhat lacking.

'Necessary in a democratic society'

8.27   The Commission in *Gay News* concluded that the law and the prosecution were 'necessary in a democratic society' and not disproportionate. The Commission

---

[36]   (1994) 19 EHRR 34.

explicitly stated that the strict liability nature of the blasphemous libel did not mean that it was disproportionate. The lack of any defence similar to the 'public good' defence under s 4, Obscene Publications Act 1959 also did not trouble the Commission.

The Commission, in *Otto-Preminger*, quoted the *Handyside* dicta relating to the need to protect offensive speech, and concluded that the seizure was not 'necessary in a democratic society'. The film was being shown in an art cinema addressed to a specially interested public, an admission fee was charged, the film was shown late at night and, most important of all in the Commission's view, there was an adequate but inoffensive warning about the contents of the film. The majority of the Commission were of the view that these restrictions were adequate to protect the rights of others by preventing the attendance of children and individuals who might be offended by the content of the film. The Commission went on to conclude that the State's reaction of a complete ban was therefore disproportionate because the measures adopted to limit the viewing were sufficient. The forfeiture, which produced permanent effects in Austria for everyone who wished to receive and impart ideas, was, *a fortiori*, disproportionate. The Court, by a majority of 6:3, however, found that both the seizure and forfeiture of the film were 'necessary in a democratic society' to protect the rights of the majority of the population from gratuitous insults to their religious feelings. The seizure of the film to 'ensure religious peace' was proportionate and within Austria's margin of appreciation. **8.28**

The majority judgment in *Otto-Preminger* has been cogently criticized[37] as unconvincing because, first, it is for viewers or readers rather than the judiciary to assess whether or not a film makes a contribution to any form of public debate capable of furthering human affairs;[38] secondly, the judgment fails to understand that social development in art often proceeds from assertion of offensive ideas to established views—freedom of expression that is limited to inoffensive speech is of little value; thirdly, penalization of dissent against strong, established religion is particularly dangerous in religious societies such as Austria where the power of religion is great. The Court should have protected dissenting voices from an intolerant majority. **8.29**

However, ignoring such criticism, the Court in *Wingrove* adopted a similar approach to that in *Otto-Preminger*, concluding that both the law of blasphemy **8.30**

---

[37] David Pannick QC, 'Religious feelings and the European Court' [1995] PL 7.
[38] This criticism reflects the views of Hoffman LJ in *R v Central Independent Television plc* [1994] Fam 192, where he stated: 'But a freedom which is restricted to what judges think to be responsible or in the public interest is no freedom.'

and the BBFC's refusal to certify the film were 'necessary in a democratic society'. The applicant attacked the BBFC's actions on a number of grounds. First, he argued that there was not a 'pressing social need' to ban a video work on the uncertain assumption that it would violate the law of blasphemy, particularly when the video could potentially be prosecuted after distribution under a panoply of laws including the offence of blasphemy. Secondly, he contended that a complete ban of the video work, which contained no obscenity and no element of vilification of Christ, was disproportionate to the aim pursued.[39] The Court rejected the applicant's submissions and concluded that the ban was both 'necessary in a democratic society' and within the State's 'margin of appreciation'. The Court acknowledged that there were strong arguments for the abolition of the crime of blasphemy and that a number of States had abolished it, but it found that there was insufficient common ground in the legal and social orders of the Member States of the Council of Europe to conclude that the imposition of restrictions on such material was unnecessary in a democratic society.[40]

8.31 In *IA* v *Turkey*,[41] the Court, by a 4:3 majority, decided that a prosecution for blasphemy did not breach Article 10 ECHR. The prosecution in issue was of the managing director of a publishing firm that had published a novel that contained offensive criticism of Mohammed and Islam. The majority, whilst paying lip-service to the oft quoted dicta in *Handyside* that Article 10 ECHR protects offensive and shocking speech, went on to conclude that the conviction was 'necessary in a democratic society'. They reached this conclusion because of the limited nature of the sanction and the nature of the expression; the majority felt that the expression went beyond merely shocking and offensive expression and included an abusive attack on the Prophet of Islam. In a powerful dissenting opinion, Judges Coista, Cabral Barreto, and Jungwiert took issue with the majority's reasoning and conclusion. The dissenters, whilst accepting that certain passages from the book caused deep offence to devout Muslims, felt that such statements could not be considered in isolation and should not form the basis for condemning an entire book and imposing criminal sanctions on its publisher. The dissenters took particular issue with the majority's reasoning in relation to proportionality and the penalty imposed. Whilst the penalty imposed in the present case was modest this was not, according to the minority, decisive because: 'Freedom of the press relates to matters of principle, and any criminal conviction has what is known as a "chilling effect" liable to discourage

---

[39] (1996) 24 EHRR 1, at para 54.
[40] Ibid, at para 57.
[41] (2007) 45 EHRR 30.

publishers from producing books that are not strictly conformist or "politically (or religiously) correct". Such a risk of self-censorship is very dangerous for this freedom, which is essential in a democracy, to say nothing of the implicit encouragement of blacklisting or "fatwas".'

The dissenters went on to acknowledge that the majority judgment was, on its face, consistent with both *Otto-Preminger-Institut* v *Austria* and *Wingrove* v *UK*. However, these two cases concerned films or videos which, in the dissenters' view, were more likely to have an impact than a novel with limited distribution. Given the limited distribution of the films in question in the earlier cases, this may not be a strong ground for distinguishing previous case law. More significantly, the dissenters noted that the judgments in *Otto-Preminger-Institut* and *Wingrove* were controversial at the time and that perhaps it was time to 'revisit' this case law, which arguably placed too much emphasis on conformism or uniformity of thought and reflected an overcautious and timid conception of freedom of the press. Unfortunately, *IA* was not referred to the Grand Chamber for such reconsideration. *IA* can be contrasted with *Aydin Tatlav* v *Turkey*[42] where a differently constituted Chamber including two of the three dissenters in *IA* unanimously concluded that a conviction and fine for blasphemy in relation to a book entitled *The reality of Islam* violated Article 10 ECHR. The Court was of the view that the book, whilst critical of Islam, was not insulting or abusive in its tone and as such the prosecution was not 'necessary in a democratic society'. Echoing the dissent in *IA*, the Court noted that although the penalty was limited, the conviction with the risk of a custodial sentence could have the effect of discouraging authors and editors from publishing opinions about religion that were non-conformist and could impede the protection of pluralism, which was indispensable for the healthy development of a democratic society. Whilst the differences in result between *IA* and *Aydin Tatlav* can arguably be explained by the different nature of the publications in question, the two decisions reveal, at the very least, some tension between various members of the Court as to how much protection blasphemous expression should receive. Until the matter is considered by a Grand Chamber this tension is likely to continue. 8.32

'Discrimination'

The English law of blasphemy was subject to scrutiny, albeit pursuant to Article 9 ECHR (the right to freedom of religion) and Article 14 (concerning a prohibition 8.33

---

[42] (App No 50692/99), 2 May 2006. See also, the Inter-American Court of Human Rights decision in *Olmedo Bustos* v *Chile* (2001) 10 BHRC 676, which held a ban on the film *The Last Temptation of Christ* was contrary to the guarantee of freedom of expression.

of discrimination) by the Commission in *Choudhury* v *UK*.[43] The case arose out of the failed private prosecution for blasphemy brought against Salman Rushdie, the author of *Satanic Verses,* and his publisher. The prosecution failed on the ground that the criminal offence of blasphemy did not extend to the Moslem religion. The applicant argued that this was a violation of his right to freedom of religion and the right not to be discriminated against. The application was unanimously declared inadmissible on the grounds that Article 9 ECHR did not extend to a right to bring any specific form of proceedings against those who, by authorship or publication, offend the sensitivities of an individual or a group of individuals. Given this conclusion that Article 9 was not engaged, Article 14 ECHR was also of no assistance because it applies only when a Convention right is in issue.

8.34 This discriminatory nature of the English law of blasphemy was invoked by the applicant in *Wingrove* v *UK* in support of his argument that the law did not pursue a legitimate aim. The Court brushed this argument aside, stating that the case related to the Christian faith and the extent to which English law protects other beliefs was not in issue. The Court would not rule in the abstract as to the compatibility of domestic law with the Convention.

The Impact of the HRA on Domestic Law

Obscenity

8.35 Article 10 ECHR has been invoked in a number of cases concerning obscene or pornographic expression. However, such invocation has invariably been unsuccessful. This lack of success is perhaps to be expected given the limited protection historically afforded to such expression by the Strasbourg Court. It is too early to judge whether the European Court's decision in *Vereinigung Blidender Künstler* v *Austria*[44] will have any significant impact on domestic courts. However, it seems unlikely given the House of Lords' opinions in *Belfast City Council* v *Miss Behavin' Ltd*.[45] A further factor that is relevant to the lack of success before the English Courts is the nature of expression in issue; unlike the art work subject to sanction in *Künstler*, most domestic litigation has concerned either hardcore pornography or material involving children.

---

[43] (App No 17439/90), 5 March 1991.
[44] (2008) 47 EHRR 5.
[45] [2007] 1 WLR 1420.

Unsuccessful challenges include *Connolly* v *DPP*,[46] an appeal against a conviction **8.36** of an individual under s 1, Malicious Communications Act 1988[47] for sending pictures of aborted foetuses to pharmacists that sold the 'morning after pill'. The Court accepted that Article 10 ECHR was engaged but that it was possible to interpret s 1 of the 1988 Act consistent with the European Convention by giving a heightened meaning to the words 'grossly offensive' and 'indecent'.[48] Dyson LJ concluded that the conviction was necessary in a democratic society for the protection of the rights of others because, inter alia, Ms Connolly's right to express her views on abortion does not justify the distress and anxiety that she intended to cause by sending the photographs, particularly given that the recipients were not in a position to influence the debate on abortion. Convictions of sex shop owners for selling R18 videos by mail order contrary to the Video Recordings Act 1984 have withstood challenge under Article 10 ECHR on the grounds that the restrictions on such sale made it harder for children to obtain such material. As such, the prosecution was necessary and proportionate notwithstanding the fact that they did not make it impossible for minors to obtain such material; the court accepted that it could be relatively easily purchased from abroad.[49] Perhaps the most surprising case in which Article 10 ECHR was considered in the context of obscene speech was the Court of Arches decision in *St Peter and St Paul's Chingford*.[50] *St Peter and St Paul's Chingford* concerned an application for a faculty from the Consistory Court permitting the installation of a mobile phone base station in the church tower. A parishioner objected to the faculty being granted on the basis that adult material might be transmitted via the base station. The Chancellor refused permission for the installation because it might result in the transmission of pornography which was not consistent with the use of the church as a place of Christian worship. T-Mobile appealed to the Court of Arches. The Court of Arches considered arguments advanced by the mobile phone company based on Article 10 ECHR.

---

[46] [2007] EWHC 237 (Admin).

[47] Malicious Communications Act 1988, s 1(1) provides that 'any person who sends to another person . . . any . . . Article which is, in whole or part, of an indecent or grossly offensive nature is guilty of an offence if his purpose or one of his purposes, in sending it is that it should . . . cause distress or anxiety to the recipient or to any other person to whom he intends that it or its contents or nature should be communicated.'

[48] *Connolly* v *DPP* [2007] EWHC 237 (Admin), at para 18.

[49] *Interfact Ltd* v *Liverpool City Council* [2005] 1 WLR 3118.

[50] [2007] Fam 67.

Although the appeal was allowed, such arguments had little impact, the Court noting the very low level of protection afforded to such speech by the House of Lords in *Belfast City* v *Miss Behavin' Ltd*.[51]

8.37 The common law offences of outraging public decency, conspiracy to outrage public decency, and conspiracy to corrupt public morals are all likely to violate Article 10 ECHR.[52] The lack of any clear indication as to what types of expression will be covered by these offences[53] suggests that they may not be 'prescribed by law'. The fact that they admit of no defence that the dissemination of the material was for the public good, nor require that the material will tend to 'deprave and corrupt', suggests a real question as to whether they are necessary in a democratic society.

8.38 The statutory offences under the Obscene Publications Acts 1959 and 1964, although not without fault, are likely to survive challenge pursuant to Article 10 ECHR.[54] The statutory defence of 'public good' allows a publication to be justified even though the material is obscene, and the further but limited safeguard provided by the bureaucratic input of the Director of Public Prosecutions into prosecutorial decisions is likely to weigh in favour of the statutory offences. There is a possible argument that the requirement to show a 'tendency to deprave and corrupt'[55] is insufficiently precise, though the Court's case law suggests that this argument is unlikely to be successful.[56]

8.39 The Protection of Children Act 1978 makes it an offence to take or make any indecent photograph or pseudo-photograph of a child,[57] to distribute such photographs,[58] or to possess such photographs with a view to their being distributed or shown by the individual himself or others.[59] There is a defence in

---

[51] [2007] 1 WLR 1420.

[52] cf *S and G* v *UK* (App No 17634/91), 2 September 1991, which ruled inadmissible a challenge to a conviction of outraging public decency.

[53] In 1976 the Law Commission recommended that the common law offence of outraging public decency should be abolished because of the vagueness of the definition of the offence. See generally, Feldman, D, *Civil Liberties and Human Rights in England and Wales* (Oxford: Clarendon Press, 1993), at 712–13.

[54] See *R* v *Perrin* [2002] EWCA Crim 747, where the Court of Appeal rejected a challenge to a conviction of the defendant for publishing a website which included coprophilia and coprophagia contrary to s 2(1) of the Obscene Publications Act 1959. The Court of Appeal concluded that Parliament was entitled to conclude that the prescription was necessary in a democratic society, per Kennedy LJ, at para 52.

[55] 1959 Act, s 1(1).

[56] Ibid, at para 46, *per* Kennedy LJ, who rejected such an argument. See paras 2.37–2.40 for consideration of this issue.

[57] s 1(a).

[58] s 1(b).

[59] s 1(c).

relation to the distribution or possession of such photographs if the individual 'has a legitimate reason for distributing or showing the photographs or having them in his possession'. However, this defence does not apply to the taking of or making of any indecent photograph under s 1(a). The lack of a defence in relation to the taking and making of indecent photographs of children may give rise to difficulties under Article 10 ECHR, as the courts have interpreted s 1(a) very broadly to include downloading such pictures from the Internet.[60] There may be legitimate reasons for such downloading; for example, a journalist investigating the extent of child pornography on the Internet might download such pictures. The journalist would have no defence open to him. Prosecutions in such circumstances may well be regarded as disproportionate and unnecessary in a democratic society although it is hoped that the requirement of consent from the DPP will prevent such prosecutions being brought. However, even if the consent requirement is sufficient to prevent such prosecutions, the lack of a 'public good' defence is still problematic because the law may 'chill' the expression and discourage responsible journalists from researching such issues. The new offence of possession of extreme pornographic images contained in Criminal Justice and Immigration Act 2008, s 63, which came into force on 26 January 2009, is likely to survive challenge in light of the various exclusions and defences in ss 64–6 of the 2008 Act.

Blasphemy

The Law Commission concluded that the offence of blasphemy was arguably a **8.40** violation of the Convention in two respects. First, it was impossible to predict in advance whether a particular publication would constitute the offence[61] and, secondly, the offence extended only to the Christian faith and thus discriminated against other faiths.[62] The lack of a 'public good' defence also indicates that the offence is overbroad and therefore arguably disproportionate. Such arguments were rejected by the European Court in *Wingrove*. Allegedly blasphemous speech has generated considerable recent controversy both in the UK, in relation to the BBC's decision to broadcast *Jerry Springer: The Opera*,[63] and internationally, in relation to the cartoons caricaturing the Prophet Muhammad initially published in Denmark and then republished throughout Europe.[64] In light of Lord

---

[60] See *R v Graham-Kerr* [1989] 88 Cr App R 302, CA and *R v Smethurst* [2002] 1 Cr App R 6.

[61] Law Commission, Working Paper No 79, *Offences Against Religion and Public Worship* (1981).

[62] Article 10, read together with Article 14, prevents States from discriminating between religions in respect of the extent to which their Convention rights are protected.

[63] See *R (Green)* v *City of Westminister Magistrates' Court and others* [2007] EWHC 2785.

[64] The cartoons were the subject of an application to the European Court of Human Rights by various individuals living in Morocco who alleged that the Danish government had breached

Bingham's injunction in *R (Ullah)* v *Secretary of State for the Home Department*[65] that domestic courts should not go beyond the protection offered by the Strasbourg Court, it seems unlikely that a domestic court would have concluded that the law of blasphemy violated Article 10 ECHR per se, notwithstanding the very strong arguments in support of such a conclusion. However, the correctness of this view will now never be tested in light of Criminal Justice and Immigration Act 2008, s 79, which abolished the common law offences of blasphemy and blasphemous libel.

---

their rights under Articles 9 and 14 ECHR by failing to prosecute the cartoonists and newspaper in question. The Court, in *Beh El Mahi and others* v *Denmark* (App No 5653/06), rejected the complaint as inadmissible because the applicants did not reside in a Contracting State.

[65] [2004] 2 AC 323.

9

COURT REPORTING AND CONTEMPT OF COURT

Introduction	9.01	'Legitimate Aim	9.12
Whose Right? Standing to		'Prescribed by Law'	9.14
Complain	9.03	'Necessary in a Democratic	
'Interference'	9.10	Society'	9.16

Introduction

Court reporting is part of the staple diet of newspapers and broadcasters in the **9.01** UK and in the other States who are party to the ECHR. From the perspective of Article 10, the starting point is the right of freedom of expression which the media, like all members of the public, have as a result of Article 10(1). From the perspective of defendants, the right to a fair trial which is guaranteed by Article 6 includes the right to a 'public hearing' and to a publicly pronounced judgment. However, as the UK domestic experience repeatedly demonstrates, there is ample scope for free reporting to conflict with the interests of defendants or others involved in the judicial process. Article 10(2) recognizes that those exercising freedom of expression have 'duties and responsibilities' and that restrictions or penalties may be imposed for a variety of reasons, including 'for the protection of the . . . rights of others' and 'for maintaining the authority and impartiality of the judiciary'. Article 6(1) accepts that: 'the press and public may be excluded from all or part of the trial in the interests of morals, public order or national security in a democratic society, where the interests of juveniles or the protection of the private life of the parties so require, or to the extent strictly necessary in the opinion of the court in special circumstances where publicity would prejudice the interests of justice.'

9.02 The recognition of these competing interests is, however, only the beginning. This chapter will examine how they have been worked out in particular situations which are most likely to affect the court reporting activities of the media.

Whose Right? Standing to Complain

Article 10

9.03 There is no doubt that media organizations or individual journalists can rely on the freedom to receive and impart information in Article 10(1) ECHR. Court orders prohibiting or restricting reporting will constitute 'interferences' even though the media or journalists are not formally party to the proceedings. For professional organizations, such as the National Union of Journalists, the position is more difficult. As has previously been explained, Strasbourg will accept that a complainant is a 'victim' for the purposes of Article 34 ECHR only if he or she (or it) has been directly affected by the alleged violation of the Convention. The union would be able to demonstrate that this was so if its own freedom of expression was affected (eg by what it could publish in its own magazine or on its own website), but otherwise it would be insufficient that it was indirectly affected because of the impact of the restriction on its members.[1]

Article 6

9.04 The requirement that trials be in public is a protection for the parties, but there is also a public interest in being able to observe how justice is being administered. Thus, while in principle the right to a public hearing can be waived, this is subject to the proviso that waiver does not run counter to any important public interest.[2] Although the right to a public trial includes the right for the public to attend trials, for the vast majority of people what is more important is the ability to learn about trials through the media. Does this mean that the media can claim to be victims of violations of Article 6 if they are improperly excluded from trials which ought to have been held in public? The Court has not ruled on this issue, but we would expect it to decide that the context of Article 6 makes clear that it is establishing a bundle of rights for litigants, not for others. The public interest in open justice may provide part of the underpinning justification for those rights, but they remain rights which can be claimed only by those who are party to the proceedings. But if the media are not able to rely on Article 6

---

[1] See *Hodgson, D Woolf Productions Ltd and National Union of Journalists* v *UK* App Nos 11553/85 and 11685/85, (1987) 51 DR 136.

[2] *Hakansson* v *Sweden* (1990) 13 EHRR 1, at para 66.

directly, they may be able to do so indirectly. In particular, the public interest justification for open trials may buttress their claims to argue for a right under Article 10 to have access to trials unless one of the qualifications on the right to a public trial in Article 6(1) can be established.[3]

Of course, if reporters or media organizations are themselves party to legal **9.05** proceedings, they will be able to claim the protections of Article 6. If they are subject to contempt proceedings, these would amount to 'criminal charges' for the purpose of the Article.[4] This is an autonomous concept which is not dependent on how the proceedings are classified in domestic law and, therefore, the anomalous character of contempt in UK law is not determinative.

The summary method of dealing with contempt that was in issue in the **9.06** *Kyprianou* case derives, of course, from the English common law. Present authority in the UK strongly encourages judges not to deal themselves with allegations that proceedings which they are trying have been put at risk by prejudicial publications. Instead, the preferred alternative is for the judge to refer the matter to the Attorney-General, who will (if he thinks it appropriate) institute proceedings for contempt in the Divisional Court. The *Kyprianou* judgment will reinforce that trend. The Grand Chamber found a violation of Article 6(1) where a Cypriot court had both initiated proceedings against a lawyer for contempt, found him guilty, and imprisoned him.

However, in a case which did not concern the press (but a verbal attack on a **9.07** prosecution witness by a defendant), the Court of Appeal said that Article 6 did not add to or alter the normal requirements under English law that the proceedings be conducted fairly. It upheld the finding of contempt even though it was 'regrettable' that the judge had taken the witness through her evidence in chief.[5] The situation in this case was marked by a witness who had been put in fear by the defendant's behaviour and so will be distinguishable from most alleged contempts by the press where there will rarely be such a strong need for immediate action by the judge dealing with the matter himself or herself.

Like other litigants, the media will not invariably be entitled to a public hearing **9.08** of their rights—see 9.38. Indeed, these may sometimes be determined on paper and without a hearing at all. Thus, appeals by the media (and others) to the Court of Appeal against a Crown Court's order to hold a hearing in camera

---

[3] *BBC* v *Rochdale Metropolitan BC* [2006] EMLR 6.
[4] *Kyprianou* v *Cyprus* (2007) 44 EHRR 27.
[5] *R* v *MacLeod* (2000) *The Times,* 20 December, CA.

are determined without a hearing.[6] In *Re A and others*,[7] the Court of Appeal held that this process was compliant with Article 6 since the Appeal Court was entitled to start from the premise that the trial court had decided that departure from the normal principle of open justice was justified as a matter of domestic and Convention law. If the appeal was successful the trial would proceed in public in the usual way.

9.09 Article 6 also applies to proceedings which will determine a person's 'civil rights and obligations'. This is also an autonomous concept, but one which remains ill-defined. The Commission decided in 1987 that a court ruling as to reporting restrictions did not determine a reporter's 'civil rights and obligations'[8] and that therefore a complaint that the ruling was made without allowing the reporter to be heard was manifestly unfounded and inadmissible. In another case the Commission held that an application for a witness summons to require the BBC to produce untransmitted film of disturbances on the Broadwater Farm estate did not determine the Corporation's civil rights or obligations but rather constituted a 'normal civic duty in a democratic society'.[9] The meaning of 'civil rights and obligations' is an area of the Strasbourg case law which is still developing so that these decisions may not be the final word on the issue. In addition, the practice of the UK courts has changed since the trial judge in the *Hodgson* case refused to hear from the media, and it is now common for courts to receive representations from the media as to why reporting restrictions should not be made or should be lifted. It is important to remember that the HRA 1998 expressly provides that the rights which it creates are in addition to any other rights which the person concerned may have.[10]

'Interference'

9.10 An issue related to standing is whether there has been an 'interference' with the applicant's 'freedom of expression'. Again, in many cases this will be undisputed. The Court has accepted that the manner and means of publication are essentially a matter of choice for the publishers: Article 10 ECHR protects not only the content of the information or ideas but also the form in which they are

---

[6] See CPR, r 67, 2(6).
[7] [2006] 1 WLR 1361.
[8] *See Hodgson, D Woolf Productions Ltd and NUJ v UK* (above); *Atkinson, Crook and The Independent v UK* App No 13366/87, (1990) 67 DR 244.
[9] *BBC v UK* App No 25798/94, 84–A DR 129.
[10] s 11.

presented.[11] Thus, in *News Verlags GmbH & Co KG* v *Austria*,[12] the Court rejected an argument of the government that an Austrian court order prohibiting a newspaper from publishing a suspect's picture in conjunction with a report of his arrest on criminal charges did not interfere with the publisher's freedom of expression because the picture had no information value.

However, the Commission's conclusion in *Loersch* v *Switzerland*,[13] that there had   **9.11**
been no interference with the journalist applicant's freedom of expression, was the reason why it ruled the application inadmissible. In that case the journalist had been refused accreditation with a court because he had refused to provide a curriculum vitae or police record, or proof of legal training. Even without accreditation the journalist was as free as any other member of the public to attend court and obtain a copy of the judgment. He could not get the readier access to judgments, or the advance notification of hearings or copies of unpublished judgments that accredited journalists could, but the Commission said that none of these rights was guaranteed by Article 10 ECHR and therefore their denial did not constitute a violation of the Convention.

'Legitimate Aim'

Any interference with freedom of expression has to be for the purpose of one   **9.12**
of the permitted exceptions listed in Article 10(2) ECHR, ie the 'interests of national security, territorial integrity or public safety, . . . the prevention of disorder or crime, . . . the protection of health or morals, . . . the protection of the reputation or rights of others, . . . preventing the disclosure of information received in confidence . . . maintaining the authority and impartiality of the judiciary'. Although from time to time the other interests may be served by reporting restrictions, 'maintaining the authority and impartiality of the judiciary' has particular importance in the present context. The European Court has said that:

> The term 'judiciary' *('pouvoir judiciaire')* comprises the machinery of justice or the judicial branch of government as well as the judges in their official capacity. The phrase 'authority of the judiciary' includes, in particular, the notion that the courts are, and are accepted by the public at large as being, the proper forum for the ascertainment of legal rights and obligations and the settlement of disputes relative thereto; further, that the public at large have respect for and confidence in the courts' capacity to fulfil that function . . . in so far as the law of contempt may

---

[11] *Jersild* v *Denmark* (1994) 19 EHRR 1, at para 31, discussed further in chapter 7.
[12] (2001) 31 EHRR 8.
[13] App No 23868/94, (1995) 80 DR 162.

serve to protect the rights of litigants, this purpose is already included in the phrase 'maintaining the authority and impartiality of the judiciary': the rights so protected are the rights of individuals in their capacity as litigants, that is as persons involved in the machinery of justice, and the authority of that machinery will not be maintained unless protection is afforded to all those involved or having recourse to it.[14]

9.13 There is no reported case in this area in which the Court or Commission has held that an interference was not pursuing one or more of the aims permitted by Article 10(2).

'Prescribed by Law'

9.14 The Court has said that the requirement that any restriction must be 'prescribed by law' means that it must be possible to ascertain with reasonable certainty whether freedom of expression in a particular context is amenable to restriction.[15] However, in the present context it has never found a violation on the basis that the restriction lacked a proper legal basis. One might find this surprising given the remarkably protean character of the common law concept of contempt of court. In one of the cluster of cases concerning *Spycatcher*, the Attorney-General took proceedings for contempt against *The Independent* for publishing information which other newspapers were injuncted from publishing. A preliminary hearing was held to determine whether such behaviour could constitute contempt. The Vice-Chancellor ruled that it could not.[16] His decision was subsequently overturned by the Court of Appeal, but it might be thought that Sir Nicolas Browne-Wilkinson's decision called into question whether this extension (or 'application' as the Court of Appeal described it) was reasonably foreseeable. Nonetheless, the Commission ruled inadmissible the complaint by Times Newspapers that its Article 10 right had been violated by its conviction for contempt of court in publishing extracts from *Spycatcher* when other papers (but not *The Times* or any of the other titles of its publishers) had been enjoined from publishing extracts.[17] It noted that the paper had been repeatedly warned by the government's lawyers that publication in these circumstances would be contempt. Although the paper had received contrary advice, it had been well aware of the risks that it ran.

9.15 Attempts to argue in the UK courts that reporting restrictions were contrary to Article 10 because of imprecision have had no greater success. In *O'Riordan* v

---

[14] *Sunday Times* v *UK* (1979) 2 EHRR 245, at paras 55 and 56.
[15] *Sunday Times* v *UK* (1979) 2 EHRR 245, at para 49.
[16] *A-G* v *Newspaper Publishing plc* [1988] Ch 33.
[17] *Times* v *UK* (App No 18897/91), 12 October 1992.

DPP,[18] a woman charged with infringing the prohibition on publishing material 'likely to lead members of the public to identify' a young girl as the victim of an alleged sex offence argued that the term 'likely' was too vague to qualify as a 'law' in the Strasbourg sense. The Administrative Court agreed that the term could have different meanings in different contexts, but in the present context its meaning was sufficiently clear and predictable to satisfy Article 10(2).

'Necessary in a Democratic Society'

Sunday Times v *UK*: the thalidomide articles injunctions

As is so often the case in connection with Article 10 ECHR, the critical issue is whether the restriction conforms to the requirement that it is 'necessary in a democratic society'. One of the earliest cases in which the Court had to consider this phrase was *Sunday Times* v *UK*.[19] This followed the decision of the House of Lords to uphold an injunction against the newspaper, so preventing it from continuing with its series of articles about thalidomide. Essentially, their Lordships considered that the articles prejudged the litigation which was ongoing between alleged victims of the drug and the manufacturers. In a seminal judgment, the European Court held that this ruling violated the rights of the publishers under Article 10. Many of its propositions are of general application in cases concerning Article 10 and are referred to elsewhere in this book, but of particular importance in the present context are the Court's following comments: **9.16**

(a) Although the Court allows the contracting states a margin of appreciation in deciding whether restrictions on freedom of expression are necessary, the scope for discretion varies according to the subject matter: more latitude is allowed in relation to restrictions thought necessary to protect morals, less in relation to the 'far more objective notion of authority of the judiciary' (at para 59). Because the margin of appreciation plays a lesser role in this context, there is correspondingly less need for United Kingdom courts to make allowance for this international concept in applying the judgments of the Court and the decisions of the Commission.

(b) Whatever the historical origin of the phrase concerning the judiciary (and some suggested that it was specifically designed to cover the unique common law institution of contempt of court), 'necessity' was a Convention concept with an autonomous meaning, and thus even contempt measures had to satisfy that yardstick.[20]

---

[18] [2005] EWHC 1240 (Admin).
[19] (1979) 2 EHRR 245.
[20] At para 60.

(c) Freedom of expression is one of the essential foundations of a democratic society. Subject to Article 10(2), it applies to information or ideas which offend, shock or disturb the state or any sector of the population:

> These principles are of particular importance as far as the press is concerned. They are equally applicable to the field of the administration of justice, which serves the interests of the community at large and requires the co-operation of an enlightened public. There is general recognition of the fact that courts cannot operate in a vacuum. Whilst they are the forum for the settlement of disputes, this does not mean that there can be no prior discussion of disputes elsewhere, be it in specialised journals, in the general press or amongst the public at large. Furthermore, whilst the mass media must not overstep the bounds imposed in the interests of the proper administration of justice, it is incumbent on them to impart information and ideas concerning matters that come before the courts just as in other areas of public interest. Not only do the media have the task of imparting such information and ideas: the public also has a right to receive them. [21]

(d) The task is not to choose between conflicting principles but to apply 'a principle of freedom of expression that is subject to a number of exceptions which must be narrowly interpreted'.[22]

9.17 It was because of this ruling that the UK government introduced the Bill which became the Contempt of Court Act 1981 and which, for the purpose of strict liability contempt, replaced the 'prejudgment' test with that of 'serious risk of substantial prejudice'.

9.18 The 1981 Act also defined more precisely the period during which the 'sub judice' period lasted and when the media are vulnerable to committing strict liability contempt. The Act established a test for strict liability contempt [23] which eliminated the prior 'prejudgment test' and relied exclusively on a test based on risk of prejudice. Even in relation to this test, the feared prejudice has to have been serious and the risk that such prejudice would occur has to have been substantial. If the risk of prejudice is incidental to a good faith discussion of public affairs or other matters of general public interest, there is no contempt under the strict liability rule.[24] There is a defence that the publication was a good faith, contemporaneous, fair and accurate report of court proceedings held in public.[25] Given the genesis of the 1981 Act, it is unsurprising that the English courts interpreted it with Article 10 ECHR in mind: an approach that anyway is now required by s 3 of the Human Rights Act 1998.

---

[21] At para 65.
[22] At para 65.
[23] See s 2 of the 1981 Act.
[24] s 5.
[25] s 4(1).

Prejudicial publicity: other cases

In *Worm* v *Austria*,[26] the applicant was a journalist who had published an **9.19** article on Hannes Androsch, a former Vice-Chancellor of Austria and Minister of Finance, who was facing criminal charges alleging tax evasion. Worm was convicted of exercising prohibited influence on the criminal proceedings. It was noted that his article had assumed the guilt of Androsch, and indeed implied that no result other than a conviction was possible. The case against Androsch was due to be tried by a panel, which included lay judges who were more likely to have been influenced by the publication. Although the European Court found that there had been no violation of Article 10 ECHR, its judgment built on the principles of *Sunday Times* v *UK:*

(a) *Sunday Times* v *UK* spoke of litigation not precluding 'prior' discussion of the same issues in the media. *Worm* added that court proceedings did not mean that there could be no contemporary discussion, and that reporting 'including comment' on court proceedings contributes to their publicity and is thus perfectly consonant with the requirement under Article 6(1) that hearings be in public.[27]

(b) The media's task of imparting information to the public and the public's right to receive this 'is all the more so where a public figure is involved ... Such persons inevitably and knowingly lay themselves open to close scrutiny by both journalists and the public at large. Accordingly the limits of acceptable comment are wider as regards a politician as such than as regards a private individual.[28] The last comment is interesting because it carries over into the context of contempt a principle which the Court had previously articulated in the context of defamation. However, the Court qualified its remarks by recalling that public figures are still entitled to a fair trial, including the right to an impartial tribunal, on the same basis as every other person and 'the limits of permissible comment may not extend to statements which are likely to prejudice, whether intentionally or not, the chances of a person receiving a fair trial or to undermine the confidence of the public in the role of the courts in the administration of justice'.[29]

In *News Verlags* v *Austria*,[30] a newspaper had publicized the arrest of a bomb **9.20** suspect in lurid prose which clearly assumed guilt, and accompanied the article with his pictures. Austrian legislation prohibited the publication of a person's picture if this was contrary to his legitimate interests. An injunction was granted against any use of the suspect's picture in conjunction with a

---

[26] (1997) 25 EHRR 454.
[27] At para 50.
[28] At para 50.
[29] At para 50.
[30] (App No 31457/96), 11 January 2000.

publication about the criminal proceedings. The European Court found this to be disproportionate since the prohibition was not confined to publications which impinged on a suspect's right to a presumption of innocence.

9.21 At the time of the Birmingham Six appeal in 1987, Channel 4 proposed to broadcast nightly news reports with actors taking the part of judges, counsel, and witnesses. The plan was stopped by the Court of Appeal which granted an injunction on the grounds that, although the broadcast would not affect the judgment of the court, the public might perceive that it had been influenced which would undermine confidence in the court's decision. Channel 4 complained that this violated its rights under Article 10 ECHR. The Commission found that the restriction did answer a pressing social need and dismissed the application as manifestly ill-founded.[31] Subsequently, the High Court of Justiciary has said that while the Court of Appeal's decision might not have infringed Article 10, it was not compatible with the strict liability test in the Contempt of Court Act 1981, s 2.[32]

Pre-trial injunctions

9.22 The *Sunday Times* thalidomide case concerned an injunction to prevent the newspaper publishing what the domestic courts considered would be a contempt of court. It was implicit in the European Court's judgment that a prior restraint on publication was not by itself enough to constitute a violation of Article 10 ECHR. The Court said this expressly in *Observer and Guardian* v *UK*.[33] However, 'the dangers inherent in prior restraints are such that they call for the most careful scrutiny on the part of the Court. This is especially so as far as the press is concerned for news is a perishable commodity and to delay its publication, even for a short period, may well deprive it of all its value and interest.' The Court's examination of the injunction in this case (which concerned Peter Wright's book *Spycatcher*) is considered in chapter 13. In brief, it held that there was no violation prior to the publication of the book in the USA, but the continuation of the injunction after that date was no longer necessary in a democratic society.

Criticism of the judiciary

9.23 Several judgments of the Court have concerned alleged violations of Article 10 arising out of criminal or civil proceedings against the media for critical attacks

---

[31] *C* v *UK* (App No 14132/88), 13 April 1989.
[32] *Al Meghrahi* v *Times Newspapers Ltd* 2000 JC 22.
[33] (1991) 14 EHRR 153, at para 60.

on judges. In principle, the Court has accepted that the public watchdog role of the press includes raising questions concerning the functioning of the system of justice. The press is one of the means by which politicians and public opinion can verify that judges are discharging their heavy responsibilities in a manner which is in conformity with the aim which is the basis of the task entrusted to them.[34] However, at the same time, the Court has had regard to the special role of the judiciary and the need for it to enjoy public confidence: 'It may therefore prove necessary to protect such confidence against destructive attacks that are essentially unfounded, especially in view of the fact that judges who have been criticised are subject to a duty of discretion that precludes them from replying.' In *Prager and Oberschlick* itself, the Court found no violation because the complainants had been unable to prove the factual assertions which they had made, or demonstrate that their value judgments were fair comment.

In *Barfod* v *Denmark*,[35] the Court found no violation of Article 10 ECHR in the conviction of a Greenlander for criminal defamation. He had published an article criticizing two lay members of a court which had ruled in favour of the local government entity of which they were employees. They had done their duty, the article said, by which, the Greenland courts had inferred, the complainant meant that they had acted partially and in contravention of their professional duty. Although the Greenland court had also accepted that the lay members should not have sat in such a case, there was nothing to show that they had in fact been influenced by bias in their result. The Court has been criticized for this decision and for failing to give more weight to the fact that the article raised a matter of genuine public concern. It relied on the margin of appreciation, and the Court may have felt obliged to show deference to a domestic court which was protective of the position of lay members of the judiciary. This again illustrates the care with which UK courts must treat the Strasbourg jurisprudence when it depends on the margin of appreciation. **9.24**

A much more robust approach was taken by the Court in *De Haes and Gijsels* v *Belgium*.[36] The applicants there were the authors of articles which had severely criticized the Antwerp Court of Appeal for giving custody of children to their father, a public notary, despite allegations that the notary had been guilty of incest and other assaults on the children. The notary had been acquitted of the criminal charges, but his defamation action against his wife and her parents was dismissed because there was no bad faith in their complaints. The Court of **9.25**

---

[34] *Prager and Oberschlick* v *Austria* (1995) 21 EHRR 1, at para 34.
[35] (1989) 13 EHRR 493.
[36] (1997) 25 EHRR 1.

Appeal judges and Advocate-General who had been involved in the custody case took proceedings against the journalists complaining that the articles accused them of bias. The Belgian courts upheld the complaints. The European Court found that the journalists' rights under Article 10 ECHR had been violated. Their articles contained a wealth of detail drawn (apparently) from the original medical reports on the children. They were unable to produce the reports themselves for fear of prejudicing the anonymity of their sources. The European Court accepted that the domestic courts ought to have looked at the copies of the reports contained in the court files. The articles were in essence comments and (unlike *Prager and Oberschlick*) it could not be said that the journalists lacked a factual foundation for their opinions. The Court did not approve of the polemical (even aggressive) tone of the articles, but it recognized that the form of expression was a matter for the journalists not the judges (whether domestic or European). The one area where the Court found that criticism was justified was a reference to the conviction of the father of one of the judges for collaboration with the Nazis. The Court said that this was an impermissible intrusion into private life. The case also needed to be seen against the backdrop of concern over child abuse in the country and the public interest in the integrity of the country's legal system. However, whereas the latter point in other cases had been a factor weighing in favour of restrictions on expression, in this case (where, as has been said, the journalists were able to persuade the Court that there was a substantial foundation for their opinions) it told in favour of free reporting.

9.26 The Court has reiterated that the public watchdog function of the press applies as much to the machinery of justice, although the necessity for an interference with freedom of expression in this field must take account of the need to maintain confidence in the judiciary, to protect them from unfounded attacks, and the inhibition which they might feel in defending themselves. Nonetheless, a violation of Article 10 was found when an Austrian paper had been punished for an article which had criticized a judge in trenchant (but not unfair) terms ('we might expect at the end of the twentieth century that a judge of even minimal enlightenment would, at the very least, deliver a judgment that differs more than somewhat from the traditions of medieval witch trials').[37]

9.27 Where a judge has entered political life, the scope for criticism protected by Article 10 is correspondingly widened.[38] And even when the criticism or insult of a judge is beyond the pale, the punishment imposed must still be proportionate.[39]

---

[37] *Kobenter and Standard Verlags GmbH* v *Austria* (App No 60899/00), 2 November 2006.
[38] *Hrico* v *Slovakia* (App No 41498/99), 20 July 2004.
[39] *Skalka* v *Poland* (App No 43425/98), 27 May 2003.

The form of contempt of court known as 'scandalizing the court' is still **9.28** nominally part of English common law. It is intended to protect the judiciary from attacks on its integrity. It has not been successfully invoked in the UK for decades, despite occasional press and media campaigns against the judges. Given that the legal system has survived without the aid of prosecutions for scandalizing the court, any future resurrection of this ancient relic would no doubt meet the challenge that the restriction did not answer a 'pressing social need' and was therefore incompatible with Article 10 ECHR. The challenge would, though, have to address the survival of scandalizing the court in many parts of the Commonwealth. As recently as 1999, the Privy Council had to consider whether a prosecution for scandalizing the court was compatible with the Mauritian Constitution.[40] This was largely based on the European Convention and guaranteed freedom of expression in almost identical terms to Article 10. Lord Steyn noted the limitations on 'scandalizing the court'. The words had to concern a judge or judges in their official capacity and pose a real risk to public confidence in the judiciary. Good faith criticism would not be an offence, neither would the exposure and criticism of judicial misconduct. He thought that hedged in this way the offence was 'reasonably justifiable' in the terms of the Constitution. The decision does not necessarily mean that the same result would follow if this form of contempt were used in England. Lord Steyn specifically commented that this form of contempt was particularly useful in small jurisdictions where confidence in the administration of justice could more readily be put in jeopardy.

Criticism by lawyers

Lawyers, like everyone else, enjoy the presumptive right of freedom of expression, **9.29** but the Court has said that the special status of lawyers gives them a central position in the administration of justice as intermediaries between the public and the courts; and because of this role it is legitimate to expect lawyers to contribute to the proper administration of justice, and thus to maintain public confidence therein.[41] When a Swiss lawyer held a press conference to publicize what he regarded as the improper behaviour of the local prosecutor's office, he was disciplined by his professional body. The Court found that the relatively modest fine which had been imposed did not breach Article 10 ECHR. At the time of the press conference, there were still legal avenues of redress open to the lawyer's clients, and these subsequently proved at least partially successful.

---

[40] *Ahnee* v *DPP* [1999] 2 AC 294.
[41] See, eg *Amihalachioaie* v *Moldova* (App No 60115/00), 20 April 2004.

This rather undermined the lawyer's case that he had had no alternative but to take his complaints (expressed in strong language) to the media.[42]

9.30 Similar comments were made by the Court in *Veraart* v *The Netherlands*.[43] It said that 'although advocates are entitled to freedom of expression, the special nature of the legal profession has a certain impact upon their conduct in public which must be discreet, honest and dignified.'

9.31 However, the Court and the Commission have emphasized two other features of cases where complaints by lawyers of violations under Article 10 have been rejected. In the first place, this was an area where the margin of appreciation was particularly important. In *Zihlman* v *Switzerland*,[44] the Commission said. 'As they have direct and continuous contact with lawyers and the administration of justice, these councils [ie professional associations] and the national courts are in a better position than an international court to determine how, at a given time, the right balance can be struck between the various interests involved, namely the requirements of the proper administration of justice and the dignity of the profession'.[45]

9.32 Secondly, the Court and the Commission have often taken into account the relatively small penalty which had been imposed in deciding that the interference with freedom of expression had not been disproportionate.[46]

Access to courts and tribunals

9.33 Can journalists rely on Article 10 ECHR to claim a right of access to trials? We noted at 9.04 that Article 6 does require a public as well as a fair hearing of a criminal charge or the determination of a civil right or obligation. However, Article 6 appears to confer rights on the parties to the legal proceedings rather than on outsiders such as the press. If (as may often be the case) the immediate parties positively want to avoid media attention, or are indifferent to whether the trial is heard in public, it may only be the media themselves who are able to make the case for open justice. Can they invoke Article 10 in their cause?

9.34 While the Court has developed the concept of 'positive obligations' in other contexts (see chapter 2), it has resisted the idea that Article 10 gives a right of access to information. Ordinarily, Article 10 assumes a willing supplier of

---

[42] *Schöpfer* v *Switzerland* [1998] EHRLR 646.
[43] (App No 10807/04), 30 November 2006.
[44] App No 21861/93, (1995) 82 DR 12.
[45] Ibid, referring to *Casado Coca* v *Spain* (1994) 18 EHRR 1.
[46] See, for instance, *Leiningen-Westerburg* v *Austria* App No 26601/95, (1997) 88 DR 85.

information and a willing recipient. It does not create a positive right to demand access to information from an unwilling supplier.[47] In the present context the position may be different. The Court itself has recognized that the normal obligation to hold trials in public often serves a public interest as well as being intended to protect the parties. Similarly, while the parties may waive their right to a public trial, this is dependent on there being no countervailing public interest. The media are the obvious candidates to put forward the views as to why there might be such a countervailing public interest, or why the exceptions to a public trial which Article 6 expressly permits are not made out. In Convention terms, the media can only do this if Article 10 is, in these limited circumstances at least, construed as conferring a positive right of access to courts which would ordinarily sit in public.

This argument was presented to the Commission in *Atkinson, Crook and The Independent* v *UK*.[48] The Commission was at least prepared to assume (without deciding) that the argument had merit. In the UK the Administrative Court has alluded to the difficulty of ordinary members of the public establishing standing to complain under Article 6 of a decision by a court to sit in private.[49] The Court did not decide the point and the position of the media to raise the matter may, in any case, be somewhat stronger. Of course, as with other Article 10 cases, the right is not absolute and must give way if there is a pressing social need in pursuit of one of the aims listed in Article 10(2) ECHR. The occasions listed in Article 6(1) when a trial can be determined other than in public are not directly relevant to Article 10, but they provided the Commission with a useful benchmark, and on the facts of the *Atkinson and Crook* case it was persuaded that any interference with the journalists' right of access was justified in a democratic society. **9.35**

Access of a more general kind was sought in *Grupo Interpres SA* v *Spain*.[50] A commercial organization had wished to obtain access to archives of court decisions in order to compile a database which it would then sell to financial institutions who needed to conduct credit checks. The local courts had refused this request and the organization argued that Article 10 had thereby been violated. The Commission rejected the application as inadmissible. It recalled that Article 10 generally did not give a right of access to information against an unwilling supplier. The court records were not generally accessible to the public **9.36**

---

[47] See *Leander* v *Sweden* (1987) 9 EHRR 433 and *Guerra and others* v *Italy* (1998) 26 EHRR 357.
[48] App No 13366/87, (1990) 67 DR 244.
[49] *R (on the Application of Pelling)* v *Bow County Court* [2000] UKHRR 165, at para 30.
[50] App No 32849/96, (1997) 89 DR 150.

since a legitimate reason had to be furnished, and this was intended to protect the private lives of litigants. All these are factors which are consistent with other parts of the Strasbourg jurisprudence. However, the emphasis on the commercial nature of the applicant's operation is more troubling. It has not elsewhere been considered a material factor that newspapers, for instance, compile their stories in order to be able to market their products. As we discuss in chapter 2 and in chapter 12, even purely commercial speech is protected by Article 10.

9.37   Where the government sets up an inquiry to investigate a particular issue, Article 6 ECHR may not be immediately applicable, since the function of the inquiry is not to determine civil rights and obligations. However, Convention rights may still be material. In July 2000, the Divisional Court considered a judicial review challenge to the Health Secretary's decision to hold the inquiry into Dr Harold Shipman's activities in private.[51] One of the objections was that this conflicted with Article 10. The government argued, following *Leander,* that there was no 'interference' with freedom of expression. However, the court preferred the view that the decision to hold the inquiry in private 'restrict[ed] a family witness waiting to give evidence from receiving information that others who are currently giving evidence wish or may be willing to impart to him, namely an accurate account of what they are saying not based simply on their own imperfect recollection after they have finished'. The media had the right to rely on Article 10 since they had their own right to receive information. What was important in this respect was that at least some of the potential witnesses before the inquiry were anxious that it should take place in public. A public inquiry was then held by Dame Janet Smith. In later cases, the Courts have doubted *Wagstaff.* The government's interpretation of *Leander* has found greater support and its discretion to determine whether or not an inquiry should be in public has been reasserted.[52] Yet the government's freedom of choice may be constrained if it is obliged to conduct an inquiry because of its positive obligations under Article 2 of the Convention to investigate matters which have caused a death or near fatality. Here the Convention may require not just an inquiry, but one which is conducted in public.[53]

---

[51] *R v Secretary of State for Health, ex p Associated Newspapers Ltd* [2001] 1 WLR 292; *R v Secretary of State for Health, ex p Wagstaff* [2000] UKHRR 875, QBD.

[52] See, for instance, *Persey v Secretary of State for the Environment, Food and Rural Affairs* [2003] QB 794, which concerned the inquiry into the outbreak of foot and mouth disease in 2001.

[53] See *R (on the application of Amin) v Secretary of State for the Home Department* [2004] 1 AC 653; *D v Secretary of State for the Home Department* [2006] 3 All ER 946, CA.

Article 6 and the extent of the obligation to hold 'public hearings'

Article 6 ECHR may be important for the media even though it does not **9.38** confer rights directly on them. For this reason, they may need to explore its limits. It clearly applies to first instance trials of criminal and civil cases. The UK's practice of holding small claims arbitrations in private was in the process of being successfully challenged in Strasbourg when the government agreed to change the procedural rules to provide for a presumption in favour of a public hearing.[54] There is more doubt as to whether hearings of pre-trial applications must be in public. An old Commission decision said they did not because they did not 'determine' civil rights or obligations,[55] but subsequent judgments of the Court indicate that this may not represent the Court's view.[56] In any case, the UK Court of Appeal has already indicated that as a matter of domestic law, greater accommodation must be made for the interests of the media in interlocutory matters[57] and this is now reflected in the Civil Procedure Rules.[58]

Other tribunals which determine civil rights and obligations will need to look **9.39** to their procedural rules to see whether adequate provision is made for public hearings. In *Diennet v France*,[59] the Court found a violation of Article 6 ECHR in the general rule of a French medical disciplinary tribunal that it should always sit in private. Such proceedings might well involve private matters, but the procedure should allow for a public hearing unless and until a private matter emerged.

Where a hearing is required to be in public, the opportunity for public access **9.40** must be real and not illusory. This may, at least in principle, include a hearing that takes place, for instance in a prison even though members of the public must then submit to identity and security checks. But the practical arrangements, eg public announcements of the time and place of hearings and the practical facilities for transport if the hearing takes place at an unusual and distant location, will be scrutinized to make sure the opportunities for the media and public to attend are real and not just theoretical.[60]

---

[54] See *Scarth v UK* (1998) 26 EHRR CD 154.
[55] *X v UK* (1970) 30 CD 70.
[56] See, eg *Robins v UK* (1997) 26 EHRR 527, at para 28.
[57] *Hodgson v Imperial Tobacco* [1998] 2 All ER 673.
[58] CPR, Part 39, r 39.2.
[59] (1995) 21 EHRR 554.
[60] See, eg *Riepan v Austria*, (App No 35115/97), 14 November 2000; *Hummatov v Azerbaijan*, (App No 9852/03), 29 November 2007.

9.41   We have seen that Article 6(1) itself envisages that there are circumstances where the usual principle of publicity may be abrogated. The ECHR does not in terms say how these should be approached, but in *Campbell and Fell* v *UK*,[61] which considered the practice of holding prison disciplinary hearings in prison and in private, the Court found the practice to be proportionate and its language in this sense thus echoed its approach to Article 10(2). In *B and P* v *UK*,[62] the Court rejected a complaint of a violation of Article 6 on the grounds that the applicants' Children Act proceedings for residence orders had been held in private. The Court thought that these were 'prime examples of cases where the exclusion of the press and public may be justified to protect the privacy of the child and parties and to avoid prejudice and in the interests of justice.' The UK was entitled to treat a whole class of cases as presumptively appropriate for private hearings with the important qualification that the need for such a measure must always be subject to the Court's control. The Practice Direction under the Civil Procedure Rules expressly recognizes that a judge considering an application to sit in private must consider the requirements of Article 6(1).[63] In view of this, it is unsurprising that a challenge to the vires of the Rules on the grounds of their incompatibility with the requirements of Article 6(1) was unsuccessful.[64] The Family Proceedings Rules which presumptively require Children Act proceedings to be in private also withstood a challenge under Article 6 and Article 10.[65] However, the FPR do only establish the default position and the presumption is not a heavy one. Especially where the issue is one of public law (eg whether a child should be taken into care) it may be displaced and this is particularly likely if there are allegations of miscarriages of justice and prior publicity.[66]

9.42   *T* v *UK*[67] had to consider the converse position. The two children accused of murdering the baby James Bulger were tried in an adult court. Although some adjustments were made for their age (eleven years old at the time), they still went through a three-week public trial which attracted widespread media attention. The European Court referred to the UN Convention on the Rights of the Child and Beijing Principles, both of which emphasized the general principle that the privacy of a child (even one accused of a criminal offence) should be respected. The government had argued that public trials (particularly of notorious crimes)

---

[61] (1984) 7 EHRR 165.
[62] (2002) 34 EHRR 529.
[63] CPR, PD 39, para 1.4A.
[64] *R (on the application of Pelling)* v *Bow County Court* [2000] UKHRR 165, QBD.
[65] *P* v *BW (Children Cases: Hearings in Public)* [2004] Fam 155, CA.
[66] *Re Brandon Webster (A Child): Norfolk County Council* v *Webster* [2007] EMLR 7.
[67] (2000) 30 EHRR 121.

served a general interest in open justice. The Court considered that a modified procedure could have coped with this by providing for selective attendance and judicious reporting. The public character of the trial was one of the reasons for the Court to conclude that the defendants had been denied the opportunity to participate effectively in the criminal proceedings, and that they had therefore been denied a fair trial. In consequence of this decision the Lord Chief Justice issued a *Practice Direction* as to the trial of children and young persons in the Crown Court.[68]

The position is less clear in relation to appeals. Strasbourg has been willing to find **9.43** private appeal hearings compatible with Article 6 ECHR, but only if there has been a public hearing at first instance, and then only if there are 'special features' of the appeal procedure.[69] In *Axen* v *Germany*,[70] a private hearing was justified on the ground that it helped reduce the court's case load, but, importantly, the first instance hearing had been in public, the appeal only concerned issues of law and, furthermore, the position would have been different if the appellate body was minded to overturn rather than approve the lower court's decision.

Separately from requiring a public hearing, Article 6 also obliges a court to **9.44** pronounce its judgment publicly. This is not taken literally. If the judgment is deposited in the court registry to which the public has access, this will suffice.[71] On the other hand, if inspection is reserved to those who can demonstrate a legitimate interest, this will not be an adequate substitute for public pronouncement of the judgment.[72] The requirement for a public pronouncement of the judgment is unqualified, but where the hearing has legitimately taken place in private, the Court has recognized that there must be an implicit exception if public pronouncement of the judgment would frustrate that measure.[73]

Publicity of court proceedings and privacy interests

Witnesses

Judicial proceedings can often intrude into the most intimate matters of a person's **9.45** private and family life. Article 8 ECHR guarantees the right to respect for a person's private and family life, his home, and correspondence. How are these

---

[68] [2000] 1 WLR 659.
[69] *Ekbatani* v *Sweden* (1988) 13 EHRR 504.
[70] (1983) 6 EHRR 195.
[71] *Pretto* v *Italy* (1983) 6 EHRR 182; *Sutter* v *Switzerland* (1984) 6 EHRR 272.
[72] *Werner* v *Austria* (1997) 26 EHRR 310, at paras 56–9; *Szucs* v *Austria* (1997) 26 EHRR 310.
[73] *B and P* v *UK* (2002) 34 EHRR 529.

interests to be reconciled? In Z v *Finland*,[74] the Court had to consider the case of a woman whose husband was accused of attempted manslaughter by deliberately subjecting women to the risk of infection with the HIV virus which he carried. An issue arose as to when the husband knew that he was infectious. In this connection the police investigated the medical records of both the husband and his wife. These were added to the court's file. The Court considered that these measures were justified in terms of Article 8(2) as being necessary in the interests of the protection of the rights of others and the prevention of crime. The husband was convicted on certain counts, but the matter went to the Court of Appeal. Although the Court had power to omit the woman's name and to publish only an edited version of its reasoning, and although the Court was aware that she would have preferred this, it chose not to do so. Its judgment (which was made available to the press) named her and disclosed her infection. The European Court found that this publication was not necessary and infringed her rights under Article 8.

9.46   The Court was clearly influenced by the extreme sensitivity of these particular data. Not only did they concern the complainant's health, but they related to a highly dangerous disease. As the Court said:

> The disclosure of such data may dramatically affect his or her private and family life, as well as social and employment situation, by exposing him or her to opprobrium and the risk of ostracism. For this reason it may discourage persons from seeking diagnosis or treatment and thus undermine any preventative efforts by the community to contain the pandemic. The interests in protecting the confidentiality of such information will therefore weigh heavily in the balance in determining whether the interference was proportionate to the legitimate aim pursued. Such interference cannot be compatible with Article 8 unless it is justified by an overriding requirement in the public interest.[75]

9.47   *Shabanov* v *Russia*[76] grew out of a libel action brought by a Russian army officer who was said by the applicants' newspaper to have neglected the health of the men under his command. The officer alleged that he had been psychologically damaged by the publication and he relied on a medical certificate which also referred to his impotence. The evidence was produced in open court and the paper ran another article referring to this. The officer lost the libel claim (the court held that the article was true) but succeeded in an additional complaint as

---

[74] (1997) 25 EHRR 371.

[75] At para 96. It is worth noting that this is an example of where the Court drew on other instruments of the Council of Europe—a recommendation adopted by the Committee of Ministers (R (89)) and the Convention for the Protection of Individuals with Regard to Automatic Processing of Personal Data.

[76] (App No 5433/02), 14 December 2006.

to infringement of his privacy. The European Court found that there had been no violation of Article 10. It said that there was a difference in the publicity given to the medical evidence in court and by the newspaper to the wider public. The national court was better placed to assess the contextual significance of the article. The judgment needs to be treated with some care. Not only did it rely on the national court's margin of appreciation, but the application was unsuccessful by only a narrow vote (4:3) and the dissenting judges gave powerful reasons as to why the officer could not have had a reasonable expectation of privacy once he had taken no steps to prevent his medical evidence being read out to the public in court.

Adverse impact of publicity on third parties

The reporting of court proceedings, particularly high-profile criminal proceedings, can sometimes have a damaging effect on family members or other third parties. Article 8 provides a measure of protection for a person's physical and mental integrity and, more generally, for a private space where he or she is free to do as he chooses. There is obvious potential here for a clash between the Article 8 guarantees and the right of freedom of expression in Article 10. The House of Lords had to confront this issue when faced with a claim for an injunction to anonymize the reporting of the trial of a woman accused of murdering her child.[77] The claimant was the victim's sibling. Expert evidence said that the child could be psychologically damaged if the mother's name was publicized. Lord Steyn listed four key principles: **9.48**

- Neither Article 8 nor Article 10 *as such* took precedence over the other.
- Where the values under the two articles were in conflict, an intense focus on the comparative importance of the specific rights claimed was necessary.
- The justification for interfering with or restricting each right had to be taken into account.
- The proportionality test had to be applied to each.

Although neither provision *as such* took precedence, the Court did emphasize the particular importance of free reporting of criminal proceedings. An injunction was refused. Since then there have been other cases where the High Court has been asked to grant injunctions because of the adverse effect of publicity on the children or other relatives of those concerned. The Court has stressed how unusual the situation would have to be for an injunction to be granted.[78] **9.49**

---

[77] *Re S (a child) (identification: restriction on publication)* [2005] 1 AC 593.
[78] See, eg *A Local Authority v PD and GD (by her guardian Cathy Butcher)* [2005] EMLR 35, Fam.

A rare example of where such a claim succeeded was where anonymity was needed to protect the young children of a woman who had pleaded guilty to knowingly infecting their father with HIV. There had been no or minimal prior publicity, the identification of the mother would have had a seriously prejudicial effect on placing the children for adoption, and publicity was likely to lead to stigmatization of the children as suffering from HIV when that was not the case with one of them, and might not be for the other who was too young to test.[79] Much more typical was the case of a man who had pleaded guilty to possession of indecent images of children. The Crown Court judge acceded to a request for an order that would effectively have prohibited his identification in order to spare his two young daughters the embarrassment, distress, and taunts which they might otherwise have to endure. The Court of Appeal ruled that the judge had no jurisdiction to entertain an application of this kind, but even if he had, he should have refused it. Although reporting of the proceedings against him would bring pain to his family, the circumstances were not sufficiently unusual to justify departure from the normal rule that criminal proceedings could be freely reported.[80]

9.50 The same principles will be applied to the reporting of coroners' inquests into a suspicious death.[81]

9.51 The courts may need to take care to avoid public disclosure of private information in the course of a case where the information has little or no relevance.[82]

Court reporting and threats to life

9.52 Sometimes a witness (or even a defendant) will claim that their life will be at risk if they are identified in connection with the proceedings. Article 2 of the ECHR provides that a person's right to life shall be protected by law. This negative obligation has been found to entail a corresponding positive obligation on the part of the State. It is a duty to take reasonable steps to protect a person against a known real and immediate threat to his or her life.[83] In *Osman* the complaint was that the State had done nothing (or too little) to protect the person concerned.

9.53 In the course of the Bloody Sunday Tribunal, the former members of the Parachute Regiment argued that they would be put at risk if they were identified

---

[79] *A Local Authority* v *W* [2006] 1 FLR 1.
[80] *R* v *Croydon Crown Court, ex p Trinity Mirror plc* [2008] QB 770.
[81] See *Re: LM (Reporting Restrictions: Coroner's Inquest)* (2008) 99 BMLR 11, Fam.
[82] See *Craxi* v *Italy (No 2)* (2004) 38 EHRR 995.
[83] *Osman* v *UK* (1998) 29 EHRR 245.

and if they had to give evidence in Derry rather than in London. The UK courts held that their fears should be accommodated. From the Article 2 perspective, what mattered was the genuineness of their subjective fears, the objective support for these fears, that the risk would be diminished by a change in venue, and the lack of any compelling reason against the change.[84] The ex-soldiers did not fear that they would be killed by the State, but they did say that the risks to them would be exacerbated by the State's action in summoning them as witnesses. In *Re Officer L*,[85] the House of Lords again had to consider the impact of Article 2 on the rights of a witness who was summoned to give evidence. It ruled that the *Osman* test still applied. In other words in order to show that the State's positive duty under Article 2 was engaged, the witness had to demonstrate that as a result of giving evidence in the ordinary way, he would be exposed to a risk of real and immediate threat to his life. The threshold was high and would not be easily satisfied.

Broadcasting coverage of court proceedings

In England and Wales the Criminal Justice Act 1925, s 41 prohibits the taking of photographs in court and the Contempt of Court Act 1981, s 9 prohibits the use of tape recorders in court without permission and the publication of any recording (with no discretion in the court to grant permission). Between them these provisions effectively prohibit the broadcasting of court proceedings. There is no equivalent blanket prohibition in Scotland. However, the settled practice has been not to allow proceedings to be televised. The issue came to the fore in connection with the trial of two Libyans for placing a bomb in the airliner that exploded over Lockerbie. They tried in The Netherlands but by Scottish judges and according to Scots law. Broadcasters were refused permission to film the proceedings with their own cameras. Their challenge *inter alia* on Article 10 grounds failed.[86] The Court held that televising the proceedings would risk prejudicing the fair trial of the accused. In a second attempt, the broadcasters referred to the fact that the proceedings were in fact being televised for reception in a limited number of sites around the world with access being allowed to selected individuals—principally relatives of the victims. In these proceedings the broadcasters sought access to this encrypted feed. Again the challenge failed. The court referred to the *Leander* line of authorities that Article 10 presumed a willing supplier of information. In this case, the people responsible for the limited

9.54

---

[84] *R (A) v Lord Saville of Newdigate* [2002] 1 WLR 1249, CA.
[85] [2007] 1 WLR 2135.
[86] *BBC Petitioners (No 1)* 2000 JC 419.

broadcasting facilities did not wish the signal to be made more widely available. Their refusal of access did not amount to an 'interference' in terms of Article 10.[87]

9.55   The Strasbourg Court rejected a complaint by a Norwegian broadcaster who had been refused permission to put out a live radio transmission of the opening and closing speeches and the verdict in a particularly notorious and grisly murder trial. The Court was prepared to assume (without deciding) that this had amounted to an 'interference' for the purposes of Article 10. It referred to *Autronic AG v Switzerland*[88] for the proposition that Article 10 protected not just the content of speech or expression but also the means of transmission or reception. However, it went on to say that this was an area where the national authorities were better placed than the Strasbourg Court to assess whether broadcasting would adversely impinge on the administration of justice. Accordingly, it found that the Member States had a wide margin of appreciation and it rejected the complaint as manifestly ill-founded.[89]

Infringement of court secrecy requirements

9.56   Where court proceedings or documents are confidential, disclosure may lead to penalties. In principle this is likely to be seen as pursuing the legitimate aim of maintaining the authority of the judiciary. However, the position is different if the material is no longer confidential. In *Harman v UK*,[90] Harriet Harman (then legal officer for the National Council of Civil Liberties) had shown to a journalist a bundle of documents which had been produced by the Home Office in an action which her client had taken for false imprisonment. The significant feature of the case was that all the documents had been read out in open court in the course of the opening speech of her client's counsel. Nonetheless, the House of Lords found her to be in contempt of court for infringing the implied undertaking to use discovered documents only for the purpose of the proceedings. Showing them to a journalist was external to that purpose. The Commission declared her complaint admissible. The matter went no further because, as part of a friendly settlement, the government agreed to change UK law by introducing an amendment to the Rules of the Supreme Court.[91] A companion complaint by David Leigh, the journalist concerned, was found to be inadmissible since he was not a victim of any violation. No proceedings for contempt had been taken against him (although he had published an article on

---

87   *BBC Petitioners (No 2)* 2000 JC 521.
88   (1990) 12 EHRR 585.
89   *P4 Radio Hele Norge ASA v Norway* (App 76682/01), Decision of 6 May 2003.
90   App No 10038/82, (1984) 38 DR 53.
91   Now CPR, r 31.22.

the basis of the documents). His claim that the House of Lords ruling would make it more difficult for him to operate as a journalist in the future was regarded as being too distant an impact to constitute an interference.[92]

Somewhat similarly, in *Weber* v *Switzerland*,[93] the complainant had been prosecuted for holding a press conference at which he had disclosed details of a criminal investigation being conducted against him by a judge. Swiss law required these investigations to remain confidential. The Court found this to be a violation of Article 10 ECHR because nine months earlier the same man had held another press conference at which he had referred to virtually the same details. This had led to no prosecution. Thus, by the time of the incident which did found the charge against him, the details were in the public domain. The Court seemed unconcerned by the fact that they had been put there by the complainant.

9.57

UK law prohibits the disclosure of jury deliberations.[94] In *A-G* v *Associated Newspapers Ltd*,[95] the House of Lords held that 'disclosure' should be given a broad meaning and included a newspaper putting into the public domain previously unpublished details of a jury's deliberations. It upheld a fine for contempt of court against the newspaper publisher, editor, and journalist for infringing this prohibition. The European Commission of Human Rights dismissed their allegation of a violation of Article 10 ECHR as manifestly unfounded. The newspaper argued that because the restriction applied in an absolute form, the national courts had not had to assess the proportionality of the restriction. It submitted that this could not be compatible with the principles of what is 'necessary in a democratic society'. The Commission rejected this argument. It said that the purposes of the prohibition on jury disclosures was to encourage frankness of exchanges in the jury room, and any possibility of intrusion on this privacy could undermine that confidence. The absolute character of the restriction was thus intimately connected with its purpose.[96] A juror who wrote to the mother of the defendant alleging that the verdict was unsafe was found to have infringed s 8 of the 1981 Act. The House of Lords rejected his argument that this violated the juror's Article 10 right. It said that the restriction was a necessary and proportionate reinforcement of the confidentiality

9.58

---

[92] *Leigh* v *UK* App No 10039/82, (1984) 38 DR 74.
[93] (1990) 12 EHRR 508 (see also, *Vereniging Weekblad Bluf!* v *Netherlands* (1995) 20 EHRR 189, discussed in ch 13).
[94] Contempt of Court Act 1981, s 8.
[95] [1994] 2 AC 238.
[96] *Associated Newspapers Ltd* v *UK* (App No 24770/94), 30 November 1994.

of jury deliberations. If a juror felt that there had been impropriety, he could raise the matter with the court authorities but not with third parties.[97]

9.59 In *Du Roy and Malaurie* v *France*,[98] the Court was also concerned with an absolute prohibition on reporting aspects of court proceedings. In this case it was a French law that did not allow publication of information concerning the joinder of civil parties to a criminal prosecution. The applicants were the editor and a journalist on a French magazine which had publicized the fact that the new management of a public company for the management of residential centres for emigrants had lodged a criminal complaint and had applied to be a *partie civile* in criminal proceedings against the former head of the company. The applicants had been fined despite arguing before the French courts that the general and absolute prohibition conflicted with Article 10 ECHR. The applicants had lost in the French courts all the way up to and including the *Cour de Cassation,* on the basis that the French law was intended to guarantee the presumption of innocence and to prevent external influence on the course of justice. However, the European Court upheld the complaint under Article 10. It said that the law was anomalous: it prevented publication of proceedings instituted by a *partie civile* but not where the prosecution was brought by the state prosecutor or an ordinary complainant. There was no objective basis for this differential treatment. Furthermore, this particular case concerned a matter of public interest and the absolute ban was disproportionate.

9.60 Although prosecutions for violations of judicial secrecy laws will not necessarily amount to a breach of Article 10,[99] the Court has found violations where the publication did not contravene the presumption of innocence of the person under investigation and, particularly, where the subject matter of the publication was a matter of important public interest.[100] In both of these last two cases (see n 100), the Court has endorsed a recommendation from the Council of Ministers.[101]

---

[97] *AG* v *Scotcher* [2005] 3 All ER, 1 HL.
[98] (App No 34000/96), 3 October 2000.
[99] See, for instance, *Tourancheau and July* v *France* (App No 53886/00), 24 November 2005.
[100] See, eg *Dupuis and others* v *France* (App No 1914/02), 7 June 2007 and *Campos Dâmaso* v *Portugal* (App No 17107/05), 24 April 2008.
[101] Recommendation R 2003 (13) on the importance of media coverage of criminal proceedings.

10

REPORTING ON ELECTIONS
AND PARLIAMENT

Introduction	10.01
Elections	10.05
Parliament	10.24

Introduction

Until the Political Parties, Elections and Referendums Act (PPERA) 2000, many **10.01** of the most familiar features of modern elections were unregulated. Election law did not even recognize the existence of parties or their national campaigns and election broadcasts. All this has now changed. PPERA 2000 imposes financial and other controls on national campaigning by political parties and third parties. These changes were introduced alongside a developing European consensus that donations and expenditure should be capped, and that there should be common campaigning standards.[1] The Electoral Commission established under Part I of PPERA 2000 oversees most aspects of our electoral process. Parties fielding candidates must register their name and emblems with the Commission, which may refuse registration on grounds of similarity with an existing party, obscenity, or offensiveness. Since January 2007 a party is also entitled to register up to twelve unique descriptions of itself for use on the ballot paper.[2]

---

[1] See especially, the Council of Europe's Parliamentary Assembly Recommendation 1516 (2001) and Committee of Ministers Recommendation R (2003) 4. In this country, see the Fifth Report of the Committee on Standards in Public Life, 'The Funding of Political Parties in the UK', CM 4507–I (1998).

[2] See PPERA 2000, ss 28, 28A, 28B, and 29. These provisions prevent unscrupulous candidates using descriptions designed to trick careless party voters into marking their box on the ballot paper. A genuine candidate or organization refused registration of the style of their choice might seek to challenge the decision under Article 10 ECHR and/or Article 3 of the First Protocol.

10.02   The Representation of the People Act (RPA) 1983 and the Electoral Administration Act 2006 regulate elections at constituency and local level. In recent years many changes have been made to the law, through these statutes, to encourage higher turnout and prevent electoral fraud.

10.03   The rules of Parliamentary procedure are more old-fashioned. Indeed, the House of Commons can still banish journalists from the precincts of the Palace of Westminster for contempt of Parliament. The only significant concession to modernization has been the decision to admit television cameras in 1989.

10.04   In this chapter we consider both the domestic and Convention law in these areas, and the effect of the HRA 1998 on the former.

Elections

10.05   Article 3 of the First Protocol to the ECHR guarantees the right to free elections and provides: 'The High Contracting Parties undertake to hold free elections at reasonable intervals by secret ballot, under conditions which will ensure the free expression of the opinion of the people in the choice of the legislature.'

10.06   Protecting the right to vote therefore involves positive obligations on the part of the State. In *Mathieu-Mohin and Clerfayt* v *Belgium*,[3] the Strasbourg Court explained that the reference to conditions necessary to ensure the free expression of the electorate implies: 'apart from freedom of expression (already protected in Article 10 of the Convention) the principle of equality of treatment of all citizens in the exercise of their right to vote and the right to stand for election.'

10.07   The statutory 'conditions' under which our elections are held include a number of provisions which bear upon the reporting of elections by press and broadcasters.

Campaigning

10.08   Meetings, displays, advertisements, publications, or any other means used to support one candidate or undermine another, are strictly controlled by the RPA 1983 if the cost exceeds a specified sum. Material may be published only with the authorization of a candidate at the election, and the costs must then be included in that candidate's statutory election expenses.[4] However, newspaper articles and broadcasts (other than advertisements) which support a particular candidate are

---

[3]   (1988) 10 EHRR 1, 17.
[4]   RPA 1983, s 75(1).

not caught by these rules.[5] The specified sum was fixed at £5 for many years. In the case of *Bowman* v *UK,* discussed in detail below, the Court held that this limit was so low that it was a disproportionate limitation on freedom of expression at election time. Accordingly, s 131 of PPERA 2000 raised the limit to £500 in a Parliamentary Election and £50 plus 0.5p for every registered voter in a local government election. However, even if it does not exceed this amount, the expenditure will still be unlawful if it is part of a 'concerted' arrangement to promote or disparage a particular candidate.[6]

A breach of s 75 is a criminal offence known as a 'corrupt practice' and the offence **10.09** extends to aiding, abetting, counselling, or procuring a breach by another.[7] This is punishable by fine, imprisonment for up to a year, and mandatory disqualification from public office for five years.[8] Newspapers must therefore take care to ensure that the advertiser is the candidate or an election agent. In a Parliamentary by-election in the late 1990s, a national tabloid exposed itself to the risk of prosecution (as well as incurring the wrath of the other parties) when its normal edition was distributed in the constituency on election day with a special 'wrap around' front and back page urging voters to support the candidate of a particular party. These extra pages were not published anywhere else in the country and were arguably not part of the newspaper. The practice has not been repeated in subsequent by-elections.

The only type of media publication caught by the new financial limits on national **10.10** third-party campaigning is political advertising through the print or broadcast media.[9] These would apply to an advert placed by, say, a company or trade union urging people to vote for a particular party. Broadcasters are also subject to regulation in relation to broadcasting of local items during elections. These are items about a particular parliamentary constituency or local government areas. Under RPA 1983, s 93 'broadcasting authorities' (being the BBC, Ofcom, and Sianel Pedwar Cymru) must produce and secure compliance with a code of practice for such broadcasts. The Electoral Commission is consulted during the preparation of the codes, which require balance and impartiality in reports and discussions.[10] RPA 1983, s 66A prohibits the publication of exit polls before the poll is closed.

---

[5] s 75(1ZZA).

[6] See RPA 1983, s 75 (1ZA), considered in *R* v *Holding* [2006] 1 WLR 1040, CA.

[7] s 75(5).

[8] RPA 1983, ss 168(a)(ii), 173(a), and 160(4).

[9] PPERA 2000, s 87(2)(a).

[10] See, eg rules 6.8 to 6.13 in the Ofcom Broadcasting Code and the BBC's Editorial Guidelines for Elections.

10.11   Section 106(1) of the RPA 1983 renders it a summary offence to make or publish a false statement of fact about the personal character or conduct of a candidate 'for the purpose of affecting the return' of that candidate, unless it can be shown that there were reasonable grounds for believing the statement to be true. In addition an injunction can be obtained, on prima facie proof of falsity, preventing publication of such a statement during the campaign.[11] Urgent injunction applications are often made by candidates aggrieved about an opposition leaflet which has suddenly appeared in the constituency, though they sometimes use this provision to prevent the media running groundless stories about them in an attempt to influence the result. However, there are important limitations. The statement must be about the candidate's 'personal' character or conduct, rather than public conduct or political views. Although there is no reported case law, injunction applications can be defeated by adequate written evidence showing reasonable grounds for believing that the story is true within the meaning of s 106(1). In *Culnane* v *Morris*,[12] a candidate brought defamation proceedings after the election, complaining of allegations made in her rival's election leaflet. The High Court held that the defendant could raise a common law qualified privilege defence. It did so notwithstanding s10 of the Defamation Act 1952 which provides that a statement published by a candidate 'shall not be deemed to be published on a privileged occasion on the ground that it is material to a question in issue in the election'. It relied upon Articles 6, 10, and 14 in reaching this conclusion. The High Court could not see any justification under Article 10(2) for denying a candidate this defence when it would in principle be available to a citizen publishing the same criticisms of the claimant at the same election. Instead it interpreted these words as meaning that a candidate could not 'claim a special privilege by virtue only of publishing words that are 'material to a question in issue in the election'.[13]

Party election broadcasts

10.12   Political advertising on television and radio has always been prohibited in this country, even at election times. The ban is now in ss 319 and 321 of the Communications Act 2003. In 1971, the Commission rejected a complaint under Article 10 ECHR seeking to challenge this principle, holding that the provision for government licensing of radio and television broadcasting in Article 10(1) allowed contracting parties to impose such a blanket ban.[14]

---

[11] s 106(3).

[12] [2006] 1 WLR 2880.

[13] Para 32.

[14] *X and the Association of Z* v *UK* (App No 4515/70), 11 July 1971.

Over twenty years later, in *Murphy* v *Ireland*,[15] the Court found no violation of Article 10 in the application of a prohibition on audio-visual advertising 'directed towards any religious or political end'. The applicant had wanted to broadcast an advert about a video dealing with Christ's resurrection. In *R (Animal Defenders International)* v *Secretary of State*,[16] the House of Lords applied *Murphy* in confirming that the prohibition in ss 319 and 321 was justified in a democratic society under Article 10(2) and therefore compatible with the Convention.

The party political, or election, broadcast is the alternative (PPB/PEBs). The importance of PEBs has grown over the years. The first radio broadcasts were in 1924 and the first televised broadcasts in 1951. Parties now regard them as an important part of their election strategy. Whether they will become less important as more people receive political information through the internet remains to be seen. The broadcasters are obliged to provide airtime for PEBs.[17] Only registered political parties may benefit.[18] The broadcasters liaise informally to decide the principles which will govern allocation of PEB airtime, having regard to the views of the Electoral Commission. In the past at general elections the lesser parties have been allocated one PEB if they are fielding candidates above a threshold number. Allocations to larger parties may depend on past electoral support. This approach was adopted at the 1997 general election. Although it discriminates against new parties, it was upheld by the Divisional Court in *R* v *BBC, ex p Referendum Party*.[19] The court accepted that the BBC and the ITC (the forerunner of Ofcom) had reached their own decisions about the best system for allocating airtime, and held that impartiality in this context could not be 'equated with parity or balance as between political parties of different strengths, popular support and appeal'. It simply meant 'fairness of allocation' of airtime, taking into account such factors and with proper allowance being made for changes in the political landscape and the potential for television to influence such changes. **10.13**

It has long been an accepted broadcasting standard that the public should be protected from offensive and harmful material. The Communications Act, s 319(2)(f) requires that this standard is in the Ofcom Code, with which commercial broadcasters must comply. The BBC's obligation is in their **10.14**

---

[15] (2003) 38 EHRR 212.
[16] [2008] 2 WLR 781.
[17] The obligation of the BBC arises under the Agreement accompanying its 2007 Royal Charter. Commercial channels are obliged to do so under their licence. They must comply with Ofcom rules requiring them to broadcast PEBs (Communications Act, s 333).
[18] PPERA 2000, s 37.
[19] [1997] 9 Admin LR 553.

Agreement with the government. In the 2001 general election the ProLife Alliance, a registered party, fielded enough candidates for a PEB in Wales. The tape it submitted to the broadcasting authorities was rejected. The broadcasters considered they would breach their obligations under this 'offensive material restriction' if they showed it. This was because it contained repeated images of aborted foetuses. In judicial review proceedings against one of the authorities, the Court of Appeal held that the refusal was unlawful as unjustified censorship of political expression. The House of Lords reversed this decision by a majority of 4:1—see *R (ProLife)* v *BBC*.[20] In *Verein gegen Tierfabriken* v *Switzerland*,[21] the Strasbourg Court had considered a ban on 'advocacy advertising' away from elections. It held that the Article 10 rights of an animal welfare association had been violated when a ban was imposed on its television commercial showing distressing images of pigs being farmed in small pens. The ProLife Alliance relied on this decision to argue that the potent effect, and wide reach, of television did not necessarily mean that disturbing images could not be shown. However, the majority in the House of Lords decided the case on a straightforward basis. The broadcasters' judgment could not be impugned on public law principles. As Lord Nicholls put it: 'The broadcasters' duty is to do their best to comply with this restriction, loose and imprecise though it may be and involving though it does a significantly subjective element of assessment'.[22]

10.15 They had not acted unlawfully in deciding that to broadcast would breach the obligation, for example by misunderstanding the standard or failing to consider the political importance of the images to the Alliance's election campaign. The Court of Appeal had erred by treating the case as a challenge to the standard itself, rather than its application to the facts by the broadcasters. *R (ProLife)* v *BBC* was perhaps a more difficult case than the approach of the majority in the House of Lords suggests. After all, four of the eight judges who considered the case at appellate level found for the Alliance. The decision of the majority does not sit easily with the numerous pronouncements of the Strasbourg Court as to the importance of protecting freedom of political expression, particularly at election time. See for example, *Castells* v *Spain*.[23]

---

[20] [2004] 1 AC 185.
[21] (2002) 34 EHRR 159.
[22] Para 12.
[23] (1992) 14 EHRR 445, at paras 65 and 67.

Bowman v UK

In the important decision of *Bowman* v *UK*,[24] the Strasbourg Court considered **10.16** the restrictions placed on freedom of expression at election time by s 75 of the RPA 1983 (see above).

The applicant complained that a prosecution brought against her under s 75 of **10.17** the 1983 Act violated her Article 10(1) ECHR rights. Immediately before the 1992 general election, she had arranged the distribution of 1.5 million leaflets in selected constituencies on behalf of the Society for the Protection of the Unborn Child. These put the case against abortion and summarized the views of the main local candidates on the issue. She was prosecuted for the version of the leaflet put out in the constituency of Halifax, where the candidates had strong pro- and anti-abortion views. Although the applicant was acquitted on a procedural technicality, the Court accepted that she was a victim because the decision to prosecute operated as a warning that she would be prosecuted for doing the same thing again at any future election.[25] The Court acknowledged that s 75 helped to secure equality between candidates, and therefore pursued the legitimate aim of protecting the rights of the candidates and the electorate.[26] The case therefore turned on the proportionality issue.

The Court emphasized once again the crucial importance of freedom of political **10.18** speech in the democratic process and that the free elections guaranteed by Article 3 of the First Protocol are 'secured in part' by freedom of expression so that 'it is particularly important in the period preceding an election that opinions and information of all kinds are permitted to circulate freely'.[27] But it also recognized, as is implicit in s 75, that on occasion the two rights may come into conflict during a campaign: 'so that it may be considered necessary, in the period preceding or during an election, to place certain restrictions, of a type which would not usually be acceptable, on freedom of expression.[28]

The Court could not accept that this was necessary in Mrs Bowman's case, **10.19** observing that s 75, and the then £5 expenditure cap, operated 'for all practical purposes, as a total barrier to Mrs Bowman's publishing information with a view to influencing voters of Halifax in favour of an anti-abortion candidate'.

---

[24] (1998) 26 EHRR 1.
[25] At para 29.
[26] At para 38.
[27] At para 42.
[28] At para 43.

In particular, it was not satisfied of the necessity for this strict interference with her freedom of expression in a democracy where the media were free to support or oppose particular candidates, and national or regional advertising on political issues at election time was unregulated.[29]

10.20 The increase in the prescribed limit (see above) undoubtedly allows more scope for local campaigning. Problems may still arise, however, particularly where it is viewed as a 'concerted' attempt to promote a particular candidate. Section 75 applies only where the campaigning is 'with a view to promoting or procuring the election of a candidate at an election'.[30] The solution, short of further amendment to the RPA 1983, may be for the domestic courts to interpret these words in a way which excludes genuine campaigning on issues of public interest, as distinct from supporting a candidate who is preferred *because* of his or her identity or party allegiance.

Election law: other possible challenges

10.21 The scope for politicians and electors to complain about lack of balance or biased reporting at election time may be limited. It is well established in the Convention case law that Article 10 ECHR does not give a citizen or private organization a 'general and unfettered right' to put forward an opinion through the media or to be interviewed in a particular way, although the same cases acknowledge that a complaint about denial of access to broadcasting time could in principle be made out in 'exceptional circumstances' if one political party was excluded while others were given broadcasting time.[31] However, there would have to be clear evidence of bias, arbitrariness, or unjustifiable discrimination. In *Huggett* v *UK*,[32] the Commission rejected a complaint about the BBC's threshold requirement that a party should be standing candidates in at least 12.5 per cent of the seats in an election before it could qualify for an election broadcast. The threshold was justified by the need to ensure that air time was given only to political opinions which were 'likely to be of general interest and command some public support'.[33]

10.22 In the earlier case of *X and the Association of Z* v *UK*,[34] a similar complaint by an organization which was not fielding any candidates at all was rejected by the

---

[29] At para 47.
[30] s 75(1).
[31] See *Haider* v *Austria* App No 25060/94, (1995) 83 DR 66, at 74, and the cases referred to there.
[32] App No 24744/94, (1995) 82 DR 98.
[33] At 101.
[34] (App No 4515/70), 11 July 1971.

Commission. Although in principle, therefore, a political party could seek to challenge the allocation of election broadcast time as discriminatory, asking the Divisional Court to take account of its Article 10(1) rights in conjunction with Article 14, the result would probably be the same as in the *Referendum Party* case. In *Haider* v *Austria*,[35] the Commission also rejected a complaint of bias by the politician against a statutory broadcasting supervisory body which had declined to question legitimate editorial and journalistic decisions taken at election time. In *Bader* v *Austria*,[36] a complaint alleging failure by the Austrian authorities to provide sufficient information to help electors to vote in the referendum on accession to the EU was rejected. The Commission reiterated that while the right to receive information under Article 10(1) ECHR prohibits restrictions on the passage of information, it cannot be used to force public authorities to disclose information against their wishes.[37]

While s 106 of the 1983 Act limits freedom of speech at election time, it may not **10.23** be incompatible with Convention rights, seeking as it does to protect candidates from wholly unfounded allegations of fact about their private lives and, thereby, to preserve the integrity of the electoral process. However, the provision that 'prima facie proof of falsity' is sufficient for the purpose of granting an interim injunction[38] may conflict with the higher test for prior restraint in s 12(3), HRA 1998, and the close scrutiny which the European Court requires in such cases.

Parliament

Parliamentary privilege

Article 9 of the Bill of Rights of 1688 (BoR) provides that 'the freedom of **10.24** speech, and debates or proceedings in Parliament ought not to be impeached or questioned in any court or place outside of Parliament.' Each House has mechanisms for disciplining members for contempt if they make false accusations in the course of debates. Aggrieved parties can also petition the House through another MP to seek a retraction.

The effect of Article 9 BoR is that there is a 'blanket prohibition' on the **10.25** examination of Parliamentary proceedings in court. The court cannot hear

---

[35] At 74.
[36] App No 26633/95, (1996) 22 EHRR CD 213.
[37] See further, *Gaskin* v *UK* (1989) 12 EHRR 36 and *Leander* v *Sweden* (1987) 9 EHRR 433.
[38] RPA 1983, s 106(3).

evidence, cross-examination, or argument challenging the truth or propriety of anything done in the course of Parliamentary proceedings.[39] So, for example, a claimant suing a Member in defamation for speech outside of Parliament could not rely on statements by the MP in Parliament to invite an inference of malice.[40]

10.26 Article 9 BoR gives rise to an absolute privilege against suit in defamation for expression in Parliament. This extends to speech and publication incidental to the proceedings themselves, for example when giving evidence to a committee or the Parliamentary Commissioner for Standards.[41] However, defamatory statements made by parliamentarians outside Parliament are not absolutely privileged, even if they simply repeat something said in Parliament. In *Buchannon* v *Jennings*,[42] a member of the New Zealand Parliament gave a newspaper interview in which he said he 'did not resile from' defamatory statements he had made about the claimant in Parliament. The Privy Council held that the claimant could produce the record of what the MP had said in Parliament when he sued for the 'repetition by reference' to these words outside the legislature. This repetition was not absolutely privileged. In simply producing the text of what had been said, the claimant was not questioning the MP's 'mind, motive or intention when saying what he did inside Parliament'.[43] Thus a 'degree of circumspection is . . . called for when a Member of Parliament is moved or pressed to repeat out of Parliament a potentially defamatory statement previously made in Parliament'.[44]

10.27 A fair and accurate report of proceedings in either House or a committee of Parliament has qualified privilege in defamation and proceedings for contempt of court.[45] This is only lost if the publisher has acted maliciously. The media can also comment honestly upon statements made in Parliament under cover of privilege, whether they are true or not, provided the report gives an accurate account of the making of the statement.[46] These principles are broadly consistent with the Strasbourg case law on political speech and honest 'value judgments'.

---

[39] See *Hamilton* v *Al Fayed* [2000] 2 All ER 224, HL, *per* Lord Browne-Wilkinson at 231B.
[40] See *Church of Scientology of California* v *Johnson-Smith* [1972] 1 QB 522.
[41] See Defamation Act 1996, s 13(5).
[42] [2005] 1 AC 115.
[43] Para 18.
[44] Para 20.
[45] *Wason* v *Walter* (1868) LR 4 QB 73; see also *A-G* v *Times Newspapers Ltd* [1973] 1 All ER 815, at 823.
[46] See Milmo, E and Rodgers, WVH (eds), *Gatley on Libel and Slander* (10th edn, London: Sweet & Maxwell, 2004), at para 12.20 and the cases referred to.

The Strasbourg Court considered Article 9 BoR in *A* v *UK*.[47] A Member of   **10.28**
Parliament had initiated a debate in the House of Commons on social housing
policy. A and her family lived in social housing in his constituency. In the course
of the debate the MP attacked them as 'neighbours from hell', accusing them
of a range of anti-social activities. A denied the allegations but they were still
heavily reported in the media. A subsequently received hate mail and abuse in
the street. She wanted to sue the MP in defamation. She complained that the
absolute immunity breached either her right of access to the domestic courts
under Article 6(1) ECHR or her right to protect her reputation under Article 8
ECHR. Without deciding the point, the Court proceeded on the basis that the
immunity was a procedural rule rather than a substantive defence to civil claims.
This was because the rule was not phrased as a substantive defence and would
have to be justified as pursuing a legitimate aim and as a proportionate measure
irrespective of whether Article 6(1) ECHR or Article 8 ECHR was engaged.
The Court recalled that in *Young and O'Faolain* v *Ireland*,[48] the Commission had
rejected a similar complaint about immunity in respect of statements made in the
Irish Dail. It had done so on the grounds that the immunity allowed legislators
to engage in meaningful debate and represent their constituents on matters of
public interest without having to 'edit their opinions' because of anxiety about
suit. The Commission considered this was a legitimate aim. The Court agreed.
It noted that the UK immunity was narrower than those which operated in
other signatory States, limited as it was to statements inside Parliament. On this
basis, and because internal Parliamentary procedures could be used to redress
grievances, the Court found that the immunity was a proportionate measure in
pursuit of the legitimate aim. There may yet, however, be scope to challenge the
absolute nature of the privilege in cases where the statement in Parliament does
not genuinely relate to a matter of public interest.

Art 9 BoR prevents any direct criticism of a Member's conduct in Parliament, in   **10.29**
the course of court proceedings.[49] This will hamper the defence in a libel action
brought *by* a Parliamentarian if it requires such criticism to be levelled. Where
it does, the claim will be stayed unless the privilege is waived by the claimant
under s 13(1) of the Defamation Act 1996.[50] This provision probably succeeds

---

[47] (2002) 13 BHRC 623.
[48] App Nos 25646/94 and 29099/95, [1996] EHRLR 326.
[49] *Hamilton* v *Al Fayed*, at 231J.
[50] See *Prebble* v *Television NZ* [1995] 1 AC 321. The right to waive in s 13(1) of the Defamation
Act 1996 was introduced into the Defamation Bill in the House of Lords after the proceedings
against *The Guardian* in *Hamilton and Greer* v *Hencke and others* were stayed by the High Court
in 1995.

in ensuring that the rights of both parties to a fair trial under Article 6(1) ECHR are protected.

Contempt of Parliament

10.30   Each House of Parliament has the power to impose a range of punishments for contempt—from mild censure, through banishment from the precincts of the Palace of Westminster, to imprisonment. The definition of Parliamentary contempt is predictably loose, and includes any act which has a 'tendency' to 'obstruct or impede' the House, or its members and officers, in the exercise of their functions. This could extend to acts, in the form of articles or broadcasts, tending to diminish the respect due to them and lower their authority. There is no clearly established defence of truth or fair comment and there are no procedural safeguards for the person accused.

10.31   It is almost inconceivable that this power would be used today to stifle criticism or disrespectful comment by the media. Indeed, by its own resolution, the House of Commons will now lay a charge of contempt only where there is some 'substantial interference with its functions'.[51] If it did, the proceedings would be open to successful challenge in Strasbourg under Articles 5, 6, and 10 ECHR. Ironically, the HRA 1998 would not assist a journalist facing such proceedings, since the courts will not pass judgment on the fairness or otherwise of Parliament's procedures for protecting its 'established privileges'.[52]

---

[51] See generally, *Halsbury's Laws of England* (4th edn) Vol 34 paras 1009 and 1010.
[52] See *per* Lord Browne-Wilkinson in *Prebble* v *Television NZ*, at 332D, and the cases referred to; and HRA 1998, s 6(3) makes clear that Parliament is not a 'public authority' for the purposes of the Act.

11

LICENSING AND REGULATION OF THE MEDIA

Introduction	11.01
Broadcast Licensing and Regulation	11.02
Newspaper Licensing	11.18
Media Regulators	11.20

Introduction

Other chapters have considered the application of the guarantee of freedom of **11.01** expression to specific subject matters. In this chapter we consider the impact of the ECHR in connection with prior licensing and subsequent regulation of the media. In particular we consider the impact of the requirements of procedural fairness under Article 6 ECHR upon the activities of media regulators.

Broadcast Licensing and Regulation

The proviso for licensing in Article 10(1)

Article 10(1) ECHR provides: 'Everyone has the right to freedom of expression. **11.02** This right shall include freedom to hold opinions and to receive and impart information and ideas without interference by public authority and regardless of frontiers. This Article shall not prevent States from requiring the licensing of broadcasting, television or cinema enterprises.'

The third sentence does not exclude licensing of broadcasting and cinemas **11.03** entirely from the guarantees in the opening two sentences. The Court has explained that the origins of the third sentence were the technical limitations on broadcasting frequencies which made some form of regulation inevitable. Although there are still technical aspects, broadcasting licensing has other functions. It was recognized that the electronic media had the potential for much greater impact than the print media, and licensing controls sought to regulate content. A literal reading of the third sentence of Article 10(1) might suggest that any licensing restrictions were excluded from the Article's guarantees. However, the jurisprudence of the Court has developed so that restrictions imposed by way of broadcasting licensing are compatible with the Convention only if they satisfy two of the requirements for restrictions on freedom of expression in Article 10(2)—they must be prescribed by law and they must be necessary in a democratic society. In effect, the licensing of broadcasting, television, and cinema has become a further 'legitimate aim' which restrictions on freedom of expression may pursue. Licensing regimes may still be directed at technical aspects of broadcasting, but they may have wider public interest objectives as well. As with restrictions imposed for the other aims,[1] they are neither automatically a violation nor automatically valid. In particular, the government must demonstrate their necessity in a democratic society.[2]

11.04   The Court had to consider a complaint by a religious organization that it had not been allowed to compete for a national radio licence. The complaint was made under Articles 10 and 14. The Court found that both complaints were manifestly unfounded. Technical limitations did still mean that national licences had to be rationed and the UK had a margin of appreciation as to how to allocate these so as to satisfy as many listeners as possible.[3]

11.05   Because licensing regimes are a form of restriction on freedom of expression, they must be 'prescribed by law'. This means that they must not merely conform to national laws, but those laws (and the licensing regime generally) must be free from arbitrariness. The criteria by which licences will be granted must be published and the assessment of individual applications by reference to those criteria must be properly reasoned.[4] In both of these cases the Court found a violation of Article 10 because the process by which licences had been refused had been insufficiently transparent. In both cases, the Court relied on Recommendation R (2000) 23 from the Committee of Ministers of the Council of Europe, which proposed guidelines on how such applications should be handled. The Privy Council has similarly found arbitrary and discriminatory

---

[1]   Specified in Art 10(2).

[2]   *Groppera Radio AG and others* v *Switzerland* (1990) 13 EHRR 321; *Autronic AG* v *Switzerland* (1990) 12 EHRR 485 and *Informationsverein Lentia and others* v *Austria* (1993) 17 EHRR 93; *Demuth* v *Switzerland* (App No 38743/97), 5 November 2002.

[3]   *United Christian Broadcasting Ltd* v *UK* (App No 44802/98), 7 November 2000.

[4]   *Glas Nadezhda Eood and Elenlov* v *Bulgaria* (App No 14134/02), 11 October 2007 and *Meltex Ltd and Mesrop Movsesyan* v *Armenia* (App No 32283/04), 17 June 2008.

decisions to refuse broadcasting licences to be contrary to constitutional guarantees of freedom of expression and recognized the parallels to rights granted by the ECHR.[5]

In the UK, the regulation of broadcasting is carried out by Ofcom (the Office of Communications) under the Communications Act 2003. Ofcom is, of course, a public authority and obliged to act in conformity with Convention Rights. A refusal to grant or renew a licence could therefore be challenged if the Article 10 requirements were not met. Attempts to do so have so far been notably unsuccessful.[6]   **11.06**

Ofcom's licencees must observe standards set by the regulator's code.[7] These include requirements which have been imposed since the inception of commercial broadcasting such as due impartiality in the presentation of news and the protection of the public from offensive and harmful material. The latter is a rather diluted version of the terms used in earlier legislation which required broadcasters to observe standards of good taste and decency. The BBC has accepted an obligation to observe similar standards in its programmes.   **11.07**

The application of the offensiveness criteria to a party election broadcast had to be considered in *R (ProLife Alliance) v BBC*.[8] ProLife Alliance had submitted a PEB which contained vivid images of aborted foetuses. The BBC refused to broadcast it without amendment on the ground that it infringed the offensiveness standard. The Alliance chose not to challenge the existence of the criterion itself (or its extension to PEBs), but it did argue that its application to its broadcast was an impermissible interference with its freedom of expression. The Court of Appeal in a robust judgment upheld its complaint, but this decision was overturned by the House of Lords. The Lords said that there was no right under Article 10 to have access to the airwaves, but access could not be refused on arbitrary, discriminatory, or unreasonable grounds. The role of the court was not to substitute its own view for that of the broadcasters as to whether the programme failed the offensiveness test, but to decide whether the decision made by the broadcasters was unlawful. The majority decided that it was not.   **11.08**

The phrase 'regardless of frontiers' in the second sentence of Article 10(1) makes it clear that the restrictions on broadcasts which originate abroad will   **11.09**

---

[5] *Observer Publications Ltd v Campbell* (2001) 10 BHRC 252, PC; *Central Broadcasting Services Ltd v A-G of Trinidad and Tobago* (2006) 21 BHRC 577, PC.

[6] See, eg *R (Wildman) v Ofcom* [2005] EMLR 3.

[7] See Communications Act 2003, s 319.

[8] [2004] 1 AC 185.

also infringe the guarantee of freedom of expression unless they are prescribed by law and necessary in a democratic society.[9]

Public service broadcasting

11.10   The existence of publicly owned broadcasters does not infringe Article 10 ECHR, but in one of its most important cases the Court held that the right to freedom of expression was violated if the publicly owned stations had a monopoly on broadcasting from within the State. In *Informationsverein Lentia and others* v *Austria*,[10] the Court repeated the fundamental part that freedom of expression played in a democracy and the media's role of imparting information and ideas of general public interest which the public was also entitled to receive. It said: 'Such an undertaking cannot be successfully accomplished unless it is grounded in the principle of pluralism, of which the state is the ultimate guarantor' (at para 38). Austria argued that the state monopoly was necessary to guarantee the objectivity and impartiality of the audio-visual media and to achieve a diversity of programmes, balanced programming, and impartiality and independence. The Court was not persuaded. It saw state ownership as the most restrictive means of achieving these aims and observed that other European States sought to pursue similar aims by measures which allowed a mix of publicly and privately owned stations to coexist. The working out of a new regime in Austria was protracted. At one stage only two private radio stations were permitted for the Vienna region. In a subsequent case the Court said this was 'surprising', but did not need to rule on whether it was compatible with the Convention since the law allowing this had been declared null and void by the Austrian courts.[11]

Broadcasting bans

11.11   Under the BBC's Licence and Agreement and under the Communications Act 2003, s 336, the Home Secretary can direct broadcasters not to include any prescribed material in their programmes. Between 1988 and 1994 the equivalent power under earlier legislation was exercised to prohibit the broadcasting of the voices of anyone who was a member of or a supporter of a number of organizations, including Sinn Fein. Consequently, if Gerry Adams, the President of Sinn Fein, was interviewed on the television or radio, his words had to be blanked out and replaced with the voice of an actor and/or subtitles. The domestic legal challenge to these directions by various journalists and TV

---

[9]   See *Groppera Radio* and *Autronic*, above.
[10] (1993) 17 EHRR 93.
[11] *Radio ABC* v *Austria* (1997) 25 EHRR 185.

producers led to the House of Lords decision in *Brind* v *Secretary of State for the Home Department*.[12] Having lost in the domestic courts, they pursued their challenge in Strasbourg. However, the European Commission on Human Rights held that their application was inadmissible as manifestly unfounded. It agreed that the broadcasting bans did interfere with the applicants' freedom of expression, but the restrictions were prescribed by law and were pursuing the legitimate aim of combating terrorism. They had a limited effect on the broadcasters' freedoms and the court had recognized the particular difficulties of taking measures against terrorism. For these reasons, and taking account of the margin of appreciation, it was not reasonably arguable that the government had failed to show that the measures were necessary in a democratic society.[13] This decision followed a rejection of complaints from Ireland which had sought to argue that similar broadcasting bans in that country were contrary to Article 10.[14]

Although the particular broadcasting bans thus survived a Convention challenge, the introduction of the HRA 1998 will require a reversal of the principle which the House of Lords set out in *Brind*. That case has come to stand for the proposition that administrative decisions could not be challenged as unlawful on the grounds that they were contrary to the Convention. From 2 October 2000, public bodies are under a duty to act compatibly with Convention rights. Any future broadcasting ban would therefore have to be measured against the demands of Article 10 ECHR in order to assess its lawfulness.   **11.12**

Access to broadcasting

Article 10 ECHR guarantees a right to impart ideas and opinions, but access to the airwaves is in practice controlled by the broadcasters and anyone who wishes to 'impart ideas or opinions' on television or radio must pass these gatekeepers. Does Article 10 control the way in which they exercise these powers?   **11.13**

In general the answer is 'No'. In a case brought by Jorg Haider against Austria,[15] the Commission held that Article 10 ECHR does not give a general and unfettered right for any private citizen or organization to have access to the broadcasting media. There may be exceptional circumstances where one political party is excluded from broadcasting facilities to which others are given access. Even here, the Commission has declared inadmissible an application under   **11.14**

---

[12] [1991] AC 696.
[13] *Brind* v *UK* App No 18714/91, (1994) 77 DR 42.
[14] *Purcell* v *Ireland* App No 15404/89, (1991) 70 DR 262.
[15] *Haider* v *Austria* App No 25060/94, (1995) 83 DR 66.

Article 10 from an independent candidate for the European Parliament who was not allowed to make a party political broadcast.[16] The Commission recognized that airtime was inevitably limited and found that the threshold test used to decide which parties would be allowed a broadcast was compatible with Article 10(2). In the *Haider* case, the applicant also complained about the hostile manner in which he had been interviewed. The Commission commented, 'with regard to interviews of politicians, it is in the interests of freedom of political debate that the interviewing journalist may also express critical and provocative points of view and not merely give neutral cues for the statements of interviewed persons, since the latter can reply immediately'.

11.15 It would be a different matter if denial of access could be shown to be politically motivated. In *Benjamin* v *Minister of Information and Broadcasting*,[17] the Privy Council had to consider the case of a phone-in host whose programme was suspended when he held a discussion on whether Anguilla should have a state-run lottery. The government wanted to close down debate on this issue (as to which it had its own strong views). The Court held that while the constitutional guarantee of freedom of expression did not entail a right to broadcast, it did give protection against arbitrary and capricious behaviour of this kind. The House of Lords followed the same principle in finding that the ProLife Alliance failed to demonstrate that the BBC's refusal to air its party election broadcast violated Article 10 (*R (ProLife Alliance)* v *BBC* (above)).

Advertising restrictions

11.16 In *R (Animal Defenders International)* v *Secretary of State for Culture Media and Sport*,[18] the House of Lords considered the prohibition on the broadcasting of political advertising. The claimant had wanted to air an advert with the title 'My Mate's a Primate' as part of its campaign against cruelty to animals. It relied on a judgment of the European Court of Human Rights which had held that the Article 10 rights of a Swiss NGO with very similar aims had been violated because its advertisement urging people to eat less meat had been banned.[19] Indeed, because of this judgment the government uniquely had not certified that in its opinion the Communications Bill complied with Convention rights. However, the Lords found no incompatibility. It decided that the reason for the ban on political advertising was soundly based. It recognized the particularly strong

---

[16] See *Huggett* v *UK* (1995) 20 EHRR CD 104; see also, *Tete* v *France* App No 11123/84, (1987) 54 DR 52.
[17] [2001] 1 WLR 1040.
[18] [2008] 2 WLR 781.
[19] *VgT Verein Gegen Tierfabriken* v *Switzerland* (2001) 34 EHRR 159—'the VgT case'.

and invasive impact of broadcasting. It thought that the need for a reasonably level playing field between competing points of view was a strong reason for not allowing those with deeper pockets an advantage. It thought that lesser measures (or those decided on a case-by-case basis) would be impossible to operate. Parliament's decision also deserved particular respect because parliamentarians were likely to be particularly sensitive to what was needed to preserve the integrity of the democratic process and this measure had had broad support despite the reservation as to whether it was compatible with Convention rights. The VgT case was distinguished because there the organization was trying to respond to commercial advertising from the meat industry (which, obviously, wanted to encourage consumption). It thought that the wider considerations and principles were also compatible with the later decision of *Murphy* v *Ireland*,[20] in which the Irish ban on religious advertising had been found not to constitute a violation of Article 10.

EU law restricts advertising in certain respects via the Television Without   **11.17**
Frontiers Directive. In Case C–245/01 *RTL Television Gmbh* v *Niederachsische Landesmedienanstalt Fur Privarten Rundfunk*, the 5th Chamber of the ECJ held that the restrictions did not infringe Article 10 ECHR. The requirements pursued the legitimate aim of striking a balance between the interests of broadcasters and advertisers on the one hand and rights holders and television viewers on the other. The restrictions in question concerned the frequency of advertising, not its content, and the ECJ observed that the Human Rights Court allowed national authorities a discretion in deciding whether there was a pressing social need for the restriction. The advertisements concerned were also a form of commercial speech where again greater latitude is allowed to national authorities.

Newspaper Licensing

The press in the UK has not been licensed for centuries. There is still a   **11.18**
requirement for the printers and publishers of every newspaper which is not owned by a company registered under the Companies Acts to submit an annual return to Companies House with the title and name of the proprietor.[21]

The European Commission has held that a system of registration for the press   **11.19**
is not incompatible with the Convention as long as there is no discretion to

---

[20] (2003) 38 EHRR 212.
[21] Newspaper Libel and Registration Act 1881.

refuse registration (if the requirements are complied with) and as long as the requirements are purely formal. Even in these circumstances, a penalty for non-compliance would have to satisfy Article 10(2) ECHR.[22] Needless to say, any scheme must also be 'prescribed by law'. A Polish scheme which required a newspaper's title to be truthful was both too vague to satisfy this requirement and gave an inappropriate degree of control to state authorities.[23]

Media Regulators

11.20 There are various contexts in which the media are regulated either in advance of publication (eg the system for classification of videos by the British Board of Classification), or after the event (such as by Ofcom, the Press Complaints Commission, and the Advertising Standards Authority, as well as through the broadcast licensing system referred to at 11.06). We consider in other chapters the approach which the ECHR requires to be taken to substantive matters. Thus, for instance, chapter 8 considers the issues which are raised by the control of material which might be considered obscene or blasphemous. Here we deal briefly with the procedural issues which might arise under Article 6 ECHR in connection with such regulatory activities.

Article 6: applicability

11.21 Article 6 ECHR applies: 'In the determination of [a person's] civil rights and obligations or of any criminal charge against him.' These two alternatives—'civil rights and obligations' and 'criminal charge'—need to be considered separately.

Civil cases

11.22 For the Article 6 protections to apply, the case must concern a 'civil right', there must be an arguable basis for that right in domestic law (a dispute or *'contestation'* in French), and the procedure must lead to the 'determination' of the right.

11.23 The phrase 'civil rights or obligations' is an example of an 'autonomous concept', that is, a term which is defined and developed by the Court in the context of the Convention and its case law. Whether a dispute concerns a civil right is influenced, but not conclusively resolved, by its categorization in the domestic legal system.[24] Ultimately this question must be answered 'by reference to the substantive contents and effect of the right' in issue (at para 89). Comments

---

[22] *HN* v *Italy* App No 18902/91, (1998) 94 DR 21.
[23] *Gaweda* v *Poland* (2004) 39 EHRR 4.
[24] *König* v *Germany* (1978) 2 EHRR 170.

about this particular autonomous concept have to be tentative, in part because the Court appears to have shied away from providing a comprehensive definition and in part because its attitude has evolved over time and is still developing. Early cases from the Court referred to the distinction between rights in private law (which were treated as 'civil') and those in public law (which were not).[25] Paradigmatic cases can be identified in this way. Thus, litigation between two private parties (eg over libel, breach of confidence, or copyright) clearly concerns 'civil rights or obligations'. Conversely, disputes of a purely public law character which do not directly affect a private law right are not within Article 6(1) ECHR. On this basis, complaints have been dismissed in relation to the admission or expulsion of aliens, the recruitment or dismissal of civil servants, and the validity of election expenses, even though, in the last case, the applicant might have lost his seat and the payments which went with elected office.[26] However, disputed public law decisions which decisively affect the relationships of private legal personalities in civil law may involve the determination of civil rights (see *Ringeisen* v *Austria*, which concerned an administrative approval of a transfer of land between the applicant and a vendor).

The form or the venue of the dispute is clearly not decisive. In particular, disputes **11.24** which directly affect pecuniary rights or obligations, or which concern the use of property, are likely to be classified as 'civil'. Of particular significance in the context of the regulation of media activities are cases which have held that the withdrawal of a licence to engage in a commercial activity is a 'civil' matter,[27] and others which have held that refusal of planning permission to develop privately owned land also concerned civil rights.[28] It is likely that the refusal of a BBFC video certificate would concern a civil right in this sense. The Court has held that disciplinary proceedings by a professional body which can lead to the loss of the right to continue in the profession would engage Article 6(1).[29] Similarly the withdrawal of the necessary certificate for an executive to take part in the gaming industry engaged Article 6.[30] Decisions by Ofcom which might lead to the revocation of a broadcasting licence would similarly involve a 'civil right or obligation'.

---

[25] *Ringeisen* v *Austria* (1971) 1 EHRR 455.
[26] *Pierre-Bloch* v *France* (1998) 26 EHRR 202.
[27] *Pudas* v *Sweden* (1987) 10 EHRR 380; *Tre Traktörer Aktiebolag* v *Sweden* (1989) 13 EHRR 309; and see *Benthem* v *Netherlands* (1985) 8 EHRR 1.
[28] *Fredin* v *Sweden* (1991) 13 EHRR 784.
[29] *Le Compte, Van Leuven and De Meyere* v *Belgium* (1981) 4 EHRR 1; *Diennet* v *France* (1995) 21 EHRR 554.
[30] *Kingsley* v *UK* (2002) 35 EHRR 10.

11.25 In order for Article 6 to apply through the gateway of 'civil rights and obligations', there must also be an arguable basis in domestic law for the right. This in part reflects the principle that Article 6 is concerned with procedural rather than substantive rights, although the borderline between procedural bars and substantive ineligibility can sometimes be elusive.[31]

11.26 Furthermore, the dispute must concern a 'right' rather than a discretionary grant, so that the ability to apply for an ex gratia payment would not attract Article 6 procedural protections. Yet here, too, firm guidance is difficult. There have been cases where a dispute concerning the initial grant of a government licence has been held to be within Article 6 (see *Benthem* v *Netherlands*[32]—licence to run a petrol station granted then removed on basis of unknown opposition at the time of determination: the applicant continued to trade while an appeal went through the administrative system and then to court; *Jorbedo Foundation of Christian Schools* v *Sweden*[33]—extension of licence to an existing private middle school to allow it to teach older children). Although these have involved some element of ongoing commercial activity, this is not necessary in principle. On the face of it, therefore, even 'first time' or speculative applications for broadcasting licences would involve the determination of a civil right, however odd this may look.

11.27 Lastly, the proceedings must lead to a 'determination' of the right or obligation. On this basis the Al-Fayed brothers' complaint about the alleged unfairness of inspectors appointed under the Companies Acts was unsuccessful: the inspectors reported to the Department of Trade and Industry but determined nothing.[34] On the same basis, the Court of Appeal has concluded that the procedure by which a person's name was included on the Department of Health's list of people about whom there are doubts as to their suitability to work with children, did not have to conform with Article 6 ECHR. Although inclusion on the register would be highly detrimental to the prospects of a person gaining employment in a post that involved contact with children, it did not in itself determine anything.[35]

Criminal charge

11.28 Once again the concept of 'criminal' proceedings is autonomous. Here, though, if the domestic system does classify the proceedings as criminal that

---

[31] See, eg *Osman* v *UK* (1999) 1 FLR 198 and *Z* v *UK* (2002) 34 EHRR 3.
[32] (1985) 8 EHRR 1.
[33] App No 11533/85, (1987) 61 DR 92.
[34] *Fayed* v *UK* (1994) 18 EHRR 393.
[35] *R* v *Secretary of State for Health, ex p C* [2000] UKHRR 639, CA.

is determinative. Thus, unsurprisingly, Article 6(1) ECHR will apply if a broadcaster is prosecuted for an offence under the Broadcasting Act 1990 (eg broadcasting without a licence contrary to s 13), or if a person is charged with an offence under the Video Recordings Act 1984.

However, this is not the limit of the applicability of Article 6. Even if domestic law would regard the proceedings as non-criminal, they may involve the determination of a 'criminal' charge for the purposes of Article 6.[36] Contempt proceedings may not be strictly criminal as a matter of domestic law, but since they potentially involve imprisonment and/or substantial fines, they are criminal for the purposes of Article 6.[37]   **11.29**

The Court will look at the nature of the conduct in question and the severity of the possible penalty. The fines which Ofcom can impose can be (and have been) very large. In June 2008 it imposed a fine of £1.1 million (then its largest ever) on GCap Media in connection with a phone-in scandal. However, it is unlikely that the proceedings which lead to these penalties come within the Strasbourg concept of 'criminal'. It is only licensees who can face these proceedings. Previous cases before the Court have distinguished between regimes which have a general application (eg for collection of the community charge or poll tax and penalties for non-payment) which have been held to be 'criminal',[38] and those applying a disciplinary scheme to a particular group, such as prisoners (unless the allegations are sufficiently serious) or the armed forces, or civil servants, or professionals who face proceedings before their association. None of the latter has been held to involve the 'criminal' procedural protections.[39]   **11.30**

Article 6(1): rights granted

Assuming that Article 6(1) ECHR applies either because the proceedings concern the determination of a person's civil rights or obligations, or because they involve the determination of a criminal charge, it provides the following guarantees: **11.31**

(a) a fair and public hearing;
(b) within a reasonable time;
(c) by an independent and impartial tribunal established by law, with;
(d) judgment to be pronounced publicly.

---

[36] *Engel and others* v *Netherlands* (1976) 1 EHRR 706.
[37] See *Harman* v *UK* App No 10038/82, (1984) 38 DR 53 and *Raja* v *Van Hoogstraten* [2004] 4 All ER 793, CA.
[38] *Benham* v *UK* (1996) 22 EHRR 293.
[39] See, eg *R* v *Securities and Futures Appeal Tribunal, ex p Fleurose* [2002] IRLR 297, CA.

11.32   The judgment must be reasoned, but the duty to give a public hearing is not absolute. Article 6(1) provides that the: 'public may be excluded from all or part of the trial in the interest of morals, public order or national security in a democratic society, where the interests of juveniles or the protection of the private life of the parties so require, or to the extent strictly necessary in the opinion of the court in special circumstances where publicity would prejudice the interests of justice.'

11.33   Article 6(1) underpins the fundamental principle of the rule of law and is to be construed broadly.[40] Yet the decisions of the European Court indicate that the touchstone, as with the common law duty, is overall fairness, rather than particular technical failings. The case law of the Court under Article 6(1) is extensive, but the following features may be of importance in the context of media regulation.

The 'tribunal'

11.34   If not a court, this must exercise essentially judicial functions. The fact that it has other non-judicial, perhaps administrative, functions does not necessarily prevent it being a tribunal,[41] neither does the fact that the members are not professional judges.[42] Where a decision affecting civil rights or obligations is taken by a body which does not meet Article 6(1) requirements, the procedure can be saved by a right of appeal or review before a court or tribunal which does so.[43] A full reconsideration of the merits may be required (as in *Albert and Le Compte* v *Belgium,* where an appeal to the Court of Cassation against a decision of a medical disciplinary tribunal, on a point of law only, was regarded as insufficient), though not necessarily. The Court has accepted that in certain specialized areas of law, where issues of policy arise, Article 6(1) may be satisfied by a two-stage procedure under which an administrative body reaches a decision, making findings of fact and exercising judgment, which is then subject to an appeal or review on a point of law. In *Bryan* v *UK,*[44] the Court found that a planning inquiry was procedurally fair, but that the inspector lacked the necessary independence from the Secretary of State. The subsequent judicial review proceedings cured this defect, however, since the inspector's findings of fact were not disputed and the procedure enabled the applicant to challenge fully the policy decisions in issue. The House of Lords reached a like conclusion in

---

[40] *Delcourt* v *Belgium* (1969) 1 EHRR 355.
[41] See *Campbell and Fell* v *UK* (1984) 7 EHRR 165, concerning the disciplinary functions of a prison Board of Visitors.
[42] *Ettl* v *Austria* (1987) 10 EHRR 255.
[43] *Albert and Le Compte* v *Belgium* (1983) 5 EHRR 533, at para 29.
[44] (1995) 21 EHRR 342.

R (Alconbury Developments Ltd) v *Secretary of State for Environment, Transport and the Regions,*[45] confirmed by the Strasbourg Court in the admissibility decision of *Holding and Barnes* v *UK.*[46]

Independence and impartiality

In considering independence, 'regard must be had, *inter alia,* to the manner of appointment of [the tribunal's] members and to their term of office, to the existence of guarantees against outside pressures and to the question whether the body presents an appearance of independence'.[47] Appointment by the executive does not, per se, deny independence, though a right to dismiss during the appointee's terms of office would do so,[48] In *Zand* v *Austria,*[49] the Commission observed that 'the irremovability of judges during their term of office, whether it be for a limited period of time or for a lifetime, is a necessary corollary of their independence from the Administration and thus included in the guarantees of Article 6(1) of the Convention'. In one of the early Scottish cases under the HRA 1998, an objection to criminal trial by a temporary sheriff, who could be removed from office at any time for any reason by a member of the executive (the Lord Advocate), was upheld.[50]   **11.35**

Impartiality is simply the absence of bias. This may be actual bias, for which the Court applies a subjective test to establish the 'personal conviction of the given adjudicator', or perceived bias ('the lack of the necessary appearance of impartiality'). In the latter case the Court looks for 'sufficient guarantees to exclude any legitimate doubt'.[51] In *Kingsley* v *UK*, the applicant's licence to manage in the gaming industry had been removed following a Gaming Board hearing tainted by an appearance of bias. The Board had already resolved that he was not a 'fit and proper person' to hold a licence, which was the issue at the revocation hearing. However, the applicant failed to quash the decision in judicial review proceedings and was denied leave to appeal by the Court of Appeal. Both Courts held that the Board had no power to delegate the revocation hearing to an independent tribunal. The applicant was therefore denied his remedy on grounds of necessity. The European Court held that in this case judicial review was plainly   **11.36**

---

[45] [2003] 2 AC 295.

[46] (App No 2352/02), 11 March 2002.

[47] *Bryan* v *UK* (1995) 21 EHRR 342, at para 37; three-year terms of office were upheld in *Campbell and Fell*, see para 80.

[48] *Campbell and Fell* v *UK* (1984) 7 EHRR 165, at paras 79 and 80.

[49] App No 7360/76, (1978) 15 DR 70, at 80.

[50] *Starrs and Chalmers* v *Procurator Fiscal, Linlithgow* 2000 JC 208.

[51] *Piersack* v *Belgium* (1982) 5 EHRR 169, at para 30; *Langborger* v *Sweden* (1989) 12 EHRR 416; and *Kingsley* v *UK* (2002) 35 EHRR 10.

inadequate to cure the defect since the concept of full jurisdiction involves that the reviewing court not only considers the complaint but has the ability to quash the impugned decision. The UK courts similarly will find 'objective bias' where there are ascertainable facts that may raise doubts as to independence or impartiality if such doubts are objectively justified (see, eg *Re Medicaments and Related Classes of Goods (No 2)*[52]). An alternative formulation given by the House of Lords is whether a fair-minded and informed observer, having considered the facts, would conclude that there was a reasonable possibility that the tribunal was biased—*Porter* v *Magill*.[53]

Public hearing and public judgment

11.37 It is not unusual for many regulatory bodies to determine disputes on the basis of written submissions. This can be compatible with both the common law duty to act fairly and the Convention requirement of a 'hearing' unless there is some aspect of the dispute that can only be fairly resolved by an oral hearing. This might be the case, for instance, if there is a crucial dispute on the facts for which there is no adequate documentary record. In deciding whether the requirement for a *public* hearing and *public* judgment is satisfied, it is necessary to consider the legal process as a whole. Thus, the availability of judicial review which will give public scrutiny to any allegation of arbitrariness, unfairness, or other illegality by the regulator and give a public judgment on these matters may be sufficient to satisfy Article 6.[54]

Protections specific to 'criminal charges'

11.38 If the proceedings constitute the determination of a criminal charge, Article 6 guarantees certain specific procedural protections in addition to the general requirements of Article 6(1). Thus, Article 6(2) provides: 'Everyone charged with a criminal offence shall be presumed innocent until proved guilty according to law.'

11.39 Article 6(3) says:

Everyone charged with a criminal offence has the following minimum rights:

(a) to be informed promptly, in a language which he understands and in detail, of the nature and cause of the accusation against him;

(b) to have adequate time and facilities for the preparation of his defence;

---

[52] [2001] 1 WLR 700, CA.
[53] [2002] 2 AC 357, at para 103.
[54] *R (Heather Moore and Edgecomb Ltd)* v *Financial Ombudsman Service* [2008] EWCA Civ 642.

(c) to defend himself in person or through legal assistance of his own choosing or, if he has not sufficient means to pay for legal assistance, to be given it free when the interests of justice so require;

(d) to examine or have examined witnesses against him and to obtain the attendance and examination of witnesses on his behalf under the same conditions as witnesses against him;

(e) to have the free assistance of an interpreter if he cannot understand or speak the language used in court.

In addition, Article 7 prohibits the imposition of retrospective criminal liability or a more severe penalty than prevailed at the time the criminal offence was committed.   **11.40**

A considerable body of case law has elaborated these rights and the specialist books on criminal procedure should be consulted if the proceedings in question are likely to be classified as the determination of a criminal charge.   **11.41**

Article 6: issues for media regulation

As indicated above, there are a number of statutory and industry-imposed regimes for the regulation of television, radio, cinema/video, the press, and advertising. The status of these bodies under the HRA 1998 is dealt with at 3.36. The impact that their decisions can have on the interests of media organizations (as well as complainant consumers) is varied. They will have to be alive to decisions which engage Article 6(1) rights. Some, such as denial/revocation of a licence or a requirement to cease an advertising campaign, will obviously do so. Others may be less obvious.   **11.42**

Where these rights are engaged, regulators should not assume that the possibility of a judicial review challenge to the proceedings after the event will cure all defects, as it did following the planning inquiry in *Bryan* v *UK*.[55] They will have to ensure that their procedural arrangements meet the Article 6 requirements, particularly in respect of the fairness of the fact-finding exercise. This may not be too traumatic. They have been subject to the public law duty of fairness for many years. In broad terms this corresponds with the Article 6 protection, in particular the requirement to accord a fair hearing. Indeed, in some respects the common law duty is broader. It applies, for instance, to all parties (including the person presenting a complaint or opposing an application for a licence or renewal). The duty to give a public hearing would have been novel in many regulatory contexts some years ago, but there has been a marked trend towards   **11.43**

---

[55] (1995) 21 EHRR 342 (see para 11.34).

more openness recently. The regulator may be able to rely upon the provisions for the exclusion of the public in some cases—for example, a contested PCC complaint about the private life of a celebrity.

11.44   The need to have an impartial and independent tribunal is also a principle of common law. However, here, as the *Starrs and Chalmers* case has illustrated (see 11.35), Convention law may be stricter. The composition of, and terms of appointment to, some regulatory bodies may require reappraisal to ensure that this requirement is met. These sometimes allow the Secretary of State considerable discretion which may give rise to challenges in particular cases. Regulators will also have to take care not to fall into the trap of prejudging issues that may return before them in the form of a decision as to a person's 'civil rights and obligations', in the way the Gaming Board did in *Kingsley* v *UK* (see 11.36). Where this is unavoidable, provision will have to be made for lawful delegation of the second decision to a body untainted by involvement in the first decision. The seminal common law case on bias was the decision of the House of Lords in *R* v *Gough*.[56] Having reviewed the Strasbourg case law, the Court of Appeal said that a 'modest adjustment' of the *Gough* test was needed (in *Re Medicaments and Related Classes of Goods (No 2)*, above). Courts would now examine all the circumstances and ask themselves whether a fair-minded and informed observer would conclude that there was a real possibility or real danger that the tribunal was biased.

---

[56]   [1993] AC 646.

12

COMMERCIAL SPEECH AND ADVERTISING

Introduction	12.01
ECHR Case Law	12.07
The Impact of the HRA on Domestic Law	12.23

Introduction

In the UK, as in most jurisdictions, commercial speech is subject to a large **12.01** number of restrictions, from the Trade Descriptions Act 1968 regulating misleading advertising to European Directives regulating a number of fields such as tobacco advertising and Codes of Practice which regulate various media such as television and radio.[1] Political advertising on television and radio is prohibited by the Communications Act 2003.[2]

In the first edition of this work, we predicted that given the relative lack of case **12.02** law from the European Court of Human Rights and the regular recourse to the doctrine of the margin of appreciation, domestic courts may find assistance from the more evolved jurisprudence of other countries, such as Canada and the USA, both of which provide a substantial degree of protection to truthful and accurate commercial speech.[3] So far, our prediction has turned out to be utterly wrong with domestic courts finding little or no assistance from the North American jurisdictions.[4] As discussed below, the incorporation of Article 10 ECHR has,

---

[1] The Advertising Standards Authority regulates non-broadcast and, since 2004, broadcasting advertising.

[2] See below, at para 12.34.

[3] See, eg *Central Hudson Gas* v *Public Services Commission* 447 US 557 (1980) and *RJR Macdonald* v *A-G of Canada* (1995) 127 DLR (4th) 1.

[4] See, eg McCombe J in *R (British American Tobacco and others)* v *The Secretary of State for Health* [2004] EWHC 2493. See also, Lord Hale's speech at para 47 in *R (Animal Defenders)* v *Secretary of State for Culture* [2008] 2 WLR 781.

with limited exceptions, had little impact on the regulation of commercial speech and advertising, and such speech continues to be heavily regulated and, in certain circumstances, prohibited.

What is commercial speech?

12.03   Numerous definitions have been advanced for 'commercial speech' yet none is entirely satisfactory. Perhaps the dominant view is that commercial speech is speech that is primarily designed to promote the commercial, economic, or financial interests of individuals or enterprises.[5] The most obvious example of commercial speech is advertising, but, as can be seen from the ECHR case law, it extends beyond advertising to include any means of conveying commercial information to the consumer. This chapter, in addition to considering 'pure' commercial speech, also considers political and religious advertising.

Why protect commercial speech?[6]

12.04   Commercial speech clearly qualifies as 'speech' or 'expression' on any normal understanding of the words, as it involves the conveying of information and ideas. To exclude commercial speech from protection under Article 10 ECHR would inevitably require courts to draw arbitrary distinctions between it and other kinds of expression. Furthermore, as the US Supreme Court has explained, consumers have an interest in receiving accurate, truthful information about products: 'As to the particular consumer's interest in the free flow of commercial information, that interest may be as keen, if not keener by far, than his interest in the day's most urgent political debate . . . When drug prices vary as strikingly as they do, information as to who is charging what becomes more than a convenience. It could mean the alleviation of physical pain or the enjoyment of basic necessities.'[7]

Competing interests

12.05   The justifications for restricting commercial speech are generally accepted to be stronger than in the case of political, and possibly artistic, speech. Clearly there is a public interest in forbidding false or misleading claims about products or services. These competing interests of consumer protection and fair competition

---

[5]   See *Demuth* v *Switzerland* (2004) 38 EHRR 20, at paras 41–2.
[6]   See Munro, CR, 'The Value of Commercial Speech' [2003] 62 CLJ 134 for a general discussion of the reasons for protecting commercial speech.
[7]   *Virginia State Board of Pharmacy* v *Virginia Citizens Consumer Council* 425 US 748 (1976), at 76–84.

mean that in every jurisdiction commercial speech is subject to considerable regulation.

Categorization[8]

The European Court of Human Rights, like the US Supreme Court, has sought to break down expression into separate categories. Expression categorized as political receives substantial protection whilst commercial expression receives limited protection with the Court deferring to States in relation to the regulation of both misleading and truthful advertising. However, expression often does not neatly fall into one category. Paid-for speech sometimes concerns matters of public concern such as the human rights violations in Rwanda and Burundi at issue in *Amnesty International (UK)* v *UK*.[9] The European Court has treated commercial speech on political matters and matters of public concern, which it has defined broadly, as entitled to heightened protection whilst pure commercial speech advertising products has received little protection. Until recently, the Court's classification of the speech in question had been determinative of the outcome of the proceedings. All cases concerning restrictions on commercial speech relating to matters of public concern including, but not limited to, political issues resulted in a finding that Article 10 ECHR had been violated.[10] However, the European Court recently concluded that a ban on religious advertising in the broadcast media was permissible notwithstanding that the advertising related to matters of public concern rather than merely the promotion of pure commercial interests.[11] Again, until recently, all cases concerning limits on expression classified as purely commercial had been found not to violate Article 10 ECHR. However, in *Krone Verlag GmbH & Co* v *Austria (No 3)*,[12] the European Court concluded that Austria's restrictions on comparative advertising did breach Article 10 EHCR. It remains to be seen whether the importance of the categorization, by the European Court, of the speech in issue will diminish. *Krone Verlag* and *Murphy* perhaps suggest that the European Court is developing a more sophisticated analysis of commercial speech which is to be welcomed.

12.06

---

[8] See Randall, MH, 'Commercial Speech under the ECHR: Subordinate or Equal?' Human Rights Law Review [2006] 6 53 for a useful overview of the European Court's approach to commercial speech and a critique of its categorization approach.

[9] (App No 38383/97), 18 January 2000.

[10] Matters of 'public concern' include the safety of microwaves, at issue in *Hertel* v *Switzerland* (1998) 28 EHRR 534, and debate about veterinary services.

[11] See *Murphy* v *Ireland* (2004) 38 EHRR 13.

[12] (2004) 39 EHRR 42.

ECHR Case Law

Commercial speech: general principles

12.07 The leading authority in the ECHR case law on the protection of commercial speech is *Markt Intern Verlag and Klaus Beermann* v *Germany*.[13] *Markt Intern* grants Member States an extremely wide margin of appreciation in regulating and banning commercial speech. The Court was evenly split 9:9, but the President, with his casting vote, concluded that there had been no violation of Article 10 ECHR. The applicants published a bulletin which included an article about the dissatisfaction of a customer who had been unable to obtain the promised reimbursement of a beauty product purchased from a mail-order firm. The bulletin requested further information from its readers as to the commercial practices of the firm. The applicants were restrained by court order from repeating the statements on the grounds that they infringed the German Unfair Competition Act 1909. The German government again attempted to argue that Article 10 was not engaged because of the commercial nature of the speech.[14] The applicant argued in reply that to restrict the scope of Article 10 to news items of a political or cultural nature would result in depriving a large proportion of the press of any protection.

12.08 The Court concluded that the speech, although addressed to tradespeople rather than the public at large, conveyed information of a commercial nature which was within the ambit of Article 10 ECHR.[15] The majority judgment, however, removed virtually all scrutiny of decisions in this field when it concluded that in the area of commercial matters, and in particular unfair competition, States were permitted a wide margin of appreciation, otherwise the Court would have to undertake a re-examination of the facts and all the circumstances of the case.[16] The Court confined its review to the question whether the measures taken at the national level were justifiable in principle and proportionate. Applying this very deferential approach the Court concluded that it could not be said that the granting of injunctions went beyond the margin of appreciation left to the national authorities, and therefore there was no breach of Article 10.[17]

---

[13] (1989) 12 EHRR 161.
[14] At para 25.
[15] At para 26.
[16] At paras 32–3.
[17] At paras 36–8.

This approach was cogently criticized by the various dissenting opinions, **12.09** which considered the majority's decision as an abdication of the Court's role of supervision, and as an unwarranted departure from earlier Article 10 jurisprudence requiring that the necessity of any interference with the right to freedom of expression needed to be 'convincingly established'.[18] The dissenting judgments took a different view of the importance of the expression at issue, stating that: 'It is just as important to guarantee the freedom of expression in relation to the practices of a commercial undertaking as it is in relation to the conduct of a head of government . . . In order to ensure the openness of business activities it must be possible to disseminate freely information and ideas concerning the products and services proposed to consumers'.[19]

Commercial speech and advertising by professionals

Barthold v *Germany*,[20] concerned an interview given by a German veterinary **12.10** surgeon (Mr Barthold) to a local newspaper, in which the vet was critical of the lack of emergency veterinary services at night in Hamburg. He went on to state that his clinic was the only one offering such a service. This interview led to proceedings against Mr Barthold for breaking the rules of professional conduct forbidding advertising and publicity, and for breaching s 13 of the German Unfair Competition Act 1909. The German courts granted interim and final injunctions requiring him to refrain from repeating the statements on the grounds that the publicity provided exceeded the bounds of objective comment on matters of justified public concern. The Court by a majority found that there had been a violation of Article 10 ECHR. The German government again sought to argue that Article 10 was not engaged because it did not extend to commercial speech, as this was a matter relating to the right freely to exercise a trade or profession which was a right not protected by the Convention.[21]

The majority judgment rejected this argument on the grounds that the speech in **12.11** question included the expression of 'opinions' and the imparting of 'information on a topic of general interest'.[22] Furthermore, the publication in issue was an article written by a journalist and not a commercial advertisement. The majority, however, explicitly refused to decide whether, as a matter of principle,

---

[18] At p 176. Joint Dissenting Opinion of Judges Golcuklu, Pettiti, Russo, Speilmann, De Meyer, Carrillo Salcedo, and Valticos.
[19] At p 177.
[20] (1985) 7 EHRR 383.
[21] At para 40.
[22] At paras 41–2.

commercial advertising came within the scope of Article 10.[23] They went on to find that the restrictions placed on Mr Barthold, while pursing the legitimate aim of 'protecting the rights of others',[24] were not 'necessary in a democratic society' because they were so strict as not to be proportionate.[25] The Court invoked the fear of the chilling effect when it stated that the very strict rules risked discouraging members of liberal professions from contributing to public debate on topics of public interest, as such comment might be treated as entailing (to some degree) an advertising effect.[26] Judge Pettiti's concurring opinion went further in discussing commercial advertising by the liberal professions, and drew on US jurisprudence to support the general proposition that: 'Freedom of expression in its true dimension is the right to receive and to impart information and ideas. Commercial speech is directly connected with that freedom . . . Even if it were to be conceded that the State's power to regulate is capable of being more extensive in relation to commercial advertising, in my view it nevertheless remains the case that "commercial speech" is included within the sphere of freedom of expression'.[27]

12.12   In *Casado Coca* v *Spain*,[28] the Court had to examine a near absolute ban on advertising by lawyers.[29] The applicant placed an advert in a local newspaper containing only neutral factual information, such as name, address, and telephone number. There was nothing in the advert that was untrue, offensive, or misleading. Neither did the advertisement criticize any fellow members of the Bar. However, contrary to the Commission's opinion, the Court concluded that there was no violation of Article 10 ECHR. The Commission took the view that the near absolute ban on factual advertising was excessive and not necessary in a democratic society. The Commission opined that such a ban infringed not only the rights of the applicant, but also the public's right to receive information. The Court again took refuge in the doctrine of margin of appreciation and concluded by a majority of 7:2 that there was no violation of Article 10. Factors that led the Court to reach this view included the limited nature of the sanction, the lack

---

[23]   At para 42.
[24]   At para 51.
[25]   At paras 52–9.
[26]   At para 58.
[27]   At pp 407–8. Judge Pettiti cited various US judgments, including *Virginia State Board of Pharmacy* v *Virginia Citizens Consumer Council* 425 US 748 (1976) and *Bates* v *Bar of Arizona* 433 US 350 (1977).
[28]   (1994) 18 EHRR 1.
[29]   Advertising was permitted in certain, very limited circumstances, namely when a practice was being set up or if there was a change of membership, address, or telephone number.

of consensus on legal advertising throughout Europe, and the complexity of the issue.[30]

The Court has taken a less deferential approach to regulation of other liberal professions. In *Colman* v *UK*,[31] the Commission considered the complete ban on advertising by general practitioners which existed, in the UK, prior to the relaxation of rules in May 1990. The Commission concluded that the application was admissible, but before the Court could consider the case it was struck out as a result of a friendly statement, whereby the government made no admission as to a breach of the Convention but agreed to pay the applicant £12,500.

12.13

In *Stambuk* v *Germany*,[32] the Court considered a fine of 2000 marks imposed on an ophthalmologist for breach of the Rules of Professional Conduct. The ophthalmologist had appeared in a newspaper article reporting on his use of laser operation techniques and his success rates, which were explained by reference to his expertise and experience. The domestic courts considered that the publication went beyond the limits of objective information and therefore constituted advertising which was prohibited by the relevant rules of professional conduct. The European Court, however, analysed the principle content of the article as providing information on matters of public concern rather than advertising services, notwithstanding the large photograph of the applicant accompanying the article. The European Court distinguished its approach to lawyers' advertising concluding that there was no similar justification for granting Member States such a wide margin of appreciation, because there was no lack of common ground among Member States regarding the principles at issue. The Court concluded that Article 10 ECHR was violated by the State's strict interpretation on the ban on advertising in the medical profession which prohibited articles that may have a possible side effect of giving publicity to the medical practitioner concerned. The interference in question did not achieve a fair balance between the interests at stake, namely the protection of health and the interests of other medical practitioners and the applicant's right to freedom of expression and the vital role of the press and, as such, it was not 'necessary in a democratic society'.

12.14

---

[30] Ibid, at paras 54–5. See also, *Lindner* v *Germany* (App No 32813/96), 9 March 1999. Challenge to disciplinary action taken against a German lawyer for advertising contrary to the rules of his profession. Declared inadmissible. The Court recognized that the regulation of professional advertising was in a state of flux in the Member States of the Council of Europe and that there was a wide range of regulations in Member States. However, it saw this as further reason for allowing Member States a wider margin of appreciation and, especially in light of the modest penalty imposed on the applicant, did not find the restriction disproportionate in the applicant's case.

[31] (1993) 18 EHRR 119.

[32] (2003) 37 EHRR 42.

Commercial speech and advertising critical of competitors or products

12.15   In *Jacubowski* v *Germany*,[33] the applicant had been dismissed as an editor of a news agency which issued a press release questioning the applicant's abilities. The applicant, who was planning to set up on his own, was restrained by injunction from sending a mailing to journalists containing newspaper articles critical of his former employer and a letter offering to meet with them to discuss future developments in the media market. The applicant contended that the injunction violated his right to freedom of expression. The Commission unanimously found a violation of Article 10 ECHR. However, yet again the Court adopted a more deferential approach and concluded, by a majority, that there was no violation having recourse to the margin of appreciation. The Court concluded that the injunction banning the distribution of the circular was not disproportionate because the applicant was still permitted to criticize the news agency. As the applicant's circular merely approved and set out passages of various newspaper articles which were already in the public domain, it is hard to agree with the majority decision. The German court yet again analysed the matters as unfair competition rather than as relating to the right of freedom of expression, and the European Court refused to criticize such an approach. This conclusion is particularly surprising given the circumstances of the circular, where the applicant had been publicly criticized by the news agency.

12.16   In *Hertel* v *Switzerland*,[34] the Court considered an injunction obtained by the Swiss Association of Manufacturers and Suppliers of Household Electrical Appliances under the Swiss Federal Unfair Competition Act 1986, prohibiting the applicant from stating, *inter alia,* that food prepared in microwave ovens was a danger to human health. The applicant, a scientist, had published a research paper in which he concluded that food prepared in microwave ovens 'may' be damaging to human health. The domestic court concluded that the applicant's article unfairly denigrated goods of others by making 'inaccurate, misleading or unnecessarily wounding statements'. The European Court treated the expression in question as concerning a matter of public interest, namely the effects of microwaves on health, rather than as merely commercial speech. This led the Court to apply a more rigorous test of the necessity of the interference, and it concluded that the injunction violated the applicant's right to freedom of expression because it was disproportionate and therefore not 'necessary in a democratic society'. The fact that the applicant's opinion was a minority one, possibly devoid of merit, was immaterial

---

[33] (1994) 19 EHRR 64.
[34] (1998) 28 EHRR 534.

because the right to freedom of expression is not limited to widely held opinions.[35]

In *Krone Verlag GmbH & Co v Austria (No 3)*,[36] the Court was, for the first time, **12.17** confronted with restrictions on comparative advertising. The advertisement in issue was promoting subscriptions of a newspaper and asserted it was the 'best local newspaper' contrasting it with another more expensive rival. The Austrian courts granted a preliminary injunction prohibiting the comparative advertising. In the main proceedings, the Austrian courts concluded that the applicant should refrain from comparing the sales prices of the two newspapers without indicating the differences in their reporting styles as regards coverage of various issues including foreign or domestic politics. Notwithstanding the wide margin of appreciation given to pure commercial speech, the European Court concluded unanimously that there had been a violation of Article 10 ECHR. The Court concluded that the restrictions were far too broad, impairing the very essence of price comparison, and further were very difficult to comply with. As such the measure imposed was disproportionate and not 'necessary in a democratic society'. It remains to be seen whether *Krone Verlag* heralds a more robust approach to commercial speech that does not relate to matters of public concern.

Political and religious advertising

A number of European States, including the UK, prohibit or severely limit **12.18** political and religious advertising, particularly in relation to the broadcast media. The rationale for such restrictions is usually said to be the desire to create a level playing field in the discussion of political issues. The restrictions on such advertising thus prevent well-funded organizations dominating the public debate.[37] Additional but very much secondary justifications include the possibility of offence caused by such advertising, particularly when it relates to moral issues such as abortion or animal cruelty.

---

[35] cf *SRG* v *Switzerland* (Application No 43524/98) where the Court rejected a complaint by a Swiss Radio and Television Company who had been ordered to pay CHF489,000 damages to a pharmaceutical company for broadcasting information critical of the side effects of multi-component painkillers referring by name to the drug produced by the pharmaceutical company. The Court, by a majority, concluded that the application was inadmissible on the grounds that it was manifestly ill-founded. *Hertel* was distinguished on the grounds that the broadcast singled out one particular medicament. SRG would have been free to broadcast a programme without mention of this drug or could have mentioned all the products of this type.

[36] (2004) 39 EHRR 42.

[37] See *VgT Verein gegen Tierfabriken* v *Switzerland* (2002) 34 EHRR 4, at paras 60–2, where the Court accepted that a desire to prevent financially powerful groups from obtaining a competitive political advantage was for the legitimate aim of protecting the rights of others.

12.19   Until recently there was a dearth of case law before the Strasbourg Court on political and religious advertising.[38] However, the European Court has now considered two cases, *VgT Verein gegen Tierfabriken* v *Switzerland*[39] and *Murphy* v *Ireland*,[40] where it addressed the level of protection of such expression, albeit reaching differing conclusions in relation to political and religious advertising. *VgT* concerned the refusal of a commercial television company to broadcast an advertisement from an animal welfare group exhorting the viewers to 'eat less meat, for the sake of your health, the animals and the environment'. The Court noted that the advertisement in question reflected controversial opinions pertaining to modern society in general. As such the margin of appreciation was reduced since what was at stake was not a given individual's purely 'commercial interests', but his participation in a debate affecting the general interest.[41] The Court concluded that the applicant was not a powerful and well-financed group seeking to unfairly sway public debate or unduly influence public opinion, but was merely seeking to participate in the ongoing general debate on animal protection and the rearing of animals. The Court noted that whilst it could not exclude the possibility that, in certain situations, a prohibition of political advertising may be compatible with the requirements of Article 10 ECHR, in the present case the grounds advanced for prohibiting the advertisement were insufficient to justify the interference with the applicant's right to freedom of expression.[42] One of the Swiss government's arguments advanced in support of the ban was that if the applicant's claim was successful it would essentially mean that the applicant had a 'right to broadcast' which would in turn substantially interfere with rights of the commercial television company to communicate information. The Court rejected this argument on the grounds that its judgment was essentially declaratory, and it was for the Member State to consider the issue of how any breach should be remedied. When the case returned to the Swiss courts they refused to amend their previous decision so as to permit the broadcasting of the advertisement because they were of the view that the

---

[38]   *Amnesty International (UK)* v *UK* (App No 38383/97), 18 January 2000, concerned a ban on political advertisement on the radio which prevented Amnesty International raising awareness of human rights violations in Rwanda and Burundi. However, before the Court could consider admissibility the Radio Authority reversed its decision and permitted the applicant to advertise. Arguably, *Lehideux and Isorni* v *France* (2000) 30 EHRR 665 concerned political advertising, as it concerned an advertisement in *Le Monde* seeking the rehabilitation of Marshal Pétain. However, the Court did not address the commercial context of the expression characterizing the discussion as part of an 'ongoing debate among historians' when considering the proportionality of a conviction under legislation prohibiting publicly defending the crimes of collaboration.

[39]   (2002) 34 EHRR 4.

[40]   (2004) 38 EHRR 13.

[41]   Ibid, at para 71.

[42]   Ibid, at para 75.

applicant had not provided sufficient reasons for such an amendment. The European Court concluded that the Swiss court's approach was overly formalistic and amounted to a further breach of Article 10 ECHR.[43] This matter had been referred to the Grand Chamber and a decision is awaited in the near future.

In *Murphy*, by contrast, the Court unanimously found that Article 10 had not been violated by a ban on religious advertising on the radio and television. The applicant wished to place a short commercial on a local radio station drawing attention to an hour-long video on the evidence for Jesus Christ which was transmitted by satellite during Easter week. The Independent Radio and Television Commission stopped the advertisement on the grounds that it breached a statutory prohibition on religious advertising. This decision was upheld by the Irish Courts. The European Court treated the expression in question very differently to the animal welfare advert at issue in *VgT*. Drawing on its previous case law concerning blasphemous speech and offensive art, the Court concluded that States should be accorded a wide margin of appreciation when regulating speech in relation to matters liable to offend intimate personal convictions within the sphere of morals and religion. *VgT* was distinguished on this basis. The Court accepted the Irish government's argument that the particular religious sensitivities in Irish society were such that the broadcasting of any religious advertisement could be considered offensive and amounting to proselytism. In support of this conclusion, the Court noted the limit on the applicant's right to freedom of expression did not prevent advertising in the print media and, further, the ban did not prevent him participating in debate on religious matters in the broadcast media.

12.20

Speech by commercial organizations on matters of public concern

Although not strictly within the definition of 'commercial speech' set out at the beginning of this chapter, the decision in *Open Door Counselling and Dublin Well Woman* v *Ireland*[44] is likely to be of relevance in the commercial expression field, particularly when restrictions on truthful advertising are in issue.[45] Open Door Counselling and Dublin Well Woman were Irish organizations that provided non-directive counselling to pregnant women. This counselling included the provision of information about abortion facilities outside Ireland, including their addresses and telephone numbers. The Society for the Protection of the

12.21

---

[43] App No 32772/02.
[44] (1992) 15 EHRR 245.
[45] See paras 12.26–12.32 below in relation to tobacco advertising.

Unborn Child obtained a permanent injunction preventing staff at the clinics from providing such information to pregnant women.

12.22 The Court concluded by a majority of 15:8 that the permanent injunction was a violation of Article 10 ECHR. The majority thought that while the Irish State had a legitimate interest in protecting the right to life of the unborn child,[46] this interest did not grant the State an unfettered and unreviewable power to act to protect this interest. While the Irish State enjoyed a considerable margin of appreciation in relation to this type of expression, this margin was not unlimited and measures were not automatically justified where the right to life of the unborn child is at stake. The Court concluded that the expression in question was subject to protection under Article 10 ECHR and that the absolute nature of the injunction was such that it was disproportionate. The Court stated that although the information in question was likely to offend, shock, and disturb a significant proportion of the Irish population, this was not sufficient grounds for restricting it, particularly when the expression in question was limited to factual and truthful statements on services which were lawful in other Convention countries and might be crucial to a woman's health and well-being. The Court, in reaching its decision, further noted that it was not a criminal offence under Irish law for a pregnant woman to travel abroad in order to have an abortion.

The Impact of the HRA on Domestic Law

Misleading, false, and deceptive advertising

12.23 Bans or other restrictions on misleading or inaccurate advertising will be unaffected by the HRA 1998. There have already been decisions of the Administrative Court upholding as compatible with Article 10 adjudications of the Advertising Standards Authority that its Code had been violated.[47] The European Commission on Human Rights has made it clear that such restrictions are permissible to protect the rights of consumers,[48] as has the European Court

---

[46] Article 40(3) of the Irish Constitution (the Eighth Amendment), which came into force in 1983, provides: 'The State acknowledges the right to life of the unborn and, with due regard to the equal right to life of the mother, guarantees in its laws to respect, and, as far as practicable, by its laws to defend and vindicate that right.'

[47] See *R* v *Advertising Standards Authority, ex p Matthias Rath BV* The Times, 10 January 2001 and *Smith Kline Beecham plc* v *Advertising Standards Authority,* 17 January 2001.

[48] See *K* v *Federal Republic of Germany* (App No 17006/90), 2 July 1991.

of Justice.[49] This, not unsurprisingly, accords with the position in the USA.[50] Restrictions and prohibitions on advertising of illegal activities, such as the sale of narcotics, will also be unaffected by the 1998 Act. Thus the prohibition of job advertisements that discriminate on the grounds of sex or race will survive challenge.[51]

Truthful and comparative advertising

The HRA 1998 has had some impact on restrictions on truthful and comparative **12.24** advertising of safe commercial products. A different approach is taken to truthful advertising of harmful products such as tobacco which is discussed below. The High Court has rejected applications for interim injunctions seeking to restrict comparative advertisements on the basis of trademark infringement because Article 10 ECHR was engaged, and therefore the party seeking the injunction had to demonstrate that they were likely to succeed at trial rather than merely that they have a real prospect of success and the balance of convenience favours the injunction.[52]

In *R (North Cyprus Tourism Centre Ltd)* v *Transport for London*,[53] the High Court **12.25** considered a ban by Transport for London on any advertising by Northern Cyprus on the basis that it was an unrecognized government illegally occupying part of Cyprus and that such advertising was likely to cause widespread or serious offence to members of the public or sections of the public. The High Court quashed Transport for London's decision on domestic public law grounds but Newman J also concluded obiter, that the ban violated Article 10 ECHR. In a somewhat cursory analysis, Newman J held that the ban was not 'prescribed by law', for a legitimate aim, or 'necessary in a democratic society'.[54]

Tobacco advertising

One of the most controversial areas of product advertising concerns tobacco. **12.26** In Canada, a challenge to various provisions concerning tobacco advertising and unattributed health warnings was held not to be justifiable since it was an unreasonable restriction on the tobacco company's right to freedom of

---

[49] See *Herbert Karner Industrie-Auktionen GmbH* v *Troostwijk GmbH* [2004] ECR I–3025.
[50] See, eg *Central Hudson Gas* v *Public Services Commission* 447 US 557 (1980).
[51] See *Pittsburgh Press Co* v *The Pittsburgh Commission on Human Relations* 413 US 3376 (1973).
[52] See *Boehringer Ingelheim Ltd* v *Vetplus Ltd* [2007] EWCA Civ 583 (concerning comparative advertising of nutritional supplements for dogs) and *Red Dot Technologies Ltd* v *Apollo Fire Detectors Ltd* [2007] EWHC 1166 (comparative advertising of fire alarms).
[53] [2005] EWHC 1698.
[54] Ibid, at paras 75–96.

expression.[55] The majority of the Canadian Supreme Court took a far more rigorous approach than is usually taken by the European Court of Human Rights and concluded that the State had failed to demonstrate that less restrictive measures would not have achieved the same legitimate aim. Thus, for example, the government adduced no evidence that a partial ban on advertising would have been less effective than a total ban. A similar approach has been taken by the US Supreme Court in relation to restrictions on advertising of alcohol products,[56] although not advertising of lawful gambling.[57]

12.27 In Europe, the Council of the EU issued a Directive[58] on the approximation of the laws, regulations, and administrative provisions relating to the advertising and sponsorship of tobacco products. The Directive prohibited all forms of advertising and sponsorship of tobacco products except at the point of sale. It also prohibited the future use of tobacco product names for non-tobacco goods and, vice versa, the use of non-tobacco product names in connection with tobacco goods. The Council relied on Treaty powers of the EU to take measures for the establishment and functioning of the internal market and the protection of the freedom to provide goods and services. In a challenge to the validity of the Directive, both the Advocate-General and the European Court of Justice found that the Directive could not be justified by the Treaty provisions on which the Council had relied, and the measure was therefore annulled for these reasons.[59] However, Advocate-General Fennelly gave extensive consideration to an alternative challenge, that the Directive was invalid because it was contrary to Article 10 ECHR (because the European Court of Justice found the Directive invalid on other grounds it did not consider this challenge). His reasoning is very interesting.

12.28 The European Court of Justice is guided by general principles of Community law. These include the protection of fundamental rights including freedom of expression,[60] and in determining the range of these rights the ECHR has special significance as a source of inspiration. Freedom of expression includes

---

[55] *RJR Macdonald* v *A-G of Canada* (1995) 127 DLR (4th) 1.

[56] See, eg *Rubin* v *Coors Brewing Co* 115 S Ct 1585 (1995) (Supreme Court declared unconstitutional a federal law that prohibited beer labels from stating the alcohol content of the product) and *44 Liquormart Inc* v *Rhode Island* 116 S Ct 1495 (1996) (Supreme Court declared unconstitutional a state law that prohibited price advertising of alcoholic beverages).

[57] See *Posadas de Puerto Rico Associates* v *Tourism Company of Puerto Rico* 478 US 328 (1986).

[58] 98/43/EC.

[59] *Germany* v *European Parliament* (Case C–376/98) [2000] ECR I–8419; *R* v *Secretary of State for Health, ex p Imperial Tobacco Ltd* (Case C–74/99) [2000] All ER (EC) 769, ECJ.

[60] *Elleniki Radiophonia Tileoraissi AE* v *Pliroforissis* (Case C-260/89) [1991] ECR I–2925, at para 44; *Vereinigte Familiapress Zeitungsverlags-und vertriebs GmbH* v *Heinrich Bauer Verlag* (Case C–368/95) [1997] ECR I–3689, at para 25.

commercial speech. Although this did not have the same value of enhancing democratic debate as did political speech, it was still to be protected: 'Thus, individuals' freedom to promote commercial activities derives not only from their right to engage in economic activities and the general commitment, in the Community context, to a market economy based upon free competition, but also from their inherent entitlement as human beings freely to express and receive views on any topic, including the merits of the goods or services which they market or purchase.'[61]

Freedom of expression could be curtailed, and one of the permitted aims of restrictions was the protection of health, but because of the fundamental character of freedom of expression, the public interest in the restriction had to be demonstrated by the public authority seeking to impose it. **12.29**

While restrictions on freedom of expression must normally be justified by showing convincing evidence of a pressing social need, Advocate-General Fennelly saw the Strasbourg Court adopting a different test in relation to restrictions on commercial speech. These would be compatible with Article 10 ECHR if the competent authorities on reasonable grounds considered the restrictions to be necessary.[62] Thus the Advocate-General applied the same test to the ban on tobacco advertising. It was relevant that the issue was the objective assessment of the likely effects of the ban rather than more nebulous matters such as the protection of morals, but if the Community legislator could show that it acted on the basis of apparently reputable specialist studies, it would not be fatal to the validity of the measure that other reputable studies came to a different conclusion. Here there were studies showing a link between tobacco advertising and the take-up of consumption and which showed the inefficacy of anything other than a total ban on advertising, and the Community did therefore have reasonable grounds to believe that a comprehensive ban on tobacco advertising would result in a significant reduction in consumption and corresponding improvement in public health. **12.30**

The Advocate-General accepted that a total ban on advertising was a particularly grave intrusion on the exercise of freedom of expression and called for particular scrutiny, but the Community had satisfied this test by its evidence that partial bans were ineffective.[63] The studies showed a potential drop in consumption of about 6.9 per cent. Because of the significant effects of tobacco on health, this meant that the restriction on freedom of expression could not be characterized **12.31**

---

[61] At para 154.
[62] At para 158, referring to *Markt Intern* and *Groppera Radio*.
[63] At para 164.

as disproportionate. The Advocate-General noted that smoking itself was not illegal (and therefore the ban prevented the promotion of a product which could be lawfully sold), but he looked to the *RJR Macdonald* case in the Canadian Supreme Court (see 12.26) to take judicial notice of the practical problems of trying to ban smoking itself. He also contrasted the *Open Door Counselling* case, in part because of its 'extremely difficult and sensitive context' (no doubt a reference to the abortion issue) and in part because the case related to the non-directive supply of information rather than to the commercial promotion of abortion.[64] Thus the Advocate-General would not have struck down the tobacco advertising ban as disproportionate. He would, though, have taken a different view about the cross-branding prohibitions in the Directive. The justifications for these restrictions were not supported by evidence, and he would have annulled these parts additionally because of their conflict with the freedom of commercial expression.[65]

12.32 In response to the ECJ's decision in *Germany* v *European Parliament*, the European Commission enacted a replacement directive to regulate the advertising of tobacco products.[66] This directive prohibits radio, internet, and print advertising of tobacco. Additionally it prohibits tobacco sponsorship of sport. This directive survived challenge before the ECJ although the primary focus of the challenge was the supposed lack of power rather than incompatibility with Article 10 ECHR.[67] The UK Parliament has also passed the Tobacco Advertising and Promotion Act 2002 which, subject to certain limited exceptions, provides for a total ban upon the advertising of tobacco products on pain of punishment for a criminal offence. One such limited exception relates to point of sale advertising. Such advertising is permitted provided that it complies with various strict limitations set out in the Tobacco Advertising and Promotion Regulations 2004. In *R (British American Tobacco and others)* v *The Secretary of State for Health*,[68] the High Court considered the legality of such limitations on point of sale advertising. The tobacco companies did not challenge the validity of the Tobacco Advertising and Promotion Act 2002, but contended that the regulations placed such strict limits on point of sale advertising that they were disproportionate and thus contrary to Article 10 ECHR. McCombe J comprehensively rejected such an argument on the basis that the intensity of review should be limited as the case concerned commercial expression

---

[64] At para 74, referring to *Open Door* (see paras 12.21–12.22) at para 75.
[65] At para 176.
[66] Directive 2003/33/EC.
[67] See *Germany* v *European Parliament* (Case C–380/03) [2007] 2 CMLR 1.
[68] [2004] EWHC 2493.

rather than political or artistic expression and that the regulations were not disproportionate to the legitimate aim of promoting health. In reaching this conclusion, he rejected the tobacco companies' argument that assistance could be gained from US Supreme Court case law which had afforded a significant degree of protection to tobacco advertising and had struck down less restrictive point of sale advertising restrictions on the grounds that they violated the First Amendment.[69] McCombe J concluded that differences in the language of the First Amendment and Article 10 ECHR was such that the case law provided limited assistance.

Advertising directed at vulnerable groups such as children

Restrictions designed to protect vulnerable groups such as children are likely to be treated with a degree of deference. The Canadian Supreme Court upheld a Quebec law prohibiting advertising directed to children under the age of 13.[70] English law regulating such advertising to children merely places limits on the type of advertising rather than a complete ban. As such, English law is likely to be held to be lawful as it is proportionate to the legitimate aim of protecting vulnerable consumers such as children.   **12.33**

Political advertising

Political advertising in the broadcast media is subject to a complete ban by virtue   **12.34**
of ss 319 and 321 of the Communications Act 2003. 'Political advertising' is defined broadly to include advertisements inserted by bodies whose objects are wholly or mainly of a political nature, advertisements which are directed towards a political end, and advertisements in connection with an industrial dispute. The government, when introducing the Act, felt unable to make a statement pursuant to HRA 1998, s 19(1)(a) that the provisions were compatible with Article 10 ECHR because of the European Court's decision in *VgT*.[71] The compatibility of the ban on political advertising was tested in *R (Animal Defenders) v Secretary of State for Culture*.[72] *Animal Defenders* concerned a non-profit making company whose aims included the suppression, by lawful means, of all forms of cruelty to animals. They wished to run a television advertisement seeking to influence public opinion in relation to the keeping of primates in zoos. The commercial broadcasters refused to transmit it on the grounds that it fell

---

[69] See *Virginia State Board of Pharmacy v Virginia Citizens Consumer Council Inc* (1975) 425 US 748, at pp 761–5 and *Lorillard Tobacco Co v Riley* (2001) 533 US 525.

[70] *Irwin Toy v Quebec* [1989] 1 SCR 927.

[71] See para 12.19 for a discussion of *VgT*.

[72] [2008] 2 WLR 781.

foul of the prohibition on political advertising. *Animal Defenders* challenged this ban seeking a declaration that the relevant provisions of the Communications Act 2003 were incompatible with Article 10 ECHR. In light of the similarity between their case and *VgT*, the claimants must have thought that they had a strong case. However, both the Divisional Court and a unanimous House of Lords rejected the challenge. The House of Lords concluded that the ban was proportionate to the legitimate aim of protecting the rights of others. In reaching this conclusion, the House of Lords noted the significant danger that if political advertising were permitted, wealthy interests would be able to dominate the debate as they do in the USA. Their Lordships considered the issue of a partial ban but accepted the government's view that such a ban would be unworkable. *VgT* was distinguished, albeit not very convincingly, on various grounds including the fact the advertisement at issue in *VgT* was a response to commercial advertisements broadcast by the meat industry. It is clear, however, that the House of Lords did not think much of the arguments advanced by the Swiss government in *VgT* or the European Court's reasoning. Their Lordships also placed weight on the subsequent decision in *Murphy* v *Ireland* which they appeared to view as indicating a shift from the Court's earlier decision in *VgT*. Lord Bingham noted that the ban was arguably too wide as it would prohibit advertisements made in response to commercial adverts such as was in issue in *VgT*. It also prohibited purely commercial advertisements by organizations with political aims. However, as the claimant's case did not fall within either of these categories, it was not necessary to consider them. It is likely that given the considerable tension with *VgT*, the claimants are likely to seek recourse in Strasbourg.

Public expression of professionals

12.35 Many professions place restrictions on what their members can say in public. Such restrictions are likely to be the subject of challenge. One example of restrictions on professionals' speech in the UK is the Bar Code of Conduct, which prohibits barristers from commenting in any news or current affairs media on current matters on which they have been briefed,[73] although there is an exception to views expressed in the educational or academic context. No such restriction applies to solicitors (including solicitor-advocates). If the restriction were challenged, the Bar Council might well be in difficulty justifying the ban as it is arguably disproportionate. Such a restriction is at risk on the grounds that if solicitor-advocates can comment on matters on which they are briefed,

---

[73] See Bar Code of Conduct, *Media Comment*, at para 709.

it is not necessary in a democratic society to have a blanket ban on barristers who are performing the same function.

Advertising by professionals

While the Court's judgment in *Casado Coca* v *Spain*[74] would appear to indicate **12.36** that broad restrictions will be immune from challenge, this judgment should be treated with caution because the reasoning in the case was based in large part on the fact that bans on advertising by lawyers were imposed by most contracting States. The recent relaxation of the rules on advertising by lawyers throughout the Council of Europe States[75] could mean that the same decision would not be reached today. Furthermore, domestic courts are likely to apply a more rigorous scrutiny because of the inapplicability of the doctrine of 'margin of appreciation'. Support for this view can be gained from the jurisprudence of the Canadian Supreme Court, which has struck down a regulation of the dentists' profession prohibiting dentists from advertising their services, with only minor exceptions such as business cards and exterior signs.[76]

---

[74] (1994) 18 EHRR 1, discussed above at para 12.12.
[75] See Ryssdal, R., (President of the European Court of Human Rights), *The Case Law of the European Court of Human Rights on the Freedom of Expression Guaranteed under the European Convention of Human Rights* (1996).
[76] *Rocket* v *Royal College of Dental Surgeons* [1990] 1 SCR 232.

13

OFFICIAL SECRETS, NATIONAL SECURITY, TERRORISM, AND PUBLIC DISORDER

Introduction	13.01	The Impact of the HRA on	
ECHR Case Law	13.06	Domestic Law	13.31

Introduction

In a wide range of fields, including that of freedom of expression, English courts **13.01** have historically refused to scrutinize, in any serious manner, claims by the British government that national security would be imperilled by the exercise of an individual's rights. Thus the House of Lords found in *Council of Civil Service Unions* v *Minister for the Civil Service*,[1] that the government's assertion of national security overrode the legitimate expectation which trade unions would otherwise have had, to be consulted. English courts have also exhibited reticence to examine national security issues in immigration cases involving Gulf War detainees[2] and those allegedly involved in international terrorism.[3] The most notorious example of judicial deference occurred in the *Spycatcher* litigation, where a bitterly divided House of Lords, in a decision defying common sense, upheld interlocutory injunctions against newspapers which had wanted to publish information and extracts from *Spycatcher*, even though, by this time, the book had been published and was widely available in a number of countries including the USA.

---

[1] [1985] AC 374.
[2] *R* v *Secretary of State for the Home Department, ex p Cheblak* [1991] 1 WLR 890.
[3] *R* v *Secretary of State for the Home Department, ex p Chahal* [1994] Imm AR 107; the UK government was later to be found to have acted contrary to the ECHR in *Chahal* v *UK* (1996) 23 EHRR 413.

13.02   This overly deferential approach can be contrasted with that taken by the European Court which, while recognizing that States have a margin of appreciation which is relatively broad in the field of national security, has been more willing to scrutinize actions of governments who have invoked the protection of national security.[4]

13.03   There are signs that some English judges are losing some of their deference to the government in matters of national security, perhaps as a result of the more robust European jurisprudence. In *R v Central Criminal Court, ex p The Guardian, The Observer and Martin Bright*,[5] the Divisional Court allowed, in part, a judicial review against orders requiring newspapers and journalists to disclose certain material relating to communications with former MI5 agent David Shayler. Judge LJ stated:

> Inconvenient or embarrassing revelations whether for the security services or for public authorities, should not be suppressed. Legal proceedings directed towards the seizure of the working papers of individual journalists, or the premises of the newspaper or television programme publishing his or her report, or the threat of such proceedings tends to inhibit discussion. When a genuine investigation into possible corrupt or reprehensible activities by a public authority is being investigated by the media, compelling evidence would normally be needed to demonstrate that the public interest will be served by such proceedings. Otherwise, to the public's disadvantage, legitimate enquiry and discussion and 'the safety valve of effective journalism' would be discouraged, perhaps stifled.

13.04   A similar sentiment was articulated by the House of Lords in *R v Shayler*.[6] Although the House of Lords rejected Mr Shayler's argument that he should be able to invoke a 'public interest' defence, it did state that since the coming into force of the HRA, courts would be expected to show a less deferential approach to government invocation of national security and scrutinize any limits on the right to freedom of expression carefully.

13.05   Since the publication of the first edition of the book, the terrorist attacks on the USA and London have led the UK government to introduce further criminal offences relating to terrorism, including the prohibition of glorification of terrorist acts.[7] It remains to be seen how the courts will resolve the inevitable tension between the right to freedom of expression and need to protect society from those who seek to encourage and incite terrorist acts.

---

[4]   See, eg *Guardian and Observer v UK* (1991) 14 EHRR 153, discussed at paras 13.08–13.15.
[5]   [2000] UKHRR 796.
[6]   [2003] 1 AC 247, discussed below at para 13.34.
[7]   Discussed below at para 13.36.

ECHR Case Law

National security: general principles

As in other areas, the Court has taken a broad approach to the existence of an **13.06**
'interference by the public authority' with the right to freedom of expression.
Interferences have included interlocutory injunctions,[8] arrest and conviction
followed by fines and/or imprisonment.[9] The Court concluded that the refusal
of the military authorities to distribute a particular magazine to their soldiers
while distributing other magazines was also an interference.[10] It has also taken
a generous approach to the issue of who benefits from the right to freedom of
expression, concluding that it extends to members of the armed forces[11] and civil
servants.[12] Similarly, 'information and ideas' is also unqualified and extends to
military secrets concerning the design and production of a guided missile.[13]

Article 10(2) ECHR, which sets out possible legitimate aims, includes 'the **13.07**
interests of national security', 'territorial integrity', and the 'prevention of
disorder'. The Court has not gone behind government assertions as to the
legitimate aims. While this approach is not surprising, it is disappointing. For
example, in *Observer and Guardian v UK*,[14] it is hard to see how the interlocutory
injunction furthered the interests of national security when the book in question
could be read in Australia, the USA, and no doubt the Soviet Union.

Publication or disclosure of secret information

The applicants in the companion cases of *Observer and Guardian v UK*[15] and **13.08**
Sunday Times v UK (No 2),[16] contested interlocutory injunctions preventing
further publication of material emanating from Mr Peter Wright's book,
Spycatcher. Mr Wright's memoirs detailed his time in MI5 and the alleged
misdeeds of the security service. After *The Observer* and *The Guardian* had
published two short articles detailing the working of the security services, the

---

[8] eg *Observer and Guardian v UK* (1991) 14 EHRR 153.
[9] eg *Hadjianastassiou v Greece* (1992) 16 EHRR 219.
[10] *Vereinigung Demokratischer Soldaten Österreichs and Gubi v Austria* (1994) 20 EHRR 56.
[11] eg *Engel and others v Netherlands* (1976) 1 EHRR 647 and *Hadjianastassiou v Greece*.
[12] eg *Vogt v Germany* (1995) 21 EHRR 205.
[13] *Hadjianastassiou v Greece*.
[14] (1991) 14 EHRR 153.
[15] (1991) 14 EHRR 153.
[16] (1991) 14 EHRR 229.

government alleged, and Millett J inferred, on the balance of probabilities, that the journalists' sources must have come from the offices of the publishers of *Spycatcher* or the solicitors acting for them and the author. On this basis, Millett J granted an interlocutory injunction to restrain any further breaches of confidence, preventing the newspapers from publishing any *Spycatcher* material.

13.09 Millett J's judgment was upheld by a majority in the House of Lords. This interlocutory injunction was intended to be temporary, but continued from 11 July 1986 until 13 October 1988 when Scott J, after a trial of the substantive issues, refused to grant a permanent injunction. The newspapers applied to the European Court, alleging that the injunction violated their right to freedom of expression under Article 10 ECHR. Neither the existence of an interference nor the issue of whether the interference was prescribed by law was disputed. The government asserted two legitimate aims: (i) maintaining the authority of the judiciary; and (ii) protecting national security.

13.10 The Court accepted both these legitimate aims.[17] 'Maintaining the authority of the judiciary' included protecting the rights of litigants. The Court agreed that the purpose of the injunction was to secure the right of the Attorney-General as a litigant.

13.11 In relation to the 'interests of national security', the government, before the domestic courts, had contended that disclosure of the information would cause damage to the security services. By the time the case reached the House of Lords, *Spycatcher* had been published in the various countries, including the USA. The government's national security argument underwent what was described by Scott J as a 'curious metamorphosis'.[18] From initially seeking to preserve the character of information that ought to be kept secret, the government's national security objective became confined to the promotion of the efficiency and reputation of the security service, notably by: (i) preserving confidence in that service on the part of third parties; (ii) making it clear that the unauthorized publication of memoirs by its former members would not be countenanced; and (iii) deterring others from following in Mr Wright's footsteps.[19]

13.12 The European Court, disappointingly, accepted that this new aim was within the ambit of protecting the interests of national security. However, the Court unanimously went on to find that the continuation of the injunction from 30 July 1987 to 13 October 1988 was a violation of Article 10 ECHR, because during

---

[17] Ibid, at paras 55–7.
[18] *A-G v Guardian Newspapers (No 2)* [1990] 1 AC 109 at 140F.
[19] (1991) 14 EHRR 153, at para 69.

this period the publication of the book began in the USA, after which it could not be said to be confidential. From that point onwards the interlocutory injunction was disproportionate. The Court rejected the government's argument that the redefined interests of national security were sufficient to justify the continuation of the injunction. The Court decided that the injunction arguably failed to advance the government's stated objectives and, furthermore, the government had other remedies such as an action for an account of profits.[20]

The Court was split as to whether there was a violation of Article 10 ECHR during the period 11 July 1986 to 30 July 1987. A bare majority concluded that there was no violation during this period because, prior to publication in the USA, the injunction was proportionate to the legitimate aim and therefore 'necessary in a democratic society'.[21] The majority were influenced by the fact that the injunction was not a blanket prohibition: while it forbade the publication of information derived from or attributed to Mr Wright in his capacity as a member of the security service, it did not prevent the applicants from campaigning for an independent inquiry into that service. Additionally, the injunction contained provisos excluding certain material from their scope, particularly material that had been previously published by other authors.[22]   **13.13**

Ten judges dissented from this conclusion and thought that there was a violation of Article 10 from the date of Millett J's granting of the interlocutory injunction. The dissenting judges differed in their reasons for this conclusion: some[23] placed emphasis on the public's right to receive information (which the majority did not address) and concluded that an interim injunction, not subsequently lifted after a short period, was 'in effect a disguised means of instituting censure or restraint on the freedom of the press';[24] while others objected to the injunction because it was an impermissible prior restraint.[25]   **13.14**

The latter dissent quoted with approval the following statement of Justice Black (joined by Justice Douglas) in the US Supreme Court decision of *New York Times* v *US* and *Washington Post* v *US*:[26] 'I firmly believe that "the press must be   **13.15**

---

[20] The US Supreme Court has held that such a remedy did not violate the First Amendment—see *Snepp* v *US* 444 US 507 (1980). This conclusion was reached on the basis that the book in question, *Decent Interval,* by former CIA operative Frank Snepp, contained no classified material.

[21] At paras 62–4.

[22] At para 64.

[23] See partly Dissenting Opinion of Judge Pettiti joined by Judge Pinheiro Farinha, at 200.

[24] At 201.

[25] See partly Dissenting Opinion of Judge de Meyer joined by Judges Pettiti, Russo, Foighel, and Bigi.

[26] 403 US 713 (1971), at 717.

left free to publish news, whatever the source, without censorship, injunctions, or prior restraint".'

13.16 One year later, in *Hadjianastassiou* v *Greece*,[27] the Court considered an application by an air force officer in charge of a project to design and produce a guided missile. The applicant was charged, convicted, and sentenced to imprisonment by a military court for disclosing military secrets by selling information from his work on the guided missile project to a private company. While the Court concluded that the court martial was insufficient to provide a fair trial, it unanimously rejected the applicant's claim under Article 10 ECHR. The information was of minor importance and there was a dispute as to whether it was available in unrestricted scientific literature. The State's interest in a particular weapon's system and the state of its progress in manufacture were also legitimate matters to be kept secret. It is important to recognize that the disclosure had been to a private company in return for payment. The applicant's reason for making the disclosure was commercial and, while Article 10 clearly applies to such communications, there was no public interest in disclosure to set against the State's interest.

13.17 The third case involving disclosure of secret material concerned a Dutch weekly magazine called *Bluf!*.[28] The magazine obtained a report produced by the Dutch security services which showed their interest in the Dutch Communist Party and the anti-nuclear movement. It also gave information about the Polish, Czech, and Romanian security services' activities in The Netherlands. The report was six years old and marked 'confidential' (the lowest classification). The magazine proposed to publish the report as a supplement, but before distribution could take place the entire print run was seized by the police. That night the magazine's staff reprinted the issue and sold 2,500 copies on the streets of Amsterdam. Several months later the authorities obtained an order that the issue be withdrawn from circulation. The European Court, adopting a similar approach to that in *Observer and Guardian*, found that the withdrawal order infringed Article 10 ECHR, in part because of the circulation which the reprinted edition had received which meant that the further restrictions were not 'necessary in a democratic society'. While *Spycatcher* had sold over a million copies as a result of the US publication, the Court applied the same principles to a far more modest distribution. Not surprisingly, the Dutch government had argued that the distribution had been effected by the magazine itself and it was objectionable to allow the applicant to rely on the publicity achieved by its own

---

[27] (1992) 16 EHRR 219.
[28] *Vereniging Weekblad Bluf!* v *Netherlands* (1995) 20 EHRR 189.

wrong. The Court was unmoved by this argument and concluded that it could not make 'necessary' a restriction which had been rendered moot by the de facto publicity that the magazine had already received. What was important was the actual state of public knowledge at the time that the restriction was imposed. In this respect the Court followed its approach in *Weber v Switzerland*.[29] In the age of the Internet, this feature of the Court's reasoning is likely to be particularly important. States will have considerable practical difficulty in preventing rapid, widespread dissemination of information.

In October 2005, the European Court rejected an Article 10 complaint brought **13.18** by George Blake, the notorious spy. Mr Blake complained that an action for account for profits for royalties that he was to receive from the publication of his autobiography was neither prescribed by law nor necessary in a democratic society.[30] The government's claim for the profits arose out of an undertaking that Mr Blake had given in 1944 not to divulge any official information gained by him as a result of his employment in the British Secret Intelligence Service. The European Court declared the Article 10 ECHR complaint inadmissible as being manifestly ill-founded notwithstanding the fact that at the time of publication none of the information contained in the autobiography was confidential. The Court concluded that the interference with freedom of expression was limited; the authorities had allowed the book to be published, sold, and distributed without restriction. As such it differed fundamentally from the injunction at issue in *Observer and Guardian* v *UK*. The Court further noted that the interference, ie the order to account for profits, was closely connected to Mr Blake's serious criminal past. The government's desire to prevent criminals from profiting from their wrongdoing was a legitimate aim and in such circumstances, the interference was 'necessary in a democratic society'. The European Court's approach accords with that taken by the US Courts.[31]

The confidentiality of diplomatic documents was the subject of *Stoll* v **13.19** *Switzerland*.[32] In *Stoll*, a Chamber of the European Court concluded that a criminal conviction of a journalist for publishing articles which quoted from a confidential report breached Article 10 ECHR because it was not necessary in a democratic society. The report was by the Swiss ambassador to the USA. It detailed strategies to be adopted in negotiations between Swiss banks and

---

[29] (1990) 12 EHRR 508, discussed at para 9.56.
[30] See *Blake* v *UK* (App No 68890/01). Mr Blake's claim pursuant to Article 6 ECHR relating to unreasonable length of proceedings was declared admissible and on 26 September 2006 the European Court concluded that there had been a violation of Article 6(1) ECHR.
[31] See *Snepp* v *US* 444 US 507 (1980).
[32] (2007) 44 EHRR 53.

the World Jewish Congress concerning compensation due to Holocaust victims for unclaimed assets deposited in Swiss bank accounts. The report was marked confidential. In finding a violation, the majority of the Court placed considerable emphasis on the fact that the applicant was a journalist and that the report was a matter of legitimate public interest. The Chamber decision in *Stoll* was the first time that the Court had found a violation of Article 10 in relation to sanctions imposed for disclosure of information that was still confidential.

13.20 However, the Chamber's decision was overturned 12:5 by the Grand Chamber.[33] Whilst the Grand Chamber concluded that the fact that freedom of the press was at issue and that the expression related to a matter of considerable public concern meant that the margin of appreciation was necessarily limited, they went on to expand the margin as a result of the lack of consensus between Member States of the Council of Europe in relation to rules aimed at preserving the confidential and secret nature of certain sensitive items. The majority found that the only legitimate aim being pursued was the protection of confidential information; they rejected arguments advanced by the Swiss government that the interference was also for the protection of national security and the rights of others. In a lengthy judgment, the majority went on to conclude that the conviction was 'necessary in a democratic society'. In reaching this conclusion, the majority placed emphasis on a number of factors including the limited nature of the penalty and the existence of competing public interests namely the public interest in informing readers on a topical issue and the countervailing public interest in ensuring a positive and satisfactory outcome to the diplomatic negotiations being conducted. The Court placed considerable emphasis on the nature of the articles in question of which they were very critical. The majority agreed with the Swiss Press Council that the journalist's chief intention was not to inform the public on a topic of general interest but to make the Ambassador's report the subject of needless scandal. The majority decision was subject to strong criticism by the judgment of five dissenting judges who argued that the majority's approach to necessity and proportionality was flawed, and departed from previous case law requiring a narrow margin of appreciation when the speech in issue related to matters of public concern. The dissenting judgment also took issue with the majority's criticism of the form and content of the article, opining that it was not for the Courts, domestic or European, to substitute their own views for those of the press as to what technique of reporting should be adopted by journalists.

---

[33] (2008) 47 EHRR 59.

Suppression of speech that threatens public order

In *Arrowsmith* v *UK*,[34] an early decision of the Commission, the applicant, **13.21** a pacifist, failed in her contention that her conviction under ss 1 and 2 of the Incitement to Disaffection Act 1934, for distributing leaflets to soldiers encouraging them to go absent without leave or refuse to serve in Northern Ireland, was contrary to Article 10 ECHR. The Commission accepted that the interference pursued a legitimate aim, namely the protection of national security (by preventing the weakening of the armed forces) and prevention of disorder in the armed forces. The applicant, relying on US Supreme Court jurisprudence,[35] sought to argue that the conviction was disproportionate and unnecessary as there was no 'clear and present danger' that the expression would bring about the substantive evils that Parliament had a right to prevent. The Court rejected this more stringent test and concluded that the conviction and sentence to nine months' imprisonment were proportionate and 'necessary in a democratic society'. The Commission's decision in *Arrowsmith* was disappointing and rightly criticized in two dissenting opinions, because the government failed to adduce any evidence at all of the threat to national security posed by the applicant's unpopular political expression.[36]

The Court adopted an equally weak approach in *Chorherr* v *Austria*,[37] which **13.22** concerned the arrest of the applicant for mounting a peaceful demonstration against the purchase of military aircraft during a military ceremony. The police asked the applicant to cease demonstrating, and when he refused he was arrested. The Court, by 6:3, considered that the arrest was to prevent disorder and that it was proportionate, taking into account the circumstances of the case and the State's margin of appreciation. The Austrian government failed to produce evidence that there was a real likelihood of disorder if the applicant had been permitted to carry on peacefully demonstrating, but this absence of evidence again failed to trouble the majority of the Court.

There is a lot to be said for a more rigorous approach when courts are faced **13.23** with expression that is alleged to be likely to cause disorder.[38] Governments tend to invoke such arguments when faced with expression that is inconvenient and unpopular. The US Supreme Court jurisprudence has progressed beyond

---

[34] (1978) 3 EHRR 218.

[35] See Justice Holmes' dissent in *Abrams* v *US* 250 US 616 (1919), at 624.

[36] This criticism was repeated in the dissenting judgment of Judge Walsh in *Observer and Guardian* v *UK*.

[37] (1993) 17 EHRR 358.

[38] This more rigorous test is equally applicable to speech that threatens national security or the territorial integrity of a State; see paras 13.26–13.30.

the 'clear and present danger' discussed above in relation to *Arrowsmith* v *UK*. *Brandenburg* v *Ohio*[39] provides a statement of the current test in US law. The court in *Brandenburg* stated: 'the constitutional guarantees of free speech and free press do not permit a state to forbid or proscribe advocacy of the use of force or of law violation except where such advocacy is directed to inciting or producing imminent lawless action and is likely to incite or produce such action'.[40]

13.24   This test, which requires evidence from the government that the speech in question is likely to produce lawless action,[41] is in our view preferable to the approach taken by the European Court and Commission. In both *Arrowsmith* and *Chorherr,* the application of this test would have led to a finding that the State's actions violated Article 10 ECHR.

13.25   A more robust approach was taken by the European Court in *Cetin* v *Turkey*[42] which concerned the banning of a newspaper in a region of Turkey that was subject to emergency laws. The Court rejected, because of a lack of evidence, the Turkish government's argument that the ban was justified as the contents of certain issues of the paper were liable to incite the population to riot and as such might have serious repercussions for public order in the region. The Court further concluded that the lack of procedural safeguards permitting a review of the administrative ban meant that the ban was not 'necessary in a democratic society'. Whilst this more robust approach is to be welcomed, the result was not surprising given the draconian nature of the interference and the lack of evidence indicating that the newspaper was having an impact on public order. It is therefore too early to say whether *Cetin* indicates a shift in approach by the European Court.

Suppression of speech that threatens national security or the territorial integrity of the State

13.26   In *Piermont* v *France*,[43] the applicant, a Member of the European Parliament, was expelled pursuant to an administrative order from French territories in the South Pacific. The Court accepted that France was pursuing the legitimate aims

---

[39]   395 US 444 (1969).
[40]   Ibid, at 447.
[41]   The *Brandenburg* test was endorsed by a panel of media and human rights experts in 'The Johannesburg Principles, National Security, Freedom of expression and access to information'. See Coliver, S et al (eds), *Secrecy and Liberty: National Security, Freedom of Expression and Access to Information* (The Hague, Netherlands: Martinus Nijhoff, 1999).
[42]   App Nos 40153/98 and 40160/98, Judgment of 13 February 2003.
[43]   (1995) 20 EHRR 301.

of preventing disorder and maintaining territorial integrity, but concluded that the orders were not necessary in a democratic society.

The Commission has taken a cautious approach in its reviews of the broadcasting **13.27** bans imposed by the UK and Irish governments. Both restricted the broadcasting of words spoken by members or supporters of specified groups (although the British ban permitted others, such as actors or newscasters, to give voice to the words which the members or supporters could only silently mouth). Furthermore, this restriction did not apply to Sinn Fein candidates during elections. The affected groups included not only terrorist organizations, but also Sinn Fein (which was not a proscribed organization but an elected political party). None of the UK broadcasters challenged the ban, but its legality was tested by journalists. They were unsuccessful in the House of Lords.[44] The Commission accepted that the measure constituted an interference with the applicant's freedom of expression, although only of a limited kind. The limited nature of the interference was an important factor in the Commission's decision that the ban did not exceed the margin of appreciation which the Convention gave to a State fighting terrorism.[45]

In 1999, the Court handed down a large number of cases against Turkey **13.28** involving Article 10.[46] These cases arose out of criminal proceedings taken against expression concerning the Kurdish conflict in Eastern Turkey. The convictions of the various applicants were for expression, both written and spoken, held by the Turkish courts to contain separatist propaganda against the Turkish nation and the territorial integrity of the State, or intended to undermine patriotic sentiment and incite hostility and hatred by making distinctions based on ethnic or regional origin or social class. The Court subjected the convictions to close scrutiny. It noted the political situation and tensions in Turkey, but as the speech was political or on matters of public concern there was little scope under Article 10(2). In each case, the European Court analysed the substance and nature of the expression in question, in light of the tense situation in Turkey, when deciding whether the interference was proportionate. Violations of Article 10 were found in eleven out of the thirteen cases. The only two cases in which

---

[44] *R* v *Secretary of State for the Home Department, ex p Brind* [1991] 1 AC 696.
[45] *Brind* v *UK* App No 18714/91, (1994) 77 DR 42; see also, *Purcell* v *Ireland* (1991) 70 DR 262.
[46] The Court handed down thirteen cases on 8 July 1999: *Ceylan* v *Turkey* (App No 23556/94), *Arslan* v *Turkey* (App No 23462/94), *Gerger* v *Turkey* (App No 24919/94), *Polat* v *Turkey* (App No 23500/94), *Karatas* v *Turkey* (App No 23168/94), *Erdogdu and Ince* v *Turkey* (App Nos 25067/94 and 25068/94), *Baskaya and Okcuoglu* v *Turkey* (App Nos 23536/94 and 24408/94), *Okcuoglu* v *Turkey* (App No 24246/94), *Surek and Ozdemir* v *Turkey* (App Nos 23927/94 and 24277/94) *and Surek* v *Turkey (Nos 1, 2, 3, and 4)* (App Nos 26682/95, 24122/94, 24735/94, and 24762/94).

the Court concluded that the conviction was necessary in a democratic society were *Surek* v *Turkey (No 1)* and *Surek* v *Turkey (No 3)*.[47] *Surek (No 1)* concerned the publication of two letters in the applicant's newspaper, while *Surek (No 3)* concerned an article which called for the use of armed force as a means to achieve national independence for Kurdistan. The Istanbul National Security Court concluded that both the letters and the article contained words which were aimed at the destruction of the territorial integrity of the Turkish State by describing areas of south-east Turkey as an independent state ('Kurdistan') and the PKK as a national liberation movement. The National Security Court further concluded that the letters and article incited violence against an individual, a public official, and a sector of the population. The majority of the European Court accepted this analysis and granted Turkey a wider margin of appreciation as a result. The majority concluded that the letters and article did incite hatred, and therefore the State's response was proportionate and 'necessary in a democratic society'. The dissenting judges criticized the test applied by the majority in the thirteen Turkish cases, namely: 'If the writings published by the applicant supported or instigated the use of violence, then his conviction by the national courts was justifiable in a democratic society.'[48] Judge Bonello rejected this yardstick as insufficient and suggested that the test should be similar to the US 'clear and present danger' test.[49] While a more rigorous test is to be welcomed, we would suggest that the test enunciated in *Brandenburg* v *Ohio* (see 13.23) is superior to Justice Holmes' clear and present danger test.[50]

13.29 In the nine or so years since the European Court handed down judgments in these thirteen cases, there has been a steady stream of complaints to Strasbourg from writers, journalists, and newspaper owners in Turkey. The European Court has found violations of Article 10 ECHR in the vast majority of such cases, concluding that the speech in issue did not incite violence and hatred or threaten the territorial integrity of the State.[51] Such a robust approach is to be welcomed,

---

[47] (App Nos 26682/95 and 24735/94), 8 July 1999.
[48] *Surek (No 1)*, at para 25; *Surek (No 3)*, at para 16.
[49] See *Abrams* v *US*, discussed at para 13.21.
[50] While Judge Bonello cited *Brandenburg* v *Ohio*, he did not appear to consider it as a development of the 'clear and present danger' test.
[51] One rare exception where the European Court found no violation of Article 10 ECHR is *Hocaogullari* v *Turkey* (Application No 77109/01) where the applicant had published an article praising the 'heroic deaths' of youths in Turkey and Vietnam who had lost their lives fighting the State. The Court concluded that the article, aimed at young people, could not be understood as calling for peace or the peaceful settlement of political problems. Instead, the tenor appears to be inciting violence and armed resistance. See also, *Falakaoglu and Saygili* v *Turkey* (App Nos 22147/02 and 24972/03)—no violation of Article 10 ECHR for prosecution of editor and proprietor of newspaper that had published the declarations of an armed terrorist group.

although it is disappointing that the Turkish domestic courts continue to impose criminal sanctions on lawful speech with such regularity.

However, it is not only the Turkish authorities that have recently fallen foul of Article 10 in relation to speech that allegedly threatens national security or the territorial integrity of the State. Moldova was also found to have breached Article 10 ECHR in closing a newspaper on the grounds that some of its articles threatened national security and territorial integrity.[52] The articles in question criticized the Moldovan government for their actions in respect of the break-away Moldavian Republic of Transdniestria. The domestic courts which closed the newspaper failed to consider which particular articles allegedly constituted a threat to territorial integrity and national security, and failed to give adequate reasons for their decision. As such, the Court was not satisfied that the Moldovan courts had applied standards which were in conformity with the principles embodied in Article 10 or that they based themselves on an acceptable assessment of the facts. Accordingly, there was a violation of Article 10. **13.30**

The Impact of the HRA on Domestic Law

The criminal law: official Secrets

English law protecting national security has improved since the repeal of s 2 of the Official Secrets Act 1911, although the statute that replaced this enactment, the Official Secrets Act 1989, is not the 'great liberalising measure' it was claimed to be at the time.[53] Section 1 of the Official Secrets Act 1911 is over-broad but convictions for espionage are likely to survive scrutiny.[54] **13.31**

Although narrower in scope than s 2 of the Official Secrets Act 1911, the 1989 Act is still problematic and has been subject to considerable academic criticism.[55] The offences contained in ss 1–6 are broadly defined. For example, s 1(1) criminalizes unauthorized disclosures by members of the security services. There is no requirement for the Crown to prove any harm or damage. Exposure to liability for this offence can be extended on written notice to others who, though not actually members of the security services, work closely with them.[56] **13.32**

---

[52] See *Kommerstant Moldovy v Moldova* (App No 41827/02).
[53] Speech by Douglas Hurd, the then Home Secretary, quoted by Shorts, E, and Than, C, *Civil Liberties: Legal Principles of Individual Freedom* (London: Sweet and Maxwell, 1998), at 210.
[54] See *Hadjianastassiou v Greece* (1992) 16 EHRR 219, at para 13.16.
[55] See, eg Fenwick, H, and Phillipson, G, *Media Freedom under the Human Rights Act* (OUP, 2006), at pp 927–48.
[56] Official Secrets Act 1989, s 1(1)(b) and (6).

In relation to Crown servants and government contractors who are not members of the security forces and have not been served with written notice, there is a narrower offence of making a *damaging* disclosure of information relating to security or intelligence. 'Damage' is defined as damage to the work of, or any part of, the security and intelligence services.[57] It is sufficient that such damage is found to 'be likely to occur' as a result of the disclosure. Further, the prosecution can succeed without proving that the particular information would be likely to cause harm but merely that it is of a class that might have this effect.

13.33   Section 5 of the Official Secrets Act 1989 makes it a specific offence for journalists and editors to publish information that they know is protected by the Act, although the prosecution must also prove that they had reason to believe that the publication would be damaging to the security services or to the interests of the UK. The precise scope of this complex offence is, at present, unclear. For example, it is still not certain whether s 5 extends to publication of the memoirs of *former* Crown servants. This issue was discussed in the speeches of the House of Lords in *Lord Advocate* v *Scotsman Publications*.[58] Lord Templeman considered that s 5 did extend to former 'Crown servants', while Lord Jauncey thought that it did not. The HRA 1998 will provide an additional argument in support of Lord Jauncey's restrictive interpretation.

13.34   The limited nature of the available defences is problematic. There is no 'public interest' defence, or a general defence of prior publication. The latter was rejected on the grounds that prior publication would be a factor to be considered in the assessment of whether the disclosure was 'damaging'. It was also contended that further publication could still cause substantial damage, especially if it adds weight to what were originally unsubstantiated rumours.[59] The absence of a general 'public interest' defence was considered by the House of Lords in *R* v *Shayler*.[60] David Shayler had been a member of the security services for nearly five years. After he left, he disclosed, without authority, a number of documents relating to security and intelligence matters to a national newspaper. Mr Shayler was charged with disclosing documents or information without lawful authority contrary to ss 1 and 4 of the Official Secrets Act 1989. Mr Shayler sought to contend that he should be able to invoke a 'public interest' defence. This argument was rejected; the House of Lords concluded that the relevant provisions of the Official Secrets Act 1989 did not violate Article 10. While such provisions

---

[57] s 1(4).
[58] [1989] 2 All ER 852.
[59] See *Reform of section 2 of the Official Secrets Act 1911* (Cm 408, 1988).
[60] [2003] 1 AC 247.

clearly interfered with Mr Shayler's right to freedom of expression, such an interference was justified because it was proportionate and pursued the legitimate aim of protecting national security. In reaching this conclusion the House of Lords felt that the 'special position' of security service employees imposed duties and responsibilities upon them not to disclose secret information. The measures were proportionate because there were means by which disclosures relating to allegations of malpractice, incompetence, or illegality could be made to the authorities including staff counsellors, Ministers, the Attorney General, and the DPP. The House of Lords rejected Mr Shayler's assertions that such avenues were ineffective in practice. The House of Lords also noted that members of the security services could make disclosures after obtaining official authorization. The refusal of such authorization would be subject to judicial review and, as such a refusal would engage the right to freedom of expression, it would be subject to rigorous and exacting scrutiny. It remains to be seen how effective the suggested safeguards are.

The HRA has had some impact in this field, however. The Court of Appeal in **13.35** *R v Keogh*[61] concluded that since the incorporation of the European Convention on Human Rights, Article 6 ECHR required that the burden of proof in establishing that an individual charged under s 2 or 3 of the Official Secrets Act 1989 knew or could reasonably be expected to know that the disclosure would cause harm, should be placed on the prosecution.

The criminal law: encouraging and glorifying terrorism

Section 1 of the Terrorism Act 2006, enacted in the wake of the 7 July **13.36** 2005 terrorist bombings in London, criminalizes the intentional or reckless publication of any statement 'likely to be understood by some or all of the members of the public to whom it is published as a direct or indirect encouragement . . . to the commission, preparation or instigation of acts of terrorism'. Indirect encouragement includes statements which glorify terrorist acts or offences (whether in the past, future, or generally), and from which it could be reasonably inferred that the conduct is to be emulated in present circumstances. Section 1(5) makes is clear that it is irrelevant whether the statement encourages any particular act of terrorism generally, and whether any person is in fact encouraged to commit any such act. Terrorism is defined very widely by s 1 of the Terrorism Act 2001. The only safeguard is that the DPP or Attorney General must consent to the prosecution. The breadth of the offence is very problematic; s 1 of the Terrorism Act 2006 lacks any requirement that the

---

[61] [2007] EWCA Crim 528.

prosecution prove either an intention by the maker/publisher to incite an act of terrorism or a likelihood that the statement will incite an act of terrorism. As such, prosecutions brought pursuant to s 1 of the Terrorism Act 2006 may fall foul of Article 10 ECHR. Whilst the European Court has not adopted the very strict approach taken by the US Supreme Court,[62] it has found convictions for glorification of terrorism in Turkey under similarly broad criminal provisions as contrary to Article 10 because of the lack of any connection between the expression and violence.[63]

The civil law

13.37 The use of injunctions by the State to suppress publication of material that relates to matters of public concern, broadly defined, is a further area which has been affected by the coming into force of the HRA 1998. Such prior restraints should be the subject of the most exacting scrutiny because, unlike subsequent punishment for unlawful disclosure, the material in issue never reaches the public. There is much to be said for the US approach in this field, which permits the granting of prior restraints only in the most limited of circumstances. In *Near v Minnesota*,[64] Chief Justice Hughes stated: 'The protection even as to previous restraint is not absolutely unlimited. But the limitation has been recognized only in exceptional cases. No one would question but that a government might prevent actual obstruction to its recruiting service or the publication of the sailing dates of transports or the number and location of troops.'[65]

13.38 This approach was further developed in *New York Times* v *US; Washington Post* v *US*,[66] which is usually known as the *Pentagon Papers* case. The *Pentagon Papers* were a 47-volume secret Pentagon study of the Vietnam War. The study was, according to an affidavit sworn by the General Counsel of the Department of Defense, classified as 'Top Secret-Sensitive'. However, a majority of the Supreme Court held that the government could not restrain the publication of extracts from the work. Justices Black and Douglas thought that prior restraints could never be justified. However, this absolutist view did not command the support of the majority, which held that the government would have been entitled to injunctions if it could establish that 'disclosure . . . will surely result in direct, immediate and irreparable damage to our Nation or its people'.

---

[62] See paras 13.23–13.24 and the discussion of *Brandenburg* v *Ohio* 395 US 444 (1969).
[63] See, eg *Karatas* v *Turkey* (Application No 24168/94).
[64] 283 US 697 (1931).
[65] Ibid, at 716.
[66] 403 US 713 (1971).

Such a high burden was not met in relation to the *Pentagon Papers*, which, **13.39** while containing material highly embarrassing to the US government and other friendly governments, was largely a historical work and as such did not expose US troops to danger. This burden recognizes the importance of the right to freedom of expression in relation to matters of public concern and requires the courts to scrutinize closely government justifications for seeking an injunction rather than treating such statements at face value. This approach stands in sharp contrast with that of the House of Lords in the *Spycatcher* litigation. Now individuals and media organizations can rely directly on Article 10 ECHR, the courts will not be able to dismiss so lightly arguments in favour of refusing government applications for injunctions.

Article 10 ECHR was successfully invoked by the *Sunday Times* in relation to the **13.40** scope of undertaking not to publish information disclosed by a former member of the Secret Intelligence Service.[67] The parties agreed that the undertaking should not apply to matters that were already in the public domain. The Attorney General, in effect, sought a requirement that the *Sunday Times* should obtain clearance either from himself or a Court before it published matters that they asserted were already in the public domain. The Court of Appeal rejected such a requirement concluding that it would not be consistent with either Article 10 ECHR or HRA, s 12.

The ability of the government to obtain interim injunctions prohibiting **13.41** disclosure of material that relates to matters of public concern is likely to decrease since the House of Lords decision in *Cream Holdings Ltd and others v Banerjee*,[68] which considered the effect of HRA, s 12(3) and is discussed in chapter 3. However, the House of Lords decision in *Cream Holdings* does not prohibit such injunctions and is therefore clearly not as protective of freedom of expression as the approach adopted by the US Supreme Court.

---

[67] See *A-G v Times Newspapers Ltd* [2001] EWCA Civ 97.
[68] [2005] 1 AC 253. See discussion at paras 3.69–3.72.

Appendices

1. Human Rights Act 1998   251
2. Convention for the Protection of Human Rights and Fundamental Freedoms as amended by Protocol No. 11 with Protocol Nos. 1, 4, 6, 7, 12 and 13   272

APPENDIX 1

Human Rights Act 1998

1998 Chapter 42

An Act to give further effect to rights and freedoms guaranteed under the European Convention on Human Rights; to make provision with respect to holders of certain judicial offices who become judges of the European Court of Human Rights; and for connected purposes.

[9th November 1998]

BE IT ENACTED by the Queen's most Excellent Majesty, by and with the advice and consent of the Lords Spiritual and Temporal, and Commons, in this present Parliament assembled, and by the authority of the same, as follows:—

1. THE CONVENTION RIGHTS

(1) In this Act 'the Convention rights' means the rights and fundamental freedoms set out in—

  (a) Articles 2 to 12 and 14 of the Convention,

  (b) Articles 1 to 3 of the First Protocol, and

  (c) [Article 1 of the Thirteenth Protocol][1],

  as read with Articles 16 to 18 of the Convention.

(2) Those Articles are to have effect for the purposes of this Act subject to any designated derogation or reservation (as to which see sections 14 and 15).

(3) The Articles are set out in Schedule 1.

(4) The [Secretary of State][2] may by order make such amendments to this Act as he considers appropriate to reflect the effect, in relation to the United Kingdom, of a protocol.

(5) In subsection (4) 'protocol' means a protocol to the Convention—

  (a) which the United Kingdom has ratified; or

  (b) which the United Kingdom has signed with a view to ratification.

(6) No amendment may be made by an order under subsection (4) so as to come into force before the protocol concerned is in force in relation to the United Kingdom.

2. INTERPRETATION OF CONVENTION RIGHTS

(1) A court or tribunal determining a question which has arisen in connection with a Convention right must take into account any—

  (a) judgment, decision, declaration or advisory opinion of the European Court of Human Rights,

---

[1] As amended by SI 2004/1574, art 2(1).

[2] As amended by SI 2003/1887, art 9, Sch 2, para 10(1).

(b) opinion of the Commission given in a report adopted under Article 31 of the Convention,

(c) decision of the Commission in connection with Article 26 or 27(2) of the Convention, or

(d) decision of the Committee of Ministers taken under Article 46 of the Convention, whenever made or given, so far as, in the opinion of the court or tribunal, it is relevant to the proceedings in which that question has arisen.

(2) Evidence of any judgment, decision, declaration or opinion of which account may have to be taken under this section is to be given in proceedings before any court or tribunal in such manner as may be provided by rules.

(3) In this section 'rules' means rules of court or, in the case of proceedings before a tribunal, rules made for the purposes of this section—

(a) by . . .[3] [the Lord Chancellor or][4] the Secretary of State, in relation to any proceedings outside Scotland;

(b) by the Secretary of State, in relation to proceedings in Scotland; or

(c) by a Northern Ireland department, in relation to proceedings before a tribunal in Northern Ireland—

(i) which deals with transferred matters; and

(ii) for which no rules made under paragraph (a) are in force.

Legislation

3. Interpretation of Legislation

(1) So far as it is possible to do so, primary legislation and subordinate legislation must be read and given effect in a way which is compatible with the Convention rights.

(2) This section—

(a) applies to primary legislation and subordinate legislation whenever enacted;

(b) does not affect the validity, continuing operation or enforcement of any incompatible primary legislation; and

(c) does not affect the validity, continuing operation or enforcement of any incompatible subordinate legislation if (disregarding any possibility of revocation) primary legislation prevents removal of the incompatibility.

4. Declaration of Incompatibility

(1) Subsection (2) applies in any proceedings in which a court determines whether a provision of primary legislation is compatible with a Convention right.

(2) If the court is satisfied that the provision is incompatible with a Convention right, it may make a declaration of that incompatibility.

(3) Subsection (4) applies in any proceedings in which a court determines whether a provision of subordinate legislation, made in the exercise of a power conferred by primary legislation, is compatible with a Convention right.

---

[3] As repealed by SI 2003/1887, art 9, Sch 2, para 10(2).
[4] As inserted by SI 2005/3429, art 8, Schedule, para 3.

(4) If the court is satisfied—
  (a) that the provision is incompatible with a Convention right, and
  (b) that (disregarding any possibility of revocation) the primary legislation concerned prevents removal of the incompatibility,
  it may make a declaration of that incompatibility.

(5) In this section 'court' means—
  (a) *the House of Lords;*
  [(a) the Supreme Court;]⁵
  (b) the Judicial Committee of the Privy Council;
  (c) the *Courts-Martial Appeal Court* [Court Martial Appeal Court]⁶;
  (d) in Scotland, the High Court of Justiciary sitting otherwise than as a trial court or the Court of Session;
  (e) in England and Wales or Northern Ireland, the High Court or the Court of Appeal;
  [(f) the Court of Protection, in any matter being dealt with by the President of the Family Division, the Vice-Chancellor or a puisne judge of the High Court]⁷.

(6) A declaration under this section ('a declaration of incompatibility')—
  (a) does not affect the validity, continuing operation or enforcement of the provision in respect of which it is given; and
  (b) is not binding on the parties to the proceedings in which it is made.

5. RIGHT OF CROWN TO INTERVENE

(1) Where a court is considering whether to make a declaration of incompatibility, the Crown is entitled to notice in accordance with rules of court.

(2) In any case to which subsection (1) applies—
  (a) a Minister of the Crown (or a person nominated by him),
  (b) a member of the Scottish Executive,
  (c) a Northern Ireland Minister,
  (d) a Northern Ireland department,
  is entitled, on giving notice in accordance with rules of court, to be joined as a party to the proceedings.

(3) Notice under subsection (2) may be given at any time during the proceedings.

(4) A person who has been made a party to criminal proceedings (other than in Scotland) as the result of a notice under subsection (2) may, with leave, appeal to the *House of Lords* [Supreme Court]⁸ against any declaration of incompatibility made in the proceedings.

(5) In subsection (4)—
  'criminal proceedings' includes all proceedings before the *Courts-Martial Appeal Court* [Court Martial Appeal Court]⁹; and
  'leave' means leave granted by the court making the declaration of incompatibility or by the *House of Lords* [Supreme Court]¹⁰.

---

⁵ As amended by Constitutional Reform Act 2005, s 40(4), Sch 9, Pt 1, para 66(1), (2).
⁶ As amended by Armed Forces Act 2006, s 378(1), Sch 16, para 156.
⁷ As inserted by Mental Capacity Act 2005, s 67(1), Sch 6, para 43.
⁸ As amended by Constitutional Reform Act 2005, s 40(4), Sch 9, Pt 1, para 66(1), (3).
⁹ As amended by Armed Forces Act 2006, s 378(1), Sch 16, para 157.
¹⁰ As amended by Constitutional Reform Act 2005, s 40(4), Sch 9, Pt 1, para 66(1), (3).

Public Authorities

6. Acts of Public Authorities

(1) It is unlawful for a public authority to act in a way which is incompatible with a Convention right.

(2) Subsection (1) does not apply to an act if—

    (a) as the result of one or more provisions of primary legislation, the authority could not have acted differently; or

    (b) in the case of one or more provisions of, or made under, primary legislation which cannot be read or given effect in a way which is compatible with the Convention rights, the authority was acting so as to give effect to or enforce those provisions.

(3) In this section 'public authority' includes—

    (a) a court or tribunal, and

    (b) any person certain of whose functions are functions of a public nature,
        but does not include either House of Parliament or a person exercising functions in connection with proceedings in Parliament.

(4) *In subsection (3) 'Parliament' does not include the House of Lords in its judicial capacity.*[11]

(5) In relation to a particular act, a person is not a public authority by virtue only of subsection (3)(b) if the nature of the act is private.

(6) 'An act' includes a failure to act but does not include a failure to—

    (a) introduce in, or lay before, Parliament a proposal for legislation; or

    (b) make any primary legislation or remedial order.

7. Proceedings

(1) A person who claims that a public authority has acted (or proposes to act) in a way which is made unlawful by section 6(1) may—

    (a) bring proceedings against the authority under this Act in the appropriate court or tribunal, or

    (b) rely on the Convention right or rights concerned in any legal proceedings,
    but only if he is (or would be) a victim of the unlawful act.

(2) In subsection (1)(a) 'appropriate court or tribunal' means such court or tribunal as may be determined in accordance with rules; and proceedings against an authority include a counterclaim or similar proceeding.

(3) If the proceedings are brought on an application for judicial review, the applicant is to be taken to have a sufficient interest in relation to the unlawful act only if he is, or would be, a victim of that act.

(4) If the proceedings are made by way of a petition for judicial review in Scotland, the applicant shall be taken to have title and interest to sue in relation to the unlawful act only if he is, or would be, a victim of that act.

(5) Proceedings under subsection (1)(a) must be brought before the end of—

    (a) the period of one year beginning with the date on which the act complained of took place; or

---

[11] As repealed by Constitutional Reform Act 2005, ss 40(4), 146, Sch 9, Pt 1, para 66(1), (4), Sch 18, Pt 5.

(b) such longer period as the court or tribunal considers equitable having regard to all the circumstances,

but that is subject to any rule imposing a stricter time limit in relation to the procedure in question.

(6) In subsection (1)(b) 'legal proceedings' includes—

(a) proceedings brought by or at the instigation of a public authority; and

(b) an appeal against the decision of a court or tribunal.

(7) For the purposes of this section, a person is a victim of an unlawful act only if he would be a victim for the purposes of Article 34 of the Convention if proceedings were brought in the European Court of Human Rights in respect of that act.

(8) Nothing in this Act creates a criminal offence.

(9) In this section 'rules' means—

(a) in relation to proceedings before a court or tribunal outside Scotland, rules made by . . .[12] [the Lord Chancellor or][13] the Secretary of State for the purposes of this section or rules of court,

(b) in relation to proceedings before a court or tribunal in Scotland, rules made by the Secretary of State for those purposes,

(c) in relation to proceedings before a tribunal in Northern Ireland—

(i) which deals with transferred matters; and

(ii) for which no rules made under paragraph (a) are in force,

rules made by a Northern Ireland department for those purposes,

and includes provision made by order under section 1 of the Courts and Legal Services Act 1990.

(10) In making rules, regard must be had to section 9.

(11) The Minister who has power to make rules in relation to a particular tribunal may, to the extent he considers it necessary to ensure that the tribunal can provide an appropriate remedy in relation to an act (or proposed act) of a public authority which is (or would be) unlawful as a result of section 6(1), by order add to—

(a) the relief or remedies which the tribunal may grant; or

(b) the grounds on which it may grant any of them.

(12) An order made under subsection (11) may contain such incidental, supplemental, consequential or transitional provision as the Minister making it considers appropriate.

(13) 'The Minister' includes the Northern Ireland department concerned.

8. JUDICIAL REMEDIES

(1) In relation to any act (or proposed act) of a public authority which the court finds is (or would be) unlawful, it may grant such relief or remedy, or make such order, within its powers as it considers just and appropriate.

(2) But damages may be awarded only by a court which has power to award damages, or to order the payment of compensation, in civil proceedings.

(3) No award of damages is to be made unless, taking account of all the circumstances of the case, including—

---

[12] As repealed by SI 2003/1887, art 9, Sch 2, para 10(2).
[13] As inserted by SI 2005/3429, art 8, Schedule, para 3.

(a) any other relief or remedy granted, or order made, in relation to the act in question (by that or any other court), and

(b) the consequences of any decision (of that or any other court) in respect of that act,

the court is satisfied that the award is necessary to afford just satisfaction to the person in whose favour it is made.

(4) In determining—

(a) whether to award damages, or

(b) the amount of an award,

the court must take into account the principles applied by the European Court of Human Rights in relation to the award of compensation under Article 41 of the Convention.

(5) A public authority against which damages are awarded is to be treated—

(a) in Scotland, for the purposes of section 3 of the Law Reform (Miscellaneous Provisions) (Scotland) Act 1940 as if the award were made in an action of damages in which the authority has been found liable in respect of loss or damage to the person to whom the award is made;

(b) for the purposes of the Civil Liability (Contribution) Act 1978 as liable in respect of damage suffered by the person to whom the award is made.

(6) In this section—

'court' includes a tribunal;

'damages' means damages for an unlawful act of a public authority; and

'unlawful' means unlawful under section 6(1).

9. Judicial Acts

(1) Proceedings under section 7(1)(a) in respect of a judicial act may be brought only—

(a) by exercising a right of appeal;

(b) on an application (in Scotland a petition) for judicial review; or

(c) in such other forum as may be prescribed by rules.

(2) That does not affect any rule of law which prevents a court from being the subject of judicial review.

(3) In proceedings under this Act in respect of a judicial act done in good faith, damages may not be awarded otherwise than to compensate a person to the extent required by Article 5(5) of the Convention.

(4) An award of damages permitted by subsection (3) is to be made against the Crown; but no award may be made unless the appropriate person, if not a party to the proceedings, is joined.

(5) In this section—

'appropriate person' means the Minister responsible for the court concerned, or a person or government department nominated by him;

'court' includes a tribunal;

'judge' includes a member of a tribunal, a justice of the peace [(or, in Northern Ireland, a lay magistrate)][14] and a clerk or other officer entitled to exercise the jurisdiction of a court;

---

[14] As inserted by Justice (Northern Ireland) Act 2002, s 10(6), Sch 4, para 39.

'judicial act' means a judicial act of a court and includes an act done on the instructions, or on behalf, of a judge; and

'rules' has the same meaning as in section 7(9).

Remedial Action

10. Power to Take Remedial Action

(1) This section applies if—

    (a) a provision of legislation has been declared under section 4 to be incompatible with a Convention right and, if an appeal lies—

        (i) all persons who may appeal have stated in writing that they do not intend to do so;

        (ii) the time for bringing an appeal has expired and no appeal has been brought within that time; or

        (iii) an appeal brought within that time has been determined or abandoned; or

    (b) it appears to a Minister of the Crown or Her Majesty in Council that, having regard to a finding of the European Court of Human Rights made after the coming into force of this section in proceedings against the United Kingdom, a provision of legislation is incompatible with an obligation of the United Kingdom arising from the Convention.

(2) If a Minister of the Crown considers that there are compelling reasons for proceeding under this section, he may by order make such amendments to the legislation as he considers necessary to remove the incompatibility.

(3) If, in the case of subordinate legislation, a Minister of the Crown considers—

    (a) that it is necessary to amend the primary legislation under which the subordinate legislation in question was made, in order to enable the incompatibility to be removed, and

    (b) that there are compelling reasons for proceeding under this section,

he may by order make such amendments to the primary legislation as he considers necessary.

(4) This section also applies where the provision in question is in subordinate legislation and has been quashed, or declared invalid, by reason of incompatibility with a Convention right and the Minister proposes to proceed under paragraph 2(b) of Schedule 2.

(5) If the legislation is an Order in Council, the power conferred by subsection (2) or (3) is exercisable by Her Majesty in Council.

(6) In this section 'legislation' does not include a Measure of the Church Assembly or of the General Synod of the Church of England.

(7) Schedule 2 makes further provision about remedial orders.

Other Rights and Proceedings

11. Safeguard for Existing Human Rights

A person's reliance on a Convention right does not restrict—

(a) any other right or freedom conferred on him by or under any law having effect in any part of the United Kingdom; or

(b) his right to make any claim or bring any proceedings which he could make or bring apart from sections 7 to 9.

12. FREEDOM OF EXPRESSION

(1) This section applies if a court is considering whether to grant any relief which, if granted, might affect the exercise of the Convention right to freedom of expression.

(2) If the person against whom the application for relief is made ('the respondent') is neither present nor represented, no such relief is to be granted unless the court is satisfied—
   (a) that the applicant has taken all practicable steps to notify the respondent; or
   (b) that there are compelling reasons why the respondent should not be notified.

(3) No such relief is to be granted so as to restrain publication before trial unless the court is satisfied that the applicant is likely to establish that publication should not be allowed.

(4) The court must have particular regard to the importance of the Convention right to freedom of expression and, where the proceedings relate to material which the respondent claims, or which appears to the court, to be journalistic, literary or artistic material (or to conduct connected with such material), to—
   (a) the extent to which—
      (i) the material has, or is about to, become available to the public; or
      (ii) it is, or would be, in the public interest for the material to be published;
   (b) any relevant privacy code.

(5) In this section—
   'court' includes a tribunal; and
   'relief' includes any remedy or order (other than in criminal proceedings).

13. FREEDOM OF THOUGHT, CONSCIENCE AND RELIGION

(1) If a court's determination of any question arising under this Act might affect the exercise by a religious organisation (itself or its members collectively) of the Convention right to freedom of thought, conscience and religion, it must have particular regard to the importance of that right.

(2) In this section 'court' includes a tribunal.

DEROGATIONS AND RESERVATIONS

14. DEROGATIONS

(1) In this Act 'designated derogation' means—
   . . .[15]
   any derogation by the United Kingdom from an Article of the Convention, or of any protocol to the Convention, which is designated for the purposes of this Act in an order made by the [Secretary of State][16].

(2) . . .[17]

---

[15] As repealed by SI 2001/1216, art 2(a).
[16] As amended by SI 2003/1887, art 9, Sch 2, para 10(1).
[17] As repealed by SI 2001/1216, art 2(b).

(3) If a designated derogation is amended or replaced it ceases to be a designated derogation.

(4) But subsection (3) does not prevent the [Secretary of State][18] from exercising his power under subsection (1). . .[19] to make a fresh designation order in respect of the Article concerned.

(5) The [Secretary of State][20] must by order make such amendments to Schedule 3 as he considers appropriate to reflect—

  (a) any designation order; or

  (b) the effect of subsection (3).

(6) A designation order may be made in anticipation of the making by the United Kingdom of a proposed derogation.

15. RESERVATIONS

(1) In this Act 'designated reservation' means—

  (a) the United Kingdom's reservation to Article 2 of the First Protocol to the Convention; and

  (b) any other reservation by the United Kingdom to an Article of the Convention, or of any protocol to the Convention, which is designated for the purposes of this Act in an order made by the [Secretary of State][21].

(2) The text of the reservation referred to in subsection (1)(a) is set out in Part II of Schedule 3.

(3) If a designated reservation is withdrawn wholly or in part it ceases to be a designated reservation.

(4) But subsection (3) does not prevent the [Secretary of State][22] from exercising his power under subsection (1)(b) to make a fresh designation order in respect of the Article concerned.

(5) The [Secretary of State][23] must by order make such amendments to this Act as he considers appropriate to reflect—

  (a) any designation order; or

  (b) the effect of subsection (3).

16. PERIOD FOR WHICH DESIGNATED DEROGATIONS HAVE EFFECT

(1) If it has not already been withdrawn by the United Kingdom, a designated derogation ceases to have effect for the purposes of this Act—

  . . .[24]

at the end of the period of five years beginning with the date on which the order designating it was made.

---

[18] As amended by SI 2003/1887, art 9, Sch 2, para 10(1).

[19] As repealed by SI 2001/1216, art 2(c).

[20] As amended by SI 2003/1887, art 9, Sch 2, para 10(1).

[21] As amended by SI 2003/1887, art 9, Sch 2, para 10(1).

[22] As amended by SI 2003/1887, art 9, Sch 2, para 10(1).

[23] As amended by SI 2003/1887, art 9, Sch 2, para 10(1).

[24] As repealed by SI 2001/1216, art 3(a).

(2) At any time before the period—
   (a) fixed by subsection (1). . .[25], or
   (b) extended by an order under this subsection,
   comes to an end, the [Secretary of State][26] may by order extend it by a further period of five years.

(3) An order under section 14(1). . .[27] ceases to have effect at the end of the period for consideration, unless a resolution has been passed by each House approving the order.

(4) Subsection (3) does not affect—
   (a) anything done in reliance on the order; or
   (b) the power to make a fresh order under section 14(1). . ..[28]

(5) In subsection (3) 'period for consideration' means the period of forty days beginning with the day on which the order was made.

(6) In calculating the period for consideration, no account is to be taken of any time during which—
   (a) Parliament is dissolved or prorogued; or
   (b) both Houses are adjourned for more than four days.

(7) If a designated derogation is withdrawn by the United Kingdom, the [Secretary of State][29] must by order make such amendments to this Act as he considers are required to reflect that withdrawal.

17. PERIODIC REVIEW OF DESIGNATED RESERVATIONS

(1) The appropriate Minister must review the designated reservation referred to in section 15(1)(a)—
   (a) before the end of the period of five years beginning with the date on which section 1(2) came into force; and
   (b) if that designation is still in force, before the end of the period of five years beginning with the date on which the last report relating to it was laid under subsection (3).

(2) The appropriate Minister must review each of the other designated reservations (if any)—
   (a) before the end of the period of five years beginning with the date on which the order designating the reservation first came into force; and
   (b) if the designation is still in force, before the end of the period of five years beginning with the date on which the last report relating to it was laid under subsection (3).

(3) The Minister conducting a review under this section must prepare a report on the result of the review and lay a copy of it before each House of Parliament.

---

[25] As repealed by SI 2001/1216, art 3(b).
[26] As amended by SI 2003/1887, art 9, Sch 2, para 10(1).
[27] As repealed by SI 2001/1216, art 3(c).
[28] As repealed by SI 2001/1216, art 3(d).
[29] As amended by SI 2003/1887, art 9, Sch 2, para 10(1).

JUDGES OF THE EUROPEAN COURT OF HUMAN RIGHTS

18. APPOINTMENT TO EUROPEAN COURT OF HUMAN RIGHTS

(1)   In this section 'judicial office' means the office of—
  (a) Lord Justice of Appeal, Justice of the High Court or Circuit judge, in England and Wales;
  (b) judge of the Court of Session or sheriff, in Scotland;
  (c) Lord Justice of Appeal, judge of the High Court or county court judge, in Northern Ireland.

(2)   The holder of a judicial office may become a judge of the European Court of Human Rights ('the Court') without being required to relinquish his office.

(3)   But he is not required to perform the duties of his judicial office while he is a judge of the Court.

(4)   In respect of any period during which he is a judge of the Court—
  (a) a Lord Justice of Appeal or Justice of the High Court is not to count as a judge of the relevant court for the purposes of section 2(1) or 4(1) of the *Supreme Court Act 1981* [Senior Courts Act 1981][30] (maximum number of judges) nor as a judge of the *Supreme Court* [Senior Courts][31] for the purposes of section 12(1) to (6) of that Act (salaries etc);
  (b) a judge of the Court of Session is not to count as a judge of that court for the purposes of section 1(1) of the Court of Session Act 1988 (maximum number of judges) or of section 9(1)(c) of the Administration of Justice Act 1973 ('the 1973 Act') (salaries etc);
  (c) a Lord Justice of Appeal or judge of the High Court in Northern Ireland is not to count as a judge of the relevant court for the purposes of section 2(1) or 3(1) of the Judicature (Northern Ireland) Act 1978 (maximum number of judges) nor as a judge of the *Supreme Court* [Court of Judicature][32] of Northern Ireland for the purposes of section 9(1)(d) of the 1973 Act (salaries etc);
  (d) a Circuit judge is not to count as such for the purposes of section 18 of the Courts Act 1971 (salaries etc);
  (e) a sheriff is not to count as such for the purposes of section 14 of the Sheriff Courts (Scotland) Act 1907 (salaries etc);
  (f) a county court judge of Northern Ireland is not to count as such for the purposes of section 106 of the County Courts Act (Northern Ireland) 1959 (salaries etc).

(5)   If a sheriff principal is appointed a judge of the Court, section 11(1) of the Sheriff Courts (Scotland) Act 1971 (temporary appointment of sheriff principal) applies, while he holds that appointment, as if his office is vacant.

(6)   Schedule 4 makes provision about judicial pensions in relation to the holder of a judicial office who serves as a judge of the Court.

---

[30] As amended by Constitutional Reform Act 2005, s 59(5), Sch 11, Pt 1, para 1(2).
[31] As amended by Constitutional Reform Act 2005, s 59(5), Sch 11, Pt 2, para 4(1), (3).
[32] As amended by Constitutional Reform Act 2005, s 59(5), Sch 11, Pt 3, para 6(1), (3).

(7)   The Lord Chancellor or the Secretary of State may by order make such transitional provision (including, in particular, provision for a temporary increase in the maximum number of judges) as he considers appropriate in relation to any holder of a judicial office who has completed his service as a judge of the Court.

[(7A) The following paragraphs apply to the making of an order under subsection (7) in relation to any holder of a judicial office listed in subsection (1)(a)—

  (a)   before deciding what transitional provision it is appropriate to make, the person making the order must consult the Lord Chief Justice of England and Wales;

  (b)   before making the order, that person must consult the Lord Chief Justice of England and Wales.

(7B) The following paragraphs apply to the making of an order under subsection (7) in relation to any holder of a judicial office listed in subsection (1)(c)—

  (a)   before deciding what transitional provision it is appropriate to make, the person making the order must consult the Lord Chief Justice of Northern Ireland;

  (b)   before making the order, that person must consult the Lord Chief Justice of Northern Ireland.

(7C) The Lord Chief Justice of England and Wales may nominate a judicial office holder (within the meaning of section 109(4) of the Constitutional Reform Act 2005) to exercise his functions under this section.

(7D) The Lord Chief Justice of Northern Ireland may nominate any of the following to exercise his functions under this section—

  (a)   the holder of one of the offices listed in Schedule 1 to the Justice (Northern Ireland) Act 2002;

  (b)   a Lord Justice of Appeal (as defined in section 88 of that Act).][33]

Parliamentary Procedure

19. Statements of compatibility

(1)   A Minister of the Crown in charge of a Bill in either House of Parliament must, before Second Reading of the Bill—

  (a)   make a statement to the effect that in his view the provisions of the Bill are compatible with the Convention rights ('a statement of compatibility'); or

  (b)   make a statement to the effect that although he is unable to make a statement of compatibility the government nevertheless wishes the House to proceed with the Bill.

(2)   The statement must be in writing and be published in such manner as the Minister making it considers appropriate.

---

[33] As inserted by Constitutional Reform Act 2005, s 15(1), Sch 4, Pt 1, para 278.

SUPPLEMENTAL

20. ORDERS ETC UNDER THIS ACT

(1) Any power of a Minister of the Crown to make an order under this Act is exercisable by statutory instrument.

(2) The power of . . .[34] [the Lord Chancellor or][35] the Secretary of State to make rules (other than rules of court) under section 2(3) or 7(9) is exercisable by statutory instrument.

(3) Any statutory instrument made under section 14, 15 or 16(7) must be laid before Parliament.

(4) No order may be made by . . .[36] [the Lord Chancellor or][37] the Secretary of State under section 1(4), 7(11) or 16(2) unless a draft of the order has been laid before, and approved by, each House of Parliament.

(5) Any statutory instrument made under section 18(7) or Schedule 4, or to which subsection (2) applies, shall be subject to annulment in pursuance of a resolution of either House of Parliament.

(6) The power of a Northern Ireland department to make—
  (a) rules under section 2(3)(c) or 7(9)(c), or
  (b) an order under section 7(11),
is exercisable by statutory rule for the purposes of the Statutory Rules (Northern Ireland) Order 1979.

(7) Any rules made under section 2(3)(c) or 7(9)(c) shall be subject to negative resolution; and section 41(6) of the Interpretation Act (Northern Ireland) 1954 (meaning of 'subject to negative resolution') shall apply as if the power to make the rules were conferred by an Act of the Northern Ireland Assembly.

(8) No order may be made by a Northern Ireland department under section 7(11) unless a draft of the order has been laid before, and approved by, the Northern Ireland Assembly.

21. INTERPRETATION, ETC

(1) In this Act—
  'amend' includes repeal and apply (with or without modifications);
  'the appropriate Minister' means the Minister of the Crown having charge of the appropriate authorised government department (within the meaning of the Crown Proceedings Act 1947);
  'the Commission' means the European Commission of Human Rights;
  'the Convention' means the Convention for the Protection of Human Rights and Fundamental Freedoms, agreed by the Council of Europe at Rome on 4th November 1950 as it has effect for the time being in relation to the United Kingdom;
  'declaration of incompatibility' means a declaration under section 4;
  'Minister of the Crown' has the same meaning as in the Ministers of the Crown Act 1975;

---

[34] As repealed by SI 2003/1887, art 9, Sch 2, para 10(2).
[35] As inserted by SI 2005/3429, art 8, Schedule, para 3.
[36] As repealed by SI 2003/1887, art 9, Sch 2, para 10(2).
[37] As inserted by SI 2005/3429, art 8, Schedule, para 3.

'Northern Ireland Minister' includes the First Minister and the deputy First Minister in Northern Ireland;

'primary legislation' means any—

(a) public general Act;

(b) local and personal Act;

(c) private Act;

(d) Measure of the Church Assembly;

(e) Measure of the General Synod of the Church of England;

(f) Order in Council—

    (i) made in exercise of Her Majesty's Royal Prerogative;

    (ii) made under section 38(1)(a) of the Northern Ireland Constitution Act 1973 or the corresponding provision of the Northern Ireland Act 1998; or

    (iii) amending an Act of a kind mentioned in paragraph (a), (b) or (c);

and includes an order or other instrument made under primary legislation (otherwise than by the [Welsh Ministers, the First Minister for Wales, the Counsel General to the Welsh Assembly Government][38], a member of the Scottish Executive, a Northern Ireland Minister or a Northern Ireland department) to the extent to which it operates to bring one or more provisions of that legislation into force or amends any primary legislation;

'the First Protocol' means the protocol to the Convention agreed at Paris on 20th March 1952;

. . .[39]

'the Eleventh Protocol' means the protocol to the Convention (restructuring the control machinery established by the Convention) agreed at Strasbourg on 11th May 1994;

['the Thirteenth Protocol' means the protocol to the Convention (concerning the abolition of the death penalty in all circumstances) agreed at Vilnius on 3rd May 2002;][40]

'remedial order' means an order under section 10;

'subordinate legislation' means any—

(a) Order in Council other than one—

    (i) made in exercise of Her Majesty's Royal Prerogative;

    (ii) made under section 38(1)(a) of the Northern Ireland Constitution Act 1973 or the corresponding provision of the Northern Ireland Act 1998; or

    (iii) amending an Act of a kind mentioned in the definition of primary legislation;

(b) Act of the Scottish Parliament;

[(ba) Measure of the National Assembly for Wales;

(bb) Act of the National Assembly for Wales;][41]

(c) Act of the Parliament of Northern Ireland;

(d) Measure of the Assembly established under section 1 of the Northern Ireland Assembly Act 1973;

(e) Act of the Northern Ireland Assembly;

---

[38] As amended by Government of Wales Act 2006, s 160(1), Sch 10, para 56(1), (2).

[39] As repealed by SI 2004/1574, art 2(2).

[40] As inserted by SI 2004/1574, art 2(2).

[41] As inserted by Government of Wales Act 2006, s 160(1), Sch 10, para 56(1), (3).

(f)   order, rules, regulations, scheme, warrant, byelaw or other instrument made under primary legislation (except to the extent to which it operates to bring one or more provisions of that legislation into force or amends any primary legislation);

(g)   order, rules, regulations, scheme, warrant, byelaw or other instrument made under legislation mentioned in paragraph (b), (c), (d) or or made under an Order in Council applying only to Northern Ireland;

(h)   order, rules, regulations, scheme, warrant, byelaw or other instrument made by a member of the Scottish Executive[, Welsh Ministers, the First Minister for Wales, the Counsel General to the Welsh Assembly Government][42], a Northern Ireland Minister or a Northern Ireland department in exercise of prerogative or other executive functions of Her Majesty which are exercisable by such a person on behalf of Her Majesty;

'transferred matters' has the same meaning as in the Northern Ireland Act 1998; and

'tribunal' means any tribunal in which legal proceedings may be brought.

(2)   The references in paragraphs (b) and (c) of section 2(1) to Articles are to Articles of the Convention as they had effect immediately before the coming into force of the Eleventh Protocol.

(3)   The reference in paragraph (d) of section 2(1) to Article 46 includes a reference to Articles 32 and 54 of the Convention as they had effect immediately before the coming into force of the Eleventh Protocol.

(4)   The references in section 2(1) to a report or decision of the Commission or a decision of the Committee of Ministers include references to a report or decision made as provided by paragraphs 3, 4 and 6 of Article 5 of the Eleventh Protocol (transitional provisions).

(5)   *Any liability under the Army Act 1955, the Air Force Act 1955 or the Naval Discipline Act 1957 to suffer death for an offence is replaced by a liability to imprisonment for life or any less punishment authorised by those Acts; and those Acts shall accordingly have effect with the necessary modifications.*[43]

22. Short Title, Commencement, Application and Extent

(1)   This Act may be cited as the Human Rights Act 1998.

(2)   Sections 18, 20 and 21(5) and this section come into force on the passing of this Act.

(3)   The other provisions of this Act come into force on such day as the Secretary of State may by order appoint; and different days may be appointed for different purposes.

(4)   Paragraph (b) of subsection (1) of section 7 applies to proceedings brought by or at the instigation of a public authority whenever the act in question took place; but otherwise that subsection does not apply to an act taking place before the coming into force of that section.

---

[42] As inserted by Government of Wales Act 2006, s 160(1), Sch 10, para 56(1), (4).

[43] As repealed by Armed Forces Act 2006, s 378(2), Sch 17.

(5) This Act binds the Crown.

(6) This Act extends to Northern Ireland.

(7) *Section 21(5), so far as it relates to any provision contained in the Army Act 1955, the Air Force Act 1955 or the Naval Discipline Act 1957, extends to any place to which that provision extends.*[44]

---

[44] As repealed by Armed Forces Act 2006, s 378(2), Sch 17.

Section 1(3)

PART I
THE CONVENTION

RIGHTS AND FREEDOMS

Article 2

Right to life

(1) Everyone's right to life shall be protected by law. No one shall be deprived of his life intentionally save in the execution of a sentence of a court following his conviction of a crime for which this penalty is provided by law.

(2) Deprivation of life shall not be regarded as inflicted in contravention of this Article when it results from the use of force which is no more than absolutely necessary:

(a) in defence of any person from unlawful violence;

(b) in order to effect a lawful arrest or to prevent the escape of a person lawfully detained;

(c) in action lawfully taken for the purpose of quelling a riot or insurrection.

Article 3

Prohibition of torture

No one shall be subjected to torture or to inhuman or degrading treatment or punishment.

Article 4

Prohibition of slavery and forced labour

(1) No one shall be held in slavery or servitude.

(2) No one shall be required to perform forced or compulsory labour.

(3) For the purpose of this Article the term 'forced or compulsory labour' shall not include:

(a) any work required to be done in the ordinary course of detention imposed according to the provisions of Article 5 of this Convention or during conditional release from such detention;

(b) any service of a military character or, in case of conscientious objectors in countries where they are recognised, service exacted instead of compulsory military service;

(c) any service exacted in case of an emergency or calamity threatening the life or well-being of the community;

(d) any work or service which forms part of normal civic obligations.

Article 5

Right to liberty and security

(1) Everyone has the right to liberty and security of person. No one shall be deprived of his liberty save in the following cases and in accordance with a procedure prescribed by law:

   (a) the lawful detention of a person after conviction by a competent court;

   (b) the lawful arrest or detention of a person for non-compliance with the lawful order of a court or in order to secure the fulfilment of any obligation prescribed by law;

   (c) the lawful arrest or detention of a person effected for the purpose of bringing him before the competent legal authority on reasonable suspicion of having committed an offence or when it is reasonably considered necessary to prevent his committing an offence or fleeing after having done so;

   (d) the detention of a minor by lawful order for the purpose of educational supervision or his lawful detention for the purpose of bringing him before the competent legal authority;

   (e) the lawful detention of persons for the prevention of the spreading of infectious diseases, of persons of unsound mind, alcoholics or drug addicts or vagrants;

   (f) the lawful arrest or detention of a person to prevent his effecting an unauthorised entry into the country or of a person against whom action is being taken with a view to deportation or extradition.

(2) Everyone who is arrested shall be informed promptly, in a language which he understands, of the reasons for his arrest and of any charge against him.

(3) Everyone arrested or detained in accordance with the provisions of paragraph 1(c) of this Article shall be brought promptly before a judge or other officer authorised by law to exercise judicial power and shall be entitled to trial within a reasonable time or to release pending trial. Release may be conditioned by guarantees to appear for trial.

(4) Everyone who is deprived of his liberty by arrest or detention shall be entitled to take proceedings by which the lawfulness of his detention shall be decided speedily by a court and his release ordered if the detention is not lawful.

(5) Everyone who has been the victim of arrest or detention in contravention of the provisions of this Article shall have an enforceable right to compensation.

Article 6

Right to a fair trial

(1) In the determination of his civil rights and obligations or of any criminal charge against him, everyone is entitled to a fair and public hearing within a reasonable time by an independent and impartial tribunal established by law. Judgment shall be pronounced publicly but the press and public may be excluded from all or part of the trial in the interest of morals, public order or national security in a democratic society, where the interests of juveniles or the protection of the private life of the parties so require, or to the extent strictly necessary in the opinion of the court in special circumstances where publicity would prejudice the interests of justice.

(2) Everyone charged with a criminal offence shall be presumed innocent until proved guilty according to law.

(3) Everyone charged with a criminal offence has the following minimum rights:

   (a) to be informed promptly, in a language which he understands and in detail, of the nature and cause of the accusation against him;

   (b) to have adequate time and facilities for the preparation of his defence;

(c) to defend himself in person or through legal assistance of his own choosing or, if he has not sufficient means to pay for legal assistance, to be given it free when the interests of justice so require;

(d) to examine or have examined witnesses against him and to obtain the attendance and examination of witnesses on his behalf under the same conditions as witnesses against him;

(e) to have the free assistance of an interpreter if he cannot understand or speak the language used in court.

Article 7

No punishment without law

(1) No one shall be held guilty of any criminal offence on account of any act or omission which did not constitute a criminal offence under national or international law at the time when it was committed. Nor shall a heavier penalty be imposed than the one that was applicable at the time the criminal offence was committed.

(2) This Article shall not prejudice the trial and punishment of any person for any act or omission which, at the time when it was committed, was criminal according to the general principles of law recognised by civilised nations.

Article 8

Right to respect for private and family life

(1) Everyone has the right to respect for his private and family life, his home and his correspondence.

(2) There shall be no interference by a public authority with the exercise of this right except such as is in accordance with the law and is necessary in a democratic society in the interests of national security, public safety or the economic well-being of the country, for the prevention of disorder or crime, for the protection of health or morals, or for the protection of the rights and freedoms of others.

Article 9

Freedom of thought, conscience and religion

(1) Everyone has the right to freedom of thought, conscience and religion; this right includes freedom to change his religion or belief and freedom, either alone or in community with others and in public or private, to manifest his religion or belief, in worship, teaching, practice and observance.

(2) Freedom to manifest one's religion or beliefs shall be subject only to such limitations as are prescribed by law and are necessary in a democratic society in the interests of public safety, for the protection of public order, health or morals, or for the protection of the rights and freedoms of others.

Article 10

Freedom of expression

(1) Everyone has the right to freedom of expression. This right shall include freedom to hold opinions and to receive and impart information and ideas without interference by public authority and regardless of frontiers. This Article shall not prevent States from requiring the licensing of broadcasting, television or cinema enterprises.

(2) The exercise of these freedoms, since it carries with it duties and responsibilities, may be subject to such formalities, conditions, restrictions or penalties as are prescribed by law and are necessary in a democratic society, in the interests of national security, territorial integrity or public safety, for the prevention of disorder or crime, for the protection of health or morals, for the protection of the reputation or rights of others, for preventing the disclosure of information received in confidence, or for maintaining the authority and impartiality of the judiciary.

Article 11

Freedom of assembly and association

(1) Everyone has the right to freedom of peaceful assembly and to freedom of association with others, including the right to form and to join trade unions for the protection of his interests.

(2) No restrictions shall be placed on the exercise of these rights other than such as are prescribed by law and are necessary in a democratic society in the interests of national security or public safety, for the prevention of disorder or crime, for the protection of health or morals or for the protection of the rights and freedoms of others. This Article shall not prevent the imposition of lawful restrictions on the exercise of these rights by members of the armed forces, of the police or of the administration of the State.

Article 12

Right to marry

Men and women of marriageable age have the right to marry and to found a family, according to the national laws governing the exercise of this right.

Article 14

Prohibition of discrimination

The enjoyment of the rights and freedoms set forth in this Convention shall be secured without discrimination on any ground such as sex, race, colour, language, religion, political or other opinion, national or social origin, association with a national minority, property, birth or other status.

Article 16

Restrictions on political activity of aliens

Nothing in Articles 10, 11 and 14 shall be regarded as preventing the High Contracting Parties from imposing restrictions on the political activity of aliens.

Article 17

Prohibition of abuse of rights

Nothing in this Convention may be interpreted as implying for any State, group or person any right to engage in any activity or perform any act aimed at the destruction on any of the rights and freedoms set forth herein or at their limitation to a greater extent than is provided for in the Convention.

Article 18

Limitation on use of restrictions on rights

The restrictions permitted under this Convention to the said rights and freedoms shall not be applied for any purpose other than those for which they have been prescribed.

PART II
THE FIRST PROTOCOL

Article 1

Protection of property

Every natural or legal person is entitled to the peaceful enjoyment of his possessions. No one shall be deprived of his possessions except in the public interest and subject to the conditions provided for by law and by the general principles of international law.

The preceding provisions shall not, however, in any way impair the right of a State to enforce such laws as it deems necessary to control the use of property in accordance with the general interest or to secure the payment of taxes or other contributions or penalties.

Article 2

Right to education

No person shall be denied the right to education. In the exercise of any functions which it assumes in relation to education and to teaching, the State shall respect the right of parents to ensure such education and teaching in conformity with their own religious and philosophical convictions.

Article 3

Right to free elections

The High Contracting Parties undertake to hold free elections at reasonable intervals by secret ballot, under conditions which will ensure the free expression of the opinion of the people in the choice of the legislature.

[PART III
ARTICLE 1 OF THE THIRTEENTH PROTOCOL

Abolition of the death penalty

The death penalty shall be abolished. No one shall be condemned to such penalty or executed.][45]

---

[45] As amended by SI 2004/1574, art 2(3).

APPENDIX 2

Convention for the Protection of Human Rights and Fundamental Freedoms as amended by Protocol No. 11 with Protocol Nos. 1, 4, 6, 7, 12 and 13

The text of the Convention had been amended according to the provisions of Protocol No. 3 (ETS No. 45), which entered into force on 21 September 1970, of Protocol No. 5 (ETS No. 55), which entered into force on 20 December 1971 and of Protocol No. 8 (ETS No. 118), which entered into force on 1 January 1990, and comprised also the text of Protocol No. 2 (ETS No. 44) which, in accordance with Article 5, paragraph 3 thereof, had been an integral part of the Convention since its entry into force on 21 September 1970. All provisions which had been amended or added by these Protocols are replaced by Protocol No. 11 (ETS No. 155), as from the date of its entry into force on 1 November 1998. As from that date, Protocol No. 9 (ETS No. 140), which entered into force on 1 October 1994, is repealed.

Registry of the European Court of Human Rights September 2003

Convention for the Protection of Human Rights and Fundamental Freedoms

Rome, 4.XI.1950

The governments signatory hereto, being members of the Council of Europe,

Considering the Universal Declaration of Human Rights proclaimed by the General Assembly of the United Nations on 10th December 1948;

Considering that this Declaration aims at securing the universal and effective recognition and observance of the Rights therein declared;

Considering that the aim of the Council of Europe is the achievement of greater unity between its members and that one of the methods by which that aim is to be pursued is the maintenance and further realisation of human rights and fundamental freedoms;

Reaffirming their profound belief in those fundamental freedoms which are the foundation of justice and peace in the world and are best maintained on the one hand by an effective political democracy and on the other by a common understanding and observance of the human rights upon which they depend;

Being resolved, as the governments of European countries which are like-minded and have a common heritage of political traditions, ideals, freedom and the rule of law, to take the first steps for the collective enforcement of certain of the rights stated in the Universal Declaration,

Have agreed as follows:

Article 1
Obligation to respect human rights

The High Contracting Parties shall secure to everyone within their jurisdiction the rights and freedoms defined in Section I of this Convention.

SECTION I: RIGHTS AND FREEDOMS

Article 2
Right to life

1. Everyone's right to life shall be protected by law. No one shall be deprived of his life intentionally save in the execution of a sentence of a court following his conviction of a crime for which this penalty is provided by law.
2. Deprivation of life shall not be regarded as inflicted in contravention of this article when it results from the use of force which is no more than absolutely necessary:
    (a) in defence of any person from unlawful violence;
    (b) in order to effect a lawful arrest or to prevent the escape of a person lawfully detained;
    (c) in action lawfully taken for the purpose of quelling a riot or insurrection.

Article 3
Prohibition of torture

No one shall be subjected to torture or to inhuman or degrading treatment or punishment.

Article 4
Prohibition of slavery and forced labour

1. No one shall be held in slavery or servitude.
2. No one shall be required to perform forced or compulsory labour.
3. For the purpose of this article the term 'forced or compulsory labour' shall not include:
    (a) any work required to be done in the ordinary course of detention imposed according to the provisions of Article 5 of this Convention or during conditional release from such detention;
    (b) any service of a military character or, in case of conscientious objectors in countries where they are recognised, service exacted instead of compulsory military service;
    (c) any service exacted in case of an emergency or calamity threatening the life or well-being of the community;
    (d) any work or service which forms part of normal civic obligations.

Article 5
Right to liberty and security

1. Everyone has the right to liberty and security of person. No one shall be deprived of his liberty save in the following cases and in accordance with a procedure prescribed by law:
    (a) the lawful detention of a person after conviction by a competent court;
    (b) the lawful arrest or detention of a person for non-compliance with the lawful order of a court or in order to secure the fulfilment of any obligation prescribed by law;

   (c) the lawful arrest or detention of a person effected for the purpose of bringing him before the competent legal authority on reasonable suspicion of having committed an offence or when it is reasonably considered necessary to prevent his committing an offence or fleeing after having done so;

   (d) the detention of a minor by lawful order for the purpose of educational supervision or his lawful detention for the purpose of bringing him before the competent legal authority;

   (e) the lawful detention of persons for the prevention of the spreading of infectious diseases, of persons of unsound mind, alcoholics or drug addicts or vagrants;

   (f) the lawful arrest or detention of a person to prevent his effecting an unauthorised entry into the country or of a person against whom action is being taken with a view to deportation or extradition.

2. Everyone who is arrested shall be informed promptly, in a language which he understands, of the reasons for his arrest and of any charge against him.

3. Everyone arrested or detained in accordance with the provisions of paragraph 1.c of this article shall be brought promptly before a judge or other officer authorised by law to exercise judicial power and shall be entitled to trial within a reasonable time or to release pending trial. Release may be conditioned by guarantees to appear for trial.

4. Everyone who is deprived of his liberty by arrest or detention shall be entitled to take proceedings by which the lawfulness of his detention shall be decided speedily by a court and his release ordered if the detention is not lawful.

5. Everyone who has been the victim of arrest or detention in contravention of the provisions of this article shall have an enforceable right to compensation.

Article 6
Right to a fair trial

1. In the determination of his civil rights and obligations or of any criminal charge against him, everyone is entitled to a fair and public hearing within a reasonable time by an independent and impartial tribunal established by law. Judgment shall be pronounced publicly but the press and public may be excluded from all or part of the trial in the interests of morals, public order or national security in a democratic society, where the interests of juveniles or the protection of the private life of the parties so require, or to the extent strictly necessary in the opinion of the court in special circumstances where publicity would prejudice the interests of justice.

2. Everyone charged with a criminal offence shall be presumed innocent until proved guilty according to law.

3. Everyone charged with a criminal offence has the following minimum rights:

   (a) to be informed promptly, in a language which he understands and in detail, of the nature and cause of the accusation against him;

   (b) to have adequate time and facilities for the preparation of his defence;

   (c) to defend himself in person or through legal assistance of his own choosing or, if he has not sufficient means to pay for legal assistance, to be given it free when the interests of justice so require;

   (d) to examine or have examined witnesses against him and to obtain the attendance and examination of witnesses on his behalf under the same conditions as witnesses against him;

(e) to have the free assistance of an interpreter if he cannot understand or speak the language used in court.

Article 7
No punishment without law

1. No one shall be held guilty of any criminal offence on account of any act or omission which did not constitute a criminal offence under national or international law at the time when it was committed. Nor shall a heavier penalty be imposed than the one that was applicable at the time the criminal offence was committed.
2. This article shall not prejudice the trial and punishment of any person for any act or omission which, at the time when it was committed, was criminal according to the general principles of law recognised by civilised nations.

Article 8
Right to respect for private and family life

1. Everyone has the right to respect for his private and family life, his home and his correspondence.
2. There shall be no interference by a public authority with the exercise of this right except such as is in accordance with the law and is necessary in a democratic society in the interests of national security, public safety or the economic well-being of the country, for the prevention of disorder or crime, for the protection of health or morals, or for the protection of the rights and freedoms of others.

Article 9
Freedom of thought, conscience and religion

1. Everyone has the right to freedom of thought, conscience and religion; this right includes freedom to change his religion or belief and freedom, either alone or in community with others and in public or private, to manifest his religion or belief, in worship, teaching, practice and observance.
2. Freedom to manifest one's religion or beliefs shall be subject only to such limitations as are prescribed by law and are necessary in a democratic society in the interests of public safety, for the protection of public order, health or morals, or for the protection of the rights and freedoms of others.

Article 10
Freedom of expression

1. Everyone has the right to freedom of expression. This right shall include freedom to hold opinions and to receive and impart information and ideas without interference by public authority and regardless of frontiers. This article shall not prevent States from requiring the licensing of broadcasting, television or cinema enterprises.
2. The exercise of these freedoms, since it carries with it duties and responsibilities, may be subject to such formalities, conditions, restrictions or penalties as are prescribed by law and are necessary in a democratic society, in the interests of national security, territorial integrity or public safety, for the prevention of disorder or crime, for the protection of health or morals, for the protection of the reputation or rights of others, for preventing the disclosure of information received in confidence, or for maintaining the authority and impartiality of the judiciary.

Article 11
Freedom of assembly and association

1. Everyone has the right to freedom of peaceful assembly and to freedom of association with others, including the right to form and to join trade unions for the protection of his interests.

2. No restrictions shall be placed on the exercise of these rights other than such as are prescribed by law and are necessary in a democratic society in the interests of national security or public safety, for the prevention of disorder or crime, for the protection of health or morals or for the protection of the rights and freedoms of others. This article shall not prevent the imposition of lawful restrictions on the exercise of these rights by members of the armed forces, of the police or of the administration of the State.

Article 12
Right to marry

Men and women of marriageable age have the right to marry and to found a family, according to the national laws governing the exercise of this right.

Article 13
Right to an effective remedy

Everyone whose rights and freedoms as set forth in this Convention are violated shall have an effective remedy before a national authority notwithstanding that the violation has been committed by persons acting in an official capacity.

Article 14
Prohibition of discrimination

The enjoyment of the rights and freedoms set forth in this Convention shall be secured without discrimination on any ground such as sex, race, colour, language, religion, political or other opinion, national or social origin, association with a national minority, property, birth or other status.

Article 15
Derogation in time of emergency

1. In time of war or other public emergency threatening the life of the nation any High Contracting Party may take measures derogating from its obligations under this Convention to the extent strictly required by the exigencies of the situation, provided that such measures are not inconsistent with its other obligations under international law.

2. No derogation from Article 2, except in respect of deaths resulting from lawful acts of war, or from Articles 3, 4 (paragraph 1) and 7 shall be made under this provision.

3. Any High Contracting Party availing itself of this right of derogation shall keep the Secretary General of the Council of Europe fully informed of the measures which it has taken and the reasons therefor. It shall also inform the Secretary General of the Council of Europe when such measures have ceased to operate and the provisions of the Convention are again being fully executed.

Article 16
Restrictions on political activity of aliens

Nothing in Articles 10, 11 and 14 shall be regarded as preventing the High Contracting Parties from imposing restrictions on the political activity of aliens.

Article 17
Prohibition of abuse of rights

Nothing in this Convention may be interpreted as implying for any State, group or person any right to engage in any activity or perform any act aimed at the destruction of any of the rights and freedoms set forth herein or at their limitation to a greater extent than is provided for in the Convention.

Article 18
Limitation on use of restrictions on rights

The restrictions permitted under this Convention to the said rights and freedoms shall not be applied for any purpose other than those for which they have been prescribed.

SECTION II: EUROPEAN COURT OF HUMAN RIGHTS

Article 19
Establishment of the Court

To ensure the observance of the engagements undertaken by the High Contracting Parties in the Convention and the Protocols thereto, there shall be set up a European Court of Human Rights, hereinafter referred to as 'the Court'. It shall function on a permanent basis.

Article 20
Number of judges

The Court shall consist of a number of judges equal to that of the High Contracting Parties.

Article 21
Criteria for office

1. The judges shall be of high moral character and must either possess the qualifications required for appointment to high judicial office or be jurisconsults of recognised competence.
2. The judges shall sit on the Court in their individual capacity.
3. During their term of office the judges shall not engage in any activity which is incompatible with their independence, impartiality or with the demands of a full-time office; all questions arising from the application of this paragraph shall be decided by the Court.

Article 22
Election of judges

1. The judges shall be elected by the Parliamentary Assembly with respect to each High Contracting Party by a majority of votes cast from a list of three candidates nominated by the High Contracting Party.
2. The same procedure shall be followed to complete the Court in the event of the accession of new High Contracting Parties and in filling casual vacancies.

Article 23
Terms of office

1. The judges shall be elected for a period of six years. They may be re-elected. However, the terms of office of one-half of the judges elected at the first election shall expire at the end of three years.

2. The judges whose terms of office are to expire at the end of the initial period of three years shall be chosen by lot by the Secretary General of the Council of Europe immediately after their election.

3. In order to ensure that, as far as possible, the terms of office of one-half of the judges are renewed every three years, the Parliamentary Assembly may decide, before proceeding to any subsequent election, that the term or terms of office of one or more judges to be elected shall be for a period other than six years but not more than nine and not less than three years.

4. In cases where more than one term of office is involved and where the Parliamentary Assembly applies the preceding paragraph, the allocation of the terms of office shall be effected by a drawing of lots by the Secretary General of the Council of Europe immediately after the election.

5. A judge elected to replace a judge whose term of office has not expired shall hold office for the remainder of his predecessor's term.

6. The terms of office of judges shall expire when they reach the age of 70.

7. The judges shall hold office until replaced. They shall, however, continue to deal with such cases as they already have under consideration.

Article 24
Dismissal

No judge may be dismissed from his office unless the other judges decide by a majority of two-thirds that he has ceased to fulfil the required conditions.

Article 25
Registry and legal secretaries

The Court shall have a registry, the functions and organisation of which shall be laid down in the rules of the Court. The Court shall be assisted by legal secretaries.

Article 26
Plenary Court

The plenary Court shall:

(a) elect its President and one or two Vice-Presidents for a period of three years; they may be re-elected;
(b) set up Chambers, constituted for a fixed period of time;
(c) elect the Presidents of the Chambers of the Court; they may be re-elected;
(d) adopt the rules of the Court, and
(e) elect the Registrar and one or more Deputy Registrars.

Article 27
Committees, Chambers and Grand Chamber

1. To consider cases brought before it, the Court shall sit in committees of three judges, in Chambers of seven judges and in a Grand Chamber of seventeen judges. The Court's Chambers shall set up committees for a fixed period of time.

2. There shall sit as an ex officio member of the Chamber and the Grand Chamber the judge elected in respect of the State Party concerned or, if there is none or if he is unable to sit, a person of its choice who shall sit in the capacity of judge.

3. The Grand Chamber shall also include the President of the Court, the Vice-Presidents, the Presidents of the Chambers and other judges chosen in accordance with the rules of

the Court. When a case is referred to the Grand Chamber under Article 43, no judge from the Chamber which rendered the judgment shall sit in the Grand Chamber, with the exception of the President of the Chamber and the judge who sat in respect of the State Party concerned.

Article 28
Declarations of inadmissibility by committees

A committee may, by a unanimous vote, declare inadmissible or strike out of its list of cases an application submitted under Article 34 where such a decision can be taken without further examination. The decision shall be final.

Article 29
Decisions by Chambers on admissibility and merits

1. If no decision is taken under Article 28, a Chamber shall decide on the admissibility and merits of individual applications submitted under Article 34.
2. A Chamber shall decide on the admissibility and merits of inter-State applications submitted under Article 33.
3. The decision on admissibility shall be taken separately unless the Court, in exceptional cases, decides otherwise.

Article 30
Relinquishment of jurisdiction to the Grand Chamber

Where a case pending before a Chamber raises a serious question affecting the interpretation of the Convention or the protocols thereto, or where the resolution of a question before the Chamber might have a result inconsistent with a judgment previously delivered by the Court, the Chamber may, at any time before it has rendered its judgment, relinquish jurisdiction in favour of the Grand Chamber, unless one of the parties to the case objects.

Article 31
Powers of the Grand Chamber

The Grand Chamber shall

(a) determine applications submitted either under Article 33 or Article 34 when a Chamber has relinquished jurisdiction under Article 30 or when the case has been referred to it under Article 43; and

(b) consider requests for advisory opinions submitted under Article 47.

Article 32
Jurisdiction of the Court

1. The jurisdiction of the Court shall extend to all matters concerning the interpretation and application of the Convention and the protocols thereto which are referred to it as provided in Articles 33, 34 and 47.
2. In the event of dispute as to whether the Court has jurisdiction, the Court shall decide.

Article 33
Inter-State cases

Any High Contracting Party may refer to the Court any alleged breach of the provisions of the Convention and the protocols thereto by another High Contracting Party.

Article 34
Individual applications

The Court may receive applications from any person, non-governmental organisation or group of individuals claiming to be the victim of a violation by one of the High Contracting Parties of the rights set forth in the Convention or the protocols thereto. The High Contracting Parties undertake not to hinder in any way the effective exercise of this right.

Article 35
Admissibility criteria

1. The Court may only deal with the matter after all domestic remedies have been exhausted, according to the generally recognised rules of international law, and within a period of six months from the date on which the final decision was taken.
2. The Court shall not deal with any application submitted under Article 34 that
   (a) is anonymous; or
   (b) is substantially the same as a matter that has already been examined by the Court or has already been submitted to another procedure of international investigation or settlement and contains no relevant new information.
3. The Court shall declare inadmissible any individual application submitted under Article 34 which it considers incompatible with the provisions of the Convention or the protocols thereto, manifestly ill-founded, or an abuse of the right of application.
4. The Court shall reject any application which it considers inadmissible under this Article. It may do so at any stage of the proceedings.

Article 36
Third party intervention

1. In all cases before a Chamber or the Grand Chamber, a High Contracting Party one of whose nationals is an applicant shall have the right to submit written comments and to take part in hearings.
2. The President of the Court may, in the interest of the proper administration of justice, invite any High Contracting Party which is not a party to the proceedings or any person concerned who is not the applicant to submit written comments or take part in hearings.

Article 37
Striking out applications

1. The Court may at any stage of the proceedings decide to strike an application out of its list of cases where the circumstances lead to the conclusion that
   (a) the applicant does not intend to pursue his application; or
   (b) the matter has been resolved; or
   (c) for any other reason established by the Court, it is no longer justified to continue the examination of the application.

   However, the Court shall continue the examination of the application if respect for human rights as defined in the Convention and the protocols thereto so requires.
2. The Court may decide to restore an application to its list of cases if it considers that the circumstances justify such a course.

Article 38

Examination of the case and friendly settlement proceedings

1. If the Court declares the application admissible, it shall
   (a) pursue the examination of the case, together with the representatives of the parties, and if need be, undertake an investigation, for the effective conduct of which the States concerned shall furnish all necessary facilities;
   (b) place itself at the disposal of the parties concerned with a view to securing a friendly settlement of the matter on the basis of respect for human rights as defined in the Convention and the protocols thereto.
2. Proceedings conducted under paragraph 1.b shall be confidential.

Article 39

Finding of a friendly settlement

If a friendly settlement is effected, the Court shall strike the case out of its list by means of a decision which shall be confined to a brief statement of the facts and of the solution reached.

Article 40

Public hearings and access to documents

1. Hearings shall be in public unless the Court in exceptional circumstances decides otherwise.
2. Documents deposited with the Registrar shall be accessible to the public unless the President of the Court decides otherwise.

Article 41

Just satisfaction

If the Court finds that there has been a violation of the Convention or the protocols thereto, and if the internal law of the High Contracting Party concerned allows only partial reparation to be made, the Court shall, if necessary, afford just satisfaction to the injured party.

Article 42

Judgments of Chambers

Judgments of Chambers shall become final in accordance with the provisions of Article 44, paragraph 2.

Article 43

Referral to the Grand Chamber

1. Within a period of three months from the date of the judgment of the Chamber, any party to the case may, in exceptional cases, request that the case be referred to the Grand Chamber.
2. A panel of five judges of the Grand Chamber shall accept the request if the case raises a serious question affecting the interpretation or application of the Convention or the protocols thereto, or a serious issue of general importance.
3. If the panel accepts the request, the Grand Chamber shall decide the case by means of a judgment.

Article 44

Final judgments

1. The judgment of the Grand Chamber shall be final.

2. The judgment of a Chamber shall become final
    (a) when the parties declare that they will not request that the case be referred to the Grand Chamber; or
    (b) three months after the date of the judgment, if reference of the case to the Grand Chamber has not been requested; or
    (c) when the panel of the Grand Chamber rejects the request to refer under Article 43.
3. The final judgment shall be published.

Article 45
Reasons for judgments and decisions

1. Reasons shall be given for judgments as well as for decisions declaring applications admissible or inadmissible.
2. If a judgment does not represent, in whole or in part, the unanimous opinion of the judges, any judge shall be entitled to deliver a separate opinion.

Article 46
Binding force and execution of judgments

1. The High Contracting Parties undertake to abide by the final judgment of the Court in any case to which they are parties.
2. The final judgment of the Court shall be transmitted to the Committee of Ministers, which shall supervise its execution.

Article 47
Advisory opinions

1. The Court may, at the request of the Committee of Ministers, give advisory opinions on legal questions concerning the interpretation of the Convention and the protocols thereto.
2. Such opinions shall not deal with any question relating to the content or scope of the rights or freedoms defined in Section I of the Convention and the protocols thereto, or with any other question which the Court or the Committee of Ministers might have to consider in consequence of any such proceedings as could be instituted in accordance with the Convention.
3. Decisions of the Committee of Ministers to request an advisory opinion of the Court shall require a majority vote of the representatives entitled to sit on the Committee.

Article 48
Advisory jurisdiction of the Court

The Court shall decide whether a request for an advisory opinion submitted by the Committee of Ministers is within its competence as defined in Article 47.

Article 49
Reasons for advisory opinions

1. Reasons shall be given for advisory opinions of the Court.
2. If the advisory opinion does not represent, in whole or in part, the unanimous opinion of the judges, any judge shall be entitled to deliver a separate opinion.
3. Advisory opinions of the Court shall be communicated to the Committee of Ministers.

Article 50
Expenditure on the Court

The expenditure on the Court shall be borne by the Council of Europe.

Article 51
Privileges and immunities of judges

The judges shall be entitled, during the exercise of their functions, to the privileges and immunities provided for in Article 40 of the Statute of the Council of Europe and in the agreements made thereunder.

SECTION III: MISCELLANEOUS PROVISIONS

Article 52
Inquiries by the Secretary General

On receipt of a request from the Secretary General of the Council of Europe any High Contracting Party shall furnish an explanation of the manner in which its internal law ensures the effective implementation of any of the provisions of the Convention.

Article 53
Safeguard for existing human rights

Nothing in this Convention shall be construed as limiting or derogating from any of the human rights and fundamental freedoms which may be ensured under the laws of any High Contracting Party or under any other agreement to which it is a Party.

Article 54
Powers of the Committee of Ministers

Nothing in this Convention shall prejudice the powers conferred on the Committee of Ministers by the Statute of the Council of Europe.

Article 55
Exclusion of other means of dispute settlement

The High Contracting Parties agree that, except by special agreement, they will not avail themselves of treaties, conventions or declarations in force between them for the purpose of submitting, by way of petition, a dispute arising out of the interpretation or application of this Convention to a means of settlement other than those provided for in this Convention.

Article 56
Territorial application

1. Any State may at the time of its ratification or at any time thereafter declare by notification addressed to the Secretary General of the Council of Europe that the present Convention shall, subject to paragraph 4 of this Article, extend to all or any of the territories for whose international relations it is responsible.
2. The Convention shall extend to the territory or territories named in the notification as from the thirtieth day after the receipt of this notification by the Secretary General of the Council of Europe.
3. The provisions of this Convention shall be applied in such territories with due regard, however, to local requirements.

4. Any State which has made a declaration in accordance with paragraph 1 of this article may at any time thereafter declare on behalf of one or more of the territories to which the declaration relates that it accepts the competence of the Court to receive applications from individuals, non-governmental organisations or groups of individuals as provided by Article 34 of the Convention.

Article 57
Reservations

1. Any State may, when signing this Convention or when depositing its instrument of ratification, make a reservation in respect of any particular provision of the Convention to the extent that any law then in force in its territory is not in conformity with the provision. Reservations of a general character shall not be permitted under this article.
2. Any reservation made under this article shall contain a brief statement of the law concerned.

Article 58
Denunciation

1. A High Contracting Party may denounce the present Convention only after the expiry of five years from the date on which it became a party to it and after six months' notice contained in a notification addressed to the Secretary General of the Council of Europe, who shall inform the other High Contracting Parties.
2. Such a denunciation shall not have the effect of releasing the High Contracting Party concerned from its obligations under this Convention in respect of any act which, being capable of constituting a violation of such obligations, may have been performed by it before the date at which the denunciation became effective.
3. Any High Contracting Party which shall cease to be a member of the Council of Europe shall cease to be a Party to this Convention under the same conditions.
4. The Convention may be denounced in accordance with the provisions of the preceding paragraphs in respect of any territory to which it has been declared to extend under the terms of Article 56.

Article 59
Signature and ratification

1. This Convention shall be open to the signature of the members of the Council of Europe. It shall be ratified. Ratifications shall be deposited with the Secretary General of the Council of Europe.
2. The present Convention shall come into force after the deposit of ten instruments of ratification.
3. As regards any signatory ratifying subsequently, the Convention shall come into force at the date of the deposit of its instrument of ratification.
4. The Secretary General of the Council of Europe shall notify all the members of the Council of Europe of the entry into force of the Convention, the names of the High Contracting Parties who have ratified it, and the deposit of all instruments of ratification which may be effected subsequently.

Done at Rome this 4th day of November 1950, in English and French, both texts being equally authentic, in a single copy which shall remain deposited in the archives of the Council of Europe. The Secretary General shall transmit certified copies to each of the signatories.

PROTOCOL TO THE CONVENTION FOR THE PROTECTION OF HUMAN RIGHTS AND FUNDAMENTAL FREEDOMS:

Paris, 20.III.1952

The governments signatory hereto, being members of the Council of Europe,

Being resolved to take steps to ensure the collective enforcement of certain rights and freedoms other than those already included in Section I of the Convention for the Protection of Human Rights and Fundamental Freedoms signed at Rome on 4 November 1950 (hereinafter referred to as 'the Convention'),

Have agreed as follows:

Article 1
Protection of property

Every natural or legal person is entitled to the peaceful enjoyment of his possessions. No one shall be deprived of his possessions except in the public interest and subject to the conditions provided for by law and by the general principles of international law.

The preceding provisions shall not, however, in any way impair the right of a State to enforce such laws as it deems necessary to control the use of property in accordance with the general interest or to secure the payment of taxes or other contributions or penalties.

Article 2
Right to education

No person shall be denied the right to education. In the exercise of any functions which it assumes in relation to education and to teaching, the State shall respect the right of parents to ensure such education and teaching in conformity with their own religious and philosophical convictions.

Article 3
Right to free elections

The High Contracting Parties undertake to hold free elections at reasonable intervals by secret ballot, under conditions which will ensure the free expression of the opinion of the people in the choice of the legislature.

Article 4
Territorial application

Any High Contracting Party may at the time of signature or ratification or at any time thereafter communicate to the Secretary General of the Council of Europe a declaration stating the extent to which it undertakes that the provisions of the present Protocol shall apply to such of the territories for the international relations of which it is responsible as are named therein.

Any High Contracting Party which has communicated a declaration in virtue of the preceding paragraph may from time to time communicate a further declaration modifying the terms of any former declaration or terminating the application of the provisions of this Protocol in respect of any territory.

A declaration made in accordance with this article shall be deemed to have been made in accordance with paragraph 1 of Article 56 of the Convention.

Article 5
Relationship to the Convention

As between the High Contracting Parties the provisions of Articles 1, 2, 3 and 4 of this Protocol shall be regarded as additional articles to the Convention and all the provisions of the Convention shall apply accordingly.

Article 6
Signature and ratification

This Protocol shall be open for signature by the members of the Council of Europe, who are the signatories of the Convention; it shall be ratified at the same time as or after the ratification of the Convention. It shall enter into force after the deposit of ten instruments of ratification. As regards any signatory ratifying subsequently, the Protocol shall enter into force at the date of the deposit of its instrument of ratification.

The instruments of ratification shall be deposited with the Secretary General of the Council of Europe, who will notify all members of the names of those who have ratified.

Done at Paris on the 20th day of March 1952, in English and French, both texts being equally authentic, in a single copy which shall remain deposited in the archives of the Council of Europe. The Secretary General shall transmit certified copies to each of the signatory governments.

PROTOCOL NO. 4 TO THE CONVENTION FOR THE PROTECTION OF HUMAN RIGHTS AND FUNDAMENTAL FREEDOMS SECURING CERTAIN RIGHTS AND FREEDOMS OTHER THAN THOSE ALREADY INCLUDED IN THE CONVENTION AND IN THE FIRST PROTOCOL THERETO

Strasbourg, 16.IX.1963

The governments signatory hereto, being members of the Council of Europe,

Being resolved to take steps to ensure the collective enforcement of certain rights and freedoms other than those already included in Section I of the Convention for the Protection of Human Rights and Fundamental Freedoms signed at Rome on 4th November 1950 (hereinafter referred to as the 'Convention') and in Articles 1 to 3 of the First Protocol to the Convention, signed at Paris on 20th March 1952,

Have agreed as follows:

Article 1
Prohibition of imprisonment for debt

No one shall be deprived of his liberty merely on the ground of inability to fulfil a contractual obligation.

Article 2
Freedom of movement

1. Everyone lawfully within the territory of a State shall, within that territory, have the right to liberty of movement and freedom to choose his residence.
2. Everyone shall be free to leave any country, including his own.

3. No restrictions shall be placed on the exercise of these rights other than such as are in accordance with law and are necessary in a democratic society in the interests of national security or public safety, for the maintenance of ordre public, for the prevention of crime, for the protection of health or morals, or for the protection of the rights and freedoms of others.

4. The rights set forth in paragraph 1 may also be subject, in particular areas, to restrictions imposed in accordance with law and justified by the public interest in a democratic society.

Article 3
Prohibition of expulsion of nationals

1. No one shall be expelled, by means either of an individual or of a collective measure, from the territory of the State of which he is a national.

2. No one shall be deprived of the right to enter the territory of the state of which he is a national.

Article 4
Prohibition of collective expulsion of aliens

Collective expulsion of aliens is prohibited.

Article 5
Territorial application

1. Any High Contracting Party may, at the time of signature or ratification of this Protocol, or at any time thereafter, communicate to the Secretary General of the Council of Europe a declaration stating the extent to which it undertakes that the provisions of this Protocol shall apply to such of the territories for the international relations of which it is responsible as are named therein.

2. Any High Contracting Party which has communicated a declaration in virtue of the preceding paragraph may, from time to time, communicate a further declaration modifying the terms of any former declaration or terminating the application of the provisions of this Protocol in respect of any territory.

3. A declaration made in accordance with this article shall be deemed to have been made in accordance with paragraph 1 of Article 56 of the Convention.

4. The territory of any State to which this Protocol applies by virtue of ratification or acceptance by that State, and each territory to which this Protocol is applied by virtue of a declaration by that State under this article, shall be treated as separate territories for the purpose of the references in Articles 2 and 3 to the territory of a State.

5. Any State which has made a declaration in accordance with paragraph 1 or 2 of this Article may at any time thereafter declare on behalf of one or more of the territories to which the declaration relates that it accepts the competence of the Court to receive applications from individuals, non-governmental organisations or groups of individuals as provided in Article 34 of the Convention in respect of all or any of Articles 1 to 4 of this Protocol.

Article 6
Relationship to the Convention

As between the High Contracting Parties the provisions of Articles 1 to 5 of this Protocol shall be regarded as additional Articles to the Convention, and all the provisions of the Convention shall apply accordingly.

Article 7
Signature and ratification

1. This Protocol shall be open for signature by the members of the Council of Europe who are the signatories of the Convention; it shall be ratified at the same time as or after the ratification of the Convention. It shall enter into force after the deposit of five instruments of ratification. As regards any signatory ratifying subsequently, the Protocol shall enter into force at the date of the deposit of its instrument of ratification.
2. The instruments of ratification shall be deposited with the Secretary General of the Council of Europe, who will notify all members of the names of those who have ratified.

In witness whereof the undersigned, being duly authorised thereto, have signed this Protocol.

Done at Strasbourg, this 16th day of September 1963, in English and in French, both texts being equally authoritative, in a single copy which shall remain deposited in the archives of the Council of Europe. The Secretary General shall transmit certified copies to each of the signatory states.

Protocol No.6 to the Convention for the Protection of Human Rights and Fundamental Freedoms Concerning the Abolition of the Death Penalty

Strasbourg, 28.IV.1983

The member States of the Council of Europe, signatory to this Protocol to the Convention for the Protection of Human Rights and Fundamental Freedoms, signed at Rome on 4 November 1950 (hereinafter referred to as 'the Convention'),

Considering that the evolution that has occurred in several member States of the Council of Europe expresses a general tendency in favour of abolition of the death penalty;

Have agreed as follows:

Article 1
Abolition of the death penalty

The death penalty shall be abolished. No-one shall be condemned to such penalty or executed.

Article 2
Death penalty in time of war

A State may make provision in its law for the death penalty in respect of acts committed in time of war or of imminent threat of war; such penalty shall be applied only in the instances laid down in the law and in accordance with its provisions. The State shall communicate to the Secretary General of the Council of Europe the relevant provisions of that law.

Article 3
Prohibition of derogations

No derogation from the provisions of this Protocol shall be made under Article 15 of the Convention.

Article 4
Prohibition of reservations

No reservation may be made under Article 57 of the Convention in respect of the provisions of this Protocol.

Article 5
Territorial application

1. Any State may at the time of signature or when depositing its instrument of ratification, acceptance or approval, specify the territory or territories to which this Protocol shall apply.
2. Any State may at any later date, by a declaration addressed to the Secretary General of the Council of Europe, extend the application of this Protocol to any other territory specified in the declaration. In respect of such territory the Protocol shall enter into force on the first day of the month following the date of receipt of such declaration by the Secretary General.
3. Any declaration made under the two preceding paragraphs may, in respect of any territory specified in such declaration, be withdrawn by a notification addressed to the Secretary General. The withdrawal shall become effective on the first day of the month following the date of receipt of such notification by the Secretary General.

Article 6
Relationship to the Convention

As between the States Parties the provisions of Articles 1 and 5 of this Protocol shall be regarded as additional articles to the Convention and all the provisions of the Convention shall apply accordingly.

Article 7
Signature and ratification

The Protocol shall be open for signature by the member States of the Council of Europe, signatories to the Convention. It shall be subject to ratification, acceptance or approval. A member State of the Council of Europe may not ratify, accept or approve this Protocol unless it has, simultaneously or previously, ratified the Convention. Instruments of ratification, acceptance or approval shall be deposited with the Secretary General of the Council of Europe.

Article 8
Entry into force

1. This Protocol shall enter into force on the first day of the month following the date on which five member States of the Council of Europe have expressed their consent to be bound by the Protocol in accordance with the provisions of Article 7.
2. In respect of any member State which subsequently expresses its consent to be bound by it, the Protocol shall enter into force on the first day of the month following the date of the deposit of the instrument of ratification, acceptance or approval.

Article 9
Depositary functions

The Secretary General of the Council of Europe shall notify the member States of the Council of:

(a) any signature;
(b) the deposit of any instrument of ratification, acceptance or approval;
(c) any date of entry into force of this Protocol in accordance with articles 5 and 8;
(d) any other act, notification or communication relating to this Protocol.

In witness whereof the undersigned, being duly authorised thereto, have signed this Protocol.

Done at Strasbourg, this 28th day of April 1983, in English and in French, both texts being equally authentic, in a single copy which shall be deposited in the archives of the Council of Europe. The Secretary General of the Council of Europe shall transmit certified copies to each member State of the Council of Europe.

PROTOCOL NO. 7 TO THE CONVENTION FOR THE PROTECTION OF HUMAN RIGHTS AND FUNDAMENTAL FREEDOMS

Strasbourg, 22.XI.1984

The member States of the Council of Europe signatory hereto,

Being resolved to take further steps to ensure the collective enforcement of certain rights and freedoms by means of the Convention for the Protection of Human Rights and Fundamental Freedoms signed at Rome on 4 November 1950 (hereinafter referred to as 'the Convention'),

Have agreed as follows:

Article 1
Procedural safeguards relating to expulsion of aliens

1. An alien lawfully resident in the territory of a State shall not be expelled therefrom except in pursuance of a decision reached in accordance with law and shall be allowed:
    (a) to submit reasons against his expulsion,
    (b) to have his case reviewed, and
    (c) to be represented for these purposes before the competent authority or a person or persons designated by that authority.
2. An alien may be expelled before the exercise of his rights under paragraph 1.a, b and c of this Article, when such expulsion is necessary in the interests of public order or is grounded on reasons of national security.

Article 2
Right of appeal in criminal matters

1. Everyone convicted of a criminal offence by a tribunal shall have the right to have his conviction or sentence reviewed by a higher tribunal. The exercise of this right, including the grounds on which it may be exercised, shall be governed by law.
2. This right may be subject to exceptions in regard to offences of a minor character, as prescribed by law, or in cases in which the person concerned was tried in the first instance by the highest tribunal or was convicted following an appeal against acquittal.

Article 3
Compensation for wrongful conviction

When a person has by a final decision been convicted of a criminal offence and when subsequently his conviction has been reversed, or he has been pardoned, on the ground that a new or newly discovered fact shows conclusively that there has been a miscarriage of justice, the person who has suffered punishment as a result of such conviction shall be compensated according to the law or the practice of the State concerned, unless it is proved that the non-disclosure of the unknown fact in time is wholly or partly attributable to him.

Article 4
Right not to be tried or punished twice

1. No one shall be liable to be tried or punished again in criminal proceedings under the jurisdiction of the same State for an offence for which he has already been finally acquitted or convicted in accordance with the law and penal procedure of that State.
2. The provisions of the preceding paragraph shall not prevent the reopening of the case in accordance with the law and penal procedure of the State concerned, if there is evidence of new or newly discovered facts, or if there has been a fundamental defect in the previous proceedings, which could affect the outcome of the case.
3. No derogation from this Article shall be made under Article 15 of the Convention.

Article 5
Equality between spouses

Spouses shall enjoy equality of rights and responsibilities of a private law character between them, and in their relations with their children, as to marriage, during marriage and in the event of its dissolution. This Article shall not prevent States from taking such measures as are necessary in the interests of the children.

Article 6
Territorial application

1. Any State may at the time of signature or when depositing its instrument of ratification, acceptance or approval, specify the territory or territories to which the Protocol shall apply and state the extent to which it undertakes that the provisions of this Protocol shall apply to such territory or territories.
2. Any State may at any later date, by a declaration addressed to the Secretary General of the Council of Europe, extend the application of this Protocol to any other territory specified in the declaration. In respect of such territory the Protocol shall enter into force on the first day of the month following the expiration of a period of two months after the date of receipt by the Secretary General of such declaration.
3. Any declaration made under the two preceding paragraphs may, in respect of any territory specified in such declaration, be withdrawn or modified by a notification addressed to the Secretary General. The withdrawal or modification shall become effective on the first day of the month following the expiration of a period of two months after the date of receipt of such notification by the Secretary General.
4. A declaration made in accordance with this Article shall be deemed to have been made in accordance with paragraph 1 of Article 56 of the Convention.
5. The territory of any State to which this Protocol applies by virtue of ratification, acceptance or approval by that State, and each territory to which this Protocol is applied by virtue of a declaration by that State under this Article, may be treated as separate territories for the purpose of the reference in Article 1 to the territory of a State.
6. Any State which has made a declaration in accordance with paragraph 1 or 2 of this Article may at any time thereafter declare on behalf of one or more of the territories to which the declaration relates that it accepts the competence of the Court to receive applications from individuals, non-governmental organisations or groups of individuals as provided in Article 34 of the Convention in respect of Articles 1 to 5 of this Protocol.

Article 7
Relationship to the Convention

As between the States Parties, the provisions of Article 1 to 6 of this Protocol shall be regarded as additional Articles to the Convention, and all the provisions of the Convention shall apply accordingly.

Article 8
Signature and ratification

This Protocol shall be open for signature by member States of the Council of Europe which have signed the Convention. It is subject to ratification, acceptance or approval. A member State of the Council of

Europe may not ratify, accept or approve this Protocol without previously or simultaneously ratifying the Convention. Instruments of ratification, acceptance or approval shall be deposited with the Secretary General of the Council of Europe.

Article 9
Entry into force

1. This Protocol shall enter into force on the first day of the month following the expiration of a period of two months after the date on which seven member States of the Council of Europe have expressed their consent to be bound by the Protocol in accordance with the provisions of Article 8.
2. In respect of any member State which subsequently expresses its consent to be bound by it, the Protocol shall enter into force on the first day of the month following the expiration of a period of two months after the date of the deposit of the instrument of ratification, acceptance or approval.

Article 10
Depositary functions

The Secretary General of the Council of Europe shall notify all the member States of the Council of Europe of:

(a) any signature;
(b) the deposit of any instrument of ratification, acceptance or approval;
(c) any date of entry into force of this Protocol in accordance with Articles 6 and 9;
(d) any other act, notification or declaration relating to this Protocol.

In witness whereof the undersigned, being duly authorised thereto, have signed this Protocol.

Done at Strasbourg, this 22nd day of November 1984, in English and French, both texts being equally authentic, in a single copy which shall be deposited in the archives of the Council of Europe. The Secretary General of the Council of Europe shall transmit certified copies to each member State of the Council of Europe.

PROTOCOL NO. 12 TO THE CONVENTION FOR THE PROTECTION OF HUMAN RIGHTS AND FUNDAMENTAL FREEDOMS

Rome, 4.XI.2000

The member States of the Council of Europe signatory hereto,

Having regard to the fundamental principle according to which all persons are equal before the law and are entitled to the equal protection of the law;

Being resolved to take further steps to promote the equality of all persons through the collective enforcement of a general prohibition of discrimination by means of the Convention for the Protection of Human Rights and Fundamental Freedoms signed at Rome on 4 November 1950 (hereinafter referred to as 'the Convention');

Reaffirming that the principle of non-discrimination does not prevent States Parties from taking measures in order to promote full and effective equality, provided that there is an objective and reasonable justification for those measures,

Have agreed as follows:

Article 1
General prohibition of discrimination

1. The enjoyment of any right set forth by law shall be secured without discrimination on any ground such as sex, race, colour, language, religion, political or other opinion, national or social origin, association with a national minority, property, birth or other status.
2. No one shall be discriminated against by any public authority on any ground such as those mentioned in paragraph 1.

Article 2
Territorial application

1. Any State may, at the time of signature or when depositing its instrument of ratification, acceptance or approval, specify the territory or territories to which this Protocol shall apply.
2. Any State may at any later date, by a declaration addressed to the Secretary General of the Council of Europe, extend the application of this Protocol to any other territory specified in the declaration. In respect of such territory the Protocol shall enter into force on the first day of the month following the expiration of a period of three months after the date of receipt by the Secretary General of such declaration.
3. Any declaration made under the two preceding paragraphs may, in respect of any territory specified in such declaration, be withdrawn or modified by a notification addressed to the Secretary General of the Council of Europe. The withdrawal or modification shall become effective on the first day of the month following the expiration of a period of three months after the date of receipt of such notification by the Secretary General.
4. A declaration made in accordance with this article shall be deemed to have been made in accordance with paragraph 1 of Article 56 of the Convention.
5. Any State which has made a declaration in accordance with paragraph 1 or 2 of this article may at any time thereafter declare on behalf of one or more of the territories to which the declaration relates that it accepts the competence of the Court to receive applications from individuals, non-governmental organisations or groups of individuals as provided by Article 34 of the Convention in respect of Article 1 of this Protocol.

Article 3
Relationship to the Convention

As between the States Parties, the provisions of Articles 1 and 2 of this Protocol shall be regarded as additional articles to the Convention, and all the provisions of the Convention shall apply accordingly.

Article 4
Signature and ratification

This Protocol shall be open for signature by member States of the Council of Europe which have signed the Convention. It is subject to ratification, acceptance or approval. A member State of the Council of Europe may not ratify, accept or approve this Protocol without previously or simultaneously ratifying the Convention. Instruments of ratification, acceptance or approval shall be deposited with the Secretary General of the Council of Europe.

Article 5
Entry into force

1. This Protocol shall enter into force on the first day of the month following the expiration of a period of three months after the date on which ten member States of the Council of Europe have expressed their consent to be bound by the Protocol in accordance with the provisions of Article 4.
2. In respect of any member State which subsequently expresses its consent to be bound by it, the Protocol shall enter into force on the first day of the month following the expiration of a period of three months after the date of the deposit of the instrument of ratification, acceptance or approval.

Article 6
Depositary functions

The Secretary General of the Council of Europe shall notify all the member States of the Council of Europe of:

(a) any signature;
(b) the deposit of any instrument of ratification, acceptance or approval;
(c) any date of entry into force of this Protocol in accordance with Articles 2 and 5;
(d) any other act, notification or communication relating to this Protocol.

In witness whereof the undersigned, being duly authorised thereto, have signed this Protocol.

Done at Rome, this 4th day of November 2000, in English and in French, both texts being equally authentic, in a single copy which shall be deposited in the archives of the Council of Europe. The Secretary General of the Council of Europe shall transmit certified copies to each member State of the Council of Europe.

PROTOCOL No. 13 TO THE CONVENTION FOR THE PROTECTION OF HUMAN RIGHTS AND FUNDAMENTAL FREEDOMS CONCERNING THE ABOLITION OF THE DEATH PENALTY IN ALL CIRCUMSTANCES

Vilnius, 3.V.2002

The member States of the Council of Europe signatory hereto,

Convinced that everyone's right to life is a basic value in a democratic society and that the abolition of the death penalty is essential for the protection of this right and for the full recognition of the inherent dignity of all human beings;

Wishing to strengthen the protection of the right to life guaranteed by the Convention for the Protection of Human Rights and Fundamental Freedoms signed at Rome on 4 November 1950 (hereinafter referred to as 'the Convention');

Noting that Protocol No. 6 to the Convention, concerning the Abolition of the Death Penalty, signed at Strasbourg on 28 April 1983, does not exclude the death penalty in respect of acts committed in time of war or of imminent threat of war;

Being resolved to take the final step in order to abolish the death penalty in all circumstances,

Have agreed as follows:

Article 1
Abolition of the death penalty

The death penalty shall be abolished. No one shall be condemned to such penalty or executed.

Article 2
Prohibitions of derogations

No derogation from the provisions of this Protocol shall be made under Article 15 of the Convention.

Article 3
Prohibitions of reservations

No reservation may be made under Article 57 of the Convention in respect of the provisions of this Protocol.

Article 4
Territorial application

1. Any state may, at the time of signature or when depositing its instrument of ratification, acceptance or approval, specify the territory or territories to which this Protocol shall apply.
2. Any state may at any later date, by a declaration addressed to the Secretary General of the Council of Europe, extend the application of this Protocol to any other territory specified in the declaration. In respect of such territory the Protocol shall enter into force on the first day of the month following the expiration of a period of three months after the date of receipt by the Secretary General of such declaration.
3. Any declaration made under the two preceding paragraphs may, in respect of any territory specified in such declaration, be withdrawn or modified by a notification addressed to the Secretary General. The withdrawal or modification shall become effective on the first day of the month following the expiration of a period of three months after the date of receipt of such notification by the Secretary General.

Article 5
Relationship to the Convention

As between the states Parties the provisions of Articles 1 to 4 of this Protocol shall be regarded as additional articles to the Convention, and all the provisions of the Convention shall apply accordingly.

Article 6
Signature and ratification

This Protocol shall be open for signature by member states of the Council of Europe which have signed the Convention. It is subject to ratification, acceptance or approval. A member state of the Council of Europe may not ratify, accept or approve this Protocol without previously or simultaneously ratifying the Convention. Instruments of ratification, acceptance or approval shall be deposited with the Secretary General of the Council of Europe.

Article 7
Entry into force

1. This Protocol shall enter into force on the first day of the month following the expiration of a period of three months after the date on which ten member states of the Council of Europe have expressed their consent to be bound by the Protocol in accordance with the provisions of Article 6.
2. In respect of any member state which subsequently expresses its consent to be bound by it, the Protocol shall enter into force on the first day of the month following the expiration of a period of three months after the date of the deposit of the instrument of ratification, acceptance or approval.

Article 8
Depositary functions

The Secretary General of the Council of Europe shall notify all the member states of the Council of Europe of:

(a) any signature;
(b) the deposit of any instrument of ratification, acceptance or approval;
(c) any date of entry into force of this Protocol in accordance with Articles 4 and 7;
(d) any other act, notification or communication relating to this Protocol;

In witness whereof the undersigned, being duly authorised thereto, have signed this Protocol.

Done at Vilnius, this 3rd day of May 2002, in English and in French, both texts being equally authentic, in a single copy which shall be deposited in the archives of the Council of Europe. The Secretary General of the Council of Europe shall transmit certified copies to each member state of the Council of Europe.

INDEX

access to broadcasting, controls on 11.13–11.15
access to courts and tribunals, media's right of
    9.33–9.37
access to information, right of 2.26–2.32
advertisements
    broadcasting restrictions 11.16–11.17
    children, to 12.33
    comparative 12.24–12.25
    misleading, false and deceptive 12.23
    political, controls on 10.12, 12.18–12.20,
        12.34
    professional conduct and 12.10–12.14, 12.36
    restrictions on 11.16–11.17
    tobacco advertising 12.26–12.32
    truthful 12.24–12.25
    vulnerable groups, to 12.33
Advertising Standards Authority (ASA), status
    as public body 3.36
American Convention on Human Rights
    (American Convention)
    right of access to information compared to
        ECHR 2.30–2.31
application form (European Court) 4.10–4.11
armed forces, limitation of freedom of
    expression of 2.47
artistic expression 2.46
    protection under Article 10 ECHR 2.16

bans on broadcasting 11.11–11.12
blasphemous libel
    offence of 8.10
        abolition of 8.12
blasphemy 2.62
    discrimination in English law of 8.33–8.34
    domestic law 8.10–8.12
    ECHR as to 8.21–8.34
    HRA 1998 as to 8.40
    overview of regulation 8.01–8.05
    rationale for offence of 8.11
    restriction of
        interference by public authority 8.21
        legitimate aim 8.24–8.26
        necessary in democratic society 8.27–8.32
        prescribed by law 8.22–8.23

Bowman v UK 10.16–10.20
Brandeis, L D, right to privacy, on 1.10–1.11,
    1.23
British Board of Film Classification (BBFC)
    status as public body 2.23, 3.36
British Broadcasting Corporation (BBC)
    as public body 3.39
    victim, whether can be 3.49
broadcasting see also media regulators
    access to, controls on 11.13–11.15
    advertising, restrictions on 11.16–11.17
    Article 10 ECHR as to 11.02–11.09
    bans 11.11–11.12
    licensing 2.33–2.34, 11.02–11.17
    party political broadcasts 10.12–10.15
    public service broadcasting, licensing of 11.10
    videos, certification of 2.23
Broadcasting Standards Commission (BSC)
    ruling on infringement of company's
        privacy 3.48
Broadcasting Standards Commission (BSC),
    status as public body 3.36

Canada
    jurisprudence
        recognition of rationales for protecting
            freedom of expression 1.08
        use by English courts 1.03, 12.02
    protection for freedom of expression compared
        with English law 1.18
    racial hatred, law as to 7.34
certification of videos 2.23
Channel 4
    status as public body 3.39
    victim, whether can be 3.49
children, advertising to 12.33
cinema
    BBFC as public body 2.23, 3.36
    licensing 2.33–2.34
civil servants, limitation of freedom of
    expression of 2.47
commercial expression 2.46, 12.24–12.25
    advertising
        children, to 12.33

commercial expression (*cont.*)
  advertising (*cont.*)
    comparative 12.24–12.25
    misleading, false and deceptive
        advertisements 12.23
    political 12.18–12.20, 12.34
    professionals, by 12.36
    religious 12.18–12.20
    tobacco 12.26–12.32
  American and Canadian jurisprudence,
      reference to 12.02
  balance between consumer protection and fair
      competition, need to maintain 12.05
  degree of protection 12.06
  ECHR case law
    advertising by professionals 12.10–12.14
    criticism of competitors or products
        12.15–12.17
    general principles on protection
        12.07–12.09
  HRA 1998, impact of 12.23–12.36
  margin of appreciation as to 2.46, 12.02
  Markt Intern and Beerman v Germany
      12.07–12.09
  meaning 12.03
  need for protection 12.03
  overview of regulation and case law
      12.01–12.02
  professional conduct as to
    advertisements 12.10–12.14, 12.36
    public expression 12.35
  protection under Article 10 ECHR 2.16
  public concern, as to matters of 12.21–12.22
  truthful advertisements 12.24–12.25
  unfair competition 12.15–12.17
**company as victim of Convention rights
    violation** 3.48
compatibility, statements of 3.22–3.26
compensation and costs, award of 4.30
contempt of court *see* court reporting
**contempt of Parliament, use to restrict
    reporting** 10.30–10.31
Convention rights *see* Human Rights Act 1998
    (HRA 1998)
court reporting 2.52–2.54
  conflict of interest between media and
      defendants 9.01–9.02
  media's right to complain about restrictions on
    Article 10 as to 9.03
    Article 6 as to 9.04–9.09
  prejudicial publicity 9.18–9.21
  public hearings
    obligation to hold, extent of 9.38–9.44

  waiver of right to hearing 2.54
  restrictions on
    legitimate aim for 9.12–9.13
    necessary in democratic society
      access to courts and tribunals 9.33–9.37
      adverse effect of publicity on third
          parties, because of 9.48–9.51
      broadcasting of proceedings, on
          9.54–9.56
      criticism by lawyers 9.29–9.32
      criticism of judiciary 9.23–9.28
      penalties for disclosure of proceedings
          9.56–9.60
      public hearings, obligation to hold
          9.38–9.44
      Sunday Times v UK 9.16–9.18
      threats to life, because of 9.52–9.53
      witnesses' privacy, protection of
          9.45–9.47
    necessary in democratic society
      prejudicial publicity, cases on 9.19–9.21
    pre-trial injunctions 9.22
    prescribed by law 9.14–9.15
    whether interference taken place 9.10–9.11
  Sunday Times v UK 9.16–9.18
  thalidomide articles injunctions 9.16–9.18
courts
  judicial notice of case law by 3.15
  media's rights of access to 9.33–9.37
criminal law
  encouraging and glorifying terrorism, as to
      13.36
  official secrets, as to 13.31–13.35
criminal libel 5.10, 5.61–5.62

damages
  defamation 5.08
  enforcement of Convention rights 3.63–3.66
  judicial acts violating Convention rights,
      for 3.66
declarations of incompatibility 3.22–3.26
defamation
  civil law of, impact of HRA 1998 on
      5.63–5.64
    irresponsible journalism 5.70–5.71
    neutral reportage 5.72
    other possible developments 5.73–5.74
    Reynolds defence for public interest speech
        5.65–5.69
  complainants 5.04–5.05
  criminal libel 5.10, 5.61–5.62
  criminal proceedings 5.06
  damages 5.08

defamatory statement, meaning of 5.01
defences
    fair comment on matter of public
        interest 5.02
    privilege 5.02
    truth (justification) 5.02
    HRA 1998, impact on law of 5.61–5.74
    injunctions to prevent repetition of libel 5.11
    interferences with Convention rights in cases
        of 5.06–5.11
    legitimate aim for restriction of Convention
        right in cases of 5.12
        prevention of disorder 5.15
        protection of reputation 5.13–5.14
    necessary in democratic society, restriction of
        Covenant right 5.16–5.21
        acceptable assessment of facts by court
            5.22–5.27
        form of expression, value judgment
            as to 5.28–5.31
        political debate 5.36–5.38
        press as watchdog 5.32–5.34
        public interest considerations 5.35–5.49
            issues of public interest or concern
                5.46–5.49
        reportage by journalists 5.50–5.60
    orders to publish 5.09
    prior restraint 5.07
democratic self-governance 1.06, 1.08–1.09
Dicey, A V, freedom of expression, on 1.14
discrimination
    blasphemy 2.62
    differential treatment, prohibition of 2.61
    ECHR as to 7.09–712
    law of blasphemy, in 8.33–8.34
    right not to be discriminated against
        2.59–2.62
disorder, prevention of *see* public disorder
domestic remedies, exhaustion of 4.21–4.25

effectiveness principle of interpreting
    the ECHR 2.06
elections
    advertising, restrictions on 10.12
    Article 3 ECHR as to 10.05
    Bowman v UK 10.16–10.20
    campaigning, controls on 10.08–10.11
    complaints about biased or unbalanced
        reporting 10.21–10.23
    overview of legislation 10.02
    party political broadcasts, controls on
        10.12–10.15
    protection of right to vote 10.05–10.07

enforcement of Convention rights
    company as victim of violation 3.48
    complaints made in advance of violation of
        Convention right 3.45
    damages 3.63–3.66
    freedom of expression, special provisions
        for 3.67–3.74
    independent proceedings 3.46
    limitation period 3.47
    methods 3.54–3.60
    pre-trial injunctions, restrictions on 3.69–3.72
    pressure groups, by 3.50
    public authorities, by 3.58
    relief without notice, restrictions on 3.68
    remedies 3.61–3.66
    standing provisions for 3.42–3.53
    victim of violation of Convention right,
        by 3.42–3.53
English law *see also* Human Rights Act 1998
    (HRA 1998)
    developments pre-HRA 1998 1.18–1.23
    historical approach to freedom of expression
        1.14–1.17
    licensing as prior restraint 1.16
    prior restraints on freedom of expression
        1.16–1.17, 2.49–2.50
    privacy, right to *see* privacy
    protection for freedom of expression
        compared with Article 10 1.18
        compared with US and Canadian law 1.18
    seditious libel, suppression of expression by
        prosecution for 1.15
environmental information, right of
    access to 2.29
European Convention on Human Rights
    (ECHR)
    Article 1, states' obligations under 4.01
    Article 10 *see under* freedom of expression *and*
        individual aspects
        broadcasting, licensing of 11.02–11.09
        court reporting 9.03
        limitations to freedom of expression
            2.35–2.50
    Article 14, right not to be discriminated
        against 2.59–2.62
    Article 3 *see* elections,
    Article 6
        court reporting 2.52–2.54, 9.04–9.09
        media, regulation of 11.21–11.44
    Article 8 *see also* privacy
        respect for private life 2.55–2.58
    Article 8 ECHR as to privacy 6.26–6.29
    blasphemy 2.62

European Convention on Human Rights (ECHR) (*cont.*)

declarations of incompatibility 3.22–3.26

discrimination 7.09–7.12

freedom of expression *see* freedom of expression

hate speech 2.65–2.66

interpretation of 2.02–2.07

    effectiveness principle 2.06

    other human rights instruments, by reference to 2.07

    teleological approach 2.03–2.05

interpretation of legislation consistently with 3.16–3.28

margin of appreciation *see* margin of appreciation

obscenity 8.13–8.20

reporting of judicial proceedings 2.52–2.54

respect for private life 2.55–2.58

restrictions on freedom of expression, as to

    hate speech 2.65–2.66

    public emergencies 2.63–2.64

    time of war 2.63–2.64

right not to be discriminated against 2.59–2.62

right of access to information compared to American Convention 2.30–2.31

text Appendix 2

European Court of Human Rights (European Court)

admissibility

    determination procedure 4.26

    exhaustion of domestic remedies 4.21–4.25

    initial inadmissibility 4.12–4.16

    victim, requirement for applicant to be classed as 4.17–4.20 *see also* victim of violation of Convention right

    violation within jurisdiction, requirement that 4.14

application form 4.10–4.11

chambers 4.05

commercial expression case law 12.07–12.22

compensation and costs, award of 4.30

complaint, procedure for making 4.08–4.11

    application form 4.10–4.11

    time limit 4.09

composition 4.03

consideration of complaint 4.27–4.29

    friendly settlement 4.27

    hearings, conduct of 4.29

    judgments, handing down of 4.29

defamation *see* defamation

grand chamber 4.05

judges 4.03

judicial structure 4.05

legal aid 4.07

national security case law 13.06–13.30

permanent court 4.03–4.04

rapporteur 4.05

recognition of rationales for protecting freedom of expression 1.09

registry 4.06

third party, intervention by 4.29

time limit for application to 4.09

expression *see also* freedom of expression

artistic 2.46

categories 12.06

commercial *see* commercial expression

hate speech, restriction of 2.65–2.66

medium of, as factor in legitimacy of restriction 2.48

public concern, as to matters of 2.46

fair comment on matter of public interest defence to defamation claim 5.02

false statement or portrayal, intrusion of privacy via 1.13

flag burning protests 2.17

freedom of expression *see also individual aspects*

activities covered by right of 2.12–2.15

armed forces, restrictions on 2.47

Article 10 ECHR

    adjudication of cases under 2.09

    broadcasting, licensing of 11.02–11.09

    court reporting 9.03

    importance given to protecting freedom of expression 2.09

    limitations to freedom 2.35–2.50

    protection for freedom compared with English law 1.18

    provisions 2.08

    whether infringement of right is violation of 2.35–2.36

artistic expression 2.46

benefitting from right, persons 2.11

Canadian law as to 1.08, 1.18

categories of expression 2.46

'chilling effect' of imprecise or vague laws on, avoidance of 2.37–2.38

civil servants, restrictions on 2.47

commercial expression *see* commercial expression

confidence, breach of *see* breach of confidence

court reporting *see* court reporting

defamation *see* defamation

Dicey, A V, on 1.14

duties and responsibilities as to exercise
of 2.47
environmental information, right of
access to 2.29
foreseeability of effect of legislation on,
need for 2.37–2.38
hate speech, restriction of 2.65–2.66
historical development in English law
1.14–1.17
HRA 1998 as to *see* Human Rights Act 1998
(HRA 1998)
interference by public authority 2.23
legitimate aim for restriction of 2.41
margin of appreciation as to *see* margin of
appreciation
media, special position of 2.18–2.21
medium of expression, as factor in legitimacy
of restriction 2.48
opinions offensive to state 2.16
prescribed by law, restriction 2.37–2.40
prior restraints on 2.49–2.50
privacy, right to *see* privacy
protection of
importance given to 1.18, 2.10
judiciary's approach to 1.20
public concern, as to matters of 2.46
racial hatred *see* racial hatred
receiving and imparting information 2.15
restrictions *see also* margin of appreciation
armed forces, on 2.47
justified to protect privacy and
confidentiality 6.21–6.25
legitimate aim 2.41
necessary in democratic society 8.27–8.32
court reporting *see* court reporting
defamation cases 5.16–5.58
obscenity cases 8.16–8.19
whether necessary and proportionate
2.42–2.43
prescribed by law 2.37–2.40
prevention of disorder, for 2.41
proportionality of 2.43
right to receive and impart information
2.26–2.32
symbolic conduct 2.17
types of expression covered by right of
2.16–2.17
friendly settlement 4.27

hate speech, restriction of 2.65–2.66
Holocaust denial 7.20–7.21
Human Rights Act 1998 (HRA 1998)
blasphemy 8.40

commercial expression 12.23–12.36
Convention rights *see also* enforcement of
Convention rights
consistent interpretation of legislation with
3.16–3.28
ECHR case law, reference to 3.11–3.15
omitted rights 3.03–3.10
public authorities' duty of compliance
3.29–3.41
declarations of incompatibility 3.22–3.26
ECHR case law, reference to 3.11–3.15
enforcement of Convention rights *see*
enforcement of Convention rights
freedom of expression, as to 3.02
interpretation of legislation consistently with
ECHR 3.02, 3.16–3.28
margin of appreciation, as to 3.13–3.14
media intrusion 6.30–6.44
national security
civil law 13.37–13.41
criminal law 13.31–13.36
obscenity 8.35–8.39
omitted rights 3.03–3.10
provisions for taking cases to European
Court 4.02
public authorities
compliance with Convention rights, duty of
3.29–3.41
enforcement of Convention rights by 3.58
incompatible primary legislation, duty in
cases of 3.30
meaning 3.31–3.40
media bodies as 3.36–3.40
prohibition of omitting to remedy
incompatibility with Convention
right 3.41
purpose 3.01
standing provisions for enforcement of
Convention rights 3.42–3.53
text Appendix 1

incompatibility, declarations of 3.22–3.26
**Independent Television Commission, status as
public body** 3.36
informants, protection by media 2.20
information, right of access to 2.26–2.32
injunctions
pre-trial injunctions 9.22
restrictions on 3.69–3.72
thalidomide articles injunctions 9.16–9.18
interpretation
ECHR, of 2.02–2.07
effectiveness principle 2.06

interpretation (*cont.*)
  ECHR, of (*cont.*)
    other instruments 2.07
    teleological approach 2.03–2.05
  legislation, of
    HRA 1998 as to 3.16–3.28
    primary and secondary legislation
      3.20–3.21

journalists
  court reporting *see* court reporting
  protection of sources 2.20
judges
  ECHR 4.03–4.05
  protection of freedom of expression,
    approach to 1.20
judgments, handing down of 4.29
judicial acts, damages for 3.66
judicial proceedings, reporting of *see* court
  reporting

legal aid
  ECHR, complaints to 4.07
legitimate aim justification for restriction of
  Convention right
  blasphemy 8.24–8.26
Lehideux and Isorni v France 7.22–7.24
libel *see also* defamation
  blasphemous 8.10, 8.12
  criminal 5.61–5.62
  seditious 1.15
licensing and regulation of media
  broadcasting, television and cinema,
    of 2.33–2.34 *see also* media
    regulators
  newspapers, of 11.18–11.19
  prior restraint, as 1.16
  suppression of expression, as tool for 1.16
licensing and regulation of media and regulation
  of media
  broadcasting *see* broadcasting

margin of appreciation 2.44
  artistic expression 2.46
  commercial expression 2.46, 12.02
  duties and responsibilities of applicant 2.47
  ECHR and HRA 1998 compared
    3.13–3.14
  HRA 1998 as to 3.13–3.14
  national security, as to claims of 13.02
  public concern, as to matters of 2.46
Markt Intern and Beerman v Germany
  12.07–12.09

media
  court reporting by *see* court reporting
  duty to impart information 2.19
  freedom of the press 2.19
  intrusion of privacy by 6.21–6.44
  irresponsible journalism in defamation cases,
    impact of HRA 1988 5.70–5.71
  licensing of *see* licensing
  objective and balanced reporting,
    media's freedom to choose methods
    of 2.21
  position under Article 10 ECHR 2.18–2.21
  protection of informants by 2.20
  racial hatred, reporting in public interest
    7.25–7.32
  reportage of defamatory statements
    5.50–5.60, 5.72
  state interference with 6.10–6.18
  victim of violation of Covenant right,
    whether can be 3.49
media regulators 11.37
  Article 6 as to
    applicability 11.21–11.30
    regulators' obligations, issues as to
      11.42–11.44
    rights granted to persons subject to
      proceedings 11.31–11.41
  civil cases, Article 6 as to conduct of
    11.22–11.27
  criminal charges, Article 6 as to use of
    11.28–11.30
  specific protections for defendants
    11.38–11.41
  impartiality of proceedings, Article 6
    provisions 11.36
  independence of tribunals, Article 6 provisions
    on 11.35
  proceedings in public, whether requirement
    satisfied 11.37
  tribunals, Article 6 provisions on conduct of
    11.34
medium of expression as factor in legitimacy of
  restriction 2.48
Meiklejohn, Alexander, democratic
  self-governance, on 1.06
Mill, John Stuart, argument from truth 1.05,
  1.08–1.09

national security *see also* official secrets
  civil law, HRA 1998's impact on use of
    13.37–13.41
  courts' approach to, overview of
    13.01–13.05

criminal law
  encouraging and glorifying terrorism 13.36
  official secrets, as to 13.31–13.35
damage to security service 180–181
ECHR case law
  general principles 13.06–13.07
  publication or disclosure of secret
      information 13.08–13.20
  suppression of speech 13.21–13.30
HRA 1998, impact of
  civil law 13.37–13.41
  criminal law 13.31–13.36
injunctions, use of 13.37–13.41
margin of appreciation as to claims of 13.02
suppression of speech for reasons of
  national security or integrity, threats to
      13.26–13.30
  public order, threats to 13.21–13.25
terrorism, courts' approach to implications
    13.05
**necessary in democratic society justification for
    restriction of Covenant right**
blasphemy 8.27–8.32
newspapers
licensing of 11.18–11.19
regulation of (aspects of) *see* media regulators

obscenity
domestic law 8.06–8.09
  HRA 1998 and 8.35–8.39
ECHR 8.13–8.20
HRA 1998 as to 8.35–8.39
overview of regulation 8.01–8.05
problem of defining 8.14
restriction of
  interference by public authority 8.13
  legitimate aim for 8.15
  necessary in democratic society 8.16–8.19
  prescribed by law 8.14
  selective enforcement 8.20
Ofcom
privacy code, reference to 3.76–3.77
status as public body 3.36
offensive expression, freedom of
importance of protecting 1.18
  expression relating to religion 2.10
opinions offensive to the state 2.16
official secrets *see also* national security
civil law, HRA 1998's impact 13.37–13.41
criminal law as to, impact of HRA 1998
    13.31–13.35
injunctions, HRA 1998's impact on use of
    13.37–13.41

publication or disclosure of, ECHR case law
    relating to 13.08–13.20
***Open Door Counselling* case** 2.15,
    12.21–12.22
**opinions offensive to state, protection
    for** 2.16

Parliament, reporting of
contempt of Parliament, use to restrict
    reporting 10.30–10.31
overview of rules of procedure 10.03
restrictions due to parliamentary privilege
    10.24–10.29
party political broadcasts, controls on
    10.12–10.15
political advertisements, restrictions on 10.12,
    12.18–12.20, 12.34
political debate
restriction of Covenant right in context of
    5.36–5.38
**political expression, protection under Article 10
    ECHR** 2.16
pre-trial injunctions 9.22
restrictions on 3.69–3.72
**prescribed by law justification for restriction of
    Convention right**
blasphemy 8.22–8.23
press
freedom of, included in freedom of
    expression 2.19
licensing or registration of 11.18–11.19
regulation of (aspects of) *see* media
    regulators
Press Complaints Commission
privacy code, reference to 3.76–3.77
status as public body 3.37
**pressure groups, enforcement of Convention
    rights by** 3.50
prevention of disorder *see* public disorder
prior restraints on freedom of expression
    2.49–2.50
defamation cases 5.07
English law, in 1.16–1.17
privacy 6.01–6.05
Article 8 ECHR 6.26–6.29
balanced with public interest 3.73–3.77
breach of confidence *see* breach of
    confidence
classification of torts 1.12–1.13
English law, in 1.11
English law pre-HRA 1998, in 1.18–1.23
intrusion via false statement or
    portrayal 1.13

privacy *(cont.)*
  media intrusion
    ECHR as to
      justification defence for restricting
          freedom of expression 6.21–6.25
      positive obligation to protect freedom of
          expression 6.26–6.29
    HRA 1998 as to 6.30–6.44
    Prosser, William, torts of privacy, on
        1.12–1.13, 1.23
    rape victim, disclosure of identity of 1.13
    right to be left alone 1.10–1.11
    threats to life, resulting in 6.48–6.50
  production orders, use of 6.06–6.09
  remedies for intrusion of 6.45–6.47
  right to, L D Brandeis on 1.10–1.11, 1.23
  searches of premises, use of 6.06–6.09
  state interference 6.06–6.09
  state interference with media sources
    compelling disclosure 6.10–6.18
    penalising whistleblowers 6.19–6.20
  telephoto lenses, use of 1.22
  warrants, use of 6.06–6.09
  Warren and Brandeis's theory of 1.10–1.11,
      1.23
  witnesses, of 9.45–9.47
private life, right to respect for 2.55–2.58
privilege defence to defamation claim 5.02
proceedings, reporting of court *see* court
    reporting
production orders, intrusion of privacy by use of
    6.06–6.09
professional conduct
  advertisements 12.10–12.14, 12.36
  public expression 12.35
propaganda, race hate 7.15–7.19
proportionality of restrictions 2.43
Prosser, William, torts of privacy,
    on 1.12–1.13, 1.23
public authorities
  blasphemy, interference with Convention
      rights in cases of 8.21
  compliance with Convention rights 3.02
  compliance with Convention rights, duty of
      3.29–3.41
  enforcement of Convention rights by 3.58
  freedom of expression, interference with 2.23
  HRA 1998 as to *see* Human Rights Act
      1998 (HRA)
  incompatible primary legislation,
      in cases of 3.30
  meaning 3.31–3.40
  media bodies as 3.36–3.40

obscenity, interference with Convention rights
    in cases of 8.13
prohibition of omitting to remedy
    incompatibility with Convention
    right 3.41
public disorder
  prevention of, restriction of Covenant right
      needed for 5.15
  suppression of expression for reasons of 2.41,
      13.21–13.25
public emergencies, ECHR restrictions
    2.63–2.64
public hearings
  extent of obligation to hold 9.38–9.44
  waiver of right to hearing 2.54
public interest and concern, matters of
  balanced with privacy 3.73–3.77
  expression on 2.46
  media's right to report on 2.18
  reporting of racial hatred 7.25–7.32
  restriction of Covenant right in context of
      matters of 5.35–5.49
public servants
  limitation of freedom of expression of 2.47
public service broadcasting, licensing of 11.10

racial hatred
  Canadian law as to 7.34
  discrimination, ECHR as to 7.09–712
  domestic law 7.02–7.08
  Holocaust denial 7.20–7.21
  Lehideux and Isorni v France 7.22–7.24
  public interest reporting of 7.25–7.32
  race hate propaganda 7.15–7.19
  racist expression, restriction of 7.13–7.24
  restraints in other human rights instruments
      7.33
  US law as to 7.34
radio, licensing and regulation of media of *see*
    licensing
rape victim, disclosure of identity of 1.13
relief without notice, restrictions on 3.68
religion
  blasphemy 2.62
  protection for offensive expression
      relating to 2.10
  religious advertising, restrictions on
      12.18–12.20
remedies *see also individual remedies e.g.* damages
  exhaustion of domestic remedies 4.21–4.25
  intrusion of privacy 6.45–6.47
reportage of defamatory statements 5.50–5.60,
    5.72

reporting of judicial proceedings *see* court
   reporting
respect for private life 2.55–2.58
restraints *see* prior restraints
Reynolds defence for public interest speech
   5.65–5.69
right to be left alone 1.10–1.11

searches of premises, intrusion of privacy by
   use of 6.06–6.09
seditious libel, suppression of expression by
   prosecution for 1.15
self-fulfilment rationale for freedom of
   expression 1.07, 1.08–1.09
self-government rationale for freedom of
   expression 1.06, 1.08–1.09
statements of compatibility 3.22–3.26
state's duty to impart information 2.26–2.32
Sunday Times v UK, injunctions against articles
   on thalidomide 9.16–9.18
symbolic speech or conduct, protection for 2.17

teleological approach to interpreting the ECHR
   2.03–2.05
telephoto lenses, use of 1.22
television, licensing and regulation of media of
   see licensing
terrorism
   encouraging and glorifying, criminal law
      as to 13.36
   national security implications, courts'
      approach 13.05
thalidomide articles injunctions 9.16–9.18
theories as to right of freedom of expression
   argument from truth (J S Mill) 1.05,
      1.08–1.09
   democratic self-governance 1.06, 1.08–1.09
   relevance for protection of freedom 1.08–1.09
   self-fulfilment rationale 1.07, 1.08–1.09
third parties, adverse effect of publicity from
   court reporting 9.48–9.51
threats to life
   court reporting, resulting from 9.52–9.53
   media intrusion, resulting from 6.48–6.50
time limit for application to ECHR 4.09
tobacco advertising 12.26–12.32
torts of privacy, classification of 1.12–1.13
tribunals, media's right of access to 9.33–9.37

truth
   acknowledged truths and accepted beliefs,
      challenge to 1.05
   argument from truth (J S Mill) 1.05
   defence to defamation claim,
      as (justification) 5.02
   defence to prosecution for seditious libel,
      as 1.15

unpopular or offensive speech, importance of
   protecting 1.18
USA
   jurisprudence
      recognition of rationales for protecting
         freedom of expression 1.08
      use by English courts 1.02, 12.02
   privacy law, theories by Warren and Brandeis
      and Prosser 1.10–1.13
   protection for freedom of expression compared
      with English law 1.18
   racial hatred, law as to 7.34

victims of violation of Convention right
   admissibility to European Court 4.17–4.20
   companies as 3.48
   defamation claims by 5.04–5.05
   enforcement of Convention rights by
      3.42–3.53
   loss of status as 4.20
   media bodies, whether can be 3.49
   rape victim, disclosure of identity of 1.13
   types of 4.17
Video Appeals Committee, status as public
   body 3.36
videos, certification of 2.23
vulnerable groups, control of advertisements to
   12.33

war, restrictions on reporting in time of
   2.63–2.64
warrants, intrusion of privacy by use of
   6.06–6.09
Warren, S D, right to privacy, on 1.10–1.11,
   1.22
whistleblowers, penalising of 6.19–6.20
Williams Committee on Obscenity and Film
   Censorship 8.06